POWER, PRESENCE AND SPACE

Patterns of ritual power, presence and space are fundamentally connected to, and mirror, the societal and political power structures in which they are enacted.

This book explores these connections in South Asia from the early Common Era until the present day. The chapters in the volume examine a wide range of themes, including a genealogy of ideas concerning Vedic rituals in European thought; Buddhist donative rituals of Gandhara and Andhra Pradesh in the early Common Era; land endowments, festivals and temple establishments in medieval Tamil Nadu and Karnataka; Mughal court rituals of the Mughal Empire and contemporary ritual complexes on the Nilgiri Plateau. This volume argues for the need to redress a historical neglect in identifying and theorising ritual and religion in material contexts within archaeology. Further, it challenges existing theoretical and methodological forms of documentation to propose new ways of understanding rituals in history.

This volume will be of great interest to scholars and researchers of South Asian history, religion, archaeology and historical geography.

Henry Albery has been a postdoctoral fellow at the Distant Worlds Graduate School, Münchner Zentrum für Antike Welten, Ludwig-Maximilians-Universität, Munich, Germany, since 2018, where a year prior he completed his doctoral thesis in Indologie und Religionswissenschaft. His research is primarily concerned with a social and political history of Buddhism in the north and northwesterly regions of South Asia in the early Common Era, focusing foremost on donative inscriptions in Brāhmī and Kharoṣṭhī and on Buddhist legal and narrative literature in Chinese, Gāndhārī, Pāli and Sanskrit. He is also a member of the collaborative project 'An English Translation of a Sanskrit Buddhist Yoga Manual' from Kuča, funded by The Robert H. N. Ho Family Foundation Grants for Critical Editions and Scholarly Translations, 2018.

Jens-Uwe Hartmann is former Professor of Indology at the Ludwig-Maximilians-Universität, Munich, Germany. After studying in Munich and Göttingen, he held the post of Professor of Tibetology at Humboldt University in Berlin before returning to Munich in 1999. In 2001, he became a full member of the Bavarian Academy of Sciences and a corresponding member of the Austrian Academy of Sciences in 2007. He has held visiting appointments at the Collège de France in Paris (2001 and 2004), the Centre for Advanced Study of the Norwegian Academy of Sciences in Oslo (2001–2002), the International College for Advanced Buddhist Studies in Tokyo (2002), the Soka University in Tokyo (2003), the UC Berkeley (2010) and the University of Stanford (2017).

His research centres on the recovery and reconstruction of Indian Buddhist literature on the basis of Indic manuscripts as well as translations into Chinese and Tibetan with a focus on canonical texts and works of poetry. His various authored and coedited works include an edition of the *Varṇārhavarṇastotra* of Mātṛceṭa (1987); a study of the *Dīrghāgama* of the Sarvāstivādins (1992); the series *Buddhist Manuscripts*, devoted to the publication of ancient Indic manuscripts from Afghanistan (2000, 2002, 2006, 2016) and *From Birch Bark to Digital Data: Recent Advances in Buddhist Manuscript Research* (2014).

Himanshu Prabha Ray is Research Fellow, Oxford Centre for Hindu Studies, Oxford, UK. She was the first chairperson of the National Monuments Authority, Ministry of Culture, New Delhi, India, from 2012 to 2015, and former Professor in the Centre for Historical Studies, Jawaharlal Nehru University, New Delhi, India. Her research interests include maritime history and archaeology of the Indian Ocean, the history of archaeology in South and Southeast Asia and the archaeology of religion in Asia. Her recent books include *Archaeology and Buddhism in South Asia* (2018), *Buddhism and Gandhara: An Archaeology of Museum Collections* (ed. 2018), *The Archaeology of Sacred Spaces: The Temple in Western India, 2nd Century BCE to 8th Century CE* (with Susan Verma Mishra, 2017), *The Return of the Buddha: Ancient Symbols for a New Nation* (2014) and *The Archaeology of Seafaring in Ancient South Asia* (2003).

ARCHAEOLOGY AND RELIGION IN SOUTH ASIA

Series Editor: Himanshu Prabha Ray, *Senior Research Fellow, Oxford Centre for Hindu Studies, Oxford; Chairperson of the National Monuments Authority, Ministry of Culture, Government of India; and former Professor, Centre for Historical Studies, Jawaharlal Nehru University, New Delhi*

Editorial Board: Gavin Flood, *Academic Director, Oxford Centre for Hindu Studies*; Jessica Frazier, *Academic Administrator, Oxford Centre for Hindu Studies*; Julia Shaw, *Institute of Archaeology, University College, London*; Shailendra Bhandare, *Ashmolean Museum, Oxford*; Devangana Desai, *Asiatic Society, Mumbai*; and Vidula Jayaswal, *Jnana-Pravaha, Varanasi, former Professor, Banaras Hindu University*

This series, in association with the Oxford Centre for Hindu Studies, reflects on the complex relationship between religion and society through new perspectives and studies on archaeology. It looks at the critical interface to provide alternative understandings of communities, beliefs, cultural systems, sacred sites, ritual practices, and habitats and their modifications, power, and agents of political legitimisation. The books in the series underline the importance of archaeological evidence in the production of knowledge of the past. They also emphasise that a systematic study of religion requires engagement with a diverse range of sources such as inscriptions, iconography, numismatics and architectural remains.

POWER, PRESENCE AND SPACE
South Asian Rituals in Archaeological Context
Edited by Henry Albery, Jens-Uwe Hartmann and Himanshu Prabha Ray

For a full list of titles in this series, please visit www.routledge.com/Archaeology-and-Religion-in-South-Asia/book-series/AR

ARCHAEOLOGY AND RELIGION IN SOUTH ASIA

OXFORD CENTRE FOR HINDU STUDIES

UNIVERSITY OF OXFORD

A RECOGNISED INDEPENDENT CENTRE OF THE UNIVERSITY OF OXFORD

This series, in association with the Oxford Centre for Hindu Studies, reflects on the complex relationship between religion and society through new perspectives and advances in archaeology. It looks at this critical interface to provide alternative understandings of communities, beliefs, cultural systems, sacred sites, ritual practices, food habits, dietary modifications, power, and agents of political legitimisation. The books in the Series underline the importance of archaeological evidence in the production of knowledge of the past. They also emphasise that a systematic study of religion requires engagement with a diverse range of sources such as inscriptions, iconography, numismatics and architectural remains.

POWER, PRESENCE AND SPACE

South Asian Rituals in Archaeological Context

Edited by Henry Albery, Jens-Uwe Hartmann and Himanshu Prabha Ray

For a full list of titles in this series, please visit www.routledge.com/Archaeology-and-Religion-in-South-Asia/book-series/AR

POWER, PRESENCE AND SPACE

South Asian Rituals in Archaeological Context

Edited by Henry Albery, Jens-Uwe Hartmann and Himanshu Prabha Ray

Routledge
Taylor & Francis Group
LONDON AND NEW YORK

First published 2021
by Routledge
2 Park Square, Milton Park, Abingdon, Oxon OX14 4RN

and by Routledge
52 Vanderbilt Avenue, New York, NY 10017

Routledge is an imprint of the Taylor & Francis Group, an informa business

British Library Cataloguing-in-Publication Data
A catalogue record for this book is available from the British Library

Library of Congress Cataloging-in-Publication Data
A catalog record for this book has been requested

ISBN: 978-0-367-13396-2 (hbk)
ISBN: 978-1-003-08383-2 (ebk)

Typeset in Sabon
by Apex CoVantage.LLC

CONTENTS

TABLES AND FIGURES

Tables

Figures

CONTRIBUTORS

Henry Albery has been a postdoctoral fellow at the Distant Worlds Graduate School, Münchner Zentrum für Antike Welten, at Ludwig-Maximilians-Universität, Munich, Germany, since 2018, where a year prior he completed his doctoral thesis in Indologie und Religionswissenschaft. His research is primarily concerned with a social and political history of Buddhism in the north and northwesterly regions of South Asia in the early Common Era, focusing foremost on donative inscriptions in Brāhmī and Kharoṣṭhī and on Buddhist legal and narrative literature in Chinese, Gāndhārī, Pāli and Sanskrit. He is also a member of the collaborative project, 'An English Translation of a Sanskrit Buddhist Yoga Manual from Kučā', funded by The Robert H. N. Ho Family Foundation Grants for Critical Editions and Scholarly Translations, 2018.

Andrew M. Bauer is Assistant Professor in the Department of Anthropology at Stanford University, USA, where his research and teaching interests broadly intersect archaeological method and theory and environmental anthropology, with particular emphasis on the politics of environmental production in pre-colonial South India. He has published several books, including *Climate Without Nature: A Critical Anthropology of the Anthropocene* (2018, with Mona Bhan), *Before Vijayanagara: Prehistoric Landscapes and Politics in the Tungabhadra Basin* (2015) and *The Archaeology of Politics: The Materiality of Political Practice and Action in the Past* (2011, co-edited with Peter Johansen), as well as numerous articles and essays.

Shailendra Bhandare is Assistant Keeper, Numismatics, Ashmolean Museum, Oxford University, UK. His publications include 'Not Just a Pretty Face: Interpretations of Alexander's Numismatic Imagery in the Hellenic East' in *Memory as History: The Legacy of Alexander in Asia*, 2007; 'Numismatics and History: The Maurya-Gupta Interlude in the Gangetic Plain' in *Between the Empires: Society in India 300 BCE to 400 CE*, New York and 'From Kautilya to Kosambi and Beyond: The Quest for a Mauryan/ Asokan Coinage,' in *Reimagining Aśoka: Memory and History*, 2012. His research interests include Indian coinage: its historical context, utility and evolution with specific attention to the early historic, medieval (Mughal) and modern periods; also, its significance for undertaking studies of broad historical interests such as cross-cultural syncretism, urbanisation and colonialism, as well as the applicability of Indian numismatics for various Indological themes such as art, iconography, epigraphy and archaeology.

Crispin Branfoot is Reader in the History of South Asian Art and Archaeology at the School of Oriental and African Studies, University of London. His writing and research have focussed on the religious architecture, sculpture and painting of southern India from the 14th to the early 20th centuries. His books include *Gods on the Move: architecture and ritual in the south Indian temple* (2007); with Roger Taylor, *Captain Linnaeus Tripe: Photographer of India and Burma, 1854–1860* (Washington DC 2014); with Archana Venkatesan, *In Andal's Garden: Art, Ornament and Devotion in Srivilliputtur* (Mumbai 2015) and as editor with Ruth Barnes, *Pilgrimage: The Sacred Journey* (Oxford 2006).

Nupur Dasgupta has been teaching at the Department of History, Jadavpur University, India, since 1991. Her area of interest is ancient Indian history and archaeology and history of science, technology and medicine (ancient—modern). She was the recipient of the Charles Wallace Fellowship at the School of Oriental and African Studies, University of London, in 2001 and was invited to be Visiting Fellow at the Department of Ancient Indian History and Culture at the Universities of Calcutta (in 2009) and Munich (in 2018) and at the Department of History, University of Calcutta, in 2019. She has authored books entitled *The Dawn of Technology in Indian Protohistory*, Calcutta, Punthi Pustak, 1997, and the translations and edition of *Suvarnatantra*: *A Treatise on Alchemy*, Kalpaz Publications, Delhi, 2009, edited jointly with C. Palit.

Frank Heidemann is Professor for Social and Cultural Anthropology at the University of Munich, Germany. His research interests include politics, religion, indigeneity, social aesthetics, visual anthropology and the history of anthropology. Most of his fieldwork was based in South India and Sri Lanka, especially in the Nilgiri Hills, on the Andaman Island, and presently on Lakshadweep Islands with a focus on Minicoy. Recently he co-edited *Manifestations of History* (with P. Zehmisch, 2016), *The Bison and Its Horn: Indigeneity, Performance and the State in South Asia* (with R. Wolf, 2014) and *The Modern Anthropology of India* (with Peter Berger, 2013).

Leslie C. Orr is a professor in the Department of Religions and Cultures at Concordia University in Montréal, Québec, Canada, where she teaches in the areas of South Asian religions and women and religion. Following the publication of her book *Donors, Devotees and Daughters of God:*

Temple Women in Medieval Tamilnadu (New York: 2000), she has continued to work and publish on the history of women's lives in South India. Other research has been oriented toward the study of Jainism and of the temples and inscriptions in southernmost Tamilnadu, especially in the late medieval/early modern period.

Lisa N. Owen is an associate professor of art history at the University of North Texas, USA. Her research focuses on India's ancient and medieval rock-cut monuments and how carved imagery and space shape devotional practices. She is the author of *Carving Devotion in the Jain Caves at Ellora* (2012) and her work appears in issues of *Artibus Asiae*, the *International Journal of Jaina Studies* and the *Journal of the International Association of Buddhist Studies*. She has also contributed essays to edited volumes on archaeology and ritual. She has received numerous grants to support her fieldwork in India, including a fellowship from the American Institute of Indian Studies, a Fulbright-Nehru Research Scholar Award and a Howard Foundation fellowship. Her current book project, *Rocks, Caves, and Divinity*, questions the saliency of employing traditional art historical categories such as 'architecture' and 'sculpture' to India's rock-cut monuments that clearly express a power of place through more complex visual systems.

Ingo Strauch is Professor for Sanskrit and Buddhist Studies at the University of Lausanne, Switzerland. He received his PhD (2000) and his habilitation (2010) in Indian philology at Freie Universität Berlin, Germany. His current research focusses on early Buddhist manuscripts from Gandhāra and Buddhist epigraphy in Brāhmī and Kharoṣṭhī scripts.

Robert A. Yelle has been Professor for the Theory and Method of Religious Studies and Chair of the Interfaculty Program in Religious Studies at Ludwig Maximilian University, Munich, Germany, since 2014. He studied at Harvard College (BA in Philosophy 1988), the University of California at Berkeley (JD 1993) and the University of Chicago Divinity School, where he received a PhD in the History of Religions (2002) based on research conducted in Calcutta, India, on a Fulbright-Hays Fellowship. Before arriving in Munich, Yelle was Associate Professor at the University of Memphis. He has received fellowships from the University of Toronto, the University of Illinois at Urbana–Champaign, New York University School of Law and the John Simon Guggenheim Memorial Foundation. Yelle is presently Editor of the American Academy of Religion/Oxford University Press book series *Religion, Culture, and History*, and was previously Executive Secretary of the North American Association for the Study of Religion (2007–2011). His monographs include *Explaining Mantras* (2003), *The Language of Disenchantment* (2013), *Semiotics of Religion* (2013) and *Sovereignty and the Sacred* (2019).

PREFACE

It has been a pleasure and a learning experience working with Jens-Uwe Hartmann and Henry Albery, my co-editors for this book. The conference from which these chapters have been drawn was generously supported by the five-year Anneliese Maier research award of the Alexander von Humboldt Foundation and was hosted in Munich by the Distant Worlds Graduate School of Ancient Studies, Ludwig-Maximilians-Universität (LMU). The research award provided me the opportunity to work closely with Jens-Uwe Hartmann since 2013 and to engage with scholars on a diverse range of themes, such as Gandharan sculptures, Buddhism, rituals and heritage. Two edited books including papers from earlier conferences have already been published, entitled *Buddhism and Gandhara: The Archaeology of Museum Collections*, Routledge 2018 and *Decolonising Heritage in South Asia: The Global, the National and the Transnational*, Routledge 2019. This book is the third, while a fourth on *The Archaeology of Knowledge Traditions of the Indian Ocean World* is in press, Routledge 2021.

The Anneliese Maier research award was instituted by the Federal Ministry of Education and Research in Germany to foster collaboration between German scholars and those from other parts of the world. I am grateful to Dr. Monika Zin for nominating me for the award. For me, the challenge was to grapple with different traditions of understanding South Asia's past as researched and taught in Germany and India. Compounding diverse disciplinary training in history, archaeology, Indology, Buddhist and religious studies is the absence of engagement with current scholarship and secondary writings in the two countries. The Indian past is often described and represented through ancient 'Brahmanical' texts written in Sanskrit, which are seen as normative and are contrasted with Buddhist sources discussed as closer to social reality. This is a paradigm that developed in writings dated to the 19th and 20th centuries, based on an understanding of religion through the post-Enlightenment traditions of Christian Europe. The award of the Annaliese Maier fellowship was both critical and significant since it provided the resources for initiating dialogue between researchers in India and Germany but also with those in other parts of the world.

I acknowledge with gratitude the cooperation and contributions of scholars who participated in the three-day conference from 23 to 25 March 2018 and subsequently revised their papers for publication. It is my privilege to thank Ute Hüsken, University of Heidelberg; Deepra Dandekar, Max Planck Institute for Human Development, Berlin; Timothy Lubin, Washington and Lee University and Vincent Tournier, EFEO, Paris, for presentations at the Munich conference. We were also fortunate that Prof. Christoph Levin and Dr. Stefan Baums agreed to chair sessions. Participation of students and teachers from LMU enlivened the discussion, while Mrs. Evelyn Kindermann and her team ensured the smooth functioning of the meeting and kept the participants well-fed.

Shashank Shekhar Sinha, Aakash Chakrabarty and Brinda Sen helped guide the manuscript as it gradually took shape. The editors are thankful for their help and encouragement and would also like to thank the anonymous reviewers for their useful suggestions.

Himanshu Prabha Ray

INTRODUCTION

The archaeology of ritual in South Asian contexts

Archaeology denotes a mode of inquiry concerned with the 'study of the ancient', a classification of 'documents' with the principal aim of determining historical series.[1] Etymologically, however, it also connotes a 'discourse on beginnings', a process purportedly concerned with origins but through which a dialogue is engendered between an archaeologised object and archaeologist subject. To that extent it is a particular strategy for dealing with the past in the terms of the present. However, such a radical understanding of archaeology as process—of reflexively classifying documents as well as the modes of documentation—has not always been practised in scholarship. One good example of this is to be found in the history of the relation between archaeology and the documentation of ritual.

Indeed, it is only in recent decades that the 'archaeology of ritual' has been more critically defined.[2] This endeavour is intended to redress a historical neglect of ritual within archaeology, a lacuna attributed to epistemological issues encountered when identifying and theorising ritual and religion in material contexts and an overdependence on ethnographic and literary sources employed to do so. Operating under a definition of ritual as a repeated and mimetic behaviour, contributors to this trend argue that ritual practice is more likely to leave traces and can therefore be examined as a discrete material process.

This book is a contribution toward the archaeology of ritual in South Asian contexts. It comprises a collection of individual case studies, whose foci geographically span the length and breadth of the subcontinent and temporally the period from the early Common Era to the present day. Whilst the chapters treat ritual within a range of different contexts, each share in the collective purpose of challenging theoretical and methodological forms of its documentation. They do so under three section headings—power, presence and space—each of which serves as conceptual lens through which ritual may be critically examined.

Before clarifying these terms and summarising the contributions in this book, it is necessary to first outline the specific course of development the archaeology of ritual underwent in the context of South Asia. This historiography has yet to be fully realised, despite scrupulous attention being given to the history of archaeology in the region and ritual in more general terms. For the purposes of this introduction, however, it is unfeasible to unpick the entangled discourses of associated literature, simply given the voluminosity of the corpus. Rather, in the following we can only hope to point the reader to some of the broader and more recent trends. In particular, the development of the archaeology of ritual in South Asia is dependent upon the institutional and discursive effects of three historical conditions—Protestantism, modernity and colonialism—for these factors in conjunction would come to have overarching ramifications for how ritual was to be conceptualised as an object of the archaeological method.

A brief historiography of the archaeology of ritual in South Asia

> All might receive the sacrament; and yet some believe it to be the body and blood of Christ, others only a sacrament of it.[3]

In deploying this pun—that the sacrament (bread and wine) is mere sacrament (sign)—William Chillingworth's (1602–1644) primary motive was in persuading his patron and addressee, Prince Charles (1600–1649), of the merits of Protestantism and the logical contradictions of Roman Catholicism. As a convert from the latter church, he sought to mediate finally, for the Anglican position, a resolution in the ongoing debates initiated by the Protestant Reformation of the 16th century. Protestantism widely held that the ecclesiastically sanctioned Roman Catholic 'ritual'—a term which entered coevally with 'sacrament' into the English language as a component of Protestant polemics[4]—was merely an external symbol, empty of meaning and embedded in superstitious, idolatrous belief.[5] True practice, rather, was now attributed to internal agency and individual faith in respect to scriptural doctrine. Chillingworth's deliberately provocative appropriation of 'sacrament' from an ontological to signifying purport thus exemplifies what is now recognised as one of the most enduring effects of Reformation thought on intellectual history: the rifting of the sign from the signified.[6]

This semiotic shift is widely regarded as having had seismic implications. It precipitated an immediate reaction from within the Christian tradition, whereby the 'misuse' of 'sacrament' and the emptying of ritual engendered outraged responses from British proponents of Catholicism,[7] as well as to doctrinal attempts from Anglican circles to reendow the 'visible signs, water or wine,' of the ritual with concrete meaning and salvific function.[8] It also caused a wider process of objectification, an empiricist and materialist focus to which Max Weber attributed the developments of capitalism and the scientific revolution of the 17th and 18th centuries.[9] From it emerged, namely, what Webb Keane terms a 'semiotic ideology': an underlying premise governing a 'representational economy', in which signifying practices upon 'words, things and persons' enacted in discrete social domains (e.g., the domestic, economic, intellectual, political and religious) were rendered mutually intelligible.[10]

In the context of 18th-century colonialism, the ideology was subsequently adopted in the incipient academic domains of archaeology, anthropology and comparative religion.[11] This resulted in the uncontested assumption that ritual was a signifying act.[12] However, the encounter with alterity had the additional hierarchising effect of introducing an evolutionary element to the discourse. No longer were rituals placed at variance with doctrine but with myth; a framework of meaning certainly, yet one divorced from truth. The purported recognition of symbols in ritual and myth thus served as a central colonial mechanism to affirm a particular form of knowledge and power.

In the inaugural volume of *Asiatick Researches*, published in 1798 precisely a half-decade after the founding of the Asiatic Society, two contributions by Williams Jones (1746–1794)[13] attempt to demonstrate that the ancient 'nations' of the orient all originate from 'one central place'—a proposition often regarded as the birth of Aryan racial and linguistic theories.[14] The myths and rituals of these peoples, reflected in their architecture, iconography and texts (oral and written), were seen to symbolically retain common elements and subsequently were marshalled to substantiate an 'ancient theology'[15] and a 'universal history'.[16] Specifically, this form of archaeologising drew on the Book of Genesis to posit that all post-diluvial peoples in Asia could be traced to Ham, son of Noah, who in Indic myth and ritual was mistakenly worshipped as a deified Sun,[17] itself symbolic of fire.[18] However, certain logical results of Jones' comparative method posed significant challenges to this history; he writes:

> I am persuaded that connexion subsisted between the old idolatrous nations of *Egypt, India, Greece*, and *Italy*, long before they migrated to their various settlements, and consequently before the birth of MOSES; but the proof of this proposition will in no degree affect the truth and sanctity of the *Mosaic* History, which, if confirmation were necessary, it would tend to confirm. The *Divine Legate* . . . could not but know the mythological system of *Egypt*; but he must have condemned the superstitions of that people, and despised the speculative absurdities of their priests; though some of their traditions concerning the creation and flood were grounded on truth. Who was better acquainted with the mythology of *Athens* than SOCRATES? Who more accurately versed in the Rabbinical doctrines than PAUL? Who possessed clearer ideas of all ancient astrological systems than NEWTON, or of scholastic metaphysics than LOCKE? In whom could the *Romish* Church have had a more

> formidable opponent than in CHILLINGWORTH, whose deep knowledge of its tenets rendered him so competent to dispute them? In a word, who more exactly knew the abominable rights and shocking idolatry of *Canaan* than MOSES himself? Yet the learning of those great men only incited them to seek other sources of truth, piety, and virtue, than those in which they had long been immersed. There is no shadow then for the foundation of an opinion, that MOSES borrowed the first nine or ten chapters of *Genesis* from the literature of *Egypt*: still less can the adamantine pillars of our *Christian* faith be moved by the result of any debate on the comparative antiquity of the *Hindus* and *Egyptians*, or of any inquiries into the *Indian* theology.[19]

To reconcile the threat of these obvious chronological inconsistencies, Jones is forced to perform some intellectual acrobatics, availing himself, namely, of the semiotic ideology. Likening Moses to Socrates, Paul the Apostle, Isaac Newton,[20] John Locke and the aforecited William Chillingworth—each of whom is here united for their ostensibly having discerned a primordial truth behind the signs with which they were respectively concerned—Jones ultimately aims to situate himself directly in this constructed ideological tradition,[21] becoming to South Asian religion what Chillingworth was to Roman Catholicism—sufficiently intimate with it signs to ascertain its significance.

For the archaeological method in South Asia, there were several insidious corollaries of these semiotic and evolutionary presuppositions. They ultimately led to the determination of what periods of history were to be regarded as important on a scheme of societal progression, trifurcating South Asian history into the Hindu (ancient), Muslim (medieval) and British (modern) periods. Apart from reinforcing the view that colonial rule should be regarded as the epitome, the model ultimately caused the superimposition of European development on South Asia, which awarded objective precedence to the ancient 'Golden Age' over the medieval 'Dark Age'.[22] Equally the rituals and myths of all 'ancient' and 'primitive' societies alike were situated on an evolutionary scale[23] and attributed certain cognitive capacities considered polar to the semiotics of empiricism (e.g., consubstantiation, multilocality and multinumerality).[24] They also governed 'where religion as an object of investigation is to be located':[25] its essence was regarded as being retained in myth, whereas external manifestations of ritual in architecture, art and performance were simply symbols thereof and to be elucidated as such—this rendered ritual the active carrier of a static religious belief. Although an awareness of this tendency led to some attempts to reverse the model and treat ritual as primary,[26] the discussion remained quite firmly within the borders of the dichotomy and, through the 19th and 20th centuries, the lasting assumption was that ritual was a repeated and communicative act expressive of something outside it.[27]

The exclusion of ritual from archaeology is indeed notable, by its absence, within early publications on South Asia. A cursory survey of volumes published in *Asiatick Researches* (1801–1818) and the *Journal of the Royal Asiatic Society of Bengal* (1832–1912) reveals that 'ritual' (also 'rites' and 'ceremonies') was a central topic, albeit limited to anthropological and philological studies of Buddhist, Jain and Vedic religion. Archaeology had other objectives. Being a secondary pursuit of colonial personnel in addition to their civil and military duties, it largely constituted an antiquarian interest in curios, resulting in the assemblage and presentation of art, coins and inscriptions in museums—the first being established by the Asiatic Society in 1786.[28] It was also enacted as part of surveying for colonial administration, which produced detailed topographical descriptions and measurements of monuments and space that proved to be of utility. But when dealing with religious artefacts these observations rarely strayed beyond a concern with architectural and iconographic typologies. Following James Prinsep's (1799–1840) decipherment of the Brāhmī and Kharoṣṭhī scripts in coinage and inscriptions, there was also the possibility of examining sites and objects historically and necessarily political chronologies became the primary concern.[29]

Under Alexander Cunningham (1814–1893) more systematic surveys were conducted within the dedicated remit of the Archaeological Survey of India, founded in 1861.[30] His central purpose was in identifying locations and mapping geographies, primarily on the basis of Greek historiographies detailing Alexander's invasions of the 4th century BCE or Chinese travelogues of Buddhist monks of the 5th and 7th centuries CE.[31] This purpose took him to a vast number of sites and created the first historical geography of the Subcontinent.[32] Along with such figures as James Fergusson (1808–1886),[33] James Burgess (1832–1916) and Bhagwan Lal Indraji (1839–1888),[34] there was also a focus on classifying art, architecture and epigraphy, mainly at Buddhist stupa sites such as Sanchi[35] and Bharhut.[36] Drawing on an increasing corpus of translated inscriptions and literature, these scholars 'textualised' material remains to explicate their meaning and to lay out a history of Buddhism in South Asia.[37] Their analyses of epigraphy also offer some of the earliest sociological reflections on the institutional nature of Buddhism as well as documentations of ritual practice apart from art and literature. However, conceptualisations of ritual (if done at all) were a firm continuation of the foregoing semiotic, evolutionary and Aryan ideologies.[38] Exemplificatory thereof is the accent given to Buddhism, a tendency which has been connected to Protestant influenced thought that subsequently portrayed the Buddha as something of a reformer of Hindu ritual.[39]

Excavations conducted by John Marshall (1876–1958)[40]—for instance, at Mohenjodaro[41] and Taxila[42]—are widely regarded as representing a shift in archaeological theory and method. Employing an admixture of horizontal and vertical excavations, his practice stands as a precursor to ethno-archaeology; namely, one concerned with society and culture in its totality.[43] Religion thus constituted a central component. Yet Marshall's classification of religious artefacts has been criticised as 'essentialising' and overly reliant on ethnographic and textual sources.[44] For instance, despite noting a lack of any material context for ritual practice at Mohenjodaro, Marshall nonetheless sought to explain potential ritual objects in light of Vedic literature and contemporary Hinduism. Thus, female terracottas, bovine figurines, decorative *pippala* leaves on pottery, phallic-like objects, the now-famous seal depicting the so-called proto-Śiva in yoga-like posture and so on, were positioned as forerunning ritual objects of Vedic religion.[45]

The 20th century saw a shift in the concerns of the Archaeological Survey of India. Dedicated positions for Arabic, Persian and Sanskrit archaeologists were created,[46] leading to an increase in the number of South Asian archaeologists, many of whom were trained under the archaeological educational programmes designed by Mortimer Wheeler (1890–1976).[47] And, following Independence, evolutionary models came to be questioned, leading to Marxist-inspired research on the socio-economic aspects of medieval periods, such as feudalism.[48] However, work by South Asian scholars in the post-Independence period, such as B. B. Lal's studies of the *Mahābhārata* and Aryan culture,[49] did not radically question the textually informed premises of archaeology—these were now reproduced to reify emergent national identities. Processual archaeology in the 1960s adjusted the historically focused, text-based archaeology by applying both new theoretical perspectives from anthropology, cognitive psychology and sociology to consider cultural development as well as practical tools that enabled the contextual re-examination of objects. Thus, many of the aforementioned objects Marshall had associated with ritual and religion were found not to derive from any context that would lend to such a view.[50] Under this method, however, both ritual and religion were broadly relegated to an 'epiphenomenal' status and thus only drawn on as secondary categories to explain inexplicable artefacts not otherwise suited to universalisable rationale.[51]

For fundamental change to occur to the archaeology of ritual, two elements required modification: it needed a workable material definition of ritual and religion beyond symbol and greater consideration of ritual as a contextual phenomenon beyond normative literary sources. Hints of both were to occur in the late 1980s and 1990s. This period witnessed widespread re-evaluation of what constitutes ritual-ness. It reformulated ritual action as a set of fixed behaviours or qualities to a quality of action and process of ritualisation. Any action could thence be distinguished as ritual by its marking of a specific intentionality apart from the quotidian.[52] This enabled it to be considered as both distinct and related to the broader social field and as being a transformative rather than a static and normative religious act. Post-processuralism also questioned positivistic categories such as ritual and religion as universal and initiated a renewed reflexive archaeologising of material phenomena, which focused on the contextually produced nature of meaning.

Scholarship today has learned these lessons and, coupled to a reinvigorated comparative method, the archaeology of ritual is now characterised as an interdisciplinary endeavour which treats ritual as a distinct experiential 'frame', universal in some functional, cognitive, linguistic, semiotic and social aspects, but conditioned by discrete economic, political and sociological determinants. Vitally, ritual objects and spaces are no longer regarded as solely symbolic but have been reendowed with a performative significance and agency; that is, ritual objects through performance are themselves rendered causally efficacious social agents.[53] Now the relation between subject and object in a ritual frame is conceived of dynamically, whereby cognition and somatics are mutually related to object and space.[54]

Such theoretical advances have been mirrored and supported by methodological attempts to study religion in South Asia 'on the ground'—to reject a historical overreliance on textual sources and to begin using them alongside epigraphic and material remains.[55] This has enabled several persistent assumptions in text-based scholarship to be fundamentally interrogated, such as the evolutionary model of textual ages—'there is no Vedic archaeology[!]'[56]—and the historical focus on ritual as the province of social hierarchs. This has been achieved particularly through the systematic analysis of epigraphy, producing greater sociological understanding of donative modes as embodied acts, and of material artefacts and space conceived as both moulding and moulded by ritual behaviour within an interactive social forum.[57] Ritual is now treated as part of 'lived religion' enacted alongside everyday beliefs and practices.[58] Under this all-encompassing scheme, ritual can and must be treated through all available witnesses and under a variety of conceptual possibilities.[59]

Summary of chapters

The chapters of this book draw on three such concepts in the study of ritual: power, presence and space. Reflecting the aforementioned theoretical and methodological advances, they use these categories to force novel questions that were hitherto impossible, generating for their respective fields a more nuanced understanding of ritual as a conceptual category and as a mode of contextually circumscribed behaviour.

Power here denotes the agency and potency conferred on subjects and objects. As already discussed, the seat of power in ritual was relocated under the semiotic ideology from an ontological to a symbolic position. Thus, ritual theory removed any inherent agency ritual objects may have had within a given system of religious thought. With renewed perspective, objective power is now widely considered a central component of ritual experience and both the ontologies and semiotics of ritual can be used to express it in a variety of social contexts. The three chapters in this section are reflective of the on-going debate regarding where power is to be located in ritual.

In the first chapter, Robert A. Yelle traces a genealogy of sacrifice within Jan Heesterman's influential work, *The Broken World of Sacrifice*. Building on existing criticism of Heesterman's model—as being overly interpretative in its reconstruction of pre-Vedic sacrifice on the basis of purported symbolic remnants in the ritual of Vedic literature—Yelle for the first time examines the premises and mythemes underlying this model within two strands of European thought in the 19th and 20th centuries. The first is the afore-described semiotic ideology of Protestant thought. He shows that Heesterman relies on similarly derived Weberian notions of 'disenchantment' and the 'routinisation of charisma' and other widespread dichotomies between the lawless sacrifice of folk religion and the structured ritual legalism of priests. Heesterman saw the original pre-Vedic sacrifice as a life and death struggle enacted by warriors, whose climax would result in a communal feast. This is contrasted with the Vedic *śrauta* ritual as a highly constrained and individual affair, wherein the sacrifice is retained symbolically as a burnt offering. Second, Yelle further exposes, more controversially, that Heesterman drew ideas from explicitly racialising Weimar- and Nazi-era notions of the *Männerbund* as the original collective social formation of Aryan warriors. Criticising the 'amnesia' of scholars who still reproduce Heesterman's ideas in scholarship, this chapter demonstrates for the betterment of the philological method the necessity of reflexivity when employing categories of ritual and sacrifice.

In Chapter 2, Shailendra Bhandare considers court rituals among Mughal rulers between the 17th and 19th centuries. Inspired by political theories of ritual, he examines the instrumental relation between both the symbolic function and the consubstantial agency of coins as ritual objects in the formation of imperial power and the articulation of divine kingship. The Mughals minted a series of coins with the likeness of the ruler which formed a central part of two court rituals' gift-economies: *Nazar*, a highly formalised process in which a privileged individual is allowed rare private audience with the ruler and, because of a sighting (*Darshan*) of the ruler, gives a gift of money in symbolic recognition of his power; and *Nisār*, constituting the reciprocal gifting of a coin by the ruler, or, more widely, the ritual scattering of coins over the head of the ruler during public events, which would later be distributed among the public. The gifting of such coins served the dual function of averting the 'evil eye'—a potentially harmful glance of a jealous subject—by enabling the subjects to have a sighting of the ruler at will and to draw the ruler's somatic power, with which the coin was regarded as being imbued. Arguing against both colonial and more recent scholarship which, again deploying Protestant-derived polemics, suggests the Mughal rulers were somehow semiotically incapable and consumed by substantiality, Bhandare demonstrates how coins enabled both the symbolic performance of power as well as effecting a cognitive and emotional experience among the observers through their sighting.

The symbolic potential of ritual in legitimising political power is also taken up by Frank Heidemann in Chapter 3. Through an anthropological study of contemporary Badaga society in the Nilgiris, he examines how ritual processions have continually served to transform the relation between, and coexistence of, traditional structures and the shifting demands of the modern polity. He argues for the possibility of archaeologising a pre-colonial judicial and state structure on the basis of contemporary ritual complexes. Badaga myths detail descent and affinal kinship relations, represented by the female deity Hette, and past migration patterns, represented by the male god Hireodeya. Heidemann demonstrates that these mythic structures are performed in annual festivals focusing on the deities. He argues that through their performance two forms of power are enabled. First, in the sense of a Foucauldian emergent power, the ritual reifies mythically determined territorial organisations, centred on original and satellite villages, and reconstructs them in terms of their relation to the modern state. Second, adopting the Weberian model of dyadic power, the rituals also provide figures of both the traditional social hierarchies (village headmen, priests and councils), and incipient economic leaders of the capitalist economy to take centre stage in ritual performance and elicit support of the participants. He thus reveals how the power of ritual has served to adapt Badaga society from the pre- to post-colonial periods.

Part Two considers *presence* as one mode of manifesting ritual power. Here the notion reflects the power of ritual media to award ubiety to an absentee ritual participant within and through a ritual object. This assumes therefore that ritual objects are endowed with not only a semiotic function but also an ontological agency. Whilst the principle of presence can serve several functions, the chapters in this section treat two in particular, including cases where a ritual object can be employed to demarcate institutional and political power or where it can stand in lieu of a ritual participant's physical presence. Because of the instrumentality of presence in affirming power, its locations are shown to be contested and in turn to transform and reshape ritual space and social structures. In both its actual and figurative employment, presence (and absence) thus acts as a central tenet of ritual and its power often served functions far beyond the borders of the ritual frame.

In Chapter 4, Henry Albery problematises the well-known function of the Buddha's ontological and semiotic presence in relics and stupas. He examines this principle as a mechanism of expansionism, central to the diffusion of Buddhism and the formation of local political power in the Indic Northwest around the turn of the Common Era. Introducing new evidence from the *Sarvāstivādavinaya* and other works preserved in Chinese he demonstrates a distinct and paradoxical ambivalence among Buddhists towards stupas and relics, whose respective destruction and theft were both legally validated and invalidated. Identifying a propagandistic reworking of these regulations in the *Mahāparinirvāṇasūtra* and *Aśokāvadāna*, he locates the works in the Northwest on the basis of archaeological, art-historical and epigraphic remains and argues that destruction and theft came to be ritualised as archaeologising activities enacted by political agents in the region. Through a systematic study of Kharoṣṭhī reliquary inscriptions, he questions existing socio-historical models of the region and provides a more nuanced social demographic of individuals engaging in relic (re)-dedications. On that basis, he suggests that regulations allowing theft were first employed by local rulers and thereafter by imperial regimes of the region in response to the fluxes of the turbulent political landscape.

Leslie C. Orr also takes up relations between presence and social power in Chapter 5 through a series of epigraphic case studies from Śaiva and Vaiṣṇava temples in Tamil Nadu between the 13th and 16th centuries. She focuses on two forms of naming rituals that typically record the donation of wealth and land to the temple: daily worship services or annual and monthly festivals occurring in conjunction with an individual's birth star. She argues that naming rituals served the repeated purpose of highlighting the presence of an absentee donor, whose name is uttered during the ritual circumambulation of the *maṇḍapa*. Examining spatiality and temporality, she notes certain mimetic patterns in the prominent positions of inscriptions on the *maṇḍapas* and the auspicious times at which they were commonly enacted. She demonstrates how the engraving of patrons' nominal presence on temple architecture is reflective of how power was shared and contested in the space of the Tamil temple.

Inspired by a line of sculptured devotees stationed in perpetual veneration toward a now empty shrine, in Chapter 6 Crispin Branfoot raises the question of how absent deities can aid our understanding of past ritual modes at Tamil temples between the 7th and 17th centuries. He makes use of anthropological, architectural, art-historical, epigraphic and textual sources to diachronically reconstruct the bygone enactments of deities' ritual processions on festival days. Moving beyond textual research of Śaiva and Vaiṣṇava literature which reveals the mythic and formally prescribed dimensions of ritual practice, art-historical research concerned with typologies, and anthropological research into contemporary practice, he applies an archaeology of performance to understand how shifting ritual patterns shaped the materiality of deities' representations, the construction of temples and urban planning, and their relation to social structures across this historical period. Branfoot demonstrates that increasing trends towards circumambulatory festival processions led to the construction of vast temples sites. From the now-absent presence of the deity, he infers that on ritual days of procession the deity would be brought and temporarily stationed within *maṇḍapas* built in expanding layers of the temples' structures which encircled the central shrine. This concentricity, he argues, created a spatial, sacred and social hierarchy determined by the degree of proximity individual social groupings were afforded to the central shrine.

The final section of the book deals with the dynamics of ritual and *space*. The chapters consider how the two are reciprocally determinative for the formation of power. Reformulations of space through land grants, agricultural expansion or distinct ritual modes are treated as reflective of broader ideological and social concerns. A better understanding of space and ritual is a matter of determining what is at stake in a socio-historical context, and examples dealt with in this section detail ritual land grants; the relation between art, architecture and practice among different social groups; agricultural expansion and ritual access and the ritual construction of institutional and ideological nodes.

In Chapter 7, Ingo Strauch examines inscriptions relating the 'permanent endowment' of money, agricultural land, animals and slaves to religious institutions. This ritual practice, he argues, served principally as a means for institutions to develop sustainable ritual centres and secure their longevity. Comparing textual sources with epigraphic evidence from Maharashtra in the 1st century CE and Andhra Pradhesh in the 3rd–4th centuries CE, he demonstrates that endowments of money and land were developed among Buddhist institutions initially to fund building maintenance but later to support ritual activities also. In the early Common Era the practice became widespread and was also adopted by other non-Buddhist groups, whereupon it was modified according to distinct moments of ritual import. Strauch thus provides evidence for how space was ritualised and transformed under specific ideological and socio-historical contexts.

In Chapter 8, Lisa N. Owen turns to a series of 6th–8th century rock-relief depictions of temples and deities at Badami, Karnataka. Because of their eluding ready classification as sites of ritual performance, these spaces have been disregarded as archaeological objects. Seeking to rectify this, Owen reconsiders the 'ritual vocabulary' of the reliefs in the broader architectural complex of Badami, examining visual and spatial features of the rock architecture to determine potential forms and experiences of ritual practice. Her interpretation is framed in terms of Śaiva and Vaiṣṇava cosmological and eschatological systems. Noting a series of juxtapositions between carvings of *liṅgas*, figural deities and a nearby reservoir, she argues that these signify associations with temporality and transformative states that were ritually enacted during post-death memorial rituals. In light of inscriptions composed in Telegu, Kanada and Nāgarī scripts, she further considers how space can provide insight into the rituals and daily life practices of the artists, visitors, pilgrims and local residents recorded at the site. She concludes that these reliefs created a 'power of place' for a broad social demographic of devotees.

In Chapter 9, Andrew M. Bauer considers the overlapping 'sacred' and 'profane' dimensions of ritual and space within a case study of 11th-century land endowments at Maski, in the Raichur Doab. Applying a politico-ecological approach, he conjunctionally examines agricultural and sociological data provided in donative inscriptions, patterns of agricultural expansion in pottery distribution and degrees of soil cultivability (colour, texture, irrigation conditions) and the value of cultigens. This enables him to argue against common scholarly assumptions, which have tended to overstress the relation between fertile land in the Doab and political conflict in the medieval period. Rather, he convincingly details a far more complex landscape, demonstrating how hydrological conditions, soil quality and agricultural technologies served to construct emic notions of fertility and how these were further attached to the formation of social status. Bauer thereby demonstrates that certain agricultural spaces, and the concomitant value of the cultigens they produced, served to marginalise certain groups, which together impacted upon these groups' ability to engage in ritual.

Moving the focus from peripheries to nodes, in Chapter 10 Nupur Dasgupta considers a group of 10th–11th century inscriptions recording land endowments in Gadag District, Karnataka, which bear witness to the emergence of temple and administrative centres among Jain, Śaiva and Vaiṣṇava institutions. Reorienting dynastic interpretations of ritual, she considers a fuller social constellation, looking at the relational roles of local administrative, intellectual and pedagogic figures in temple spaces. She demonstrates that, faced with broader political changes, 'provincial agencies' (e.g., village headmen) ensured the continuation of ritual complexes, sometimes increasing patterns of patronage at temple sites and initiating the construction of monuments in an effort to define a regionally circumscribed sacred landscape. Many land grants were 'donations for learning', a specific ritual practice that marked the institution of educational centres and grants for the promotion of grammatical and philosophical study. These new spaces facilitated intercourse between the aforementioned figures and generated a burgeoning of literary composition and the propagation of local ideologies. Dasgupta shows, therefore, that ritual space was paramount to the creation of this local intellectual tradition and cultural identity.

Notes

1 But here used in the wider sense of written, constructed and behaved forms of documentation as per Michel Foucault, *The Archaeology of Knowledge*, London: Routledge Classics, 2002, pp. 6–9.

2 To cite but a few works, Timothy Insoll, *Archaeology, Religion, Ritual*, London and New York: Routledge, 2004; Evangelos Kyriakidis (ed), *The Archaeology of Ritual*, Los Angeles: Cotsen Institute of Archaeology, 2007; Lars Fogelin, 'The Archaeology of Religious Ritual', *Annual Review of Anthropology*, 2007, 36: 55–71; Julian Droogan, *Religion, Material Culture and Archaeology*, London:

Bloomsbury Academic, 2013; Edward Swenson, 'The Archaeology of Ritual', *Annual Review of Anthropology*, 2015, 44: 329–45; Caitlín E. Barrett, 'Archaeology of Ancient Religions', *Religion: Oxford Research Encyclopedias*, Oxford: Oxford University Press, 2016.

3 William Chillingworth, *The Religion of Protestants: A Safe Way to Salvation*, London: James Nichols, 1686 [1637], p. 624.

4 Ritual is a likely etymological derivation of the Sanskrit *ṛta* ('order'), but it is primarily a derived term from the Latin *rītus* ('ceremony') and *rītuālis* ('belonging to the ceremony'). Presuming that citations in the Oxford English Dictionary may be considered representative, the term was introduced into English, primarily within Protestant literature of the 16th and 17th centuries, with two shades of meaning: as a book detailing the form and order of ceremonial rites or as a synonym to 'rites' and 'ceremonies' performed by various religious traditions. *Oxford English Dictionary: The Definitive Record of the English Language*, https://www-oed-com, accessed 17 October 2019, s.v. ritual. For an etymology and historical usage, see Talal Asad, *Geneaologies of Religion: Discipline and Reasons of Power in Christianity and Islam*, Baltimore: John Hopkins University Press, 1993, p. 58ff; Jens Kreinath, 'Ritual', *International Encyclopedia of Anthropology*, ed. H. Callan, New York: John Wiley & Sons, 2018, pp. 1–11 (pp. 1–2).

5 See Jonathan Z. Smith, *To Take Place: Toward Theory in Ritual*, Chicago: University of Chicago Press, 1987, p. 100.

6 This has been traced to Huldrych Zwingli (1484–1531). J. P. S. Uberoi, *Science and Culture*, Oxford: Oxford University Press, 1978, p. 25ff.

7 See, for example, Thomas More, *The Yale Edition of the Complete Works of St. Thomas More. Volume 13, Treatise on the Passion, Treatise on the Blessed Body, Instructions and Prayers*, ed. Garry E. Haupt, New Haven: Yale University Press, 1976 [1534], p. 138.

8 See, for example, *The Sermons of John Donne in Ten Volumes: II*, eds. George R. Potter and Evelyn M. Simpson, Berkeley and Los Angeles: University of California Press, 1955 [1631], pp. 255, 258.

9 Max Weber, *Die protestantische Ethik und der 'Geist' des Kapitalismus*, ed. Klaus Lichtblau, Johannes Weiß, Wiesbaden: Springer VS, 2016.

10 Webb Keane, *Christian Moderns: Freedom and Fetish in the Mission Encounter*, Berkeley and Los Angeles: University of California Press, 2007.

11 Peter van de Veer, 'Religion in South Asia', *Annual Review of Anthropology*, 2002, 31: 173–87.

12 One of the earliest exemplifications of this premise is to be found in George Forster, *Sketches of the Mythology and Customs of the Hindoos, Most Respectfully Inscribed to the Honorable the Court of Directors of the East-India Company*, London, 1735, esp., pp. 2, 38.

13 See *Asiatic Researches; or, Transactions of the Society Instituted in Bengal, for Inquiring into the History and Antiquities, the Arts, Sciences, and Literature, of Asia. Volume: The First*, Calcutta: Brojendro Lall Doss, 1884 [1798], pp. 118–235, 343–55.

14 On the reception of Jones' ethno-linguistic theories see Thomas R. Trautmann, *Aryans and British India*, Los Angeles: University of California Press, 1997; Michael J. Franklin, *Orientalist Jones. Sir William Jones, Poet, Lawyer, and Linguist, 1746–1794*, Oxford: Oxford University Press, 2011, esp. 39ff.

15 Urs App, *William Jones' Ancient Theology*, Sino-Platonic Papers, 191, Philadephia: University of Pennsylvania, 2009.

16 Dilip K. Chakrabarti, *A History of Indian Archaeology from the Beginning to 1947*, New Delhi: Munishram Manoharlal Publishers, 2001, pp. 18–21.
17 Jones' theory relies on the mythologist Jacob Bryant, *A New System, or, an Analysis of Ancient Mythology: Wherein an Attempt Is Made to Divest Tradition of Fable: And to Reduce the Truth to Its Original Purity*, vol. I–III, London, 1775–76.
18 *Asiatic Researches*, p. 233, 352.
19 *Ibid*, pp. 232–3.
20 On this connection, see Trautmann, *Aryans and British India*, pp. 42–3.
21 A biography of Jones written by John Shore in 1805 posthumously canonised this status, likening him to other 'Protestant scholar-heroes' and 'innovators in science', such as Francis Bacon, Newton and Locke, see *ibid*, pp. 99–101.
22 Jason Hawkes, 'Finding the "Early Medieval" in South Asian Archaeology', *Asian Perspectives*, 2014, 53(1): 53–96 (p. 54ff).
23 Edward Tylor, *Primitive Culture: Researches into the Development of Mythology, Philosophy, Religion, Language, Art, and Custom*, vol. I–II, London: John Murray, 1920 [1871].
24 For example, Lucienne Lévy-Bruhl, *How Natives Think*, trans. Lillian A. Clare, New York: Washington Square Press, 1966.
25 Gregory Schopen, *Bones Stones and Buddhist Monks: Collected Papers on the Archaeology, Epigraphy, and Texts of Monastic Buddhism in India*, Honolulu: University of Hawaii Press, 1997, p. 13.
26 William Robertson Smith, *Lectures on the Religion of the Semites: The Fundamental Institutions*, New York: The Macmillan Company, 1927 [1886], pp. 16–20.
27 Catherine Bell, *Ritual: Perspectives and Dimensions*, Oxford: Oxford University Press, 1997, p. 1ff; Asad, *Geneaologies of Religion*, p. 55ff; Barbara Boudewinjse, 'British Roots of the Concept of Ritual', in Arie L. Molendijk and Peter Pels (eds), *Religion in the Making: The Emergence of the Sciences of Religion*, Leiden: Brill, 1998, pp. 277–95.
28 Himanshu Prabha Ray, 'The History of Archaeology in India: Introduction', in *Archaeology as History in Early South Asia*, New Delhi: Aryan Books International, 2004, pp. 12–33 (pp. 16–17).
29 Sourindranath Roy, 'Indian Archaeology from Jones to Marshall (1784–1902)', *Ancient India*, 1953, 9: 4–28 (pp. 5–6); Chakrabarti, *A History of Indian Archaeology*, pp. 16–47.
30 For detailed discussion, see *ibid*, p. 48ff.
31 Alexander Cunningham, *Ancient Geography of India I: The Buddhist Period Including the Campaigns of Alexander, and the Travels of Hwen-Thsang*, London: Trübner & Co., 1871.
32 R. Coningham and R. Young (eds), *The Archaeology of South Asia: From the Indus to Asoka, c.6500 BCE—200 CE*, Cambridge: Cambridge University Press, 2015, p. 75ff.
33 James Fergusson, *The Illustrated Handbook of Architecture: Being a Concise and Popular Account of the Different Styles of Architecture Prevailing in All Ages and All Countries*, London: W. Clowes and Sons, 1859.
34 James Burgess and Bhagvānlal Indrājī, *Inscriptions from the Cave-Temples of Western India: With Descriptive Notes, & Co.*, Bombay: Government Central Press, 1881.
35 Alexander Cunningham, *The Bhilsa Topes: Or, Buddhist Monuments of Central India Comprising a Brief Historical Sketch of the Rise, Progress, and Decline*

of Buddhism; with an Account of the Opening and Examination of the Various Groups of Topes Around Bhilsa, London: Smith, Elder and Co, 1954.

36 Alexander Cunningham, *The Stûpa of Bharhut: A Buddhist Monument Ornamented with Numerous Sculptures Illustrative of Buddhist Legend and History in the Third Century B.C.*, London: W. H. Allen and Co., 1879.

37 Upinder Singh, *The Discovery of Ancient India: Early Archaeologists and the Beginnings of Archaeology*, New Delhi: Permanent Black, 2004, p. 44.

38 On the Aryan race in relation to Vedic and Buddhist religion, see Cunningham, *Bhilsa Topes*, p. vff, 15–16; Fergusson, *Handbook of Architecture*, p. 2ff.

39 Phillip Almond, *The British Discovery of Buddhism*, Cambridge: Cambridge University Press, 1988.

40 Chakrabarti, *A History of Indian Archaeology*, p. 120ff; Ray, 'The History of Archaeology', p. 21ff.

41 John Marshall (ed), *Mohenjodaro and the Indus Civilization,* vol. I, London: Arthur Probstein, 1931.

42 John Marshall, *Taxila: An Illustrated Account of Archaeological Excavations Carried Out at Taxila Under the Orders of the Government in India Between the Years 1913 and 1934*, vol. I–III, Cambridge: Cambridge University Press, 1951.

43 K. Paddayya, 'Theoretical Archaeology in India: An Anthropological Perspective', in Gwen Robbins Schug and Subhash R. Walimbe (eds), *A Companion to South Asia in the Past*, Chichester: John Wiley & Sons, 2016, pp. 437–49 (pp. 437–8).

44 Lars Fogelin, 'History, Ethnography, and Essentialism: The Archaeology of Religion and Ritual in South Asia', in Evangelos Kyriakidis (ed), *The Archaeology of Ritual*, Los Angeles: Cotsen Institute of Archaeology, University of California, 2007, pp. 23–42.

45 Marshall, *Mohenjodaro*, p. 48ff.

46 Ray, 'The History of Archaeology in India', p. 23.

47 Coningham and Young, *Archaeology of South Asia*, p. 80ff.

48 Hawkes, 'Finding the "Early Medieval"', p. 56ff.

49 B. B. Lal, *Historicity of the Mahabharata: Evidence of Literature, Art and Archaeology*, New Delhi: Aryan Books International, 2013.

50 H. D. Sankalia, *New Archaeology: Its Scope and Application to India*, D. N. Majumdar Lectures 1974, Lucknow: Ethnographic and Folk Culture Society, 1977.

51 Insoll, *Archaeology, Religion, Ritual*, p. 48ff.

52 See Smith, *To Take Place*; Caroline Humphrey and James Laidlaw, *The Archetypal Actions of Ritual: A Theory of Ritual Illustrated by the Jain Rite of Worship*, Oxford: The Clarendon Press, 1994, p. 71; Catherine Bell, *Ritual Theory, Ritual Practice*, Oxford: Oxford University Press, 1992; *idem*, *Ritual: Perspectives and Dimensions*.

53 Alfred Gell, *Art and Agency: An Anthropological Theory*, Oxford: Clarendon Press, 1998.

54 Fogelin, 'The Archaeology of Religious Ritual', p. 63.

55 Gregory Schopen, 'Burial "Ad Sanctos" and the Physical Presence of the Buddha in Early Indian Buddhism', *Religion*, 1987, 17(3): 193–225; Michael Willis, *The Archaeology of Hindu Ritual: Temples and the Establishments of the Gods*, Cambridge: Cambridge University Press, 2009, p. 3.

56 Dilip K. Chakrabarti, 'The Archaeology of Hinduism', in Timothy Insoll (ed), *Archaeology and World Religion*, London and New York: Routledge, 2001, pp. 33–60.

57 Lars Fogelin, 'Ritual and Representation in Early Buddhist Ritual Architecture', *Asian Perspectives*, 2003, 42(2): 129–54; Coningham, 'The Archaeology of Buddhism', in Robin Coningham and Timothy Insoll (eds), *Archaeology and World Religion*, London and New York: Routledge, 2002, pp. 61–95; Himanshu Prabha Ray, 'The Archaeology of Sacred Space', in Himanshu Prabha Ray and Carla M. Sinopoli (eds), *Archaeology as History in Early South Asia*, New Delhi: Aryan Books International, 2004, pp. 350–75.

58 Rubina Raja and Jörg Rüpke, 'Archaeology of Religion, Material Religion, and the Ancient World', in Rubina Raja and Jörg Rüpke (eds), *A Companion to the Archaeology of Religion in the Ancient World*, Chichester: John Wiley & Sons, 2015, pp. 1–26 (p. 3ff).

59 See Bell, *Ritual: Perspectives and Dimensions*, *Ritual Theory*; Jens Kreinath, J. M. Snoek, and Michael Stausberg (eds), *Theorizing Rituals, Volume 1: Issues, Topics, Approaches, Concepts*, Leiden and Boston: Brill, 2006; Swenson, 'The Archaeology of Ritual'.

Part I

POWER

1

IMAGINING SACRIFICE IN ANCIENT INDIA

A genealogy of Heesterman's *Broken World*[1]

Robert A. Yelle

Introduction: staging the primal scene of sacrifice

In his 1993 work, *The Broken World of Sacrifice*, the late Dutch Indologist Jan Heesterman (1925–2014) offered a summation of his decades-long argument that the Vedic sacrificial texts contained the traces of an older, lost tradition.[2] In Heesterman's reconstruction, sacrifice was originally a life-and-death struggle between competitors for certain material, social and existential goods: 'the overall contest pattern of preclassical sacrifice . . . was a real struggle for the ultimate stakes of life and death'.[3] He describes this primal scene as a 'battleground'[4] or 'undisguised raiding affair'[5] where the 'sacred frenzy of the warrior'[6] endured through the 'apogee of the sacrifice' in 'the unpredictable exuberance of the communal meal'.[7] According to Heesterman, traces of this original model remain visible in the Vedic corpus, in symbolic chariot races, references to securing the 'head' of the sacrifice (which may refer to decapitating one's opponent) and the vestigial meal that is the *odana*.

His account is structured by the contrast between an original, ecstatic scene that may be dimly glimpsed behind the extant texts—as if these were palimpsests—and what became of the sacrifice as it degenerated into a mechanistic form of ritual. The Brahmins resolved the tension of the sacrificial agon by removing its competitive element, and making it a solo performance that was, moreover, tightly scripted. The logical end point of this process of denaturalisation was the Upaniṣadic identification between Ātman and Brahman, or self and universal, in which no uncertainty remained and even the sacrifice itself could be reduced to the internal yoga of the *prāṇāgnihotram*:

> While the sacrificial contest reenacted the enigmatic relationship of life and death, ritualism—stripping away the contest—posited the absolute rule of ritual beyond life and death. It thereby opened

> up a definitive split between the dynamic sacrality of the life-and-death nexus and the static transcendence of the Vedic injunction—between the awesome uncertainty of the sacred and the dead certainty of the transcendent. . . . [I]t is ancient Indian ritualism . . . that offers the clearest and by far the best documented case of such an 'axial' breakthrough. . . . When . . . a breakthrough like Vedic ritualism did occur, it 'disenchanted' a world held in thrall by the sacred brokenness of the contest.[8]

Before the Vedic period, sacrifice had been a communal affair; indeed, what Marcel Mauss referred to as a 'prestation totale', at which social groups came together and reestablished their bonds through the festive rivalry of the 'Three F's'—Feasting, Fighting and Falling in Love. The *Mahāvrata* festival, for example, shows 'the remnants of a rowdy and orgiastic New Year's festival'.[9] After the Brahmin priests domesticated the sacrifice, it became an individualistic, even antisocial, affair that led logically to movements of renunciation and asceticism.

Heesterman's reconstruction has been admired for its boldness as well as questioned for its speculative leaps by other scholars of the *Vedas*.[10] Stephanie Jamison posed, among other criticisms, the following:

> A more dubious method of reconstruction is the constant derivation of the figurative and symbolic from the literal. Heesterman regularly argues that apparent symbolic representations in śrauta ritual are denatured, 'deconstructed' survivals of actual, literal procedures in the older system. For example, the presence of a chariot or even a chariot wheel points to a real, lengthy journey embedded in the older sacrifice; a symbolic contest (with dice or with words) to a real fight to the death. . . . [T]o what extent are we required (or allowed) to assume that a particular element in a ritual is the diachronic schematization of something originally real?[11]

More cuttingly, Christopher Minkowski stated: 'The misfortune is that each of [Heesterman's] brilliant insights is, as it were, dragged up the side of an ideological volcano and sacrificed whole to the angry, catastrophic god of [his] grand theory'.[12]

Despite such critiques, Heesterman's historical reconstruction of the development of Vedic sacrifice remains as one of the last important interpretations of this key tradition. To my knowledge, there has been no serious effort to trace the genealogy of his account in the history of European ideas, as opposed to that part which may derive directly from a reading of the Vedic texts. I will argue that Heesterman's account is premised on a series of tropes, mythemes and narratives that reveal much more about the European mind than they do about the ancient history and prehistory of the subcontinent. His depiction of the primal scene of sacrifice as a combat among warriors drew both on his countryman Johan Huizinga's focus in *Homo Ludens* (1938) on agonistic play as the key to culture and on various early 20th-century and Weimar- and Nazi-era studies of the Aryan or Indo-German *Männerbund*, or 'male band', as the original social formation. Heesterman's account of the degeneration of sacrifice at the hands of priests resembles narratives of the decline of ancient Israelite sacrifice from a joyous communal meal into empty ritualism, narratives that received influential expression by the late-19th-century Protestant Bible scholars Julius Wellhausen and William Robertson Smith. More generally, Heesterman's account echoed Max Weber's thesis of the routinisation of charisma;[13] he actually appropriated Weber's term 'disenchantment' to label the ancient Indian developments. The fact that each of these older theories has by now been criticised itself as encoding certain biases, whether theological or racialist, lends urgency to the task of a genealogical critique.

Protestant narratives of the decline from sacrifice to ritual

First let me summarise a few more of the main points of Heesterman's theory. Sacrifice normally consists of three components: immolation or killing, generally (although not always) of an animal or even a human being; the destruction of an offering and a meal.[14] The element of destruction signals abandonment, and it is what distinguishes the sacrifice from the gift.[15] Heesterman acknowledges that 'there are well-known cases in which one of the three basic elements is missing. . . . Thus the holocaust or the biblical *'olah* is wholly burnt without any part being eaten. Here oblational destruction has taken over from the otherwise normal meal'.[16] However, the presence of the three elements in some combination is what defines sacrifice. Contradicting a long scholarly tradition that regards sacrifice as a type or subset of ritual, Heesterman posits a fundamental distinction between these two categories. Where sacrifice is spontaneous, natural and communal, ritual is artificial, mechanistic and sharply separated from social life: 'the ritualists have remolded the animal sacrifice so as to eliminate the "inauspicious" awesomeness and excitement of blood and killing. The result . . . is an utterly flat, though intricate, sequence of acts and mantras, perfectly regulated and without ups or downs, which agrees with the ritualists' aim of taming sacrifice'.[17] Heesterman's archive is the developed system of *Śrauta* or 'solemn' rites in the Vedic texts, which are complex and carried out by specialists. These rituals are some of the most elaborate and well-documented that we know of. The form of ritual is adapted to its purpose, which is to provide a 'fail-safe, risk-free mechanism that will automatically deliver the goods of life . . . that took out the sting of death and absolutized the capacity of sacrifice for establishing order'.[18] Ritual replaced the 'awesome uncertainty' of sacrifice with 'dead certainty'.

This required a denaturation of sacrifice, as shown not only by its increasingly scripted nature, but also by the loss of its communal dimensions—represented above all by the displacement of the festival meal—as well as by the rise of a specialised cadre of priests. Tamed by ritual, 'sacrifice . . . no longer even contains a festive meal'.[19] The burnt oblation, or the element of destruction by fire, took over until 'little room was left for the direct and tangible manipulation of life and death epitomized in the two other moments of sacrifice, the immolatory kill and its material purpose, the sacrificial meal. . . . Sacrifice was dematerialized as it was desocialized'.[20] The focus of sacrifice as a social event had been the communal meal, which, because of its involvement in an 'ever-shifting web of conflict and alliance', had to be pushed to the margins.[21] The potlatch was broken up and the punchbowl taken away; all that remained was the vegetarian *odana* meal, as an afterthought.

The villains in Heesterman's drama are the Brahmin priests, who gradually take over as sacrifice gives way to ritual. The original sacrificer was a warrior consecrated unto death, who entered into combat for the goods of sacrifice and enjoyed the Three F's as previously mentioned. 'Briefly and crudely, before there were priests there were warriors'.[22] A key example is the *Vrātya*, an ambivalent figure in the Vedas, whom Heesterman describes as an 'aggressive warrior moving about in sworn bands'.[23] Indeed, one of the earliest statements of his theory of sacrifice appears in a 1962 article on these figures, whom Heesterman described as 'partak[ing] of the nature of both sacrificers and priests. . . . Ritual technique did not yet require rigorous specialization, nor were warriors and priests rigidly exclusive groups'.[24] Indeed, Heesterman argued that even in the Vedas 'the institution of sacrifice did not lead to a clearly defined and highly profiled priesthood', as this required the development of temples under royal patronage, such as happened in the ancient Near East.[25]

At this point, we have enough of a sketch of Heesterman's theory that we are prepared to begin our genealogy. In general terms, this theory belongs to the familiar genre of narratives of decline. (While writing this I can't help thinking about the recently deceased Hayden White's book, *Metahistory*.) One of the most famous such narratives was promoted by the German sociologist Max Weber, who described the two interrelated processes of 'disenchantment' and the 'routinisation of charisma' through its replacement by bureaucratic or legal authority. Weber described charisma as an inherently personal, spontaneous and lawless force, which can inhere just as easily in berserkers or murderers as in religious figures such as Jesus or the Buddha.[26] Heesterman's warrior-sacrificers are from the same mould. Like Weber's charisma, Heesterman's sacrifice is fundamentally lawless: 'Rather than establishing and guaranteeing order, sacrifice overthrows order by the violent irruption of the sacred'.[27] Describing ritualisation as a movement away from the radical uncertainty of the earlier sacrificial contest, Heesterman conjures up a romanticised, ideal picture of an 'unbroken' world of sacrifice that existed *in illo tempore*. Similarly, for Weber, our present 'disenchanted' moment has replaced the arbitrary and personal force of charisma with 'calculability' (*Berechenbarkeit*).[28]

This connection is hardly speculative, given that Heesterman specifically cites Weber in several places. However, this reliance is problematic, as it has now been established that Weber's ideas of disenchantment and the routinisation of charisma borrowed from earlier Christian theological tropes, including the idea that miracles ceased at the end of the Apostolic Age—tropes that were redeployed against the Roman Catholic Church by Protestants from early in the Reformation.[29] Apart from these older precedents, Weber drew directly on the late-19th-century Protestant theologians Rudolph Sohm and Julius Wellhausen in developing his account of the routinisation of charisma. The identification of a pure, spontaneous religion that deteriorates into legalism was a Protestant trope that had been deployed against both Catholic law and Jewish *halakhah* by, respectively, Sohm and Wellhausen.[30] Whereas Sohm described the decline from the charismatic organisation of the primitive Christian community into the legal and institutional organisation of the Roman Catholic Church, Wellhausen described the fall in ancient Israelite religion from the prophets to the priests and into legalistic ritualism. Both narratives reinforced the superiority of Protestantism as a restoration of the charisma of the primitive Christian Church. Heesterman's polemic against ritual, and his insistence that the priesthood came late to India, appear to reflect these older theological polemics.

One of Heesterman's sources will help to reinforce this point. Ernst Arbman published his book *Rudra* in 1922. In it he draws a very sharp distinction between folk and priestly religion, in terms that anticipated Heesterman's later distinction between sacrifice and ritual. Arbman contrasts 'the artless, popular (*volkstümliche*) sacrifice' to 'the artificial and overladen ceremonial' that is the developed *Śrauta* ritual:

> The laborious, minutely elaborated (*ausgestaltete*) ceremonial, with which the sacrificial process itself is braided (*umsponnen*), the stereotypical basic scheme, according to which all rites should be carried out, the sacrificial-technical details, the hieratic formulas, which are often built on purely theological patterns of thought (*Gedankengänge*), and not least the expansive mass of non-popular (*unvolkstümlicher*), in part exclusively priestly-conventional pantheon, are features, which show their origin clearly enough.[31]

Arbman deplores the 'paralyzed formalism of the brahmanical sacrifice', in which sacrifice is no longer 'a bringing of gifts and an act of worship' but has become instead 'a magical procedure' that includes 'movements and formulas, hymns and prayers, fasting and asceticism' and so on.

> With this machinery man labours with his own hand (*auf eigene Faust*) to reach his goals and no longer needs the help of the gods. . . . They do not avail themselves any more of divine powers (*Machtressourcen*) in order to reach their goals, but must help themselves out with sacrifices and various ritualistic works (*Werken*) . . . If the effective power of the sacrifice should be thought to touch upon the personal intervention of the gods, then this intervention follows the same mechanistic route—exactly as when someone presses on a button—not as the result of free influence.[32]

Arbman concludes, 'From the above it has been shown that the Vedic sacrifice in its typical form represented an exclusively priestly cult, that in its external system as much as in its ideational content differs sharply from the popular (*volkstümlichen*) worship of the gods'.[33]

As it should scarcely be necessary to point out, Arbman here applies to Vedic ritual a number of the standard Protestant criticisms of Catholic ritual, including its mechanistic nature, rigid formalism and belief in the power of ritual works *ex opere operato*.[34] Heesterman's account of the decline from sacrifice to ritual closely parallels Arbman's description of the difference between popular and priestly ritual.

Wellhausen argued that the prominence of the whole burnt offering in the Priestly Code was a later development that coordinated with the rise to dominance of the priestly class, the centralisation of worship at Jerusalem and the proliferation of offerings made directly to priests.[35] Originally, sacrifice consisted of a communal meal and represented a spontaneous expression of community and solidarity in ancient Israel. It was the priests who cast us out of this Eden, by replacing such celebrations with the burnt offering and other modes of sacrifice that were 'deprived of their natural spontaneity, and degraded into mere "exercises of religion" '.[36] Wellhausen's thesis concerning the development of sacrifice was taken over by his colleague and fellow Protestant theologian William Robertson Smith, who endorsed the idea that ancient Israelite religion was focused on sacrifice as an act of commensality. Émile Durkheim borrowed from Smith in defining the social function of religion in producing group solidarity, particularly in ecstatic communal rituals. Sacrifices that eventuated in feasting obviously fit such theoretical models much better than did the burnt offering. Such interpretations were biased by Protestant attitudes against ritual and echoed interpretations of the Eucharist, going back to Luther, as a meal rather than a sacrifice.

Such narratives of decline through priestly ritualism appear to have been carried over, *mutatis mutandis*, into Heesterman's accounts of Vedic sacrifice. Heesterman makes two claims that were also central to Wellhausen's account; namely, that the burnt offering came gradually to replace the communal meal and that the specialised priesthood was a late innovation. One obvious difference is that Wellhausen's account lacked the element of gladiatorial combat that was central for Heesterman.

How should we account for these parallels? Although I have found no evidence that Heesterman was influenced directly by Wellhausen, there were plenty of routes for an indirect influence. Weber's work on ancient Judaism adopted Wellhausen's decline narrative and applied it to describe the fall from prophetic charisma into priestly legalism.[37] More likely this parallel reflects the shared current of *Kulturprotestantismus*. The anti-ritual bias and characterisation of the Eucharist (*Abendmahl*) as something other than a sacrifice was a common heritage of the Reformation. Furthermore, plenty of German Indologists, such as Arbman, had already applied to Brahmins the polemics that had originally been applied against Catholic priests and Jewish rabbis. Such polemics had long argued that these groups corrupted their respective traditions and possibly even their sacred scriptures—which accordingly required 'fixing' these texts back to their original form. Indeed, the primary example in European tradition of the kind of speculative reconstruction in which Heesterman engages was the critical study of the Hebrew Bible that emerged from the Reformation. Whereas Wellhausen represented the culmination of this tradition, there were many other examples to hand that served as models for Heesterman and other Indologists.

Heesterman echoes these older theological polemics when he claims that 'there is at least one well-documented case of a sacrifice *without* sacrificial ritual—the Crucifixion'.[38] As this was, according to Christians, unique and perfectly effective, 'it was . . . not in need of any ritual. It is thus even more remarkable that, however slowly and tortuously, a ritual came to be elaborated'.[39] Once again, it seems that Heesterman's distinction between ritual and sacrifice is practically designed to privilege the Protestant over the Jewish and Catholic views of sacrifice.

'Before there were priests, there were warriors'

More direct evidence exists for the source of Heesterman's idea of pre-Vedic sacrifice as a conflict among warriors. He cited some representatives of an older tradition of primarily German philology that was implicated in promoting the idea of the Aryan 'men's federation' or 'male band' (*Männerbund*), the notion that the original Indo-European or, as it is often called, 'Indo-German' culture consisted of roving bands of warriors who conquered subject peoples, spreading mayhem along the way. Heesterman drew on this literature beginning in the 1950s and 1960s—thus, after World War II and the full public awareness of the problematic role that such Aryanist ideas had played in supporting the Nazi ideology. More remarkably, he continued to repeat such ideas until the 1990s, apparently without any more sober colleagues in Indology noting that he was doing so. Indeed, there still remain some who continue to repeat these ideas. This reinforces the need to uncover their problematic past as a necessary propaedeutic, a form of mental hygiene that hopefully will pave the way for a better, more scientific philology.

As we have seen, Heesterman's speculative history began with a depiction of the original sacrifice as something like a frenzied potlatch conducted, in competitive fashion, by warriors rather than priests. Weber's idea that berserkers illustrate charismatic authority was only one small precedent for this primal scene. Other sources were Heesterman's countrymen Johan Huizinga and George Held, as well as more problematic figures implicated in elaborating the mythology of the Aryan warrior, including the Austrian Otto Höfler, the Swede Stig Wikander and the German Jakob Wilhelm Hauer. That none of these connections is noted in the published reviews of Heesterman's work constitutes a striking and disturbing episode of amnesia for the discipline, which it is my purpose now to correct.

Huizinga's famous work *Homo Ludens* (1938) served as a relatively benign source for several of Heesterman's specific tropes, including especially the idea that culture begins in a form of agonistic play that is indistinguishable from ritual. Huizinga stresses all the competitive elements of ritual in early cultures, including combat, dice-play and the potlatch, which we can define as centrally focused on a form of competitive gift-giving through one-upmanship. Both Huizinga and Heesterman followed Marcel Mauss in emphasising the manner in which this primal scene constitutes a 'prestation totale' or form of total cultural exchange between groups, not only of food but also of marriage partners, in a manner that may be dualistic and competitive.[40] Huizinga anticipates Heesterman in highlighting the potentially violent nature of these events:

> When the people foregather at the sanctuary they gather together for collective rejoicing. Consecrations, sacrifices, sacred dances and contests, performances, mysteries—all are comprehended within the act of celebrating a festival. The rites may be bloody, the probations of the young men awaiting initiation may be cruel, the masks may be terrifying, but the whole thing has a festal nature.[41]

Huizinga refers to the specific forms of play on which Heesterman's reconstruction relies, including gambling with dice and the riddle-contest, in connection with the *Mahābhārata* and the *Upaniṣads* respectively.[42] For the former, he relies also on Held, whose reconstruction of the *Mahābhārata* Heesterman also applies, *mutatis mutandis*, to the Vedas.[43]

Held's work, *The Mahābhārata: An Ethnological Study*, was published in 1935. It interprets the Indian epic as evidence of an older history in which different clans, corresponding to the Kauravas and Pāṇḍavas of the story, assembled for a giant potlatch and practised exogamy.[44] Behind the myth was a ritual, in which combat, the *soma*-sacrifice, chariot races and gambling with dice all occurred.[45] Originally, the Śūdra participated with the Brahmin in these events, until 'they [were] more and more excluded' and 'the prohibitions of marriage with the Sudras gradually became stricter'.[46] The Vrātyas represented one such clan group, already by Vedic times ostracised from the Brahmins.[47] The existence of such societies at the time of the *Brāhmaṇas* indicates that the 'clan-organization is falling into decay' and with this 'class-exogamy'.[48] Held's theory is really a thesis regarding the origin of the caste system as a form of endogamy opposed to the earlier exogamy practised among even Brahmins and Śūdras. He is critical of the thesis that explains caste on racial grounds and that identifies Śūdras as the aboriginal, non-Aryan population.[49] He further refrains from opining on whether the Vrātyas were a non-Aryan people.[50] However, he characterises Rudra as a 'pure "Aryan" god' because of his 'terrifying and formidable' nature.[51] The Brahmins however attacked the clan associations such as the Vrātyas, with their *sabhā* or potlatch, and in the interest of preserving the new principle of endogamy, gradually altered the ritual:

> Now the Brahminic ritual, i.e. the official ritual, has in the course of ages been subjected to a meticulous elaboration. Investigators are generally agreed that this minute elaboration of the religious ritual ultimately resulted in its celebration becoming more and more restricted to a special class of people who had come to be considered ritual experts, viz. the caste of the Brahmins . . . whose members fancied themselves the upholders of the entire cosmic order, as their very name, indeed, implies. It was only their meticulous practice of the sacred rites that could produce the desired effects. The ritual ceremonial gradually became an intricate technical practice by means of which, provided it was made use of in the right manner, the right man in the right place might move heaven and earth to do his bidding.[52]

Held, as previously mentioned, wisely refrains from racialising the Vrātyas and the Śūdras, much less the Kauravas and Pāṇḍavas. Huizinga's concept of agonistic play is color-blind and extends to Africa as well as to ancient Greece and Vedic India. Heesterman is, rather like Held, somewhat noncommittal, although in his 1962 article on the Vrātyas he declared these to be 'authentic Aryans'[53] as well as true warriors, who reflected the original, pre-Brahminical agents of the sacrifice. In *The Inner Conflict of Tradition*

(1985), citing Held's theory, Heesterman characterises the potlatch and its subsequent breakup in the following terms:

> To eliminate conflict and violence, the community had to be broken up and the parties separated. This, not ethnic 'apartheid,' is the reason why the ārya and śūdra varṇas had to be separated from each other. Originally both had taken part in the agonistic sacrificial festival as opposite parties—a situation preserved in an innocuous form in the Vedic mahāvrata ritual.[54]

Here the different groups, which ultimately become separate castes, are characterised only as 'varṇas', rather than races or ethnicities. Heesterman consistently accounted for the evolution of Vedic society and culture in orthogenetic terms, as an internal development, as opposed to resorting to extraneous forces or groups as, most recently, Johannes Bronkhorst has done in order to account for the ideas of karma and rebirth.[55] It was this same impulse, in fact, that led Heesterman to declare the Vrātyas 'authentic Aryans', within the original system rather than outside of it. One problem here is the ambiguity in the word 'Aryan', which in the declaration just quoted, detached from the contrast between 'ārya' and 'śūdra varṇas', is difficult to interpret as anything other than an ethnic descriptor. Behind such language, as we shall see, lay an explicit racialisation of these categories in some of Heesterman's sources, such as Jakob Wilhelm Hauer, for whom the Vrātyas were racial Aryans, indeed the reflection of older Indo-German warrior traditions.[56] Heesterman's own invocation of such ideas of racial unity was very faint by comparison.[57]

In their controversial 2014 book, *The Nay Science*, Vishwa Adluri and Joydeep Bagchee present a far-reaching critique of the biases that informed German Indological reconstructions of the *Mahābhārata* in the 19th and early 20th centuries. Although they overreach and caricature an entire discipline rather than some of its individual practitioners, Adluri and Bagchee successfully document the long survival of certain biases and tropes in at least some main areas of *Mahābhārata* research. For example, Christian Lassen's idea that the great composition originated with a warrior epic that recounted a racial conflict between Aryans and Dravidians, but that was subsequently corrupted by the Brahminical priestly tradition, with the addition from Adolf Holtzmann, Jr., that the original epic reflected an Indo-German tradition, served as background for Held's own, tamer reconstruction, on which Heesterman explicitly relied.[58] Adluri and Bagchee emphasise how Holtzmann used Brahmanism to express his own Protestant disdain for Roman Catholic ritualism.[59] They generalised this critique to German Indology more broadly.[60] As we have seen, this critique would appear to apply to Heesterman as well.

Yet the idea of the Aryan warrior owed more to another tradition, pagan rather than Christian. Behind Held's and Heesterman's image of exogamous clans engaged in feasting and fighting lay the notion that Aryan society was divided originally into warrior bands, the so-called *Männerbünde*.[61] Heesterman himself stated: 'Probably the best studied material regarding this function of the war band is that of the ancient Germanic peoples'.[62] Some of the main figures here were Otto Höfler and Stig Wikander.[63] Wikander relied on some of the same sources as Heesterman, such as Arbman and Hauer, in elaborating his thesis concerning these original Aryan warrior groups.[64] Rather than attempt to characterise Wikander's book, I shall quote Bruce Lincoln:

> It is less the scholarly failings of *Der arische Männerbund* that concern me (although these exist, to be sure) than its extrascholarly dimensions. This is, after all, a book on the topic of 'Aryan' warbands that was written in the late 1930s, just after its author had spent a considerable period of time in Berlin. It begins, moreover, by acknowledging the strong influence of Otto Höfler's Nazi-tinged *Kultische Geheimbünde der Germanen*, and notes with special approval the recent upsurge of scholarly interest in Germany on questions of Indo-European religion and society.[65]

Lincoln proceeds to note Wikander's 'positive attitude' toward the demonic. This is reflected especially in the latter's discussion of the Avestan references to the *aēšma*, or warrior's frenzy,[66] of which an echo can perhaps still be heard in Huizinga's reference to the experience of play as 'being seized', or what Höfler in 1934 called *Ergriffenheit*,[67] a concept that, as Steven Wasserstrom and Gustavo Benavides both have detailed, was used to justify similar forms of ontic seizure or irrational exuberance in contemporary times.[68] In *Broken World*, Heesterman also refers directly to *aēšma* and states, 'what was ruled out [by the Brahmins] was the sacred frenzy of the warrior'.[69]

The *Männerbund* discourse is now widely recognised as a speculative reconstruction, ideological rather than scientific in nature. This discourse is actually quite varied. The work that is generally regarded as the source for all subsequent discourses on the *Männerbund* is Heinrich Schurtz's *Altersklassen und Männerbünde* (1902).[70] Schurtz's text, however, is not Aryanist; it is a global survey of men's associations among all the peoples of the world but especially among the indigenous peoples or what used to be called *Naturvölker*. The Aryanisation of this discourse proceeded especially with the school surrounding Rudolf Much in Vienna, among whose students were Lily Weiser-Aall (née Weiser), Richard Wolfram and Otto Höfler, whose *Kultische Geheimbünde der Germanen* (1934) became perhaps the key text of this genre.[71] Some key elements in this discourse were ideas of the *Männerbund* as a band of roving warriors-cum-hunters, either led or possessed by a berserker god identified as Wotan/Odin.[72] These bands were supposedly the original form of Indo-German social organisation that continued into more recent eras, as traced through folklore and evidenced in carnivalesque practices such as those of Fastnacht and the Perchten- and Krampuslauf.

The connection of such ideas with the Vrātyas described in the Vedas was argued especially by Jakob Wilhelm Hauer, whose deep complicity in both National Socialist politics and Aryanist racial ideology has been detailed by others, including not only Adluri and Bagchee but also Horst Junginger[73] and Stefan Arvidsson.[74] Two of Hauer's books are most relevant here: *Die Anfänge der Yogapraxis*, which was published in 1922 but which the author states was composed partly in an English prison during World War I, and *Der Vrātya*, which was published in 1927.[75] Hauer identified the Vrātyas as the ancestors of the yogins, but also as warriors, 'wild ecstatics of the warrior caste',[76] and as forerunners of the Kṣatriya caste.[77] He emphasised their participation in sexual magic, fertility rites, or orgies.[78]

> They can be equated with the northern berserkers, who also as 'ripping animals' with magical-demonic power in monstrous, warlike, wild ecstasy storm against the enemy and drive them into flight or at night in transformed shape, while their bodies lay sleeping, roamed around the land and exterminated the enemy, a strange mixture of wild ecstatics and demonic beings. . . . The Vedic vrātyas were members of heretical cultic societies with diverse rites and with an expansive knowledge of sacrifice bordering on the mystical.[79]

Although Heesterman called Hauer's book 'weak in its translation and interpretation of the ritual texts',[80] he nevertheless adopted his predecessor's ideas that the Vrātyas represented an older, warrior tradition of the Aryan *Männerbund*, whose chief ritual consisted of the potlatch-like festival of the Mahāvrata.[81] Hauer's own characterisation of the Germanic soul provides a precedent for Heesterman's theory of the lost tension and conflict in pre-Vedic sacrifice, or what he called the 'inner conflict of tradition'. Thus Hauer:

> A monstrously wide-tensed polarity is especially characteristic of the Indo-German peoples. . . . Such a polarity needs however a great power of unification, a power that was not available in all periods of Indo-German history. There were times in which the tension-spring that held the two poles was broken, so that the power went astray and circled only one pole. . . . And there were the great epochs of Indo-German history, when the polarity manifested itself in its greatest tension in great men and living communities.[82]

Another well-known figure in the *Männerbund* discourse deserves some discussion, because, although never (to my knowledge) cited by Heesterman, he represented the first application of Schurtz's idea to the Vedas: Leopold von Schröder, *Mysterium und Mimus im Rigveda* (1908).[83] Von Schröder engaged in a far-reaching and speculative reconstruction of the original basis of Vedic ritual in a pattern of ecstatic folk-religion among the Indo-Germans. Almost all of the elements that would come to be present in later applications of the *Männerbund* idea to the ancient Indian data are already present in von Schröder: dancing youths, competitions (foot races, chariot races, sword dances, dice games), free love and, above all, Rudra and the Maruts as the signs of this ecstasy. In an appendix, von Schröder connected his systematic reconstruction of a pre-Vedic ecstatic religion with Schurtz's *Männerbund* idea, which he cited as independent corroborating evidence.[84] Where Schurtz had traced such men's associations across the globe, von Schröder's focus was on proving that the Aryans in particular had passed through such a developmental stage. He named precisely the hymns to Rudra and his embodiment in ecstatic mimetic performances in the Vedas as 'in all probability an inheritance from the primitive age of the Aryans'[85] that had been progressively erased in the later ritual:

> The cultic drama, the mystery, as it lies before us in the dialogue songs of the Rig Veda, is no beginning, but rather an end. Nothing further followed in this line. And one grasps very well the reason. The cultic drama, the mystery, was not in accordance with the sense of those men, who in the time after the Rig Veda constructed and fixed the Indian ritual of sacrifice. The lively procession (*Auftreten*) of the gods in their own person, represented by men, their dancing and singing, would have appeared indecent to a later age, particularly to one that was priestly and ever more antiquated (*verzopften*) and petrified. . . . And this [custom] was not merely contested, rather it actually perished, disappeared in the Vedic priestly ritual without a trace, forever. Much that was popular (*volkstümlich*), that stemmed from the old times, the priestly ritualists of the Vedic times stylised as sacred, and so let become paralysed: races and target-shooting (*Scheibenschiessen*), lighting fires and swinging and still more besides. Other things of this sort were allowed to completely disappear. And among those evidently was the cultic drama, the mystery.[86]

Von Schröder drew the parallel between Rudra and Wotan/Odin as ecstatic warrior gods.[87] He connected the idea of the Aryan *Urmythos* of stealing fire, an idea developed earlier by Adalbert Kuhn,[88] with the Vedic sacrificial fire,[89] establishing a precedent for Heesterman's later argument that aspects of the Śrauta ritual encoded, in obscure form, an older practice in which the sacrificial fire had been stolen from an opponent. Von Schröder also identified traces in the Rig Veda of an earlier chariot race that had constituted part of the sacrificial festival.[90] However, he interpreted the procession of the sacrificial fire by chariot as a symbol of the sun,[91] rather than as Heesterman had done, as a vestige of the practice of stealing fire.

There are so many and such close parallels between Heesterman and von Schröder that we must ask what remains in the former's reconstruction that was original. Of course, there were many differences in the details of their interpretation. Also, where von Schröder focused mainly on the *Rig Veda*, Heesterman concentrated on the *Śrautasūtras*. The fact that Heesterman did not need even to mention von Schröder's pioneering work can be interpreted in several ways. In the intervening half-century between von Schröder's work and the first articulations of Heesterman's reconstruction, there had meanwhile appeared many other works of this genre. All the pieces that were already more or less assembled in von Schröder's work had been circulating in the scholarly discourse for decades. Heesterman had only to pick up these pieces and rearrange them into a pattern of his own choosing. If we assume, however, that Heesterman knew and refrained from citing von Schröder's work, then this could have been because his predecessor's methodology and conclusions were more obviously problematic. Where von Schröder ranged much more widely and speculatively over the Indo-European terrain, Heesterman preferred to stick to his Vedic data. Von Schröder also, like many other proponents of the *Männerbund* thesis, strongly emphasised the erotic nature of the lost 'mystery cult'. The sexual dimension in Heesterman's account is repressed to a minor footnote; it appears only in the context of his reconstruction of the original festival as an orgiastic 'prestation totale', the point of which, also for many of his direct predecessors in the *Männerbund* discourse, had been the exchange of sexual partners or the conclusion of marriage contracts between groups.

Behind many of these narratives of decline, as various scholars who have studied the *Männerbund* literature have pointed out, was not merely the longing for ecstasy, but more concretely the dream of sociality, especially the desire for the company of other men, the wish to belong to a band of happy warriors—and perhaps to fall into the arms of some Aryan camp-follower. This was an almost palpable yearning, yet it also gave vent to particular imaginings of the body politic, particularly in the primal scene of its very formation. Whereas such visions of an ideal social order were used to justify, and served as models for, some contemporary political movements in a way that was profoundly problematic, we now recognise increasingly that these visions were retrospective projections: unscientific speculations based on tendentious readings of highly selective evidence from a past that, precisely because it was inaccessible, could no longer talk back. Here again I quote Bruce Lincoln:

> Any project of reconstructive scholarship—i.e. anything that seeks to describe phenomena situated in an era before that for which we have textual evidence—of necessity yields nothing more than a hypothesis or imaginative construct. That being said, it is instructive to observe how frequently and powerfully such constructs reflect (and in some measure are determined by) their author's extra-scholarly values, desires, and commitments. The deeper the past of which one speaks ('Proto-Indo-European' being a prime example), the blanker the screen onto which one projects one's 'imaginative construct' and the freer one is to introduce all manner of things only weakly, if at all, supported by evidence and defensible logic.[92]

That all of this problematic background still leaves a clear impression on the theory of one of the leading Vedicists of the past generation, who moreover was quite explicit when citing his sources, should give us practitioners of Indology cause for concern and grounds for pause and reflection. One observation reinforced by this brief study concerns the manner in which theories, even highly speculative ones, can be circulated within a closed community of researchers in such a way as to appear mutually reinforcing.[93] The system, while not entirely closed, does resemble something of an echo chamber. The only solution to this problem is the searching and critical self-examination we name genealogy. As Justice Louis Brandeis said, sunlight is the best disinfectant. I hope to have shed a little light on a dark topic today.

Notes

1 I would like to acknowledge the advice and assistance, in preparing this chapter, of Elisa Freschi, Peter Jackson Rova, Horst Junginger and Bruce Lincoln. Wenzel Braunfels, my research assistant, helped both with finding relevant literature and with suggesting improvements in a few of the translations from German into English.

2 I recall first encountering Heesterman in a class on Indian history, the only class I took with Ronald Inden while a graduate student at the University of Chicago. Ron's critical, often tongue-in-cheek approach to Indology was clearly on display in his path-breaking book from 1990, *Imagining India,* Cambridge, MA: Blackwell, 1990, which served as one model for my own book examining colonial discourses about Hinduism, Robert A. Yelle, *The Language of Disenchantment: Protestant Literalism and Colonial Discourse in British India*, New York: Oxford University Press, 2013. This chapter reflects even more deeply the influence of another of my teachers, Bruce Lincoln, whose own turn toward a critical, genealogical approach in *Death, War, and Sacrifice: Studies in Ideology and Practice*, Chicago: University of Chicago Press, 1991, intersects with the topic of the present chapter, as will be seen later.

3 Jan Heesterman, *The Broken World of Sacrifice: An Essay in Ancient Indian Ritual*, Chicago: University of Chicago Press, 1993, p. 200.

4 *Ibid*, p. 52.

5 *Ibid*, p. 163.

6 *Ibid*, p. 83.
7 *Ibid*, p. 208.
8 *Ibid*, pp. 5–6. See also *idem*, 'Ritual, Revelation, and Axial Age', in Shmuel N. Eisenstadt (ed), *The Origins and Diversity of Axial Age Civilizations*, Albany: SUNY Press, 1986, pp. 393–406 (pp. 397, 399).
9 Heesterman, *Broken World*, p. 55.
10 There are a number of published reviews of Heesterman's *Broken World*, including the following: N. Allen, review of *The Broken World of Sacrifice: An Essay in Ancient Indian Ritual*, by Jan Heesterman, *Man*, 1994, 29(4): 998–99; Francis X. Clooney, review of *The Broken World of Sacrifice: An Essay in Ancient Indian Ritual*, by Jan Heesterman, *The Journal of Religion*, 1995, 75(1): 159–61; S. W. Jamison, review of *The Broken World of Sacrifice: An Essay in Ancient Indian Ritual*, by Jan Heesterman, *Method & Theory in the Study of Religion*, 1996, 8: 103–8; Christopher Minkowski, review of *The Broken World of Sacrifice: An Essay in Ancient Indian Ritual*, by Jan Heesterman, *Journal of the American Oriental Society*, 1996, 116: 341–44; Laurie Patton, review of *The Broken World of Sacrifice: An Essay in Ancient Indian Ritual*, by Jan Heesterman, *Journal of Asian Studies*, 1994, 53: 1299–300; Karel Werner, review of *The Broken World of Sacrifice: An Essay in Ancient Indian Ritual*, by Jan Heesterman, *Bulletin of the School of Oriental and African Studies*, 1995, 30: 197. Relevant also are the reviews of Heesterman's earlier book; see David Shulman, review of *The Inner Conflict of Tradition: Essays in Indian Ritual, Kingship, and Society*, by Jan Heesterman, *Numen*, 1985, 32: 289–91; N. J. Allen, review of *The Inner Conflict of Tradition: Essays in Indian Ritual, Kingship, and Society*, by Jan Heesterman, *Indo-Iranian Journal*, 1987, 30: 306–9.
11 Jamison, 'Review of *Broken World*', p. 106.
12 Minkowski, 'Review of *Broken World*', p. 343.
13 See the reference to Weber in Heesterman, *Broken World*, p. 4.
14 *Ibid*, p. 9.
15 *Ibid*, pp. 17–18.
16 *Ibid*, pp. 10–11.
17 *Ibid*, p. 73. See also *Idem*, 'Vrātya and Sacrifice', *Indo-Iranian Journal*, 1962, 6: 1–37 (p. 37): there occurred 'a "purification" of the ritual . . . into a highly refined and systematized code of abstract symbols . . . the exclusive domain of the pure expert'.
18 *Idem*, *The Inner Conflict of Tradition: Essays in Indian Ritual, Kingship, and Society*, Chicago: University of Chicago Press, 1985, p. 84.
19 Heesterman, *Broken World*, p. 81.
20 *Ibid*, p. 188, see also p. 109.
21 *Ibid*, pp. 207–8.
22 *Ibid*, p. 186. See also *Idem*, *Inner Conflict*, p. 99: 'If we look for what may have been the original context and content of such visions, there is another instance, where, again in the flattest possible manner, the story of a band of warriors is told'.
23 *Idem*, *Broken World*, p. 178.
24 *Idem*, 'Vrātya', p. 32.
25 *Idem*, *Broken World*, p. 184.
26 Max Weber, *Economy and Society*, ed. Guenther Roth and Claus Wittich, Berkeley and Los Angeles: University of California Press, 1978, pp. 241–2, 1112.
27 Heesterman, 'Axial Age', p. 396.
28 For the definition of disenchantment as calculability, see Max Weber, *Wissenschaft als Beruf*, Munich and Leipzig: Duncker & Humblot, 1919.

29 Robert A. Yelle, *Sovereignty and the Sacred: Secularism and the Political Economy of Religion*, Chicago: University of Chicago Press, 2019, chap. 2. See also Yelle, *The Language of Disenchantment*, chap. 1.
30 Julius Wellhausen, *Prolegomena to the History of Ancient Israel*, Edinburgh: A. & C. Black, 1885, repr., Cleveland: Meridian Books, 1957; Rudolph Sohm, *Kirchenrecht, Vol. 1, Die geschichtlichen Grundlagen*, Leipzig: Duncker & Humblot, 1892, esp. 22–3, 26; Rudolph Sohm, *Kirchenrecht, Vol. 2, Katholisches Kirchenrecht*, Munich: Duncker & Humblot, 1923, pp. 168–71, 180–2; Walter Lowrie, *The Church and Its Organization in Primitive and Catholic Times: An Interpretation of Rudolph Sohm's "Kirchenrecht"*, London and Bombay: Longmans, Green, 1904, is partly a translation and partly a paraphrase and extension of Sohm's work. For the influence of Wellhausen and Sohm on Weber, see discussion and references in Robert A. Yelle, '"An Age of Miracles": Disenchantment as a Secularized Theological Narrative', in Robert A. Yelle and Lorenz Trein (ed), *Narratives of Disenchantment and Secularization: Critiquing Max Weber's Idea of Modernity*, London: Bloomsbury, 2020, pp. 129–48 (pp. 142–5).
31 Ernst Arbman, *Rudra: Untersuchungen zum altindischen Glauben und Kultus*, Uppsala: Appelberg, 1922, p. 65. All translations from original German sources are my own.
32 *Ibid*, pp. 95–6, see also p. 133.
33 *Ibid*, pp. 147–8.
34 Arbman quotes B. Oltramare's use of the *ex opere operato* idea but rejects his formulation as Oltramare still regards the gods as necessary for the effectiveness of the ritual.
35 See Robert A. Yelle, 'From Sovereignty to Solidarity: Some Transformations in the Politics of Sacrifice from the Reformation to Robertson Smith', *History of Religions*, 2019, 58: 319–46.
36 Wellhausen, p. 100, see also p. 72: 'The burnt-offering has become quite independent and comes everywhere into the foreground, the sacrifices which are unconnected with a meal altogether predominate'.
37 See Yelle, '"An Age of Miracles"'.
38 Heesterman, *Broken World*, p. 45.
39 Heesterman, *ibid*, p. 46, even notes: 'The Reformation, though rejecting the dogma of the transubstantiation, could not radically withdraw from the sacrificial understanding of the Lord's Supper.' This claim requires further nuance: whereas, following Luther, no Protestants regarded the Eucharist as a literal sacrifice, the internal debate among Protestants was whether—and if so in what sense—the Eucharist might be metaphorically labelled a sacrifice.
40 See Johan Huizinga, *Homo Ludens: A Study of the Play-Element in Culture*, London: Routledge & Kegan Paul, 1949, regarding play communities as clans, phratries, or brotherhoods (p. 12), and regarding how exogamous groups come together through ritual play (p. 53).
41 *Ibid*, p. 21.
42 *Ibid*, p. 57 (dice); pp. 107–8, 146 (riddles). See also the reference to Vedic sacrifice at *ibid*, p. 15. For a historical sketch of the study of dice-play in the Vedas, see Harry Falk, *Bruderschaft und Würfelspiel: Untersuchungen zur Entwicklungsgeschichte des veidischen Opfers*, Freiburg: Hedwig Falk, 1986, pp. 73–4.
43 See esp. Heesterman, *Inner Conflict*, p. 199: 'Now it can be shown, as G. J. Held did almost half a century ago, that originally the varṇa concept, instead of prescribing strict separation, implied a system of connubial and other exchanges'.
44 G. J. Held, *The Mahabharata: An Ethnological Study*, London: Kegan Paul, Trench, Trubner & Co., Ltd, 1935, p. 245.
45 *Ibid*, p. 271.

46 *Ibid*, p. 92.
47 *Ibid*, p. 238.
48 *Ibid*, p. 241.
49 *Ibid*, pp. 89–94.
50 *Ibid*, p. 238.
51 *Ibid*, p. 217.
52 *Ibid*, pp. 337–8.
53 Heesterman, 'Vrātya', pp. 18, 36.
54 *Idem*, *Inner Conflict*, p. 200.
55 *Ibid*, p. 57. See also *idem*, 'Warrior, Peasant, and Brahmin', *Modern Asian Studies*, 1995, 29: 637–54 (p. 647): 'For all their mutual hostility, then, the two opposite worlds were closely tied in with each other. Together they formed a single universe that found its unity in conflict'; *idem*, 'Householder and Wanderer', *Contributions to Indian Sociology*, 1981, 15: 251–71 (p. 253): 'Whatever additional outside stimuli there may have been, the renunciatory tendency can be seen to arise orthogenetically from within the vedic sacrificial tradition itself'. See also Thomas R. Trautmann, review of *The Inner Conflict of Tradition: Essays in Indian Ritual, Kingship, and Society*, *The Journal of Asian Studies*, 1988, 47(3): 681–3.
56 Held states that he did not have access to Hauer's writings on the Vrātyas. Held, p. 238n1.
57 One example is M. Sparreboom and J. Heesterman, *The Ritual of Setting Up the Sacrificial Fires According to the Vadhula School*, Vienna: Austrian Academy of Sciences, 1989, p. 95n1, where we read: 'In the Netherlands (till 1922) Sanskrit formed part of the Dutch language and literature curriculum. In those happy times, when the unity of the *humaniora* was still felt to be self-evident, there was nothing curious about a neo-philologist presenting a thesis on a Sanskrit (or Vedic) subject as many, including the historian J. H. Huizinga, did'.
58 Vishwa Adluri and Joydeep Bagchee, *The Nay Science: A History of German Indology*, New York: Oxford University Press, 2014, chap. 1 and 2, esp. pp. 41, 44, 46, 48, 57. Ironically, Adluri and Bagchee cite Heesterman's *Inner Conflict* as an example of a more valid approach to Indology, without recognising his reliance on some of the very theories that they criticise. *Ibid*, p. 144fn220.
59 *Ibid*, pp. 92, 115.
60 *Ibid*, pp. 331, 423.
61 Stefan Arvidsson, *Aryan Idols: Indo-European Mythology as Ideology and Science*, Chicago: University of Chicago Press, 2006, chap. 4, esp. 207–22, summarises the history of the Männerbund idea. There is by now a fairly large literature surveying various aspects of this idea. See Hans Peter Hasenfratz, 'Der indogermanische Männerbund : Anmerkungen zur religiösen Bedeutung des Jugendalters', *Zeitschrift für Religions- und Geistesgeschichte*, 1982: 148–63; Harm-Peer Zimmermann, 'Männerbund und Totenkult: Methodologische und ideologische Grundlinien der Volks- und Altertumskunde Otto Höflers 1933–1945', *Kieler Blätter zur Volkskunde*, 1994, 26: 5–28; Gisela Völger and Karin von Welck, *Männerbande/Männerbünde: Zur Rolle des Mannes im Kulturvergleich*, 2 vols., Köln: Rautenstrauch-Joest-Museum Köln, 1990; Ulrike Brunotte, 'Männerbund zwischen Jugend- und Totenkult: Ritual und Communitas am Beginn der Moderne', in Brigitte Luchesi and Kocku von Stuckrad (eds), *Religion im kulturellen Diskurs*, Berlin: Walter de Gruyter, 2004, pp. 401–22; Claudia Bruns, *Politik des Eros: Der Männerbund in Wissenschaft, Politik und Jugendkultur (1880–1934)*, Köln: Böhlau, 2008; Stefanie von Schnurbein, *Norse Revival: Transformations of German Paganism*, Leiden: Brill, 2016, pp. 232–43.

62 Heesterman, *Inner Conflict*, p. 19. Falk, on whose conclusions Heesterman also drew for support, also speaks approvingly of the idea ('Geschichte der Forschung', pp. 14–17). Falk explains his decision to replace the term *Männerbund* with *Bruderschaft*: 'Grund dafür ist, daß es nicht die "Männer" mit Familie und Beruf sind, die sich in Bünden organisierten, sondern die Jugendlichen in der Ausbildung und vor allem die "Halbstarken" zwischen Lehrzeit und dem Ehestand'. Falk, *Bruderschaft und Würfelspiel*, p. 11. Another, unstated reason might have been the unsavory connotations that the word *Männerbund* had acquired by the time Falk was writing in 1986.
63 Otto Höfler, *Kultische Geheimbünde der Germanen*, vol. 1, Frankfurt: Moritz Diesterweg, 1934; Stig Wikander, *Der arische Männerbund*, Lund: Håkan Ohlsson, 1938, esp. chap. 4, 'Die Mythen des Männerbundes'. On Wikander, see Mihaela Timus, 'Quand l'Allemagne était leur Mecque: La science des religions chez Stig Wikander', in Horst Junginger (ed), *The Study of Religion Under the Impact of Fascism*, Leiden: Brill, 2007, pp. 225–8.
64 Wikander, *Der arische Männerbund*, pp. 69 (Arbman), 73 (Hauer).
65 Lincoln, *Death, War, and Sacrifice*, p. 147.
66 Wikander, *Der arische Männerbund*, p. 85. See Geo Widengren, *Die Religionen Irans*, Stuttgart: Kohlhammer, 1965, p. 23; Lincoln, *Death, War, and Sacrifice*, pp. 133–5.
67 Huizinga, *Homo Ludens*, p. 17; Höfler, *Kultische Geheimbünde der Germanen*, p. vii: 'Diese Arbeit handelt von Gegenständen, die weit auseinander zu liegen scheinen: von den germanischen Totenmythen und von Kulten ekstatischer Ergriffenheit, von kriegerisch-politischen Verbänden, die in uralten Zeiten wurzeln, aber bis in späte Epochen lebendig bleiben, von der religiösen, sozialen und geschichtlichen Bedeutung dieser Bünde und von der Entstehung des deutschen volkhaften Dramas'.
68 Steven Wasserstrom, *Religion After Religion: Gerschom Scholem, Mircea Eliade, and Henry Corbin at Eranos*, Princeton: Princeton University Press, 1999; Gustavo Benavides, 'Irrational Experiences, Heroic Deeds and the Extraction of Surplus', in Horst Junginger (ed), *The Study of Religion Under the Impact of Fascism*, Leiden: Brill, 2007, pp. 263–70.
69 Heesterman, *Broken World*, p. 83.
70 Heinrich Schurtz, *Altersklassen und Männerbünde: Eine Darstellung der Grundformen der Gesellschaften*, Berlin: Georg Reimer, 1902.
71 Richard Wolfram, *Schwerttanz und Männerbund, 3. Lieferung, II. Hauptstück, Der Männerbund*, Kassel: Bärenreiter, 1936; Arvidsson, *Aryan Idols*, pp. 180–1.
72 Höfler, *Kultische Geheimbünde der Germanen*, pp. 323–41.
73 Horst Junginger, 'Introduction', in Horst Junginger (ed), *The Study of Religion Under the Impact of Fascism*, Leiden: Brill, 2008, pp. 1–106 (pp. 25, 147–51). See also Petteri Pietikäinen, 'Futures Past: C. G. Jung's Psychoutopia and the "German Revolution" of 1933', in Horst Junginger (ed), *The Study of Religion Under the Impact of Fascism*, Leiden: Brill, 2008, pp. 591–603 (pp. 597, 603).
74 Arvidsson, *Aryan Idols*, pp. 231–2.
75 Jakob Wilhelm Hauer, *Die Anfänge der Yogapraxis*, Stuttgart: Kohlhammer, 1922, p. vi; Jakob Wilhelm Hauer, *Der Vrātya: Untersuchungen über die nichtbrahmanische Religion Altindiens, Vol. 1, Die Vrātya als nichtbrahmanische Kultgenossenschaft arischer Herkunft*, Stuttgart: Kohlhammer, 1927.
76 Hauer, *Anfänge*, p. 169.
77 *Ibid*, p. 186.
78 *Ibid*, pp. 175–6; *idem*, *Vrātya*, pp. 38–9, 238–40, 274–5. See also Geo Widengren, 'Harlekintracht und Mönchskutte, Clownhut und Derwischmütze', in

Orientalia Suecana, vol. 2, pt. 2, Uppsala: Almqvist & Wiksells, 1953, pp. 41–111 (pp. 91–2).
79 Hauer, *Vrātya*, pp. 211–17.
80 *Ibid*, p. 2.
81 In addition to Heesterman 'Vrātyas and Sacrifice', see also *idem*, 'Warrior, Peasant and Brahmin', pp. 643–4.
82 Jakob Wilhelm Hauer, 'Die vergleichende Religionsgeschichte und das Indogermanenproblem', in Helmut Arntz (ed), *Germanen und Indogermanen: Volkstum, Sprache, Heimat, Kultur*, vol. 1, Heidelberg: Carl Winters, 1936, pp. 177–202 (p. 192).
83 Leopold von Schröder, *Mysterium und Mimus im Rigveda*, Leipzig: H. Haessel, 1908.
84 *Ibid*, pp. 469–81.
85 *Ibid*, p. 65.
86 *Ibid*, p. 70.
87 *Ibid*, pp. 118–23.
88 Adalbert Kuhn, *Die Herabkunft des Feuers und des Göttertranks: Ein Beitrag zur vergleichender Mythologie der Indogermanen*, Berlin: Ferd. Dümmler, 1859.
89 Von Schröder, *Mysterium und Mimus*, p. 217.
90 *Ibid*, p. 352.
91 *Ibid*, p. 438.
92 Bruce Lincoln, personal communication.
93 Examples are the way that Heesterman, *Broken World*, often cites Hertha Krick, *Das Ritual der Feuergründung*, Vienna: Austrian Academy of Sciences, 1982, although the latter's depiction draws explicitly on Heesterman himself. See Krick, *Das Ritual der Feuergründung*, p. 2. As Wenzel Braunfels pointed out to me, this allows Heesterman to cite himself, while appearing to rely on independent research, in a process comparable to money laundering. Heesterman uses Falk in a similar fashion. See Falk, *Bruderschaft und Würfelspiel*, pp. 11, 190–3, who upholds Heesterman's thesis overall while criticising some aspects.

2

RITUALS OF POWER

Coinage, court culture and kingship under the great Mughals

Shailendra Bhandare

It has been well-observed by theorists of ritual[1] that rituals were not all pomp and circumstance; they also were an important and integral 'cement' in the construction of imperial order and power structures. The ritualisation of the practices in the court gave an excuse for the rulers to be at the centre of the ritual complex and draw to them the ultimate authority to preside over people's lives. Rituals have a cognitive impact on people's perceptions about political reality and, as Kertzer has commented, 'rulers for millennia . . . have attempted to design and employ rituals to arouse popular emotions in support of their legitimacy and to drum up popular enthusiasm for their policies'.[2] Rituals also are 'a means of influencing people's ideas about political events, political policies, political systems and political leaders. . . . Political understandings are mediated through symbols, and ritual, as a potent form of symbolic representation, is a valuable tool in our construction of political reality'.[3] As Cannadine and Price have observed, 'ritual is not a mask of force, but is itself a type of power'.[4] Rituals might not always be 'ancient' and 'continuous'; they are often remodelled and made to fit into an 'invented tradition', which is, as famously noted by Eric Hobsbawm, 'essentially a process of formalization and ritualization, characterized by reference to the past', so that it appears to have a 'a continuity with the past'.[5]

The history of the establishment of the Mughal rule in India is intricately linked with coinage in more than one way. The 'rupee' or 'rupiya', which is the national denominational term for modern currency of not only India but also a host of different nations, was in effect a Mughal innovation, although it was apparently first issued by 'Sher Khan', or Sher Shah Suri, on the testament of the Mughal Chronicler, Abu'l Fazl.[6] An effectively controlled, trimetallic regime, producing coins which could be trusted for their metallic purity as well as their weight, was the hallmark of Mughal currency. Having a reliable and popular currency led to an epoch of great prosperity during the Mughal times, and its outcome, including magnificent monuments and great strides in arts and letters, serve as an indirect indicator of the secure financial underpinning the Mughal currency provided for such great endeavours.

As Islamic rulers, the right of *Sikkā*—to have the name of the ruler on circulating currency—constituted a fundamental right in the exercise and legitimation of kingship for the Mughals. However, it was not just a passive engagement; surviving numismatic evidence suggests that the Mughal emperors were also deeply interested in their coinage. Noted numismatist–historians like S H Hodivala have written in detail about this engagement by drawing parallels between the textual sources of Mughal history and numismatic elements such as coin types, the inscriptions on them and mints.[7] However, the way in which coins were integrated in the Mughal court culture has not yet been fully described. In this chapter, I intend to take the opportunity to do so. In the following pages, I would outline how coins were viewed by the Mughals as an essential part of the courtly apparatus, how they were integral to the precepts of the articulation of the Mughal kingship and how they broadly fit into ritualised use of money, both in token and real terms of constituting an element of 'gift economy'.

Kingship: a Mughal perspective

By far the greatest interlocutor of the ideals of kingship during the Mughal times was Abu'l Fazl, who wrote his treatise '*Ain-i Akbari* on governance, political ideology and statecraft during Akbar's rule (1556–1605 CE). In his view, the Mughal king ruled through a divine dispensation and God himself held royalty in ultimate dignity. The king maintained the rule of law and so suppressed insubordination and the 'spirit of rebellion'; therefore, the king was the 'origin of stability and possession'. He equates royalty to a 'divine light of illumination' in the following words: 'Royalty is a light emanating from the God, and a ray from the Sun, the illuminator of the Universe, the argument of the book of Perfection, the receptacle of all virtues. Modern language calls this light *Farr-i Yazidi* (the Divine Light) and the tongue of antiquity called it *Kiyan Khwarrah* (sublime Halo)'.[8] The belief that God himself chooses the king he wishes to rule stemmed from the Central Asian concepts of kingship that Mughals inherited. As Ram Prasad Khosla has observed, it is reflected even in Timur's memoirs.[9] Even if the king's powers were absolute, they were not considered to be above the Holy Law, or *Shari'a*; however, God alone was the king's ultimate judge.

Divine providence as the basis of kingship also meant that the Mughal king was shrouded in a degree of mystical sanctity. He was 'above all', considered to be the God's vice-regent and as such the sole interlocutor of God's will. He was thus a 'Shadow of the Divine'. This status created a chasm between the king and his subjects and, to maintain the degree and awe of that chasm, the Mughal court developed elaborate rituals around the king's charisma. Obeisance, subordination and magnanimity were at the core of these rituals. Some of the sayings of Akbar quoted by Abu'l Fazl[10] reflect this exalted status of the king, who was very different than that of the lesser mortals, even if they ended up being courtiers or close associates of the king. It will be worthwhile to reproduce some here verbatim, because these have a very important bearing on how the Mughal king was envisaged and thus, honoured, obeyed and glorified as a ruler.

- 'The very sight of kings has been held to be a part of divine worship . . . to behold them is a means of calling to mind the Creator'.
- 'Sovereignty is a supreme blessing for its advantages extend to multitudes'.
- 'In the reciprocity of rule and obedience, the sanctions of hope and fear are necessary to the well-ordering of the temporal government and the illumination of the interior recesses of the Spirit'.
- 'A monarch should be ever intent on conquest, otherwise his neighbours rise in arms against him'.

Sentiments like these encapsulate the attitude of the 'learned elite' of the court like Abu'l Fazl towards their king and it would be a matter of wonder if this did not permeate to the subjects. Evident in these is a way in which subjects would interact with the king. The fact that the king considered himself a 'Shadow of the Divine' also meant that he was at the centre of the 'universe' and a created a culture around himself which reflected his centrality to the cosmic order. R S Tripathi and John Richards have discussed at length how the Turko-Mongol ideals of kingship influenced the conceptualisation and articulation of kingship for the Mughals and how the kingly authority was formulated under Akbar and Jahangir.[11,12] Eva Orthmann has described how Mughal kings as early as Humayun considered the cosmological centrality to be a part of the functioning of their court. Humayun, who had a keen interest in astronomy, is known to have created a seating order in his court where his nobles sat in concentric circles over a cosmologically designed carpet, known as the 'carpet of mirth'. He also held court under a cosmic tent, referred to as the 'tent of the twelve Zodiac signs'. The form and drawing of an Islamic horoscope, with sections for planetary positions, was created as a design for the roof over Akbar's seat in the *Daulatkhānā* at Fatehpur.[13] Needless to say, the sun played a crucial role in conceptualising kingship, particularly considering the idea of 'light' and 'glory' in envisaging the king. Mughal emperors regularly appear surrounded by a solar halo or nimbus, the 'Sun in Leo' was the insignia of the Mughals and words like *Jalāl* (glory) or *Noor* (light) formed a part of the Mughal kings' names. Insights like these contribute to our understanding of how the conception and ideals of Mughal kingship were translated into the elaborate mechanisms and ordering about the Mughal court, which set it up as a theatre for rituals concerning the king and his prowess.

The concept of kingship underpinned the way protocol emerged in the Mughal court but some peculiar cultural concepts also played a role in it. One of these concepts was that of the 'evil eye'. Very much preponderant in the wider Islamic world, it is defined as 'popular belief that a person can glance or stare at someone else's favourite possession and, if envious of the other person's good fortune, hurt, damage, or destroy it'.[14] The bearers of the 'evil eye' would lurk among the population and some categories, like widows, strangers, physically disabled or malformed persons, or those with a squint or other such ocular dysfunctionalities were considered particularly potent to carry its malevolent powers.[15] The spell of the 'evil eye' could be remedied, either by averting it 'by specific words, gestures, amulets and other apotropaic objects, designs and devices'.[16] As one can imagine, the most prominent target for attracting the 'evil eye' would be the monarch, who was by far the most 'fortunate' of the population in being powerful, rich and the 'chosen' of the God. The situations in which the king would present himself to be a target were embedded in kingly rituals of the court of both semi-private and public kind—the king regularly held court, or went on a hunt or campaign, and this gave a chance not only for his noblemen but also for their entourages to see him in person; he often processed in grand assemblages where the general public came out to see him; he also held the ceremony of ritualised sighting or *Darshan* at a royal window so that his subjects were assured of his good health and sound physique. All these potentially presented a chance that someone would cast an 'evil eye' on the king. Although a lot of information is available on how the concept of the 'evil eye' affected parts of the king's retinue and what measures were taken to avert its ill effects (for example, we know that a particular grass was burnt in the Mughal stables to free the precious horses from the 'evil eye' they might attract from the menial staff who looked after them), there is not much written about the vulnerability of the Mughal king in particular to this superstition. However, plenty of evidence that the king was never considered immune from the 'evil eye' is available in the visual sources of Mughal history—for example, see the discussion by Minissale[17] about hexagonal emeralds being considered as an antidote to counter the effects of the 'evil eye' with some paintings of the emperor Shahjahan showing him holding one. As we shall see further, coins played an important role in averting the casting of the 'evil eye' over persons of royal significance while they engaged in their courtly ceremonies, customs and rituals.

Kingship and coinage were integrally linked in the Mughal State per tenets of Islam—the king's right to rule was validated by striking coins in his name (*Sikkā*) and his mention in the Friday prayers (*Khutbā*). These two rights were inalienable for an Islamic king and the Mughal rulers were no exceptions to them. Mughal coins therefore often carried the full name of the ruler, including the components *Laqab*, *Kunyat* and *Ism* and the Shahada, or profession of Islamic Faith, along with the names of the *Rashidoon* caliphs on them.

An effective decoding and contextualisation of available numismatic evidence show how intimately coin design and issue were connected to the happenings in the emperor's life as well as court. The Mughal emperors took this engagement to new heights. Coinage became an integral part of the apparatus of Mughal court culture. The emperor's public image, rights, duties and privileges became involved and reflected in the coins struck in his name. Monetary exchanges became a norm of protocol and other practices in the court. Occasions, such as the emperor's birthday or celebration of particular festivals, provided the stage where money could be used in theatrics of the court, often with deeper and indexical meanings. The emperor's munificence towards the masses, be it in almsgiving or scattering of coins in processions, was often reflected by the choice of issuing special, made-to-purpose coins for such reasons. In the following paragraph, I will describe and contextualise some instances of this engagement. As supplementary evidence, I will draw from other sources of Mughal history such as chronicles and visual arts.

An 'especiall favoure': the 'portrait medallions' of Jahangir

It is evident from the description of the 'initiation ritual' to the 'Divine Community' that two objects—referred to as *Shast* and *Shabeeh* (loosely translated as 'token'/'testament' and 'likeness')—were given to the 'disciples and servants' when they were initiated. Abu'l Fazl furnishes a clear description of this ritual and from his account it can be gleaned that the ceremony took place on a Sunday, 'when the world-illuminating Sun is in its highest splendour'. At an auspicious time, the incumbent was brought to the emperor with his turban in his hand and then he 'put his head on the feet of His Majesty'. The emperor then raised him up again, put the turban back on his head and 'then gave the novice the *Shast* on which was engraved the 'Great Name' and His Majesty's symbolic motto *Allāhu Akbar*'.[18],[19] Badayuni, while describing a ceremony that took place on the Nowruz day of AH993, mentions that several courtiers embraced the Divine Community, swearing a total allegiance—inclusive of life, reputation, religion and property—to the emperor.[20] They were brought forward in batches of 12 and he 'gave them a *Shabeeh* (likeness); they looked on it as the standard of loyal friendship, and the advance guard of righteousness and happiness, and they put it wrapped up in a jewelled case on the top of their turbans'. Jahangir, upon succeeding to his father's throne, kept the ceremony going at least for the first few years. He notes in his memoirs[21] of appointing Shaikh Ahmad

Lahori to the office of *Mir-i 'Adl*, or Chief Justice, and it was under the purview of this office that the recommendations for those who were considered fit to receive this privilege were made. At the time of initiation, few words of 'advice' were given to the incumbent and he agreed to the basic principles of the Divine Community—to maintain *Sulh-i Kul* or the rule of 'Universal Peace', to swear loyalty to the emperor and not to kill any living being by hands, except in battles and in pursuit. Judging from all these accounts, it is evident that the *Shast* and *Shabeeh* were in fact a single object—a token which carried the 'likeness' of the emperor and the 'great name', or 'symbolic motto', which as we have seen, made an oblique reference to Akbar.

Hodivala has rightly suggested[22] that a unique gold piece in the British Museum (Figure 2.1) is perhaps the object which represented the 'testament and likeness', which was given at the initiation ceremony and the earliest instance of a Mughal medallion/coin bearing a royal portrait. It bears a three-quarter profile bust of Akbar which is remarkably similar to the one seen in a famous Mughal miniature showing Jahangir admiring a portrait of his father (Musee du Louvre, accession number OA 3676 B Recto; Figure 2.2). A feature noted by Abu'l Fazl, namely, the 'Great Name' *Allāhu Akbar*, is inscribed to the left of the bust. The piece also bears the Hijri date 1014 and the 'Julus' or regnal year 1, which both suggest that it was struck after Akbar's death but before Jahangir had been officially crowned the new emperor (as per convention, his first year after coronation would be referred to by the word 'Ahd' and not by the numeral '1'). Jahangir appointed Lahori as chief justice on 19th Dhu'l-hajjah 1014, almost six months after the death of Akbar, and the Nowruz of that year fell almost

Figure 2.1 Gold *Shast* with portrait of Akbar, struck soon after Jahangir's accession in CE 1605, The British Museum, accession number 1930,0607.1

Source: Photograph by author

Figure 2.2 Portrait of Jahangir with Akbar, Musée du Louvre, accession number OA-3676B Recto

Source: Wikimedia Commons

a month later, on 11th Dhu'l-q'ada 1014.[23] Since this was the very first Nowruz of the new emperor's reign, it is plausible that an 'initiation ceremony' was held on this day and the acolytes received pieces with the likeness of the deceased emperor, the founder of the order. The piece on reverse shows a full sun which, as we know, was a significant constituent in the idea of kingship for the Mughals and played a key role in staging and timing of the ritual of initiation.

To have a testament struck with the likeness of the deceased emperor was rather unusual but as Hodivala has suggested,[24] it was probably due to the fact that right at the beginning of his reign, Jahangir chose not to rock the boat too much—he had been in rebellion against his father for a long time and had many opponents at the court—and show respect to the former emperor instead. The precise date when the ritual initiations into the 'Divine Community' stopped is not known, but Jahangir almost immediately into his reign resurrected the use of the Islamic Profession of Faith (*Shahadā*) on his circulatory coins and largely did away with the 'Great Name' *Allāhu Akbar*, barring a couple of rare exceptions. However, it is plausible to assume, as Hodivala has speculated, that Jahangir might have struck similar pieces with his own portrait rather than that of his father, for the same purpose in other rounds of initiations, if they indeed took place after Jahangir's formal accession, before being stopped completely.

In the 6th year of his reign, Jahangir took the practice to a new level. Textual substantiation of this is available from more than one source, but Khafi Khan's *Muntakhab ul-Lubāb* offers this passage:[25]

> In this year (i.e. the 6th), he gave orders that a piece of gold of one *tola* weight, stamped on one side by the likeness (*shabeeh*) of the Padshah, and displaying on the other, the figure (*sūrat*) of a lion ridden by (i.e. surmounted by) the Sun, should be given to the favourite/close Amirs (*umrāye muqarrab*) and special servants (*fiduyān-i khās*) and they were to keep it (i.e. wear it) respectfully on the sash of the turban or on the breast front as a life preserving amulet (*harz-i jān*).

The same author mentions that in the 21st year of Jahangir's reign he ordered even heavier pieces to be struck, which weighed five *tolas*. By far the best testimony for granting such an object to an important person (if not a 'favourite Amir' or 'special servant') is found in the diaries of Sir Thomas Roe:[26]

> I went to visitt the King, who, as soone as I came in, called to his woemen and reached out a picture of him selfe sett in gould hanging at a wire gould chaine with one pendant foule pearle which he delivered to Asaph Chan.... Asaph Chan came to me, and I offered

> to take it in my hand; butt hee made a sign to putt off my hatt and then putt it about my neck, leading me right before the King. Hee made me sign to me to give the king thancks which I did after my owne custome. Wheratt some officers called me to *Size-da* but the King answered no, no, in Persian.

This encounter had an amusing preamble, described by Roe earlier in his diary,[27] which involved Roe offering a picture (a European miniature of a woman) to Jahangir and the Emperor challenging him that his court artists could do a better job. A few days later, Jahangir showed five pictures to Roe, who rather grudgingly—and blaming the poorly lit conditions in which the pictures had been shown to him—admitted that they were indeed better than the one he had. The Emperor was pleased and asked Roe to demand 'whatsoever you desire', to which Roe politely replied: 'Whatsoever came from his Majesties hands I would receive as a marke of honor'. Jahangir offered him a picture of himself and Roe said to him that he 'would desire one for my selfe and which I would keepe and leave it to my posterity as an ensigne of his Majesties favour'. Jahangir then ordered one to be made and the assembly was dismissed. This meeting took place on August 6th, and Roe finally received his promised gift on August 17th.

Roe took the gesture to 'judge the king's liberallitye'. He notes that the 'gift was not worth in all 30 li yet it was five tymes as good as any hee gives in that kind, and held for an especiall favour, for that all the great men that weare the kings image (which none may doe but to whom it is given) recive noe other then a medal of gould as bigg as sixpence, with a little chayne of 4 inches to fasten it on their heads, which at their owne charge some sett with stones or garnishe with pendant pearls'.[28]

The description of the ultimate use of this royal gift[29] matches precisely with that given by Khafi Khan. It can be seen from the account that the bestowal of this privilege brought along other 'freedoms'—Roe was not required to do the *Sajdāh*, or full prostration to the king, and when he was prompted by other courtiers to do one, the king himself intervened to comment that it was not required. This was a tremendously significant step, for it meant that Roe was exempt from the token gestures of servitude. A full and total allegiance to the emperor was one of the cornerstones of Mughal court culture, so this exemption would effectively mean that Roe was treated indeed with an 'especiall favour', the sign of which was the present of the portrait medallion to him.

A number of these objects survive in private and institutional collections. They are categorised in three types:

1. Struck in 6th regnal year and weighing around 11 gm each—these have a labelled bust of the emperor and the chronological mention, but no mention of the mint name (Figure 2.3–5).

Figure 2.3 Gold portrait medallion of Jahangir, struck in 6th regnal year, The British Museum, accession number MAR.836.b

Source: Photograph by author

Figure 2.4 Gold portrait medallion of Jahangir with globe, struck in 6th regnal year, The British Museum, accession number RPK,p206.8.Zod

Source: Photograph by author

Figure 2.5 Gold portrait medallion of Jahangir with 'wine cup', struck in 6th regnal year, The British Museum, accession number OR.7432

Source: Photograph by author

2. Struck in the 7th regnal year and weighing a quarter of the full units—the emperor is depicted as a full length seated portrait which is not labelled, but his full name appears on reverse (Figure 2.6). No mint is mentioned.
3. Struck in the 8th and 9th regnal year while the court had moved to the holy city of Ajmer—these also show a full length seated portrait and have poetic inscriptions which allude to the Emperor, in addition to the mention of the mint-name (Figure 2.7–8).

Of these, one of the busts from the 6th regnal year series, and the full-length portraits on other pieces, show Jahangir with a cup-like object in his hand. This has been widely construed to be a 'wine cup'[30] and, accordingly,

Figure 2.6 Gold 1/4th mohur, struck in 7th regnal year, showing full-length portrait of Jahangir seated on throne, Münzkabinett, Kunst-Historisches Museum, Vienna, no accession number

Source: Photograph by author

Figure 2.7 Gold mohur of Jahangir struck at Ajmer in 8th regnal year, with full length portrait of Jahangir, The British Museum

Source: Photograph by author

Figure 2.8 Gold mohur of Jahangir struck at Ajmer in 9th regnal year, with full length portrait of Jahangir enthroned, Ashmolean Museum, HCR7680

Source: Photograph by author

the depiction is suggested to depict Jahangir's penchant for alcohol, which of course he does not deign to acknowledge in his memoirs, which are replete with mentions of wine parties. Hodivala goes as far as referring to him as a 'thirsty toper'![31] Along with this particular aspect of the depiction, a few other features of the other depictions are also discussed—to quote Hodivala, 'in one variety something like a book is held in the hand. In another, there is a fruit in the left hand and the right hand rests on the left forearm'.[32] In the depiction in which he holds the wine cup in his right hand, he has 'the supposed book' in the left hand. Hodivala also discusses features such as the nimbus behind the emperor's head mainly to refute interpretations offered by Stanley Lane Poole, who wrote on these pieces in some detail in his catalogue of the Mughal coins in the British Museum.[33] However, that discussion does not concern us here very much. Suffice it to point out a couple of lacunae in Hodivala's analysis of these depictions and then offer an argument to suggest how the depictions were in fact linked with the Mughal idea of kingship and court rituals.

By far the most important aspect where Hodivala has gone wrong is his judgement about the emperor holding a 'book' in one of his hands. It was originally identified as a 'book' by Lane Poole, and, while Hodivala offered a critique of Lane Poole's assertion that the 'book' might have been the Quran, he did not challenge the basic identification of the object as a book.[34] Hodivala waxes lyrical on what this 'book' might have been, if not the Quran, and offers several highly romantic suggestions, including a collection of poems or a *Diwān* by the Farsi poet Hafiz. Evidently Hodivala's analysis is influenced by the historical memory of Jahangir as a complacent Mughal emperor, given to pleasures of life such as alcohol and poetry. It is an analysis undoubtedly influenced by the Romantic appeal evident in James

Fitzgerald's translations of Umar Khayyam's *Ruba'iyāt,* in which imagery of such reclusive, almost ascetic, oriental men given to simple pleasures of the pre-industrial world occurs via the 'book in one hand, wine in the other' sort of imagery. Hodivala has even cited the famous verse of Khayyam, as translated by Fitzgerald.[35]

Hodivala's assertions were first rectified by R B Whitehead,[36] who correctly identified this particular object as a piece of expensive cloth or carpet that was placed on the balustrade of a window or a balcony, or an extended railed platform. This was used as hand/palm rest, while the emperor sat immediately behind the balustrade, at a window or balcony. It is seen in many examples of such depictions—the Musée du Louvre miniature of Jahangir admiring a picture of Akbar that we have referred to earlier shows the carpet under Jahangir's and Akbar's hands: Jahangir has one thrown on the balustrade he sits next to, and so does Akbar in the picture Jahangir holds. By far the most realistic example would be the alabaster bas relief of Shahjahan in the Rijkmuseum collection (Object number AK-NM-12249, Figure 2.9), in which the sculptural nature of the bust of Shahjahan against a balustrade has been used effectively to indicate the folds of this cloth, thereby leaving no doubt about its nature.

The identification of this object as a 'carpet/cloth over a balustrade' is crucial to understand the context of the depictions of the emperor; in fact it changes it completely from an isolated, visually static, portrait one might expect to see in other objects of similar purpose, such as the European miniature that Roe showed to Jahangir.

The fact that the emperor's bust is set against a balustrade covered with carpet /cloth suggests that the emperor is depicted on the coin in a very particular instance—that of his 'sighting' by the public, which was a ritualised act of the Mughal court, drawn from the Indic tradition of *Darshan*, or presenting oneself to be seen in a public fashion, so that the subjects could draw power from the emperor's visage and be assured about his good health and physique. Typically, the sightings happened at a specific window or balcony which was called *Jharokhā-i Darshan.* The ritual is mentioned by Thomas Roe in his diary: 'He [Jahangir] comes every morning to a wyndow called the Jarruco looking into a playne before his gate, and shows him selfe to the common people'.[37] The appropriation of the practice has been credited to Humayun; however, Akbar devised it to be done at the moment of sunrise.[38] Badayuni offers a very vivid account of what happened afterwards and, as usual, his acerbic pen scoffs at the 'vile swindling wicked hordes' of all sorts of people gathered in a 'most terrible crowd'. As the emperor stepped out in the balcony, there was a clamour in the crowds, who all prostrated, and 'cheating thieving Brahmins' tried to flatter him by telling him he was 'an incarnation like Ram, Kishen and other infidel kings'. They showed him Sanskrit verses written on old papers predicting the rise of a great conqueror in India who would honour Brahmins and cows and govern the Earth with

Figure 2.9 Alabaster bas-relief of Shahjahan, Rijkmuseum, Amsterdam, The Netherlands, accession number AK-NM-12249

Source: Image in public domain from the Rijkmuseum http://hdl.handle.net/10934/RM0001.COLLECT.25629

justice. The emperor, much to the chagrin of Badayuni, 'believed every word of this nonsense'.[39]

However, the ritual of *Darshan* was not just this mayhem; it also gave the opportunity for the emperor to hear supplications and pleas, to inspect new war and pack animals and to observe soldiery of favourite *mansabdars* and princes. It became an important ritual in dispensation of justice. Jahangir famously installed a 'golden chain' for people to pull and demand justice anytime they felt the need to redress their grievances. The *Darshan* was by no means confined to times when the emperor was in his quarters; it also happened when he was on the move, in instances such as military campaigns or in other royal pursuits like pilgrimages or hunts. A German traveller named Heinrich von Poser, who accompanied Augustine Hiriart (Herryard), the French jeweller to Lahore in August 1621, notes that the first glimpse of Jahangir he caught was while he was 'at a small window' in a camp, on 15 January 1623, while Jahangir was en route to Lahore.[40] Incidentally, Augustine Hiriart was yet another European who had been given a 'likeness in gold' by Jahangir as a special gift, which he mentions in a letter written to his compatriots in Istanbul in 1620: 'He has given me two elephants and two horses, a house valued at 8000 livres, and his likeness in gold to put on my hat, which is a mark of honour, corresponding to the Order of the Holy Spirit in France'.[41],[42]

That this ritual happened only at predetermined times meant that the sighting of the emperor was not something for public consumption at will. To see him beyond these short public appearances was a privilege given to a very select few at a time. Larger gatherings where he could be sighted were equally ritualised as court assemblies. The fact that one could sight the emperor at will, was thus almost an impossibility. This is precisely what the presentation medallions were meant to achieve—the recipient could 'see' the emperor at his will because he had been sanctioned this rare privilege through the agency of the gold object. The reason why this gift was 'five times more worth than what it is' was because it had this rare privilege attached to it. The portrait medallions were therefore not just objects of status; they brought with them the potency and power which one would usually draw upon sighting the emperor. They were thus an embodiment of his presence but in a token form, and that is what made them a part of the rituals of power exercised at the Mughal court. It was this power that ultimately made them 'life preserving amulets'.

The identification of the object Jahangir holds as a 'wine cup' has earned the coins the sobriquet 'Bacchanalian coins'. Jahangir's penchant for alcohol is well attested and therefore to link it to the coin depiction is tempting, albeit facile. But the coins depict Jahangir in specific courtly roles: on the coins dated 6th regnal year, he is evidently giving a *Darshan* and, on later coins, he is shown seated in court, exactly as courtiers would have sighted him. On the 9th regnal year issue struck at Ajmer, even the hexagonal throne is visible, leaving no doubt that this was an effigy of the emperor at court. Both were sighting opportunities highly regarded for their status, by the general public as well as the courtiers and other incumbents of the court. Now even though Jahangir and many of his successors enjoyed drinking wine, this was never practised while in court. As Harbans Mukhia has noted, the space of the Mughal court was treated like a space for worship. Complete temperance and silence were the prerequisites for maintaining the decorum of the court. Jahangir was particularly strict in enforcing temperance in the court—his guards would smell the breath of courtiers and anyone with the slightest hint of liquor would be turned away. Even drinking water while the emperor sat on his throne was a rare occurrence.[43] Moreover, the objects upon which the image was impressed were used as high-status objects that substituted a personal sighting of the emperor, which was deemed a privilege and a source of 'life preservation'. It therefore seems highly unlikely that Jahangir would choose to show himself engaging in an act that was positively despised by the followers of the Hindu and well as the Islamic religion during his times. An alcoholic he might have been, but Jahangir was acutely aware of this problem and consciously tried to wean himself off the habit. Two of his brothers had been lost to alcoholism. He notes: 'I myself drink wine, and from the age of 18 years up till now, when I am 38, have persisted in it. When I first took a liking to drinking I sometimes took as much as twenty cups of double-distilled spirit; when by degrees it acquired a great influence over me I endeavoured to lessen the quantity, and in the period of seven years I have brought myself from fifteen cups to five or six. My times for drinking were varied; sometimes when three or four sidereal hours of the day remained I would begin to drink, and sometimes at night and partly by day. This went on till I was 30 years old. After that I took to drinking always at night. Now I drink only to digest my food'.[44] So what precisely is the message behind these portraits?

It is also possible to regard the depictions as a representation of the king's connoisseurship. Appreciation of talent, be it related to the arts or the crafts, was one of the ideals of kingship and a kingly duty. Mughal rulers are often depicted holding art objects such as paintings, jewels (stones, aigrettes and the like) or natural objects such as flowers, which please human sense and sensibilities. Sometimes, the object held is not just an object of artistic or technological merit but also has a deeper meaning. One such object is the small orb which Jahangir playfully holds on one of the 6th regnal year issues in the British Museum's collection. There are other depictions of Jahangir holding round globe-like objects[45] and it is quite clear that these depictions constitute a visual pun on the emperor's name—the globe is indicative of the Earth or the 'world', and the emperor is the one who 'grasps the World' which is the literal meaning of his regal name. So romantic it may sound, but the so-called 'wine cup' or 'Bacchanalian' portraits of Jahangir appear to have less to do with the emperor's love for alcohol and more with the emperor's image as a connoisseur of refinement and taste.

Going along these lines, it is also possible to argue that the object that looks like a goblet or a cup is not a utilitarian object but an object of appreciation. Indeed, the known examples of jade and crystal cups from Mughal workshops are examples of superb craftsmanship and exquisite taste in fashioning, finishing and ornamentation. Indeed, there is a description of an expensive wine cup in Roe's account[46]—on Jahangir's birthday, he invited Roe to a party at which 'all men do make merry' and asked him if he would drink with them. After a bit of hesitation Roe agreed, and the emperor called for a 'cupp of goulde' to be sent to him to drink wine from and then to accept as a present. The wine was too strong for Roe, and it made him sneeze, which caused a great amusement to the assembly! Roe describes the 'cupp was of gould, sett all over by Turkyes and Rubies, the cover of the same sett with great turkises, rubyes and emeralds in works, and a dish suteable to sett the cup upon'. These stones were small, but 'in number about 2000 and in goulde about 20 oz', so evidently this was an object of value and offered to Roe as yet another article indicative of royal appreciation.

Nazar: ritualised gift exchange and Mughal coinage

It was customary in Mughal courtly assemblages that the incumbents did not enter in the king's presence 'empty handed'. This was mainly because he was an exalted human being and his sighting was a gratifying act. This core concept was embedded in the protocol observed at the court. The order of assembly, the position where noblemen stood, the objects or weapons they were allowed to carry in the court, all were embedded in a complex code which involved a power hierarchy that emanated downwards from the emperor. The combination of hierarchy, protocol and etiquette were imbibed into court rituals. At the forefront of these rituals was the *Nazar* or, implying the act of gratification through seeing the emperor, which involved presenting a token gift, usually of money, to the emperor. The glossary 'Hobson-Jobson' wherein it is spelled as 'Nuzzer', defines it as 'primarily "a vow or votive offering"; but, in ordinary use, a ceremonial present, properly an offering from an inferior to a superior, the converse of *in'ām*'.[47] Interestingly, the almost homophonous word *Nazar*, spelled with the letter 'Zoy' in the middle, also means 'sighting'. Incumbents such as foreign dignitaries to the court brought forth other gifts and presents, referred to as *Peshkash*, which were offered subsequent to the *Nazar*. The emperor responded by ritually returning the gifts, acknowledging them, by presenting the incumbent with robes or cloth, usually referred to as *Khilat*. The *Nazar* ritual was traditionally a gesture of political obeisance and a tacit acknowledgement of the symbolic power of the Mughal sovereign.[48]

The ritual of *Nazar* finds mention in many accounts, including those of travellers and ambassadors to the Mughal court. In the *Tuzuq-i Jahangiri*, Jahangir notes several counts where incumbents to his court presented various sums of money as *Nazar*: 'On this day Muk͟hliṣ Khan, according to order, came from Bengal, and had the good fortune to kiss the threshold. He gave 100 muhars and 100 rupees as *Nazar*';[49] 'Abdu-s-Salām, s. Muʿaẓẓam K., having arrived from Orissa, had the good fortune to wait on me: 100 muhars and Rs. 100 were laid before me as his *Nazar*'.[50] Cohen describes the exact enactment of the ritual in the court of the Nizam of Hyderabad and there is no reason to believe that the ritual in the Mughal court would be anything substantially different: 'Nobles would, after bowing deeply, present their *nazr*. Coins would be placed on a silken or cotton square of cloth and held out—with head bowed—by both hands. In some Darbars the Nizam simply touched the offering and returned it to the donor. At other times, he took the offering and in exchange gifted the donor with a *khilat* or *sar-o-pā* (complete outfit). In either case, the offering was not meant to enrich the recipient or impoverish the donor'.[51] Sharma has indicated that the ritual was not necessarily confined to the court; the emperors often marched in processions, en route to hunts or in celebration of events or festivals, and it was a norm for noblemen to present *Nazar* to the emperor while he processed, when they sighted him as the procession passed their houses.[52]

Among the repertoire of Mughal miniatures, this ritual gifting has been depicted in many instances. A painting from the Cleveland Museum of Art attributed to Miskin, who flourished under Akbar (accession number 2013.320, Figure 2.10), shows the scene of Humayun's court. It is divided into two registers. The top register shows Humayun enthroned in his tent which is set up in an outdoor setting, suggesting this is a peripatetic court.[53] In the lower register, we see an incumbent, in this case identified as an ambassador, who is shown placing a coin into a plate that a courtier extends before him. The coin itself is not visible but the gesture of the Ambassador and the carrying of a money bag in his other hand leave little doubt as to infer what is being shown here. Conceivably, the money placed in this plate would then be taken to the emperor as a gesture of *Nazar*, when the ambassador would be taken into his presence.

Although most Mughal coins are usually struck from dies which are larger than the coin blanks on which they are struck, it is a commonplace occurrence that parts of the coin design go off the visible field when imprinted on the coin blank from the die. However, in case of some coins, the flan/blank is a larger size than usual and accommodates the full die impression. Blanks were fashioned from metal rods longitudinally cut into round or rectangular pieces[54] before they were heated and struck between a pair of dies to yield coins. Conceivably, to manufacture blanks of a larger-than-normal size, extra care had to be taken, making the process more labour-intensive. The fact that such care had been taken while manufacturing the coins meant that the coins were struck for a special purpose, intentionally producing blanks of the larger size. Although it is impossible to ascertain what this 'special purpose' might have been, there is a tendency among numismatists to suggest that one of the purposes was a court ritual, like *Nazar*. The coins are commonly called 'Nazarana' issues by numismatists.[55]

The practice of striking coins for special purposes had been in vogue even before the Mughal rule. Some coins struck in denominations higher than the usual circulatory ones might have been produced for a purpose, like

Figure 2.10 An ambassador before Humayun, c. 1610, attributed to Miskin, India, Mughal, early 17th century

Source: Cleveland Museum of Art, image in public domain from Cleveland Museum of Art www.clevelandart.org/art/2013.320

providing an ease of storage. Goron and Goenka[56] have listed some such multiple denomination issues for the Sultanate of Bengal. Some such coins were produced specifically for marking specific events. A multiple-denomination silver coin of Humayun has been recently published[57] and the date on it suggests that it might have been struck to celebrate Humayun's conquest of Kabul, which was an event of strategic importance in the course of his recapture of India. Hodivala has produced a detailed discussion of 'gigantic coins' struck by various Mughal emperors and their role in ceremonial gift giving.[58] Conquest was marked sometimes by producing novel coins—Akbar struck a lovely coin with the effigy of a hawk (Figure 2.11) to celebrate his conquest of the fort of Asirgarh, which paved way for the Mughals to overrun the Deccan in the early 17th century. But the practice of striking coins of normal denominations and designs on specially prepared blanks much larger than normal size appears to have been started during Shahjahan's reign. This is evident from large-sized rupees from Akbarabad (Agra) mint (Figure 2.12), struck in his 18th regnal year in AH1054 (corresponding to late AD1644–early 1645). What was the reason that prompted the issue of these coins is not known but most likely, they were struck for the inauguration of the new regnal year which happened on 1 Jumada-II, AH1054 corresponding to 4th August 1644.

The practice of striking special coins for courtly ceremonials was considered so significant in terms of their celebratory importance that existing specimens show they were struck at important political junctures, for example, the Afghan occupation of Delhi under the Durrani king Ahmed Shah. In January 1761, the Afghan and the Maratha combines met at the

Figure 2.11 Mohur of Akbar struck to celebrate the conquest of Asir fort, Ashmolean Museum

Source: Photograph by author

Figure 2.12 Specially struck rupee of Shahjahan, Akbarabad (Agra) mint, 18th regnal year, diam. 35mm, Ashmolean Museum

Source: Photograph by author

third battle of Panipat in which the Marathas were routed. The Afghans, under the command of Ahmed Shah Durrani, occupied Delhi twice, before and after, this significant event in Indian history. Delhi was occupied in late January 1760 by the Afghans almost a year before the Panipat debacle following a Maratha wipe out and chase from the Punjab. The city remained in Afghan hands till 3rd August 1760 when the Marathas, under the command of Sadashiv Rao, expelled the Afghans. The Marathas, under grave financial constraints, were forced to march northwards, plundering Afghan garrisons which ultimately led to their entrapment at Panipat by end of December 1760. After the battle, which took place on 15th January 1761, the Marathas were chased southwards by the Afghans, who re-occupied Delhi on 29th January 1761. This post-Panipat Afghan occupation of Delhi lasted till 20th March 1761, when Ahmed Shah left for Qandahar, his capital, leaving his protégé Najib Khan Ruhela as chief plenipotentiary at Delhi and nominally restoring the throne to the absentee Mughal emperor Shah Alam II.[59]

Specially struck wide flan coins are known for the both the stints in which the Afghans held Delhi during this period. The first occupation issues are dated AH1173 and 14th regnal year (Figure 2.13), while the second occupation issues have AH1174 and 15th regnal year impressed upon them (Figure 2.14). In both instances Ahmed Shah is known to have held court at Delhi, in which many of his Ruhela kinsmen paid homage to the Afghan overlord, so it is plausible that these coins were struck for the *Nazar* ceremony that surely must have been held in these courts.

Figure 2.13 Specially struck rupee of Ahmad Shah Durrani, Shahjahanabad (Delhi) mint, 14th regnal year, during the pre-Panipat Afghan occupation, diam. 40mm, Ashmolean Museum

Source: Photograph by author

Figure 2.14 Specially struck rupee of Ahmad Shah Durrani, Shahjahanabad (Delhi) mint, 15th regnal year, during the post-Panipat Afghan occupation, diam. 38mm, private collection, Dubai

Source: Photograph by author

The issue of *Nazar* coins became an interesting flashpoint towards the end of the Mughal Empire. The emperor Shah Alam II (r. 1760–1806) became a British puppet after his protectors the Marathas were defeated decisively by the British in several theatres of the 2nd Anglo-Maratha War (1802–1803). The British sought to manage the public perception of the Mughal emperor in the aftermath of these events. The status of the emperor was gradually and systematically abrogated from an imperial 'superior' to an 'equal' entity with his British masters. The first step in the systematic abrogation of the emperor's authority was a curb on the mint that was operated producing coins in his name and auspices in Delhi.

In 1813, the Company passed a resolution that it was going to take over the mint in Delhi and introduce mechanised minting of rupees exactly similar to those produced in its mint at Farrukhabad. The traditional minting of coins by hand in the name of emperor was to cease. But at the same time, it was decided to allow the striking of some coins in the name of the then-emperor, Muhammad Akbar II, 'intended only to be presented to His Majesty on the anniversary of his accession for the purpose of being distributed on that occasion as complimentary presents'.[60] This is a very clear reference that these coins were ceremonial in nature and struck especially for the *Nazar* ritual. The establishment of a mechanised mint at Delhi could not materialise for technical and other reasons and two years later it was decided to drop the scheme altogether as the Government by now was not keen on the idea of having a separate mint in Delhi. But since not having a mint at the seat of the imperial authority at all would 'hurt the feelings of the fallen Majesty and of the populace', it was decided that the 'continuance of the custom', that is, striking a few coins at the anniversary of the accession to allow for the court ritual of presenting the *Nazar* to be continued, would be 'requisite to satisfy the feelings of His Majesty'.[61, 62] Accordingly, the mint was shut down for regular coinage and the staff running it were made redundant (after a plea, they were given some compensation for the loss of their income), and the mint was operated only to strike special coins for *Nazar*. Although the letter quoted by Stevens and Garg mentions the custom was observed at the accession anniversary ceremony, Sharma has indicated that the ritual took place four times a year, when the Resident officially met with the emperor at his court.[63]

The existing specimens of these rupees struck especially for *Nazar* reveal the general characteristics—they are all struck on flans specially prepared in broad size and usually carry the full impression of the die, including the dotted margin (Figure 2.15). From a catalogue furnished by Stevens,[64] it is evident the striking of these ceremonial coins continued till the very end of the rule of Muhammad Akbar II in 1837.

The ritual of presenting *Nazar* was a prerogative that reasserted the regal status of the emperor, thereby acknowledging the 'superiority' of the imperial house over the British. This unequal power status was allowed to continue albeit with its token semblance for a few more years. However, in 1827, at a meeting held in the court of Muhammad Akbar, the then Governor-General Lord Amherst categorically reasserted the status of 'equality' between the Company, which he represented, and the emperor by omitting the *Nazar* ceremony from the meeting protocol. The meeting was followed

Figure 2.15 'Nazar' rupee struck in the name of Muhammad Akbar II, in his 31st and last regnal year (CE 1837), Ashmolean Museum

Source: Photograph by author

by 'debilitating injunctions against the courtly ceremonials and conventions',[65] in which Europeans in general were barred from presenting the *Nazar* to the emperor, or indeed receiving it from other noblemen. Henceforth, the *Nazar* ritual ceased to be exercised by the British but presumably it continued among the other noblemen of the court.

In the aftermath of the Anglo-Afghan War in late 1830s, the British systematically reduced the status of the Mughal emperor to 'King of Dehli'. The practice of *Nazar* was finally stopped, even within the confines of whatever was left of the Mughal court, by the winter of 1842–1843 by the orders of Lord Ellenborough.[66] At this juncture even the striking of coins for ceremonial purposes in the mint at Delhi came to be forbidden. The chronological details seen on the *Nazar* coins struck in the name of the last Mughal emperor Bahadur Shah II corroborate this decision—none struck after the 6th regnal year, which corresponds to 1842–1843, are known.[67]

Nisār coins: power, protection and piety

Like coins struck specifically for the *Nazar* ritual, the other category of Mughal coins issued for a specific court ritual were the *Nisār*s. By far the most extensive treatment of these has been by Hodivala,[68] who produces details from a number of Mughal and other texts to provide a context for them. As he has rightly observed the root of the appellation is the tri-literal root 'N-th-r' which means 'to spread or scatter'. As defined in the dictionary of Steingass,[69] *Nusār* and *Nusārat* mean 'what is scattered, the crumbs from a table; a small coin at weddings'. The word denotes objects, such as coins, precious stones, and other articles which are 'waved around the head of the emperor or other great personages and thrown among the crowd to scramble for at coronations, weddings, birthday anniversaries, royal entries and progresses through the great cities and other festive celebrations'. The practice of scattering or offering coins as an index of the king's munificence was a 'pan-Asiatic' practice and Hodivala has given examples from the wider Islamicate world from Iran to Indonesia.[70] In the pre-Islamic world it certainly existed in the Byzantine Empire, in which political officers or 'consuls' held a privilege of scattering coins in the public.[71] From a numismatic viewpoint, we have examples of the Roman emperor Constantine's gold coins which show the emperor riding in a quadriga and scattering coins with his raised right hand.[72] Closer to home in India, the Gupta king Chandra Gupta II is shown offering a stream of coins while performing a sacrifice[73] on some of his gold coins.

The purpose for, manner in, and events for which coins were scattered differed under the Mughals. As Hodivala says, the ritual was done 'as a form of sacrifice, an offering to Nemesis, as a means of deprecating the anger or envy of gods in moments of sudden or unprecedented good fortune, a charm for averting the evil-eye or a thank offering'.[74] What he does not discuss is the significance of the ritual or what precisely was the role of this ritual in the Mughal ideals of kingship. He has also limited the discussion to events in which there was actual scattering of the coins. But going by the excerpts that he produces, it is evident that scattering was only one of the ways the ritual of *Nisār* could be enacted. Before the coins were scattered, they went through other ritual protocols. Also absent from his discussion is the fact that *Nisār* was also a part of the *Nazar* ritual we have just discussed. There are many instances reported in Mughal chronicles that, when court incumbents presented a certain amount as *Nazar*, another sum was presented at the same time designated as *Nisār*. Beveridge and Rodgers in their translation of the *Tuzuq-i Jahangiri* have translated the term as 'alms' or 'charity'—thus, we find mentions that when Khurram, the son of Jahangir, met him at Mandu after the successful Deccan campaign, he 'presented 1,000 ashrafis and 1,000 rupees as *Nazar* and the same amount by way of alms';[75] or Bahadur Khan Uzbeg, coming from Qandahar, 'had the good fortune to pay his respects: by way of *Nazar* he gave 100 muhrs, and by way of charity offered Rs. 4,000'.[76] Another instance is the visit of the Maratha king Shivaji to the court of Aurangzeb at the celebration of the emperor's 50th lunar birthday. When Shivaji was brought before Aurangzeb in court attendance, he presented 2000 rupees as *Nazar* and 5000 rupees as *Nisār*.[77] The sums of *Nazar* and *Nisār* appear to be institutionalised depending on the rank and status of the incumbent, and in some instances, we find the *Nisār* sum was greater than that of the *Nazar* sum.

Another act where coins were used was the ritual showering. It was normal for the emperor, or other important persons to be showered with coins, and then give them away to the gathering. In the aforementioned meeting between Jahangir and Khurram, Jahangir 'came down from the *jharokha* and poured over his head a small tray of jewels and a tray of gold (coins)'.[78] He then meted out the same treatment to an exceptional elephant that was sent to him as tribute from the Adil Shahi Sultan of Bijapur: ' as it appeared acceptable to me, I myself mounted (i.e. drove it) and took it into my private palace, and scattered a quantity of gold coins on its head, and ordered them to tie it up inside the royal palace'.[79] This shows that the act of pouring money was not only limited to a person of endearing qualities but on animals which were prized possessions, as well. One would presume coins lost through such rituals would then be picked up by the gathering.

Largesse using coins was practised in the Timurid court, as the European emissary Ruy Gonzales de Clavijo found out when he visited Timur at Samarqand—silver coins were brought in and showered over the gathering, which then picked them up as a token of their gratitude and the king's power.[80] In other instances, the emperor gave away coins and other precious objects such as 'nuts, almonds, fruit and spices' which were all made of thin beaten sheets of gold and silver. We find a reference to this in Thomas Roe's account: 'he ascended his Throne, and had basons of nuts, almonds, fruits, spices of all sort, made in thinne silver, which he cast about, and his great men scrambled prostrate upon their bellies; which seeing I did not, hee reached one Bason almost full, and powred into my cloke'.[81]

Giving away coins as 'alms or charity' was very much a norm of the Mughal court. Important court gatherings and events such as the festivities of Nowruz and the emperor's weighment on his solar and lunar birthdays were the usual settings for such ritual munificence. The weighment ceremony was a ritual the Mughal emperors had adopted from the Indian tradition.[82] The emperor would be weighed against metals, cloth, grain and other distributable items or commodities, and afterwards these would be distributed to the poor.

Hodivala draws a long list of instances from the *Tuzuq-i Jahangiri* in which Jahangir describes the ritual scattering of money.[83] Most instances involved a procession or transit, where the emperor and his retinue might simply have moved from one place to another and perhaps back. Entering and exiting the cities, proceeding on to hunts or campaigns, visiting gardens and passing through smaller towns en route to provincial headquarters were the usual theatres for the ritual. In most instances, we see Jahangir parading on an elephant which would be a symbol of his regal authority, and in most cases he presents himself as the actor of the ritual, although only in one instance it is mentioned that he scattered coins with his own hands.[84]

There are a couple of examples of the ritual being depicted in miniature paintings, which do not corroborate the description that royal personages indulged in the ritual; that is, scattered the coins themselves. In the 'St. Petersburg Album', now in the collection of the Institute of Oriental Studies, Russian Academy of Sciences, St. Petersburg has a painting from the *Jahangirnāmā* by the artist Abu'l Hasan (Fol. 21a, accession number E-14) which showcases a scene of joy and celebration at the accession of Jahangir (Figure 2.16). The composition is replete with the usual modes of celebration—drums being beaten and trumpets blown—but it also shows a host of characters moving to the right, either with presents, like weapons, birds and money, or in gestures of supplication and/or wondrous amusement. Understandably, their focus of attention is the newly created emperor; however, he is not visible in the painting, as it is most likely a part of the diptych spread over two page of the album.[85] In this scene in the lower register, there is a portly man throwing coins in the air from a plateful held in his hands (Figure 2.17), and menial members of the public are shown scrambling to grab them as they fall to the ground. A second example is the study showing the entry of the Mughal prince, 'Azam Shah into the city of Ahmadabad', from the Howard Hodgkin Collection, at one time on loan to the Ashmolean Museum (http://jameelcentre.ashmolean.org/object/LI118.22, Figure 2.18). Unlike the previous example, here the subject of the composition is fully visible—the prince, who is identified by a small label inscription, is being carried on a high palanquin chair by eight bearers. He is followed by another prince, identified as 'Wala Jah'. Above the figure of 'Azam Shah, partly covered by the sun-shield (*Aftabgir*) held by a bearer accompanying him, are outlines of two men who carry bags of money and are shown throwing coins from them into the great crowd assembled as a backdrop. There are no coins visible; however, the scramble to grab them is pretty much evident, as it is in the previous instance.

The most important aspect of the ritual of *Nisār* is the centrality of the 'body' and 'sight' in it. Much like the *Nazar* ritual, the dynamic that evolved by actually sighting the subject around which the ritual was carried appears to play a significant role in it. It was no wonder therefore, that *Nisār* was also subsumed in the *Nazar* ritual, as indicated by the two designated components of the ritual presenting of money to the emperor. As the example of Jahangir mentioned previously shows, the ritual was not confined only to important persons, or indeed to the performative protocol of the court; even animals were subject to it. The primary reason why such orchestrated 'throwing away' of money was performed appears to be the imbalance between the qualities and 'fortunes' of the object of the ritual and the resultant 'envy' of the rest, who partook in sighting him. This would no doubt lead to the 'evil eye' being energised. Money thus acted as an agency to ward its effects off in a talismanic way. Before the money was flung away, or offered in charity, it was, as Hodivala notes (vide supra), 'waved around the head of the emperor or other great personages'. Conceivably, such actions, apart from identifying the subject of the ritual very clearly, also symbolically

Figure 2.16 'Celebrations at the accession of Jahangir' by Abu'l Hasan, Jahangirnama. St. Petersburg Album. ca. 1615–1618, Institute of Oriental Studies, St. Petersburg. Accession number Fol. 21a, E-14

Source: Wikimedia Commons

Figure 2.17 Detail of Figure 16—a man scatters coins in the crowd and people scramble to pick them up

'gathered' the ill effects of the 'evil eye', so they can be cast away with the money. As we have seen, certain categories of people were regarded as particularly potent carriers of the 'evil eye' and in certain situations, like imperial processions, the main actors like royal personages had no choice over who they were being sighted by. The act of throwing coins into the crowd

Figure 2.18 'Prince Azam Shah enters Ahmadabad', attributed to Kalyan Das Chitarmal, Ashmolean Museum, lent by Sir Howard Hodgkin, LI118.22

Source: Photograph courtesy of the Visitors of the Ashmolean Museum, University of Oxford

served the excellent purpose of distracting the malevolent gaze of such less-fortunate people from the emperor or other illustrious persons or animals.

Coins scattered or given away as *Nisār*, while acting as apt distractions, served a different purpose for the recipients. The emperor, the 'shadow of the divine' and the 'chosen of the Almighty', imbued power in his body. This power was transferred through to the recipients when they beheld objects which had been in physical touch with him. As McLane has observed, there appeared to be a 'predisposition to ascribe charismatic, transcendent qualities' to sighting highest office-holders. 'In Islamic terms, this experience was similar to *Barakā*, the blessing or sense that the "Divine reaches into the World" when in presence of a person of exceptional character and force or genealogical background.'[86] One of the manifestations of the passing of *Barakā* was the ritual showering with money of the Mughal emperor at the time of weighing ceremonies. The money which thus had cascaded, touching the emperor's body, was considered particularly valuable for charity as it carried the *Barakā* of the emperor along with it. A detail from one of the *Padshahnama* album, showing the ritual weighment of Shahjahan (Royal Collection Trust, Windsor, no. RCIN 1005025.n, Figure 2.19) on his 42nd lunar birthday, shows a group of Sheikhs holding their hands out in supplication and anticipation, while a bearer stands facing them with a small plate full of votive objects. Although coins are not clearly shown here, it is conceivable for the plate to have them, perhaps alongside other objects like

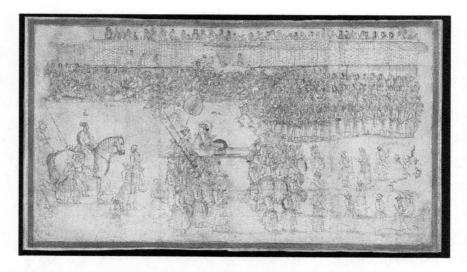

Figure 2.19 'The Weighing of Shah-Jahan on his 42nd lunar birthday (23 October 1632)', by Bhola, 1656–1657, accession number RCIN 1005025.n, Royal Collection Trust/© Her Majesty Queen Elizabeth II 2019

Source: www.rct.uk/sites/default/files/collection-online/d/5/451394-1395767749.jpg

flowers made of precious metals,[87] which were destined to be showered over the emperor after his weighing was over. Showering with money was also shown as a metaphor for divine appreciation. In a miniature painting from the Bodleian Library, University of Oxford's collection (Bodleian Library MS. Douce Or. a.1, Fol.55b, Figure 2.20), Shahjahan is shown receiving three artists (painters) while seated on an outdoor pavilion next to a river or lake. The painting no doubt reflects on connoisseurship as an essential element in the conception of kingship. To emphasise Shahjahan's role as a connoisseur exemplar, the composition also shows a group of winged cherubim gathered in the sky above. Four of them carry golden dishes in their hands, full of small gold coins, which they shower on the emperor who sits below admiringly receiving paintings from the painters' hands.

Piety was another way *Nisār* was used. Acts of ceremonial largesse were an important function in Mughal court. The emperor gave away money to alleviate particular unfortunate effects such as illnesses or death in the royal family, or adversities such as famines or pestilence. More positive and cheerful events such as marriages and festivals also prompted an almsgiving spree. Jahangir notes, 'on Sunday the 26th . . . was held the marriage feast of Parwiz and the daughter of Prince Murad. The ceremony was performed in the house of Her Highness Maryam-Zamani. The entertainment was arranged in the house of Parwiz, and all who were present were exalted with all kinds of honour and civilities. Nine thousand rupees were handed over to S͟harif Amuli and other nobles, to be given in alms to faqirs and other poor people'.[88] There are many other instances recounted in the *Tuzuq* where alms were distributed, such as a solar eclipse,[89] personal illness[90] or an unlucky conjunction of stars.[91] The *Padshahnama* mentions[92] that in his 4th regnal year, while Shahjahan was stationed at Burhanpur, a major famine broke out in the area. As a gesture of charity, it was decided that while he remained at Burhanpur, every Monday 5,000 rupees should be given away as largesse. Thus, over 20 consecutive Mondays, a total of 100,000 rupees were given away. It is impossible to know if any of this was issued in specially struck coins (see later section); however, one would assume if the daily sum was to be sufficient for more persons, it would be expedient to donate it as small denominations such as quarters or eighths of rupees.

In the same regnal year, Shahjahan's beloved wife Mumtaz Mahal died at Burhanpur. A spate of charities and almsgiving was unleashed at such events. While a person was on deathbed, it was considered particularly significant to engage in charity in his name. While Aurangzeb lay dying at Ahmadnagar in 1707, his courtier Hamid ud-Din Khan offered to give away an elephant in charity (*tasadduq*) so the emperor could be saved from ill influences. Aurangzeb agreed but forbade the giving away of elephant as a 'Hindu custom' and instead ordered, 'give 4,000 rupees to the chief Qazi for distribution among the poor'.[93] A mid-18th-century late Mughal school painting from the British Library's manuscript of the Farsi poet Nizami Ganjavi's

Figure 2.20 'Shahjahan receiving three artists or scholars', Bodleian Library MS. Douce Or. a. 1, fol. 55b,

Source: https://digital.bodleian.ox.ac.uk/inquire/p/b3d19177-3159-430c-8038-b6037b98c14d

work *Khusrau wa Shireen* shows a funeral scene (accession number Or.2933 f.95v, Figure 2.21) of Buzurjumid, a character in the long poem. At the head of the funeral cortège, we see a man carrying a moneybag giving away alms to a group of people holding out their hands in anticipation.

Jahangir was the first emperor to herald the practice of issuing special coins for the *Nisār* ritual. From the instances mentioned earlier, as well as a note in the *Tuzuq* it is apparent that the quarter rupee coin was the most favoured denomination for the ritual of scattering coins. Immediately after his accession, Jahangir notes: 'At a propitious hour I ordered that they should coin gold and silver of different weights. To each coin I gave a separate name . . . to that of 1 *tola*, [I gave] the name of *Jahāngīrī*. The half *Jahāngīrī* I called *Sulṭānī*; the quarter, *Nisārī* (showering money); the dime, *k̲h̲air-i-qabūl* (the acceptable)"[94] It must be said that available numismatic evidence suggests the list here is incomplete and inaccurate in parts. Jahangir never mentions the word *Nisārī* ever again, instead he uses the word *Charan* in vogue from his father's reign to denote the quarter rupee denomination. There are surviving examples of the 'dime' (by which the translators presumably mean a 1/8th rupee) which bears the inscription *Khair-i-qabūl*, but it would be better to regard it without the *izafah* in the middle, simply as *Khair qabūl* which would translate as 'grace accepted/received'. The inscription thus echoes the sentiments of the recipient of the largesse, who

Figure 2.21 'Buzurjumid leading the funeral procession accompanied by water-sprinklers and men giving coins to bystanders', miniature from an abridged version of *Khusrau u Shirin* by Nizami, British Library, Or.2933 f.95v

Source: Flickr Commons, www.flickr.com/photos/britishlibrary/12459605264

would have gratefully received it. From existing coins, however, we know that this inscription was not limited to only the 1/8th rupee denomination; coins as small as 1/32nd of a rupee are known to bear the legend (Figure 2.22). The mention in the *Tuzuq* does not include the name *Noor Afshan*, but it is known from extant specimens of largesse coins of 1/16th rupee denomination struck from the mints of Ajmer, Agra, Burhanpur and Lahore (Figure 2.23). The name means 'light scatterer' and evidently has a

Figure 2.22 Silver 1/32nd rupee coin of Jahangir with *Khair Qabul* legend, Ahmadabad mint, 0.41 gm

Source: Classical Numismatic Gallery, Ahmadabad, Auction 26, lot 324, 21–2–2017 www.coinarchives.com/w/openlink.php?l=2608830|2545|324|218dfec4cd8c3426e3e8c8d6cdae9414

Figure 2.23 Silver 1/16th rupee coin of Jahangir, with *Noor Afshan* legend, Ajmer mint, 0.70 gm, Ashmolean Museum

Source: Photograph by author

pun suggestive of the function of the coins, as well as a part of the emperor's name (Noor ud-Din). It also has a resonance with the name *Gul Afshan* (flower scatterer) given to a garden established on the banks of the River Yamuna by Babur, and a delight of Jahangir.[95] Barring these rather florid names, most other largesse coins of Jahangir bear the simple legends *Nisār -i Jahangiri* or *Nisār -i Jahangir Shahi* (Figure 2.24).

The *Nisār* coinage under Jahangir's son Shahjahan went a step ahead in design—now we see poetic couplets exclusively compiled to be put on coins which make a direct reference to the fact the coin is destined to be scattered or given away. An example would be a 1/4th rupee *Nisār* struck about the time of Shahjahan's investiture struck at Lahore and it refers to him with his pre-accession name 'Khurram' (Figure 2.25). The couplet on this coin reads:

مهر کند سپهر زر از سر افرازی
نثار شاه جهان شاه خرم غازی
Muhr Kunad Sipahar-i-zar az Sar Afrāzi
Nisār -i-Shāh-i-Jahān Shāh Khurram Ghāzi

(Made the stamp on the Golden Heaven with Eminence, *Nisār* of the King of the World, king Khurram, the warrior).

Apart from these *Nisār*, coins were struck bearing simple nominative legends like *Nisār -i Shāhjahān, Nisār -i Shāhjahān Bādshāh Ghāzi* and *Nisār -i Sahib Qirān Sāni* throughout Shahjahan's reign from a number of mints, namely Agra/Akbarabad, Akbarnagar, Kashmir, Kabul, Shahjahanabad, Daulatabad, Burhanpur, Patna, Delhi and Lahore. It is conceivable that

Figure 2.24 Silver 1/4th rupee coin of Jahangir with *Nisār Jahangiri* legend, Ashmolean Museum, 2.54 gm, Ashmolean Museum

Source: Photograph by author

Figure 2.25 Silver 1/4th rupee of Shahjahan struck at Lahore as *Nisār* with his pre-accession name 'Khurram' included in a special poetic couplet, Ashmolean Museum, 2.6 gm

Source: Photograph by author

Figure 2.26 Silver 1/4th rupee *Nisār* coin of Shahjahan, struck at Akbarabad (Agra), dated AH1042/5th regnal year

Source: Collection of Jan Lingen, The Netherlands; photograph by author

some of these might have been struck for occasions where the emperor might have been present. It might be tempting to attribute a 1/4th rupee *Nisār* coin struck at Akbarabad in AH1042/RY5 (Figure 2.26) to the event of the emperor's weighment in the *Padshahnama* painting we have discussed earlier. However, we know that the emperor never visited Patna or Akbarnagar

(Rajmahal in Bengal) so the *Nisār* coins struck there in his name might have been used for rituals involving other royal persons, like his son Shah Shuja'a who was the governor of Bengal towards the latter part of his reign. Some *Nisār* coins might be identified as celebratory issues, prompted by conquests of important towns or forts in campaigns: a 1/4th rupee *Nisār* struck at Balkh in Northern Afghanistan has recently been published[96] and it is undoubtedly a celebratory issue struck either for scattering in a victory procession, or as almsgiving in the event of such a fortuitous event. The *Padshahnama* mentions that the procession of Mughal standards marched in at an auspicious time into Balkh after the troops of Nazr Muhammad the Janid ruler vacated the city following a Mughal victory. Murad Bakhsh, the son of Shahjahan and the leader of the Mughal campaign into Transoxiana, held court at Balkh on 7th July 1646. A few days later, on 12th July, a reward of 2000 rupees was sent for the 'consolation of some of the people at large and inhabitants of Balkh'.[97]

The practice of striking special *Nisār* coins continued into the reign of Aurangzeb and his successors; however, the designs became more simplified with only nominative legends appearing on them. *Nisār* coins struck in the names of Shah Alam Bahadur, Jahandar Shah, Farrukhsiyar and Muhammad Shah are known with such simplified legends, wherein the words *Nisār-i* are preceded by the emperor's name. Most of these are 1/4th rupee, as that denomination was indeed preferred for charitable issues. Perhaps the last celebratory *Nisār* coin struck in India was the unique 1/4th rupee struck during the Afghan occupation of Delhi, in his 5th invasion of India by Ahmad Shah Durrani (Figure 2.27) leading to the battle of Panipat in

Figure 2.27 1/4th rupee of Ahmad Shah Durrani, king of Afghanistan, struck at Shahjahanabad (Delhi) during the Afghan occupation in CE 1760

Source: The British Museum, photograph by author

January 1761. We have already noted the issue of special *Nazar* coins in this period. Although the word *Nisār* is absent in the inscription on the coins (it only bears the normal coin couplet of Ahmad Shah with the addition of a cartouche with 'Ahmad' written inside it in the centre) the facts that it deviates a great deal from the design of circulatory coins struck during the occupation suggests it was produced for a specific purpose and that it is a wide flan, specially produced coin of 1/4th rupee denomination, leave little doubt that it must have been struck for charity or largesse.

Epilogue: coins in 'rituals of power' of Mughal court

The previous discussion highlights the role coins played in Mughal court culture, underpinned by the idea and ideals of Mughal kingship. Mughal court culture revolved around the centrality of the concept of kingship and therefore, coins were an integral part of it. The fact that, as Islamic rulers, the Mughal emperors held the right to strike coins in their names or *Sikka* as a royal prerogative brought coins directly within the ambit of objects which became indexical of kingship, alongside other symbols like standards and banners.

Two aspects related to the emperor emerge more important in the visual articulation of his status—his body and his viewing or sighting. As a person chosen with divine intercession and a 'shadow of God', the emperor's body was imbued with special powers replete with magical qualities like *Barakā*, or blessing. This power could be transferred to recipients using various channels, some of which were accessed in a ritualised sense. The recipients of this power were usually considered extremely fortunate and to have access to objects that facilitated this transfer was considered a privilege. Among the objects which were passed on and considered to be significant vectors of such power transfer, was the *Khilat* or robes which the emperor had used once or twice[98] and objects with his effigy on them. They would be used as charms or 'life propitiating ornaments', as Khafi Khan affirms when he describes Jahangir's intention of giving his likeness struck on gold to his favoured Amirs. The object not only indicated a special status of the person in the court as a member of the emperor's 'inner circle' but also offered him an opportunity to sight the emperor at his own will. Sighting the emperor as a member of his close retinue, or 'discipleship' as it was often referred to, was a great privilege. As John Richards remarks, 'selection as a royal disciple was a signal honour. Those who wore tiny portraits of the emperor were an elect group of imperial servants'.[99]

The fact that sighting the emperor was such a privilege prompted other rituals around it, both in a public and private sense. They were based on positive as well as negative aspects of the sighting, which held the viewer and the viewee in a peculiar dynamic. The exalted status and the aura of the emperor gave the viewers a chance to imbibe and draw power from him, but it also exposed the emperor, as a viewee, to the ill effects of the sighting, such as the 'evil eye'. The Mughals were particularly sensitive about it and made arrangements to ward it off by means of devising protocols that would enable the ill effects to go away. One such remedy was to perform acts of piety such as charity. The sighting of the emperor by an incumbent would prompt a small gift called *Nazar,* while the ill effects the sighting might bring forth—given that the emperor was immensely more fortunate than the incumbent and thus would be a subject of the incumbent's envy—were warded off by offering money for charity or alms, usually called *Nisār*. In a way this was a ritual institutionalisation of social customs and beliefs translated into a monetised form, and special coins were struck to articulate the particularity of their purpose.

Once ritualised in this fashion, the 'invented tradition' of rituals like offering *Nazar* and *Nisār* set off its own hierarchical modalities. They were constructed on themes of obeisance, gratitude and tribute. The sums which represented the monetised values of these offerings varied by rank of the incumbent to the court or the purpose for which the audience was being sought. It was this hierarchised effect of a ritual transaction that brought the custom into a zone of consternation when power equations between the Mughals and their political successors, the British, changed in the early 19th century. The token subordination of the British to the emperor was done away with, first by abolishing the mint for circulatory coins at Delhi and then by stopping even the issue of ceremonial coins essential for the ritual.

The warding off of the effect of the 'evil eye' by public charity assumed the nature of a processual spectacle, when the Mughal emperors offered the opportunity to their subjects by appearing in public in full sight, en route to and from a destination, be it for hunting, pilgrimage or peregrinations that came about owing to the peripatetic nature of the court. Specially struck coins were scattered, after they were ritually encircled over the emperor's body, into the public. It achieved two effects: it projected the emperor as a munificent and spectacular ruler to his subjects, but it also diverted attention of the public away from continually sighting (or gazing at) the emperor and thus averted the 'evil eye'.

The use of coins was integral to such practices and it sheds an important light on the engagement of the Mughal emperors with the money that circulated bearing their name. The very fact that Jahangir suggested specific names for his coins, almost immediately after his accession and with almost poetic allusions, shows how intimately he was connected with their issue and function. As we have seen, other forms of appreciative inputs that the Mughals were particularly fond of, like composing special couplets, were also integrated into the making of these special coins. The rituals added to the 'performativity' of the Mughal court. Indeed, the Mughal court was, as Thomas Roe had observed, 'a just theatre' where the king was set about up on a balcony 'like a King in a play, and all his nobles below on a stage covered with carpets'.[100] It helps in understanding how presumably quotidian objects like coins played their role in the envisaging and construction of performative rituals of the Mughal court. While offering a critique of court rituals of gift-giving and addressing why, in particular, the emperor Jahangir appeared so unimpressed with the gifts that Sir Thomas Roe had brought for him, Bernard Cohn has suggested, 'Europeans of the seventeenth century lived in a world of signs and correspondences, whereas Indians lived in a world of substances'.[101] This view has been rightly criticised by Truschke, who has quoted Ania Loomba to remark, 'Roe's well-received offerings at Jahangir's court suggest that the Mughals often emphasized the symbolism of gifts above their raw economic worth'.[102] The contextual placement of coins in court rituals highlights the Mughal penchant for such symbolisms involved in protocols and performances that were intentionally conceived, constructed and articulated around the central idea of Mughal kingship. The fact that the rituals were also monetised transactions gives us an insight into how ideologies were cleverly transmuted into a fiscal apparatus during the Mughal period, with the emperor, and the anthropology of his kingship at its core.

Notes

1 David Kertzer, *Ritual, Politics and Power*, New Haven and London: Yale University Press, 1988; D. Cannadine, and S. Price (eds), *Rituals of Royalty: Power and Ceremonial in Traditional Societies*, Cambridge: Cambridge University Press, 1987.
2 *Ibid*, p. 14.
3 *Ibid*, p. 79.
4 Cannadine and Price, *Rituals of Royalty*, p. 19.
5 E. Hobsbawm and T. Ranger (eds), *The Invention of Tradition*, Cambridge: Cambridge University Press, 2012.
6 *'Ain-i Akbari* of Abu'l Fazl Allami, vol. 1, trans. H. Blochman, Calcutta: Asiatic Society of Bengal, 1873, p. 31.
7 S. H. Hodivala, *Historical Studies in Mughal Numismatics*, Calcutta: Numismatic Society of India, 1923.
8 *'Ain*, vol. 1, p. iii of preface.
9 Ram Prasad Khosla, *Mughal Kingship and Nobility*, Allahabad: The Indian Press Ltd., 1934, p. 9.
10 *'Ain-i Akbari* of Abu'l Fazl Allami, vol. 3, trans. H. Jarrett, Calcutta: Asiatic Society of Bengal, 1894, pp. 398–400.
11 R. P. Tripathi, 'The Turco-Mongol Theory of Kingship', in Muzaffar Alam and Sanjay Subrahmanyam (eds), *The Mughal State*, New Delhi: Oxford University Press, 1998.
12 John F. Richards, 'The Formulation of Imperial Authority Under Akbar and Jahangir', in John F. Richards (ed), *Kingship and Authority in South Asia*, New Delhi: Oxford University Press, 1998.
13 Eva Orthmann, 'Court Culture and Cosmology in the Mughal Empire: Humayun and the Foundations of the din-i Ilahi', in Albrecht Fuess and Jan-Peter Hartung (eds), *Court Cultures in the Muslim World: Seventh to Nineteenth Centuries*, London: Routledge, 2011, pp. 202–20.

14 'Evil Eye', in *The Oxford Dictionary of Islam*, ed. John L. Esposito, *Oxford Islamic Studies Online*, www.oxfordislamicstudies.com/article/opr/t125/e597, accessed 8 August 2019.
15 John Elliott, *Beware the Evil Eye Volume 4: The Evil Eye in the Bible and the Ancient World*, Eugene, OR: Cascade Books, 2017, p. 159.
16 *Ibid*, p. 160.
17 Gregory Minissale, *Images of Thought: Visuality in Islamic India 1550–1750*, Newcastle-upon-Tyne: Cambridge Scholars Publishing, 2006, p. 66.
18 Hodivala, *Historical Studies*, pp. 151–2.
19 *'Ain*, vol. 1, pp. 165–6.
20 Hodivala, *Historical Studies*, p. 151.
21 *Tuzuq-i Jahangiri, or Memoirs of Jahangir*, vol. I and II, trans. and ed. Alexander Rogers and Henry Beveridge, vol. 1, London: Royal Asiatic Society, 1909–1914, p. 60.
22 Hodivala, *Historical Studies*, p. 153.
23 *Ibid*.
24 *Ibid*.
25 Hodivala, *Historical Studies*, p. 147.
26 *The Embassy of Sir Thomas Roe to the Court of the Great Mogul 1615–1619*, ed. William Foster, vol. 1 and 2, London: Hakluyt Society, 1893, pp. 244–5.
27 *Ibid*, pp. 213, 227.
28 *Ibid*, pp. 244–5.
29 Some historians have mistaken this gift to be a 'painting', while Roe's own account clearly says it was a 'medal of gold'. See Audrey Truschke, 'Deceptive Familiarity: European Perceptions of Access at the Mughal Court', in Dries Raeymaekers and Sebastiaan Derks (eds), *The Key to Power? The Culture of Access in Princely Courts 1400–1750*, Leiden: Brill, p. 92—"Roe was inducted into Jahangir's inner circle with a proper ceremony that featured Jahangir gifting Roe a small royal painting that he was to wear").
30 Hodivala, *Historical Studies*, p. 155.
31 *Ibid*, p. 159.
32 *Ibid*, p. 155.
33 *Ibid*, pp. 155–6.
34 *Ibid*, p. 158.
35 *Ibid*, p. 160.
36 R. B. Whitehead, *Catalogue of Coins in the Panjab Museum, Lahore: Vol. II, Coins of the Mughal Emperors*, Oxford: Clarendon Press, 1914, pp. 20–1.
37 *The Embassy*, p. 106.
38 Nirmal Kumar, 'Rituals of Power and Power of Rituals: A Study of Imperial Rituals and Invented Traditions in 16th Century North India', *Proceedings of the Indian History Congress*, 58, 1997: 246–7.
39 *The Muntakhabu-'l Tawarikh by 'Abdu-'l-Qādir Ibn-i-Mulūk Shāh known as Al-Badāoni, Vols. I, II and III,* trans. and eds. George S. A. Ranking, Sir Wolseley Haig and W. H. Lowe, vol. II, Calcutta: Asiatic Society of Bengal, 1898–1925, section 326.
40 William Irvine, 'Austin of Bordeaux', *Journal of the Royal Asiatic Society*, 1910: 1344.
41 Hodivala, *Historical Studies*, pp. 154–5.
42 Sanjay Subrahmanyam, *Europe's India: Words, Peoples, Empires, 1500–1800*, Cambridge, MA and London: Harvard University Press, 2017, p. 12.
43 Harbans Mukhia, *The Mughals of India*, Malden, MA and Oxford: Blackwell Publishing, 2008, pp. 86–7.

44 *Tuzuq*, vol. II, p. 8.
45 For a detailed study of the role the depictions of the role 'globe'-like objects played in Jahangir's visuality, see Sumathi Ramaswamy, 'Conceit of the Globe in Mughal Visual Practice', *Comparative Studies in Society and History*, 2007, 49(4): 751–82.
46 *The Embassy*, vol. 1, p. 256.
47 Henry Yule, *Hobson-Jobson: A Glossary of Colloquial Anglo-Indian Words and Phrases, and of Kindred Terms, Etymological, Historical, Geographical and Discursive*, new ed. William Crooke, London: J. Murray, 1903, p. 634.
48 Yuthika Sharma, 'Art in Between Empires: Visual Culture and Artistic Knowledge in Late Mughal Delhi, 1748–1857' (unpublished Ph.D. thesis, Columbia University) -s://academiccommons.columbia.edu/doi/10.7916/D8959QRH), p. 125.
49 *Tuzuq*, vol. 2, p. 108.
50 *Ibid*, p. 197.
51 Benjamin Cohen, *Kingship and Colonialism in India's Deccan 1850–1948*, New York: Palgrave Macmillan, 2007, p. 78.
52 Sharma, *Art in Between Empires*, p. 146.
53 Lisa Balabanlilar, 'The Emperor Jahangir and the Pursuit of Pleasure', *Journal of the Royal Asiatic Society*, Third Series, 2009, 19(2): 174.
54 *'Ain*, vol. 1, p. 21.
55 Anecdotal evidence (private conversations with Steve Album of Santa Rosa, California) suggests that it was Charles K. Panish, the American expert on coins of South Asia who first used this term. He volunteered his services to the American Numismatic Society (ANS) for over three decades, performing work for years as a virtual acting curator, attributing, rearranging, and re-labelling over half of the South Asian coins, particularly in the collection of Indian States. He was also a major benefactor, donating 9,682 coins to ANS over the course of several decades. The mention of the word 'Nazar / Nazr' as an adjective for a category of coins does occur in early numismatic tracts such as Webb's Currencies of the Hindu States of Rajputana (See W. W. Webb, *The Currencies of the Hindu States of Rajputana*, London: Constable & Co., 1893, pp. 77, 95, 99–100, 116, 131, 150).
56 S. Goron and J. P. Goenka, *The Coins of the Indian Sultanates*, New Delhi: Munshiram Manoharlal, 1991, p. 192.
57 H. Tareen, 'Kabul Victory 5-Shahrukhi of Humayun', *Journal of the Oriental Numismatic Society*, 2018, 232: 26–7.
58 Hodivala, *Historical Studies*, pp. 53–80.
59 For a detailed history of these events, see Jadunath Sarkar, *Fall of the Mughal Empire*, vol. 2, London: Sangam Books, 1991, pp. 139–226.
60 Sanjay Garg, 'The Closure of Delhi Mint 1818', in D. W. MacDowall, Savita Sharma and Sanjay Garg (eds), *Indian Numismatics, History, Art and Culture: Essays in Honour of Dr. Parmeshwari Lal Gupta*, vol. II, New Delhi: Agam Kala, 1992, p. 234.
61 P. J. E. Stevens, *The Coinage of the Hon. East India Company: Part 1 - The Coins of the Bengal Presidency*, London: A. H. Baldwin and Sons, 2012, p. 426.
62 Garg, 'The Closure of Delhi Mint', p. 235.
63 Sharma, *Art in Between Empires*, p. 125.
64 Stevens, *The Coinage of the Hon. East India Company*, pp. 437–8.
65 Sharma, *Art in Between Empires*, p. 247.
66 S. Lane-Poole, *The History of the Moghul Emperors of Hindustan: Illustrated by Their Coins*, London: Constable, 1892, p. lxxxvi.
67 Stevens, *The Coinage of the Hon. East India Company*, p. 442.
68 Hodivala, *Historical Studies*, pp. 177–85.

69 *A Comprehensive Persian-English Dictionary, Including the Arabic Words and Phrases to Be Met with in Persian Literature*, ed. Francis Joseph Steingass, London: Routledge & K. Paul, 1892, p. 1387.
70 Hodivala, *Historical Studies*, pp. 177–9.
71 M. F. Hendy, *Studies in the Byzantine Monetary Economy c.300–1450*, Cambridge: Cambridge University Press, 1985, pp. 194–5.
72 David Sear, *Roman Coins and Their Values*, vol. 4, London: Spink, 2011, no. 15623, p. 425.
73 A. S. Altekar, *The Coinage of the Gupta Empire*, Varanasi: Numismatic Society of India, 1957, p. 128.
74 Hodivala, *Historical Studies*, p. 181.
75 *Tuzuq*, vol. 1, p. 394.
76 *Tuzuq*, vol. 2, p, 232.
77 Jadunath Sarkar, *History of Aurangzib,* vol. V, Calcutta: M. C. Sarkar & Sons, 1952, p. 72.
78 *Tuzuq*, vol. 1, p. 395.
79 *Ibid.*
80 Hodivala, *Historical Studies*, p. 178.
81 *The Embassy*, vol. 2, pp. 411–12.
82 Kumar, 'The Rituals of Power and Power of Rituals', pp. 249–50.
83 Hodivala, *Historical Studies*, p. 180.
84 *Tuzuq*, vol. 2, p. 197.
85 John Huy and Joritt Britschgi, *Wonder of the Age: Master Painters of India, 1100–1900*, New York and Ahmadabad: Metropolitan Museum of Art / Mapin, 2011, p. 75, no. 29.
86 John McLane, *Land and Local Kingship in Eighteenth-Century Bengal*, Cambridge: Cambridge University Press, 1993, p. 16.
87 Hodivala, *Historical Studies*, p. 182.
88 *Tuzuq*, vol. 1, p. 81.
89 *Ibid*, pp. 281–2.
90 *Ibid*, p. 267.
91 *Ibid*, p. 81.
92 The Badshah Namah by Abd Al-Hamid Lahawri, ed. Mawlawis Kabir Ai-Din Ahmad and Abd Al-Rahim Under the superintendence of Major W. N. Lees, 2 vols, Bibliotheca Indica 56, Calcutta: The Asiatic society of Bengal, 1868–72, vol. 1, p. 362.
93 Sarkar, *Aurangzib*, vol. 5, p. 257.
94 *Tuzuq*, vol. 1, p. 11.
95 *Ibid*, pp. 4–5.
96 S. Bhandare, 'Numismatic reflections on Shahjahan's Balkh Campaign—1646–47', *Numismatic Digest*, 2015, 39: 175.
97 *Ibid*, p. 178.
98 *The Embassy*, vol. 2, p. 334.
99 John F. Richards, *The New Cambridge History of India, I.5: The Mughal Empire*, Cambridge: Cambridge University Press, 1995, p. 105.
100 *The Embassy*, vol. 1, p. 112.
101 Bernard Cohn, *Colonialism and Its Forms of Knowledge: The British in India*, Princeton: Princeton University Press, 1996, p. 18.
102 Truschke, 'Deceptive Familiarity', p. 92.

3

RITUAL AS PERFORMED CONSTITUTION

Badagas in the Nilgiris district

Frank Heidemann

Introduction

Franz Boas' vision of anthropology combined archaeology, cultural anthropology, linguistics and physical anthropology into one academic field. More than a century later, disciplines have moved apart. Generally speaking, archaeologists reconstruct the past from artefacts, and anthropologists work with the method of participant observation, focusing mainly on the present. Both the kind of data and themes of investigation appear to be rather different. But I would argue the scope for joint projects is much larger than existing cooperation. In the Nilgiris, where I work as an anthropologist among the Badagas, hardly any excavation took place.[1] I focused on contemporary politics, followed headmen on their daily routine, watched meetings of the village councils and participated in temple festivals. To understand the legitimation of power, I had to include the system of kinship, the genealogy of Badaga gods, migration myths and the territorial order of the region. The elder among the Badagas discuss their pre-colonial past and use their (mythical) history as a rationale for the present. Some aspects of what I learned can be found in the early monographs, published just two decades after the first European came to the Hills in early 19th century.[2] In retrospect, my ethnographic work included a reconstruction of the public order as it existed before the arrival of the British and made the Nilgiris a hill station with modern institutions, European bungalows and a plantation economy.[3] My argument is against the view of David G. Mandelbaum, who claimed that the hill-dwellers 'had no explicit legal standards; they had virtually nothing of the apparatus of the state.'[4] In the following I try to contribute to the archaeology of an unwritten, pre-colonial constitution of the Badaga people, today manifest in the annual temple rituals.

The terms *power* and *ritual* have a long career in cultural and social sciences. Evolutionary, functional and structural approaches offered contradicting definitions; most of them have been extended, reformulated or rejected. Max Weber´s definition of power—in short: the ability to impose one's will upon others against resistance—was refused by Michel Foucault, who stressed the emergent character and the connection of power and knowledge.[5] The concepts of ritual and its sociological effects point to the symbolic potential, the ability to transform, to control, to depict and to create a meaningful world. I do not intend to begin with a new clarification of these terms but would like to present an ethnographically based case study from South India. The rituals under discussion are annual festivals and the concept of power will refer to both, Weber's dyadic model and Foucault's discursive approach. I like to show, how power and ritual are interconnected aspects of the social construction of Badaga society.

Badagas are the peasants on the Nilgiri plateau in eastern Tamil Nadu. They live in more than 300 villages, speak their own language and worship their own gods. In pre-colonial and colonial times they were the dominant group and maintained economic and ritual relations with the neighbouring Todas, Kotas and Kurumbas. In the early 20th century, after the Nilgiris became a British Hill station, Badagas began to cultivate so-called European vegetables for the local markets.[6] From the 1940s onwards, peasants in the Aravenu area converted their fields into tea gardens and a few Badagas opened bought leaf tea factories. Today, many families live in the small towns of the plateau, in Indian metropolitan cities or have moved overseas, maintaining close relations with their kin in their native villages. In general, they prefer to marry according to Badaga kinship rules, to bring up their children with their mother tongue and many individuals return to their native villages to participate in the annual temple festivals. The old system of leadership co-exists with modern leaders. The village headman (*gowder*), who is responsible for judicial disputes and external affairs, organises the annual temple festival and stands in the limelight of the event. On these festival days, also other offices and individuals are honoured: the village priests (*pujari*), representatives of affinal groups living within village boundaries, new-rich factory owners and local politicians. The ritual performances display an enormous complexity and require knowledge about the kinship system and the territorial order. The pattern of descent, affinity, territory and worship constitute an interwoven totality.

In the late 1980s, I participated in dozens of temple festivals, visited all 132 Badaga villages in Porangadu, the eastern part of the hills, and talked to many Badaga elders.[7] Most of the information was centered on individual villages or limited to particular valleys. After I had combined different versions and created genealogical models, I discussed the results with my interlocutors. The maps and graphs that follow are the digest of the shared knowledge of Badaga elders. For an archeological project there is little material evidence of these patterns, because houses built in lines and circular cowsheds look alike in most of the villages. The old place of worship for the village god was the *dodda mane* (great-house), the first built home in the village and one of several in a row of houses. The only structure that indicates a special status of a village is the *akka bakka*, a kind of ritual gate formerly made out of wood and later carved from stones. *Akka bakka* were erected exclusively in head villages, from where satellite villages were founded. In many villages, processions pass through these gates. They are so low that each person passing the gate has to bend down, and in doing so—as the elders say—pays respect to the status of the village.

The *dodda mane* and the *akka bakka* are the old insignia of a head village. The first stands for religious autonomy and the second for political sovereignty and jurisdiction. At the occasion of a religious festival, the procession will take care to visit both places. Other aspects may be a matter of discussion or dispute. In the past 30 years, new elements from pan-Indian Hinduism have been introduced and the participation of Kurumbas as musicians and ritual specialists has been discontinued in several villages. At no other occasion do internal affairs and inter-ethnic relations find such public and explicit expression. Badagas perform rituals at the boundaries of their villages and honour their in-laws and other invited groups. The migration paths of Badaga myths become visible when *pujari* and *gowder* lead the procession from village to village. Badaga religious rituals are what Geertz in his analysis of the Bali theatre state called models of and models for reality.[8] In short, they depict and constitute society.

In his monumental work *Verwandtschaft als Verfassung* (Kinship as Constitution), Georg Pfeffer reminds us that unlike in our own, contemporary nation states in the global north, most societies in history were organised without a formal constitution.[9] Kinship offers a way to think and to experience the common ground of local societies, and structures the mode of conduct between the sexes, age groups, affinals and agnates, the own and the other contemporaries. The same patterns govern hierarchies, the division of labour, inheritance and property rights, residential order and ritual obligations. Badaga society is divided into several endogamous groups. The highest position is occupied by Lingayats, and at the bottom of the hierarchy are Toreyas. The largest and politically dominant group are 'Gowder' (a common term in academic writing but not in use among the Badagas for the endogamous group, who also used 'Gowder' as an honorific term and for village headmen). They constitute about 80% of the Badaga society, call themselves just 'Badaga' and practise what Louis Dumont called the inclusion of the contrary.[10] Their social system will be described in the following pages.

Badagas follow the Dravidian kinship system. They address a father's brother's son as 'brother' and make a distinction between elder and younger brothers. Therefore, 'brother' and also 'father's brother' are classificatory terms and should not be confused with biology. Badagas follow a patrilocal residence, but families without a son can invite the son-in-law to settle in the village. In several villages there are house-lines of 'in-laws', that is, the male successor of a former son-in-law. More strictly than the rule of residence is the identification of a person with his father's lineage, which can go back to the village founder. Badagas prefer to marry cross-cousins. The ideal spouse for a male person is a 'mother's brother's daughter', also a classificatory term. Therefore, men prefer to marry spouses from the mother's native village. A young woman can marry into the patriline of her mother. As a result, children of different sex are separated, and their successors are potential marriage partners, a pattern characteristic for Dravidian kinship.[11] However, Badaga society knows several exceptions. For example, Haruva, a very small high-ranking vegetarian group, practises exogamy. When one of their daughters marries into a non-vegetarian group, she will cook meat, but remains vegetarian, and a daughter-in-law has to become a vegetarian after wedding.

Badaga society is based on several principles, and the Dravidian kinship system is just one aspect. Unlike most societies in Pfeffer's opus, Badagas had and have a centralised political system, a hierarchy of head-village (*uur*) and hamlet (*hatti*), and clearly marked jurisdictions. As peasants they have a pragmatic attitude to life and an ambivalent attitude towards ritual purity. This religiously based principle explains the high status of Lingayats and is the basis for the devotion of their gods, but at the same time they reject its application to other aspects of life and are proud to allow re-wedding of widows. Most of these principles are expressed in the religious festivals, especially in the worship of their own gods. In the following, I shall first introduce the two main gods and Badaga myths and then describe the basic pattern of their religious festivals. At the end I would like to take up a theme from an earlier article, where I described Badaga religious rituals as a performed constitution with a half-life of one year.[12]

Kula Devaru

In the past 200 years Badaga included several pan-Indian Gods into their system of worship, but political power is strongly connected to the worship of their *kula devaru* (*kula* refers to a kind of Badaga totemic group, *devaru* = god). Badaga used to translate this term as 'own god', because *kula devaru* are worshipped by their own kin exclusively. Hette (lit. father's mother, mother's mother, old woman, ancestress) and Hireodeya (great god) are the *kula devaru* of Badagas *par excellence*. They stand respectively for female and male principles and are indissolubly linked to kinship and territory. It is difficult to assess the status of Hette and Hireodeya within Badaga religion, because temples and a few festivals for other gods appear more impressive; but most Badagas claim that Hette occupies the highest position among the gods they worship. In the second half of the 19th century, Andreas Feodor Jagor estimated the number of temples and shrines in more than 300 Badaga villages and hamlets at more than 1,000, and the number of named and built places of worship is still growing.[13] Compared to the large numbers and impressive architecture of recent temples for Gaṇeśa, Mariamma and others, Hireodeya temples (less than three dozen in number) and (even fewer) Hette temples appear negligible. In the first comprehensive essay on the Nilgiri peoples, Henry Harkness expressed a fear that Hette and Hireodeya might lose their importance.[14] One and a half centuries later Paul Hockings described both gods as 'minor deities'.[15] In contrast, William A. Noble referred to Hette as 'the Badagas' own, most popular goddess'.[16] The small number of temples for the *kula devaru* can be explained by the fact that Hireodeya can only be worshiped in the original villages that were first settlements, whence satellite hamlets were later established. Hette is goddess for all non-Lingayat Badagas, and the importance of her main temple in Beragani is not questioned by recent constructions elsewhere. V. W. Karl comments: '"Hethay" and "Hireodea" are only venerated but not worshipped and do not have large temples like Śiva or Mariamma'.[17]

In the 21st century, numerous Badagas, who have settled in Indian metropolitan cities or abroad, return for Hette's festival and much of what they see is recorded visually. The growing number of Badaga platforms in social media and uploaded videos on YouTube suggest that the fear Harkness felt no longer exists a century later. In colonial and post-Independent history, a clear move towards pan-Indian gods of the Śaivite tradition must be noted, and their festivals apparently gained in importance. But after extensive labour immigration began in the 1970s and Badagas lost their formerly undisputed dominance in the political elections, a turn towards *kula devaru* became obvious; although in recent years the labour influx has subsided to the point where there has been a slight decrease in the district population.[18]

Hette (in social media, including YouTube, often spelt 'Hethai') is worshipped as the Badaga goddess par excellence and as an ideal woman. Several myths describe her as a girl or young woman who solved conflicts between two affinal Badaga groups and sacrificed her life. The versions of her selfless life and her death vary. She committed *sati*, drowned, hanged herself or vanished without trace.[19] N. N. Bokka Matha Gowder from Naduhatti village tells a detailed and widespread version about a young man who had to leave his parents' house and worked in a family for a bond to marry their elder daughter and settle as an in-law in her village. But that girl eloped with another and a conflict arose over the broken promise. Her younger sister, who became Hette, said she would fulfill the promise and become the bride after menarche. The dispute between the two families was solved, but the bridegroom fell ill and died before the wedding could occur. Out of grief, Hette committed suicide, and after her death it became evident that the girl was a goddess: the location where she died (or disappeared) became sacred.[20] Some versions of this narrative were written down by Badaga elders in Tamil and English and appeared in print or exist as manuscripts.[21] Irrespective of competing narratives, the main and undisputed central place of worship is beside the northeastern village of Beragani.[22] Thus 'Beragani Hette' is used synonymously with 'Hette' or '*dodda* Hette' (Great Hette).

Hireodeya is the forefather and founder of Gowder villages. His narratives are linked to the migration history from the former state of Mysore into the Nilgiri Hills. A central motive of all versions is that the forefathers fled from their homes because a Muslim lord claimed their sister as a bride. They migrated southwards to the Nilgiris and by 1600 were known as *Badaga*, literally 'northerner'.[23] On the plateau the forefathers of all Gowder, seven brothers, were looking for a suitable place to settle. While hunting they were following a deer, rested in several places, and in their dreams God told them where they should stay. In each first-built house, the *dodda mane*, they worshipped an artefact, often said to be a brass vessel. Later, temples were built in the name of Hireodeya, who is thus both a historical personage and a god. The successors became the headmen of the village and the sacred item was moved into the temple. The original dwellings became head-villages with a Hireodeya temple and an *akka bakka*. Later generations founded satellite villages (*hatti*), which, irrespective of economic and demographic growth, depend on the head-villages (*uur*) until today, forming a commune of a dozen or more contiguous hamlets.

According to the migration history, the two Gowder brothers Accini and Kurudu are the forefathers and their sister Elinge Hatte (who is not worshipped as a goddess) is the foremother of the eastern part of the Nilgiri plateau (Porangadu) (see Figure 3.1). Accini became the founding father

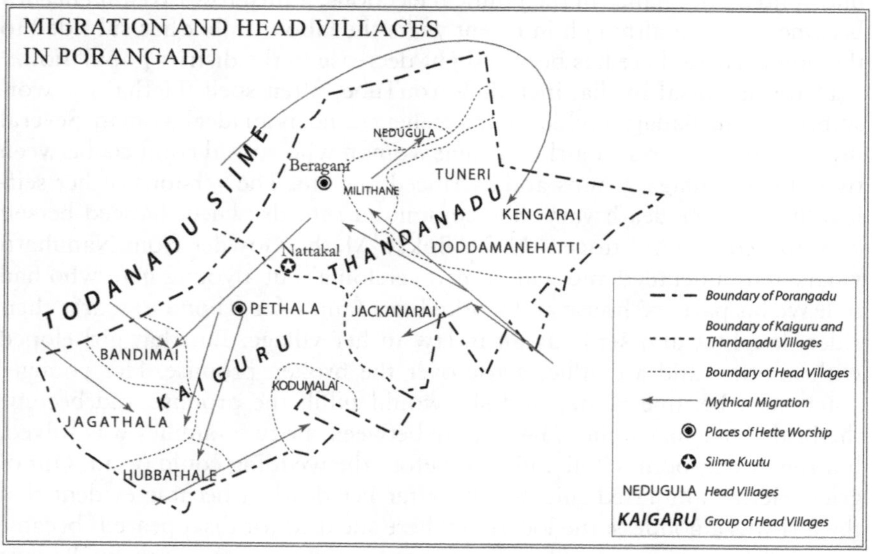

Figure 3.1 Map showing migration and head villages in Porangadu (Drawn by Uma Bhattacharya)

of Milithane and the satellite villages of Konavakkorai, Battagorai and Kairukambai. In addition, from Milithane the head-village Nedugula was founded. Kurudu's first son, Kamajjal, left his parents' village because it is the younger son who should stay in the natal house and care for the elders. Kamajjal became the prospective husband of Hette, but, as mentioned previously, he died before marriage. The second son, Hali, was married three times. The successors from his first wife founded 42 *hatti* belonging to the *uur* Thandanadu. His second wife, Malle, died after her third son was born. His third wife, Masi, looked after these boys and gave birth to three girls. To avoid a conflict with the first wife, the families of the second and third wives lived in Pethala, where the six children grew up. The boys became the founders of 21 *hatti* (see figure 3.2 below). Masi's moral standards and self-sacrifice contributed to her later status as a goddess. As a mother of three daughters she is without (male) successors but still is venerated as Pethala Hette. In the course of the annual Hette festival, she meets her 'sister' Beragani Hette on the fifth day, a Friday, in Nattakal.

A recurring element in all myths is the migration of a group of people carrying a sacred item, which was worshipped in the *dodda mane* and later moved into a temple. Having a Hireodeya temple and an *akka bakka* identify these original villages as *uur*. Both represent religious and political autonomy; one cannot exist without the other. At first sight it appears as a contradiction that Pethala, founded by Malle and Masi, should have the status of an *uur*. A close reading of the myths offers clarity. When Malle, Hali's second wife, came to the first wife's village to conduct an initiation ceremony for her first-born son, a conflict between the two wives arose. Without being noticed, Malle stole one holy item from the temple and returned to her own place. On her way, carrying that item under her clothing and the baby boy in her arms, she pronounced a curse and claimed her own territory. At home she conducted the initiation ritual. With the consent of her husband she founded her own village, where Masi Hette, the third wife, raised the three sons after Malle's death. Like other villages of the seven brothers, a Hireodeya temple and an *akka bakka* were built in this settlement. The neighbourhood around Pethala became known as Kaigaru and is considered as a complimentary part to Thandanadu.

The other ancestors among the seven brothers continued their migration further west. From the west a different group of migrants came to Porangadu and founded the *uur* of Bandimai, Jagathala and Kodumalai. Within the Porangadu *siime* (district) more than 120 *hatti* emerged, most of them offspring from some neighbouring village. Mainly agnates settled around each *uur*, but within the territories affines settled in the neighbourhood or founded their own *hatti*. In some cases, their jurisdiction changed with residence, in other cases they maintained their fathers' village affiliation. In the most easterly part of the *siime* Wodeya with a Lingayat faith settled. Their four exogamous units variously worship Mahalingasamy, Ragarama,

Malleswara and Virabhadra. They live in 16 *hatti* and have their *akka bakka* in Tuneri. Close by these *hatti*, 12 hamlets of Toreyas are located and are subsumed under two *akka bakka* in Doddamanehatti and Kengarai. Their exogamous units are based on their previous origin on the plateau; they come either from the *siime* of Mekunadu or from Todanadu. Within the territory of Thandanadu the Toreya village of Bamudi, and within Jackanarai the Toreya village of Sackata emerged. In short, more than 120 *uur* and *hatti* of Porangadu appear as neatly placed villages in the midst of tea and vegetable fields which, in the eyes of the informed locals, show invisible links to ancestors, gods, genealogies and jurisdictions.

Annual festivals for Hette and Hireodeya

In the myths of origin men appear as strong and pragmatic, at times also stubborn, and often as promoting conflicts. As village founders, they demarcate boundaries and procreate lineages. Women who turned into goddesses solve conflicts and transgress boundaries. This is also reflected in the annual rituals when Badagas from all parts of the Nilgiris come to Beragani and Pethala. From both places, processions head for Nattakal, where both goddesses meet. Hette's festival is a moment of unification. The festivals for Hireodeya take place within the limits of an *uur*. In mythology, especially in the process of migration and settlement as well as in the genesis of the social order, male and female elements are interwoven. Forefathers who became Hireodeya claim political autonomy and jurisdiction based on a sacred object; they started the worship and legitimised an *akka bakka*. Hette stands for chastity, morality and purity and is the undisputed highest entity among the *kula devaru*.

The annual Hette festival is the largest annual gathering of Badaga people and takes place before the main agricultural season starts, usually in December or January. The short account of Edgar Thurston and K Rangachari from 1909 remained basically unchanged for over a hundred years.[24] During the eight days' festival members of a Chettiar caste from the Coimbatore plains weave new cloth for Hette. Priests wash the fabric and dress the idol. Badaga devotees come to her temple, donate eatables, money or buffaloes to be grazed on Hette's fields—the only sacred herd among Badagas. The sharing of cooked food on the temple ground is a commensal event. From the 1980s 'modern' or 'polluting' elements were avoided; even leather sandals and leather watch bands were objected to as polluting items. A pre-puberty boy replaced the formerly adult Hette priest from Beragani and is in charge of the daily *puja*. Visiting priests should avoid buses to reach the temple and walk. Photography and videography were not permitted in order to keep the festival in the *hettappa's* (forefather's) style. Early in the present century hundreds of vehicles get parked by the roadside leading to Beragani, festival photographs are printed in daily newspapers, and audiovisual documentation is found in electronic social media. Non-Badaga devotees of Hette from elsewhere and VIPs are welcome to join the festival. A short summary of the festival as it took place during December 19 to 26, 1988, is given in the following section.

On Monday and Tuesday, a procession visits the *uur* and many *hatti* of Thandanadu and Milithane. Representatives of village headmen and several temples carry Hette sticks and two large ritual umbrellas representing Hette (green umbrella) and Ayya (literally 'father's father', as reference to Hireodeya, red umbrella). Hero stones (*sattukallu*) and many houses are whitewashed, even the roadside is cleaned, and villagers receive the procession with white sheets spread out on their path. The procession announces the arrival with rhythmic shouting of '*a hau hau, a hau hau*'; village representatives walk towards the elders and receive them with burning camphor. Devotees pray for Hette, some fall into trance and receive the blessing of the elders. On Wednesday visitors from Kaigaru and other villages of Porangadu arrive at Beragani, offer Hette's buffaloes salted water, present foodstuff to the temple, and young male volunteers cook rice and vegetable for all, to serve 3,000 visitors on the lawn in front of Hette's house. Thursday is a day of rest. On Friday two processions from Beragani and Pethala representing the two Hette and the two regions of Porangadu reach Iruppukal for *pujas* and proceed to Nattakal, where the main *puja* is performed. On this day, non-Badaga devotees of Hette and VIPs pay respect to both goddesses and receive the public acknowledgement of a large gathering. On Saturday, devotees gather at Kakkoreyya hill next to Beragani, where a statue of Kakkoreyya, an avatar of Śiva associated with weaving, is worshipped.[25] Several men dance in the hot sun, fall down in trance and utter predictions. On Sunday, the cloths, which Chettiars from Mulatorai have woven in the preceding days, are carried to a stream to be washed. On Monday, a procession conducts two brass images, some 40 cm tall, to the same spot. They represent Hette and Hireodeya and are dressed in clothes and turban.[26]

By comparison, the annual festivals for Hireodeya do not attract much public attention. A few elders and a Kurumba ritual practitioner conduct the main rituals. *Dodda abba* (great festival) takes place before the first sowing.[27] In some villages, a Wodeya priest conducts the first *puja* for Mahadesvara at a stream (often the village boundary), and owners of cows carry milk (if possible after the first lactation) to offer Gangamma. The priest prepares *prasaad* and offers it to god. Later a kind of ball game is played, which somewhat resembles cricket. Men use a bat to hit a bundle of clothes as a substitute for a ball. An oil lamp (*diivige*) must burn all night in the *dodda mane*. Elders and a Kurumba stay all night at the Hireodeya temple. Before dawn the Kurumba will drive an ox and with a plough will make the first furrow in a nearby field or use a ritual knife to open up the soil. He will sow the first seeds, bless the field and call three times a long '*dooo*'. By doing so, the agricultural season is blessed and the work on the fields may begin.

Devva abba (God festival) is celebrated before the first harvest in June.[28] After *puja* at the Malleswara shrine, salt is given to buffaloes, and the first harvest is fixed to the *akka bakka*. In Thandanadu, the *uur* of the largest lineage on the eastern plateau, the celebrations last one week and include the blessing of a newborn generation.

In contemporary society, the relationship of Hette and Hireodeya is not a disputed topic. Both are *kula devaru* and at the same time incarnations of Pārvatī and Śiva. They can be considered as husband and wife and in several myths appear as a couple.[29] In the eastern part of the plateau the story of Beragani Hette suggests that she died before her marriage, as a virgin. To be both a virgin and a foremother does not appear as a contradiction, because a father's mother's sister and mother's mother's sister are addressed as *hette*, and although they may be unmarried they are still one of the forebears. For Porangadu, the eastern *siime*, the relationship of Hette and Hireodeya can be summarised as follows. The forefather Kurudu had two sons. The first, Kamajjal, died before his marriage could take place, and the second, Hāli, had three wives (see previous mention). An obvious symmetry emerges. Kurudu had four (potential) daughters-in-law. The first became Beragani Hette (located in Thandanadu) and the second gave birth to the male ancestors of Thandanadu. The fourth became Pethala Hette (located in Kaigaru) and the third gave birth to the male ancestors of that region (see Figure 3.2).

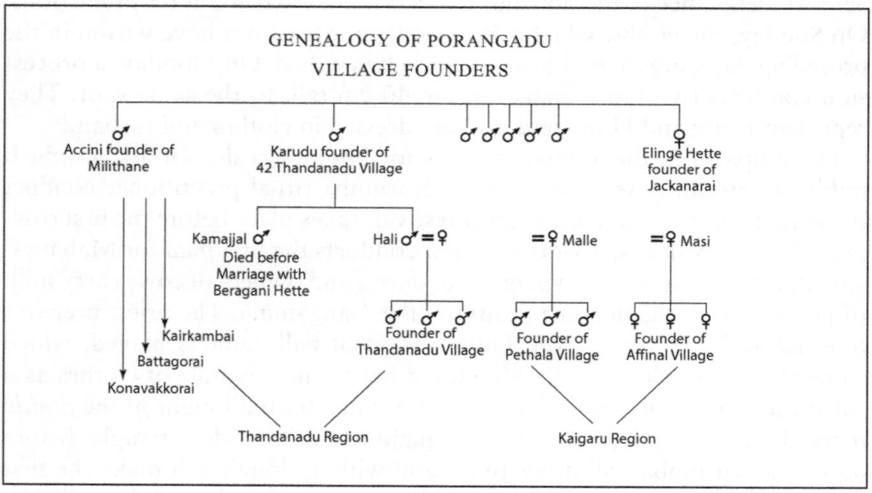

Figure 3.2 Genealogy of Porangadu village founders (Drawn by Uma Bhattacharya)

The political system

Since time immemorial, the Nilgiri Hills have been divided into four administrative regions, or *siime*. Each *siime* has a central council (*kuutu*). The *siime kuutu* of Todanadu, the largest unit, is the *primus inter pares*, also called *naku betta kuutu* ('four-hills-council'). This council resolves disputes between two or more *siime* and any cases that are forwarded from one of the *siime kuutu*. In the east, in Porangadu, the *siime kuutu* is in Nattakal, at the boundary of Thandanadu and Kaigaru, and is called 19-*uur-kuutu*. The headman of Thandanadu and a religious figure in charge of the Beragani temple preside over this council. (It is at the location of this council that Beragani Hette and Pethala Hette meet during their annual festival.) The name 19-*uur-kuutu* suggests the existence of 19 *uur* and 19 *akka bakka*, but in Porangadu only 12 Badaga villages have this status and a respective gate. Some elder Badagas suggest that once Kotas, Todas and Kurumbas in the *siime* must have owned *akka bakka*, but no evidence supports this.

The normative legal procedure follows a clear hierarchy of councils (see Figure 3.3). Each *hatti* will discuss its issues in its own *kuutu*. Unsolved cases can be forwarded to their respective *akka bakka*, and only at the request of an *uur* does the 19-*uur-kuutu* take matters up. However, there are two approved exceptions. The five *akka bakka* in Kaigaru may approach the Kaigaru *kuutu*, which is in between the *uur* and the *siime* level, and the large number of Thandanadu villages may call for the Bamudi *kuutu*, which has a convenient location and unites villages of one valley. Many more permissible exceptions exist between the level of *hatti* and *uur*. In Kaigaru the successors of the three sons of Malle Hette live in 21 *hatti* and have the means to call for a sub-*kuutu* each. In other cases, several villages located in a clearly

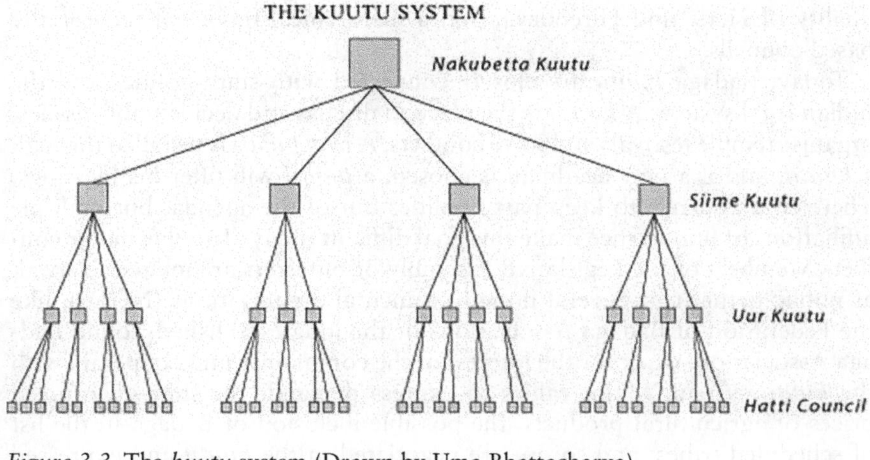

Figure 3.3 The *kuutu* system (Drawn by Uma Bhattacharya)

demarcated region have a sub-*kuutu*, too. Each of the total 20 sub-*kuutu* is directly linked to a temple dedicated either to Hette, Hireodeya, Halamale, Kali, Krishna, Ganesh, Mahalingasami, Ketaraya or Jedayasami.[30] The systems of festivals, temples, offices and councils constitute an impressive totality linked to myth and kinship, but in the social process these institutions are linked to pan-Indian Hinduism and to modern state authorities.

In Badaga history, power and ritual form an amalgam and appear as *one* phenomenon. Analytically, the religious and the political systems can be clearly distinguished, but their interconnectedness is indubitable. *Kuutu* and temples refer to the same social and territorial units. In ritual practice, a temple festival depends on a committee to organise the event, and a *kuutu* requires a temple to ask a god to be a witness. This cultural logic is expressed in the insignia of a head-village (*uur*) with its duality of *dodda mane* and *akkka bakka*. The power connected with the festivals is at least twofold. On the one hand, the Gowder, as an individual person, acts on his (and his village's) behalf. His way of acting must be seen as a demonstration of the headman's power, and it is hard to distinguish the status of his office and his personality. In the sense of Max Weber's concept of power, he exercises power in dyadic relationships. On the other hand, temple festivals create and manifest an ideological order and display a system of knowledge, which Foucault saw as the basis of a different kind of power. The devotees form a procession, visit the constitutive parts of the village, and visualise a complex spatial order, in which migration myths, kinship, leadership and religious concepts like purity are inscribed. Mandelbaum's claim about the pre-colonial order with 'no explicit legal standards' needs to be re-considered, because the judicial system followed a clear hierarchy form *hatti* to *uur* to *siime*. From all what we know today, the old Badaga social system followed a Dravidian kinship system, a religious order based on the duality of Hette and Hireodeya, and a hierarchical model of territorially based councils.

Today, Badaga *kuutu* are closely connected with state politics and the Indian legal system. A *kuutu* is the place to discuss and decide public issues, organise temple festivals and solve conflicts. A new *pujari* is installed through a *kuutu*, and if a new headman is chosen, a *pujari* will offer his blessings. There is a tendency to keep party politics out of the agenda, but multiple affiliations of importance make this goal difficult today. To solve major conflicts Members of the Legislative Assembly or ministers are invited to speak at public gatherings. Several nongovernmental organisations (NGOs), like the Federation of Badaga Associations or the long-established Young Badaga Association, work for the interest of the community and cooperate with the *kuutu* system. Major rallies to express demands for state-guaranteed prices of agricultural products, the possible inclusion of Badaga in the list of scheduled tribes, and so on, are negotiated in the *kuutu* and expressed through NGOs and political parties.[31] By and large, *kuutu* have abandoned discussing criminal activities, but still solve conflicts that arise under the civil legislation. *Kuutu* work faster than state courts, and are free of cost for the opposing parties, but they lack power to implement their verdicts. Elders ensure that their judgements are compatible with the Indian Penal Code and may seek advice on this from Badaga lawyers. In legal practice, state judges may ask the complainants about the verdict of the *kuutu* and the headman ask about parallel legal actions.

Badaga daily life is structured by facts and forces, which they classify as *ikala* (present time, or 'modern') and *akala* (distant time, or 'traditional'). All aspects concerning the state, its laws and administration, new technologies and contemporary consumption patterns is *ikala*, while village-based institutions like headman and priest, village councils and annual festivals for *kula devaru* is *akala*. Each field of social interaction owns specific norms of conduct and is based on a specific ontological base. I would argue that we could distinguish two kinds of constitutions, respectively 'modern' and 'traditional' types. The clearest expression of the first is the Indian constitution and the laws of the state. The latter is not written, but often performed on annual temple festivals and on village councils. Occasionally, these two types lead to tension; for example, when the two legal systems suggest different judgements. In other cases, Badagas make use of both qualities and weave *akala* and *ikala* into one event. In Badaga weddings, the bridegroom and the bride wear a white cotton dress, the man with a turban and the women with a Badaga akala headcloth; later they change into a Western suit and a sari. At public events, seats on the stage are reserved for traditional and modern leaders, for persons in white and persons in suits or saris.

Badagas lead public debates about their history and origin, their identity and their language and their territorial and ritual order. In the last decades, they re-activated an inter-ethnic ritual system in the Moyar Ditch and constructed new temples.[32] They modify their political and ritual constitution; they make history. In his *Archaeology of Knowledge*, Foucault claims, that 'in our time, history is that which transforms *documents* into *monuments*'.[33] New lyrics are composed for old Badaga tunes, and motives and scenes from Badaga mythology, partly forgotten, are incorporated in fiction films and made alive and public. Obviously, the constitution of the Badaga *akala*-world is not static at all, but certain aspects appear to be rather stable. The political and religious system, the worship for the God Hireodeya and the Goddess Hette, the Badaga councils and division of the territories on the plateau, were documented in the nineteenth century as they appear today.

Ritual and power

In the last four decades the relationship of ritual and power has changed drastically. When I began my fieldwork on the Nilgiri plateau in the early 1980s, temple festivals and council meetings were the sole events to legitimise power. In those days, Badaga headmen shared the powerful positions with a small number of dignitaries. The basis for power was located exclusively in the village. Politicians were dependent on votes from the villages and the owner of bought leaf tea factories required the daily supply of tea leaves. The *pujari* was the person to legitimise the headman and to bless the dignitaries. Over the years, the headmen's power lessened, while politicians and industrialists became more powerful. Today, power is based in villages and towns. Politicians compete for the party's nomination as a candidate, a decision that takes place in the party's head office. Factory owners need bank loans and administrative approvals and maintain good relationships to clerks, bankers, lawyers and judges. Still, they need support from the village headmen for votes and tea leaf. In ritual contexts and in public events in the small towns the modern leaders appear in company with the headmen, who indicate village support for the dignitaries. Headmen and politicians sit on stages and in meetings shoulder-to-shoulder and demonstrate the unity of their own community. In parts, the role of the *pujari* to legitimise power was passed to the headman, who appears as *pars pro toto* for the village.

In spite of these changes, involvement in the ritual system is a fundamental requirement for any powerful person in contemporary Badaga society. Politicians, factory owners, traders, professionals and other public persons need to appear at weddings, funerals and—more importantly—at religious festivals. They contribute to the expenses of the event or make donations to the temple; they are among the first to walk in the procession and sit on stages and address the audience. Religious festivals increase their status with the presence of so-called VIPs, and they need festivals to mark their status. An entrepreneur, who plans to build a factory, asks for local support at council meetings, and a politician visits the Hireodeya temple at the time of election. In the recent past, modern aspects of power utilised traditional institutions to strengthen their foundation. The largest gathering in the history of the Nilgiris, the Badaga Rally on 15 May 1989, was organised by the Federation of Badaga Associations, but the basic network connecting the association with the villages followed the structure of the *kuutu* system.[34] The headman of the paramount council, the *naku betta kuutu*, who was hardly known in the east and in the south of the hills, became the patron of this rally and addressed ten thousands Badagas in the stadium of Ootacamund.

Today, the pre-colonial pattern of public order and the laws and rules of the Indian state co-exist in the Nilgiris. Not much different from legal pluralism and the co-existence of Eastern and Western medical systems, we can speak of two constitutions (in the broadest sense of the term) as potent sources of power and authority in Badaga society. *Akala* and *ikala* leaders possess the knowledge respectively of myths, gods, rituals, kinship and legal regulations, government subsidies, election procedures, etc. The knowledge of myths, rituals, *kula devaru*, kinship rules, which was four decades ago shared by many, is now kept in small circles. Many elderly headmen passed away and their successors moved to South Indian metropolitan cities. Most people in the villages know the local myths and all agnatic and affinal relationships but lost the ability to link social orders from different parts of the Nilgiris. It is almost forgotten, which successors followed Accini or Kurudu. Many details and the general view on the structure of Badaga society might be forgotten, but since the same principles appear in almost each location, the cultural logic is not lost. These principles weave territory, ritual and kinship to a uniform pattern, which underlies almost all local variants.

In a nutshell: Badaga rituals relate to a spatial and political order, which is explained in mythical migration and ancient kinship relations. According to the mythological narrative, holy items were carried by the forefathers and became objects of worship. The first forefathers were village founders and are worshipped as gods, and their successors act as priests and village headmen. The first settlements became—irrespective of their size—head villages, with a Hireodeya temple dedicated to the founder and an *akka bakka* as a symbol for political and judicial autonomy. Male successors founded new villages as integral part of the religious and political system. Affinal relationships constitute links to villages of brides and to the residence of female successors. Religion, politics and kinship are central components of a spatial order, which is re-affirmed in ritual performances. The male god Hireodeya created villages and the female goddess Hette is worshipped as the foremother of all Badagas. The ritual practice of the Badaga people appears as a meaningful totality in the light of mythical narratives and ongoing kinship relationships.

Evidence for this pattern of public order can be found in ritual performances, place names and kinship relationships. The old places of worship were the *dodda mane*, the first house built in the village, alike to all other houses in the same row. For *dodda abba*, a temporary temple was built with a thatched roof in the forest near the head village. Today, each head village owns an *akka bakka* built of stone, replacing the old wooden structures. In a few valleys and on hilltops we can find today old kraals, overgrown with vegetation. According to Dieter B. Kapp, old dolmens, which were not claimed by the Badagas, were erected by the forefathers of Kurumba people.[35] Temples dedicated to pan-Indian Gods follow a typical South Indian architecture and were built in the 20th and 21st century in and around Badaga villages. In short, there is little material evidence for the ritual complex and the performed constitution of *akala* in Badaga society.

Notes

1 Allen Zagarell, 'Megalithic Culture', in Paul Hockings (ed), *Encyclopaedia of the Nilgiri Hills*, vol. 2, New Delhi: Manohar, 2012, pp. 583–7.

2 Henry Harkness, *A Description of a Singular Aboriginal Race Inhabiting the Summit of the Neilgherry Hills, or Blue Mountains of Coimbatoor in the Southern Peninsular of India*, London: Smith, Elder and Co, 1832.

3 Paul Hockings (ed), *Encyclopaedia of the Nilgiris*, 2 vols., New Delhi: Manohar, 2012.
4 David G. Mandelbaum, 'The Nilgiris as a Region', in Paul Hockings (ed), *Blue Mountains: The Ethnography and Biogeography of a South Indian Region*, New Delhi: Oxford University Press, 1989, pp. 1–19, 6.
5 Richard Ned Lebow (ed), *Max Weber and International Relations*, Cambridge: Cambridge University Press, 2017.
6 Paul Hockings, *So Long a Saga: Four Centuries of Badaga Social History*, New Delhi: Manohar, 2013.
7 Frank Heidemann, *Akka Bakka. Religion, Politik und duale Souveränität der Badaga in den Nilgiri Südindiens*, Berlin: Lit, 2006, pp. 118–26.
8 Clifford Geertz, *Negara: The Theatre State of Nineteenth-Century Bali*, Princeton: Princeton University Press, 1980.
9 Georg Pfeffer, *Verwandtschaft als Verfassung: Unbürokratische Muster öffentlicher Ordnung*, Baden Baden: Nomos, 2016.
10 Louis Dumont, *Homo Hierarchicus: The Caste System and Its Implication*, Chicago: University of Chicago Press, 1980.
11 Margaret Trawik, *Notes on Love in a Tamil Family*, Berkeley: University of California Press, 1990.
12 Frank Heidemann, 'Der Kult der sieben Mariamman am Nordrand der Nilgiri Südindiens', *Mitteilungen der Berliner Gesellschaft für Anthropologie, Ethnologie und Urgeschichte*, 1997, 18: 57–67.
13 Andreas Feodor Jagor, 'Die Badaga im Nilgiri Gebirge', *Verhandlung der Berliner Gesellschaft für Anthropologie, Ethnologie und Urgeschichte*, 1876: 190–204 (p. 202).
14 Harkness, *A Description of a Singular Aboriginal Race*, p. 110.
15 Paul Hockings, 'The Badagas', in Paul Hockings (ed), *Blue Mountains: The Ethnography and Biogeography of a South Indian Region*, New Delhi: Oxford University Press, 1989, pp. 206–31 (p. 223).
16 William A. Noble, 'Nilgiri Dolmens (South India)', *Anthropos*, 1976, 71: 90–128 (p. 115).
17 V. W. Karl, 'The Religion of the Badagas' (unpublished Bachelor of Divinity, Bangalore, United Theological College, 1945), p. 27.
18 Frank Heidemann, 'Das Fest für die Göttin', in Angelika Malinar (ed), *Hinduismus Reader*, Göttingen: Vandenhoek und Ruprecht, 2009, pp. 130–7.
19 R. K. Haldorai, *Goddess Hette of the Nilgiri Badagas*, Udhagamandalam: Nelikolu Publishing House, 2005.
20 Heidemann, *Akka Bakka*, pp. 173–9.
21 Haldorai, *Goddess Hette*.
22 Hockings, *Encyclopaedia*, pp. 410–15.
23 The first text by an European eye-witness: Jacome Finicio, Two Mss on the Todmala, 1603, reprinted in W. H. R. Rivers, *The Todas*, London: MacMillian, 1096, Appendix.
24 E. Thurston and K. Rangachari, *Caste and Tribes of Southern India*, vol. I, Madras: Government Press, 1909, pp. 96–8.
25 H. B. Grigg, *A Manual of the Nilagiri District in the Madras Presidency*, Madras: Government Press, 1880, p. 226.
26 Heidemann, *Akka Bakka,* pp. 181–90.
27 Thurston and Rangachari, *Castes and Tribes*, vol. I, pp. 94–5; Karl, *The Religion of the Badagas*, pp. 12–14.
28 Thurston and Rangachari, *Castes and Tribes*, vol. I, p. 95; James W. Breeks, *An Account of the Primitive Tribes and Monuments of the Nilagiris*, London: India Museum, 1873, p. 54.

29 Haldorai, *Goddess Hette*, pp. 51–113.
30 Heidemann, *Akka Bakka*, p. 165.
31 Frank Heidemann, 'Objectivation and Social Aesthetics. Memoranda and the Celebration of "Badaga Day"', *Asian Ethnology*, 2014, 73: 91–109.
32 Heidemann, *Der Kult der sieben Mariamman*.
33 Michel Foucault, *The Archaeology of Knowledge*, London: Routledge, 1972.
34 Heidemann, *Objectivation and Social Aesthetics*.
35 Dieter B. Kapp, 'The Kurumbas´ Relationship to the "Megalitic" Cult of the Nilgiri Hills (South India)', *Anthropos*, 1985, 80: 493–534.

Part II

PRESENCE

4

STUPA DESTRUCTION, RELIC THEFT AND BUDDHIST PROPAGANDA

(Re)-dedicating the Buddha's relics in the Indic Northwest

Henry Albery

Introduction

One often encounters the statement that the institutional history of Buddhism is parallel to the spread of the Buddha's corporeal relics (*śarīra*, *dhātu*).[1] This observation highlights that the division and widespread (P. *vitthārika*, Skt. *vaistārika*)[2] distribution of relics, and their interment within stupas, functioned as Buddhism's primary means of transferring from an existing locale and localising anew its 'presence' elsewhere.[3] Certainly this mode of expansionism was widely propagated in Buddhist discourse and is seemingly confirmed *ex post facto* by the remains of monumental stupas littered throughout the Indic sphere. Yet the precise mechanisms by which this process occurred remain obscure and there are some quite obvious substantial and functional differences between stupas and relics which complicate the matter. Unlike stupas, whose institutional value resides in their being fashioned in perpetuity, their fixedness, and their power to signify, relics are divisible, transportable, and the essential power that is signified.[4] One ineludible consequence of this at once contradictory and complimentary relation thus left the Buddhists in a paradoxical predicament—that their institutional diversification necessitated its own destruction—and such circumstance subsequently engendered a dichotomy in the practices towards stupas and relics that were deemed acceptable. Naturally concerned with their ministration, stupa destruction and relic theft were on the one hand proscriptively codified as particularly egregious forms of turpitude, precipitating correspondingly negative results for the perpetrator. Concurrently, however, certain orders of said acts were ritually prescribed, producing contrastingly wholesome benefits for the effector.

Proscriptions and prescriptions of stupa destruction and relic theft

Gregory Schopen first observed that relics and stupas have a 'functional equivalence' with the Buddha; that is, they were 'cognitively classified as "legal persons" of rank' and thus one should neither damage a stupa nor steal or sell any material items regarded as belonging to it. On the matter of vandalism, he quotes three Brāhmī inscriptions from Sanchi, dated to c. 1st century BCE, which state that anyone who destroys a stupa or transfers structural elements thereof to another monastic institution 'commits an act like the five whose results are without interval' (*pacānatariyakāraka*).[5] As Peter Skilling has more recently shown, these inscriptions constitute rather early examples of an expanded list of five crimes in Theravāda commentarial works whose results are regarded as being 'without interval' (*ānantarika*)—matricide, patricide, dominicide, drawing the blood of a Tathāgata, and schisming the monastic community—now encompassing acts of violence towards stupas and relics.[6] And a further listing in Sarvāstivāda scholastic literature similarly defines a group of actions 'equivalent to those without interval' (*ānantaryasabhāga*)—corrupting a mother or female noble one, killing a bodhisattva or a student, stealing the monastic community's capital, and destroying a stupa[7]—each of which effects rebirth in the correspondingly named hell, Avīci ('without interval').[8] Such formulations were indeed widespread and several other instances can be cited from literature.[9]

But this picture is a little more complicated. Not all forms of violence were regarded as transgressive, and stupas and relics thus found themselves subject to ideologies and practices of an altogether different class. This ambivalence is discernible in one monastic regulation of the *Moheseng qilü* 摩訶僧祇律 (*Mahāsāṃghikavinaya*):[10]

> On destroying a stupa: If [a monk] angrily destroys a stupa of the Fortunate One, he commits a *sthūlātyaya* ('gross offence'). Actions that are crimes have many results. If one desires to repair and improve [the stupa], it is not a crime.[11]

Because of the primacy of the stupa, its wanton vandalism is prohibited as a *sthūlātyaya*, a violation of middling severity that can be expiated through confession before the monastic community.[12] Conversely, some forms of destruction (presumably delineated for those anxious of being indicted for the former) were authorised when intended for structural amelioration.

This regulation corresponds to a host of textual materials which evidence that the matter of a stupa's destruction, whether due to vandalism or neglect and weathering, was indeed a quotidian issue. Several works stipulate precise regulations on how monastics should fund and organise any maintenance and repair; for instance, by selling off assets[13] or taking valuable items from within the stupa itself,[14] as well as the materials they should use to do it.[15] Apparently, monastics often showed little initiative in stupas' upkeep and therefore several narratives were also composed to render the task normative for individuals of other social groupings.[16] Oftenest the responsibility is given to a ruler, envisaged either in the form of direct financial support[17] or as a transfer of taxes to the monastic institution, and in such cases the application of state resources is invariably dichotomised in terms of a Buddhist and non-Buddhist ruler; one disposed towards establishing systems of redistributive taxation and the other removing financial support in an act of wilful neglect. Because of the transience of rulers' sponsorship, in their stead, other individuals with surplus wealth, such as 'women of the inner court' (*antaḥpurikā*)[18] and 'caravan leaders' (*sārthavāha*),[19] are commonly tasked with the maintenance.

More acute legal quandaries arose in establishing appropriate systems of relic acquisition. Indeed, the aforementioned issue inherent to Buddhism's expansionist policy required the determination of instances in which, as Kevin Trainor put it, 'relic theft is not a theft'.[20] He draws attention to several examples from post-5th century CE Theravāda commentarial and *Vaṃsa* literature, wherein, for instance, justifications are forwarded for the 2nd century BCE dedication of relics in the Mahāthūpa in Sri Lanka by King Duṭṭhagāmaṇī. In these discourses, arhats are depicted as having made aspirations (*patthanā*) to steal relics from the *nāgas* in Rāmagrāma, as using their supernatural powers (*iddhi*) to do so, and as receiving authenticating predictions (*vyākaraṇa*) of their theft from the Buddha. Trainor opines that the grounds upon which relic acquisition is determined to be malefactious or not resides in the act's intentionality. If conducted without attachment, then any conflict with the *Theravādavinaya*—wherein theft is defined as a *pārājika* ('grave offence') and results in prompt expulsion from the monastic community[21]—is circumvented.[22] But this corpus is entirely silent on the specific case of relic theft. It mentions relatedly elsewhere in the *Bhikkunīvibhaṅga* a superficially similar incident, also found in the *Vinayas* of several other monastic institutions (*nikāya*),[23] wherein the destruction of a nun's stupa and the scattering of her relics by a monk are left entirely without critique![24]

As far as I have been able to ascertain, the matter of relic theft is in fact exclusive to (Mūla)-Sarvāstivāda legal discourse. Thus, in the *Upāliparipṛcchā* section of the *Shisong lü* 十誦律 (**Sarvāstivādavinaya*):[25]

> [Upāli] further asked: 'If one steals the Buddha's relics what crime is effected?' [The Buddha] responded, saying: 'A *sthūlātyaya*.[26] If with respectful intention, one thinks thus, "The Buddha is truly my teacher", then taking with [such] pure intention is not a crime.'[27]

This cursory passage simply implies that any perceived transgression in relic theft can be mitigated by virtue of the proper intention. Greater nuance, however, is supplied in another regulation in the *Upālipariprcchā* section of the *Sapoduobupini modeleqie* 薩婆多部毘尼摩得勒伽 (**Sarvāstivādanikāyavinayamātṛkā*) to deal with *pārājika*:[28]

> Taking a Buddha's relic that has an owner, if stolen for one's livelihood [and if it values] a full[29] [five *māṣa*],[30] it is a *pārājika*; not a full [five *māṣa*], it is a *sthūlātyaya*.[31] Even if it increases unwholesomeness,[32] taking [for] both others and oneself is not a *sthūlātyaya*. If it is for the sake of performing worship, [one thinks thus], 'The Buddha is my teacher, I should perform worship', [and the relic values] a full five *māṣa*, [it is] a *duṣkṛta* ('misdemeanour').[33]

Appreciating the true purport of this peculiar guideline is not without its difficulties. For the historical circumstance in which the regulation was devised, relic theft had evidently become sufficient an issue to warrant definition, and monastics subsequently sought to secure control over the act. A component thereof was to determine, and if necessary avoid, matters of ownership, as well as to modulate the weight (i.e., the monetary value) of an illicitly acquired relic to the standardised unit of five *māṣa*—the higher the value the greater the infraction.[34] This suggests that relics were in abundance, had become items of trade, were hence being weighed and sold as any other commodity, and that larceny was perhaps rife among monastic institutions. Licit trade of relics, however, is given the lightest classification of a *duṣkṛta*, an infringement redeemable through admission before a single monastic, with the proviso it is enacted in the interests of the common weal; namely, if it is ritually intended and institutionally advantageous.[35]

Relic theft as propaganda

Relics were not only at risk of being stolen by monastics and consequently a rule was defined, albeit in slightly different terms, for non-monastics not inhering within the purview of institutional discipline. Thus, in the *Fo shuo youposai wujiexiang jing* 佛説優婆塞五戒相經 (**Upāsakapañcaśīlatvasūtra*):[36]

> If a householder with the intention of stealing steals relics, in committing the transgression [the act] could be regretted.[37] If with a respectful intention one thinks thus, 'The Buddha is truly my teacher', then taking with [such] pure intention is not a crime.[38]

Although this and the previous passages leave us guessing as to the precise circumstances in which relic theft may have been committed, one further occurrence of the justificatory intention, 'the Buddha is truly my teacher'

(佛亦我師), may provide a clue. This is found once again in a section of the **Sarvāstivādavinaya*, only now intra-textually recast as political propaganda within a unique witness of the *Mahāparinirvāṇasūtra*.

In brief,[39] following the Buddha's *parinirvāṇa*, cremation, and installation of his relics[40] by the Mallas of Kuśinagara, seven other claimants emerge from among the contemporaneous polities of the Gangetic Basin: six collectives[41]—the Mallas of Pāpa, Bullakas of Calakalpakā, Krauḍyas of Rāmagrāma, Brahmins of Viṣṇudvīpa, Licchavis of Vaiśālī, Śākyas of Kapilavastu—and King Ajātaśatru of Magadha.

> At that time, King Ajātaśatru directed his great minister, the Brahmin Varṣakāra, saying: 'Go to Kuśinagara where all the Mallas are. Bear my message, and extend my immeasurable greetings: "Are [you] strong, at ease, and well in body and mind?" Say to all: "The Buddha is truly my teacher and is mine to be honoured. Today in your domain he [entered] *parinirvāṇa*. Please divide the relics; I desire to erect a stupa in Rājagṛha to perform worship. One who shares with me is good. If you don't share with me, I will raise an army and forcibly seize [them from] you."' Orders received, the minister promptly assembled a four-fold army unit and went to Kuśinagara.[42]

Ultimately, no military action is required because a Brahmin of the family Dhūma from Droṇagrāma intercedes and apportions the relics eight-fold, each of which is rededicated in a stupa within the groups' respective domains. The resolution, however, does not detract from the fact the threat of war,[43] and theft is in principle legitimised by Ajātaśatru's intention in precisely the same terms as the aforementioned regulations. The episode later closes with a rather telling reflection (presumably of the scholiast) that discursively validates the act beyond the confines of the narrative: 'first there was the Buddha's *parinirvāṇa*, thereafter ten stupas were established, and since then innumerable stupas have been established'.[44]

Although unstated, this latter remark would appear to anticipate the events of the *Aśokāvadāna*, a topically related narrative wherein similar apologiae for theft are also utilised.[45] This cycle recounts that the Mauryan Aśoka subsequently takes a fourfold army unit, opens up seven (or eight) of the so-called Droṇa stupas, and thereafter divides the relics and rededicates them within numerous Dharmarājikā stupas throughout his polity. Once more, the potential gravity of destruction and theft is mitigated[46] by the ruler's intention to disperse the relics and establish them anew.[47]

Collectively, the purpose of the *Mahāparinirvāṇasūtra* and *Aśokāvadāna* is to wed Buddhism's diffusion to a political agenda by conveying the principle that relics are central to the formation of sovereign power. Instituted in the intertextual conversation[48] between the two, therefore, is a potentially perpetual model of expansion premised on a codified ritual practice of stupa destruction and relic theft enacted by political agents.

Reception history of the Mahāparinirvāṇasūtra and Aśokāvadāna

Much has been said as to the obscure geneses of these narrative cycles, as well as to the historical veracity of their recount. Nevertheless, an entire lack of material remains for stupas prior to the 3rd century BCE and only indicatory archaeological and epigraphic evidence of Aśoka engaging in the practice have hindered any firm conclusions in this regard.[49] By contrast, millennia of reception history have had the peculiar effect of enabling their propaganda to achieve cogency and thence precipitate the very acts they propagandise in instances of politically inspired mimicry. Two brief aperçus shall serve to illustrate the point.

Excavations of stupas by servants of the British Empire in the late 19th and early 20th centuries led to the discovery and subsequent distribution of relics among the Buddhist rulers and institutions of South East Asia with the purpose of placating uprisings;[50] in one case, the political violence of the *Mahāparinirvāṇasūtra* is cited as something of a moral contrast to the perceived righteousness of their own cynical act.[51] Over a millennium prior, the transmission of the *Aśokāvadāna* to China in the 4th century CE occasioned several rulers to initiate what Erik Zürcher terms 'a peculiar kind of archaeological field-work', whereby several Dharmarājikā stupas presumed to have been established within China by Aśoka were identified by court officials, excavated, and their relics ultimately rededicated.[52]

Time has thus told us repeatedly of this nexus between relics and the formation of political power. These cases make clear that stupa destruction and relic theft were politicised as archaeological acitivities, ritualised, and that these literary topoi often came to be enacted as concrete instruments of constitutional apparatus—the pattern, it seems, is perennial.

Since the majority of the legal discourses presented here to treat stupa destruction and relic theft were translated into Chinese no earlier than the 4th century CE, it cannot be ruled out that their regulations and associated propaganda were conceived for the specific conditions of that period. Presuming, however, that they once derived from an Indic sphere, there is perhaps one historical context that comes to the fore.

Stupas and relics in the Indic Northwest

The Indic Northwest (eastern Afghanistan and Pakistan) around the turn of the Common Era exhibits a rare, if not unique, convergence of sources that pertain to the dedication of the Buddha's relics. The epigraphic corpus—itself but a fraction of the overall number of stupas, reliquaries, and associated objects excavated in the region[53]—comprises an unprecedented 70 Kharoṣṭhī inscriptions found on 65 objects (five are rededicatory)[54] dateable to between the late 2nd century BCE and 2nd century CE (Table 4.1).[55] Deriving from the latter half of this period also, a host of reliefs from stupa sites render scenes of relic acquisition and dedication, many of which are familiar to events described in the *Mahāparinirvāṇasūtra*[56] and *Aśokāvadāna*.[57] Such a surfeit in dedications is quite peculiar to this historical context and the idiosyncrasy thus raises some rather fundamental questions as to the conditions that precipitated the spur, whence such an abundance of relics was thought to have derived, and the function Buddhist propaganda may have served in this regard. In several respects, these narrative cycles served as both localised models and repositories for accounts of rulers' acts towards stupas and relics in the Indic Northwest.

The *Mahāparinirvāṇasūtra* and *Aśokāvadāna* respectively attribute the introduction of relics into the region to a time immediately posterior to the Buddha[58] or to Aśoka.[59] Although the latter account is widely viewed in scholarship as being corroborated on architectural and numismatic grounds by several stupas—most famously the Dharmarājikā near Taxila, Punjab,[60] and Butkara I in Mingora, Swat[61]—their attribution to the Mauryan Period has been more recently challenged[62] and some favour a date in the 2nd century BCE because of a greater preponderance of Indo-Greek coinage at these and other sites.[63] Contrarily, Kharoṣṭhī[64] and Brāhmī[65] inscriptions of the early Common Era explicitly designate the two aforementioned stupas, as well as four others of unknown location, as 'Dharmarājikā'. Notwithstanding the strong possibility these appellations are products of a period later than the one they imply, and to that extent were propagandistically self-serving, such evidence implies that Aśoka's ritual landscape of the however imagined past was very much a component of the actual present and that it informed local knowledge regarding Buddhism's institutional history in the region.

That this was undoubtedly the case is underpinned by several internal tenets of the *Aśokāvadāna* cycle. Many scholars have shown that the contents of the Sanskrit version bespeak an archaeological context remarkably similar to the one we encounter in the post-2nd century CE Northwest.[66] The existence of a c. 1st century CE Kharoṣṭhī manuscript collection retained in the British Library to contain an 'Avadāna of King Aśoka' (*avadaṇo rayasa aśogasa*)[67] confirms this presence in general terms. As do some lesser studied *Aśokāvadānas* of two collections entitled *Za piyu jing* 雜譬喻經 (**Saṃyuktāvadānasūtra*)—one attributed to Lokakṣema支婁迦讖 (2nd century CE)[68] and another to an unknown translator working in the Latter Han Period (c. 25–220 CE)[69]—which are notable for their retaining alternative, localised versions of specific narrative elements that are potentially shared with the region's relief art. These tropes include Aśoka's offering of dirt to the Buddha;[70] his successful acquisition of relics from a *nāga*-king in a lake in the northern region[71] through a merit-weighing contest (in most other witnesses he unsuccessfully attempts to take the relics from Rāmagrāma);[72] and his establishment of stupas, here numbered distinctly at 1,200 (not the more often-encountered tradition of 84,000).[73]

Several *Aśokāvadānas* also preserve a nebulous memory of the politically turbulent conditions of the post-Mauryan period. Collectively they relate that a series of rulers—the Śuṅga Puṣyamitra,[74] as well as the Indo-Greeks, Indo-Scythians, Indo-Parthians,[75] and Tocharians (Kuṣāṇas)[76]—destroy stupas and kill monastics in the region, ultimately precipitating the conditions for the Dharma's evanescence. Jan Nattier attributes the Chinese witnesses' composition to either the Sarvāstivādins or Dharmaguptakas active in the Northwest between the early 2nd and 3rd centuries CE.[77] However, she questions their account, perceiving a discrepancy between the negative presentation of these rulers, their (in some cases) sporadic laudation in textual sources elsewhere, and apparent engagement in Buddhist donative activity in epigraphic sources. Two possible solutions are offered: either the narratives preserve 'a negative initial impression' of these rulers when 'none, presumably, were Buddhists' or the rulers had become 'a standard *topos* for "non-brahmanic barbarians" '.[78]

Certainly, the latter cannot be ruled out; the destructive actions of these non-Buddhist rulers clearly serve to contrast with those of Aśoka in the progression of the narrative. Nonetheless, the undoubted kernel of historicity the accounts retain would provide adequate explanation for, on the one hand, the sudden appearance of relics and ensuing wave of dedications in the Northwest, and, on the other, the concomitant demand for monastics to develop regulations and propaganda both pro- and pre-scribing destruction and theft. Certain themes also are not limited to these narratives; for instance, anxieties concerning the Dharma's disappearance (*antardhāna*) or duration (*sthiti*) were current among the Buddhists of this period, as several contemporaneous Kharoṣṭhī manuscripts quite explicitly inform.[79] Furthermore, the historical narrative (whence Nattier's discrepancy derives) to maintain these putatively Buddhist rulers supported Buddhism is not overly nuanced (see later section) and the readiness to reject the possibility they engaged in such destruction could well be attributed to an irenic view persistent within scholarship in this regard.

Yet if these Buddhist accounts were in any way veracious on the matter of political vandalism, one would expect to encounter corroborating traces. But in consideration of the evidence at hand we are presented with a conundrum. Destruction by earthquake appears ubiquitously in archaeological reports of pre-3rd century CE stupas—this issue being acute to stupas in the Northwest which often exhibit periodic phases of cosmetic refurbishment and structural restoration or enlargement,[80] as well as the depositing of coinage within layers of the structure conceivably to fund such repairs[81]—but is entirely absent in both epigraphic[82] and textual sources. Conversely that of the intentional variety is almost entirely lacking from the archaeological record but represented across all other authorities. Several possible factors could explain this incongruence but for a lack of independent textual verification for vandalism, such as the sort potentially offered by the Chinese travelogues available for later periods, any conclusions are rendered mere conjecture. Yet even in the few cases where vandalism is demonstrable, the aforementioned irenic bias has seemingly hindered this possibility being fully explored.[83] Notwithstanding further archaeological evidence that would substantiate Buddhist accounts of political destruction, it would regardless remain impossible to speak of behavioural uniformity at a regional level and to extrapolate findings from a single site to determine, say, the implementation of political policy towards Buddhist institutions. These issues must therefore remain open.

A more fruitful avenue is to be found in greater systematic analysis of the corpus of inscribed relic dedications. This enables the nature of political engagement with Buddhism to be nuanced in several respects (a task which exceeds the bounds of the present chapter)[84] as well as affording a degree of clarification with regard to concrete instances of stupa destruction and relic acquisition, which are raised on more than one occasion therein.

Inscribed relic dedications: a brief socio-historical analysis

All inscribed relic dedications (Table 4.1) arise during a period of intense political flux, spanning the successive reigns of the Indo-Greeks (c. 180–75 BCE), Indo-Scythians (c. 75 BCE—30 CE), Indo-Parthians (c. 30–55 CE), and early and middle Kuṣāṇas (c. 55–187 CE) who had invaded the Northwest from Central Asia. Only three inscriptions can be tentatively attributed to the first period,[85] after which time the practice gradually increases in the second[86] and third,[87] and burgeons during the fourth,[88] wherein approximately half of all relic dedications were made.

Across this broad frame, the demographic of the practice underwent a number of metamorphoses. Figures of several social groupings are represented in the role of donor or beneficiary, ranging from rulers and the familial, judicatory, and military figures associated with their administration to individuals who do not bear a title indicative of social status (e.g., occupational) and can only be deemed as belonging to a socio-economic stratum with sufficient wealth to fund a ritual dedication. Unusually perhaps, monastic figures are the exception; although where they do arise they are invariably[89] individuals serving specific pedagogic functions[90] or administrative roles associated with managing the economic and structural affairs of the stupa.[91] Equally, monastic institutions are rarely represented, with those named including the Kāśyapīyas,[92] Mahīśāsakas,[93] and the Mahāsāṃghikas,[94] but most predominantly the Dharmaguptakas[95] and Sarvāstivādins.[96]

Before the Kuṣāṇa Period, relic dedications were almost exclusively the provinces of rulers and those related to them, these occurring at more than twice the incidence of those of non-political (at least not overtly) social groupings. The practice was thus chiefly a political concern and its agents presumably utilised this ritual sphere to affirm associated power. This power was largely produced at a local and microstructural level. Beyond their being referenced in date formulas, one does not observe any of the Indo-Greek, Indo-Scythian, or Indo-Parthian[97] suzerains engaging directly in the practice. Nor indeed do devices on their coinage draw on a specifically Buddhist iconographic or symbolic repertoire. Rather, relic dedications were enacted by, or in conjunction with, regional governors (G. *meridarkh*; Gk. *μεριδάρχης*)[98] and (great)-satraps (Skt. (*mahā*)-*kṣatrapa*),[99] presumably governing as a contemporaneous suzerain's regional potentate.

The engagement of figures at this level is confirmed by the appearance of one great satrap named Jihoṇika (c. 30–55 CE), known to coinage[100] and epigraphy,[101] in one *avadāna* extant in a Kharoṣṭhī manuscript.[102] Therein he is mentioned in connection with the activity of 'transporting (something) widely' (*ve[stra]gena bahadi*) within Gandhāra. Noting common collocations with Skt. *vaistārika*, Timothy Lenz suggests the narrative 'could imply the diffusion of relics or Buddhist doctrine' in the region.[103] If this surmise is correct, it may be concluded, and indeed substantiate what we glean from the epigraphic corpus, that the Buddhists had developed a highly localised propaganda, specifically intended for individuals presiding at the echelons of regional governance.

With the advent of Kuṣāṇa rule, the landscape of dedicatory practice changes dramatically. Now certain Kuṣāṇa suzerains, including Kujula Kadphises,[104] Kaniṣka I,[105] and Huviṣka,[106] are found participating in the ritual. Dedicating relics as political practice hence was no longer a local phenomenon but had transformed into an instrument of imperialism. This finding could be correlated with Kaniṣka I ultimately initiating the usage of Buddha figures as part of his 'official iconography' in coinage,[107] in addition to his quite regular appearance in Buddhist discourse. Of particular relevance in this latter regard, Max Deeg has argued that several structural elements and features of the *Aśokāvadāna* provided the model for Kaniṣka I's own hypothetical **Kaniṣkāvadāna*, indicating the two cycles developed concurrently in the early Common Era.[108] For instance, the *Mūlasarvāstivādavinaya* and Chinese travelogues preserve identical past-life stories as explanation for Aśoka's and Kaniṣka's stupa establishments;[109] and several other narratives relate that a ruler of the Xiao Yuezhi 小月氏 named Zhawang 吒王 (*Caṇḍakaniṣka)[110] invaded and laid siege to a city in Madhyadeśa, stealing the Buddha's alms-bowl—a *pāribhogika* ('item of use') or 'secondary' relic—and kidnapping Aśvaghosa in order that both he and the alms-bowl could be appropriated for Gandhāra.[111]

It is also during the Kuṣāṇa period that the practice becomes more widespread. Now the vast majority of donors no longer bear an appellation indicative of status and this indefinable, by definition inclusive, social group—encompassing individuals with the economic surplus to fund the purchase of relics and valuable items often donated therewith, in addition to a stupa's construction or repair—constitutes approximately 40% of all dedications.

Foremost, however, the sudden rise in the practice can be credited to the rulers (*rāja*), princes (*kumāra*), generals (*stratega*; Gk. *στρατηγός*), wives (*bhāryā*), women of the inner court (*antaḥpurikā*), and other figures related to two local dynasties, the Apracarājas[112] and Oḍirājas.[113] From coinage and inscriptions, the former are known to have governed at the cusp of the Indo-Scythian and Indo-Parthian periods, perhaps in the regions of Dir, Bajaur and Peshawar (Gandhāra). And the latter are attested epigraphically at the advent of the Kuṣāṇa period, reigning in Swat (Uḍḍiyāna).[114] Both groups are particularly notable for their appearance in Buddhist narrative literature[115] as well as for their inscriptions sharing in topoi related in both the *Mahāparinirvāṇasūtra* and *Aśokāvadāna*, imparting issues of stupa destruction, and employing rare doctrinal formulations concerning relic acquisition and rededication.

Relic rededications in the Indic Northwest

In light of the sheer volume of relic dedications, it is abundantly clear the practice was *en vogue* during these centuries. Although only postulatory in principle and not tangibly, this overall circumstance could conceivably have necessitated the type of institutional rules regulating relic trade as those stipulated in the Sarvāstivāda discourses treated in the foregoing. With the market, as it were, awash with relics, it is likely they were commodified and that such directives were resultingly devised with the intention perhaps of hindering their appreciation and ensuring that Buddhist institutions alone profited from their sale. That they had indeed become merchandise is deducible from patterns in the material nature of dedications.

It is rather difficult to determine the status of many relic dedications. Even though a majority of 48 inscriptions refer to *śarīra* or *dhātu*, not all specify these are the Buddha's, and the remainder could potentially be the remains of other figures considered worthy of a stupa (e.g., a monastic figure).[116] Nor, more generally, were all reliquary deposits excavated in the region found with any relic-like substance (e.g., bones, ashes). And some contained what could be regarded as imposter relics (e.g., animal bone).[117] Constituting nothing perceptibly more than osseous or torrefied matter, relics are unrecognisable as such and hence redundant apart from a betokening reliquary or stupa. That many were 'relic dedications' in name only suggests they were in high demand but not in endless supply, and that their perceived presence was utilised by some more concerned with the power they awarded. This latter phenomenon is perhaps reflected in the material quality of dedications in the Kuṣāṇa period—that is, when the practice increases in frequency and becomes more socially inclusive—which lacked corporeal relics and had degraded in their material value.[118] Presuming, however, that processes of relic acquisition and authenticity were indeed at stake, proof of provenance must have been of import to those engaged in their ritual dedication.

In many cases, relics were demonstrably acquired from existing stupas and rededicated thereafter. This phenomenon has been identified both archaeologically, when coins found in a deposit are chronologically incongruent with other items therein or the associated stupa's architectural technology,[119] and epigraphically, when an object is twice inscribed,[120] when it explicitly refers to a previous dedication,[121] or when garbled inscriptions are understood as poor copies of others unearthed from earlier deposits.[122] Collectively, these authorities suggest the possibility to acquire relics was afforded under three scenarios: that a stupa had deteriorated from neglect, that it had been totally ruined by natural calamity, or that it was intentionally destroyed.

The first case is recorded on a twice-inscribed, cylindrical steatite reliquary (Figure 4.1), reportedly from Shinkot in the Bajaur region of Pakistan,[123]

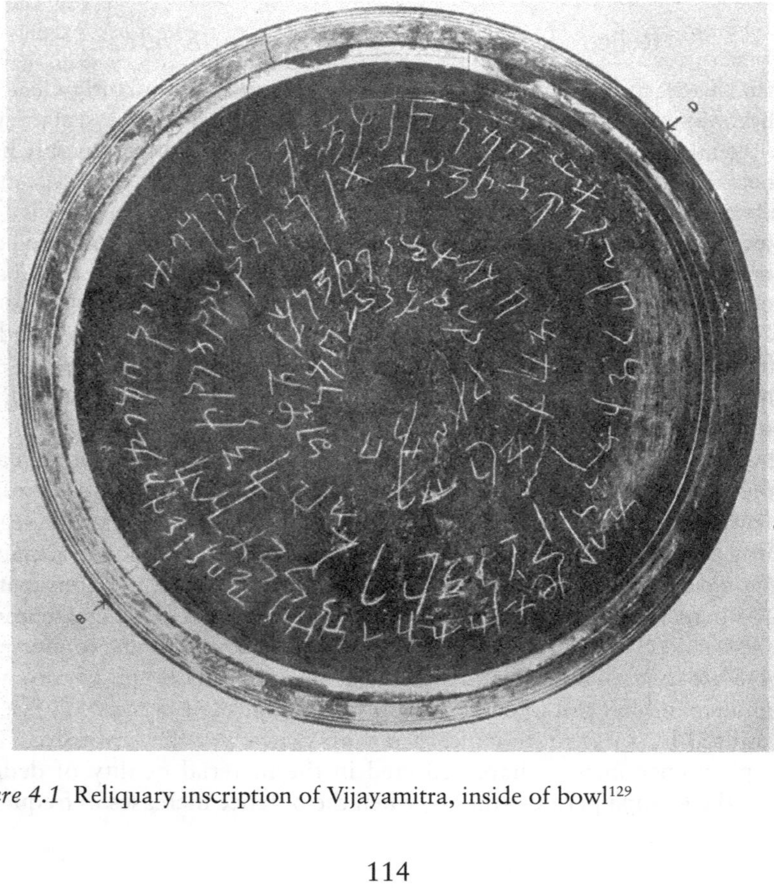

Figure 4.1 Reliquary inscription of Vijayamitra, inside of bowl[129]

which simultaneously evidences the earliest instance of a relic dedication and rededication in the region. Several points of contention remain among epigraphers regarding the dates and authenticity of the inscriptions (a resolution for which is currently not prospective)[124] but it likely bears two groups: one dated to the reign of the Indo-Greek Menander (c. 155–130 BCE)[125] and another to the 5th year (=3/4 CE) of the Apracarāja Vijayamitra (c. 2 BCE—30 CE).[126] The latter records in one line:

> [i]me śarira palugabhuṯao na sakareṯi tasa śariaṯi kalaḏe na śadhro na piṃḍoyake yi pitri griṇayaṯi tasa ye patre vapomua.[127]
> The relic became broken, is not worshipped, [and] so disintegrated over time. Neither *śrāddha*, nor *piṇḍa* and water are brought for the ancestors,[128] [and] so the bowl is not fully covered.

Between the reigns of Menander and Vijayamitra, some unspecified circumstances thus appear to have prevented those who would normally attend to the relics from doing so. One can only conjecture as to the potential grounds—the aforementioned fluctuating political conditions may provide adequate explanation—but of import here is that the dilapidated structure provided Vijayamitra with the opportunity to repair it and to acquire and rededicate the relics, inaugurating what would subsequently become a defining political behaviour among local rulers in the region.

The second issue is conveyed by an inscribed gold scroll, likely from Swat,[130] which records that the Oḍirāja Seṇavarma, in the 4th year of his reign (late 1st century CE), rededicated relics and enlarged the Ekaüḍa-stupa formerly established by his ancestor Vasuseṇa, whose own dedicatory inscription is quoted.[131]

> [2d] iśa Ekaüḍami vijuvapati tae dahiasa thuvasa vipariṇame kiḍe se me sarve upaḍa vitate mulaśave ukṣivita[132] avaśita[133] tatra pratiṭhava[3a]ṇia lihitia Utaraseṇaputre Vasuseṇe Oḍiraya Iṣmahokulade se imo Ekaüḍo pratiṭhaveti[134]
> [2d] When the Ekaüḍa was struck by lightning an alteration to the burnt stupa was made by me. Everything was torn up and spread out [and] the original-*śava* was raised up and removed. Therein was an inscription concerning [3a] the establishment: 'Son of Utaraseṇa, Vasuseṇa, the Oḍirāja and descendant of the Ikṣvākus; he establishes the Ekaüḍa'.

Apparently lightning was not an uncommon issue.[135] And in this case the incident was also politically opportune for the Kuṣāṇas, who had likely annexed the region in the recent past, as it provided them with the ritual possibility of publically articulating the Oḍirāja Seṇavarma's subjugation to their suzerainty. This is reflected in their being named in a list of beneficiaries with the comparatively lofty titles 'Son of the Gods, Sadaṣkaṇa, son of the Great King, Supreme King among Kings, Kujula Kadphises' ([8g] Maharaja rayatirayakuyulakataph[śp]aputro Sadaṣkaṇo devaputra).

The inscription and ritual act additionally allowed for Seṇavarma to affirm his own identity, stating that he and the Oḍirājas belong to the Ikṣvākus,[136] the solar lineage ancestry shared with Śākyamuni Buddha. This claim is also known to the legend recorded by Xuanzang 玄奘 whilst in Swat during the 7th century CE, which relates that the Buddha, having quelled the *nāga* Apalāla on his famous journey along the 'Northern Route' (*uttarāpatha*),[137] visits the palace of King Utaraseṇa (*wadaluoxina*嗢呾羅犀那), whom he names as a member of the Śākya lineage. The Buddha informs Utaraseṇa's mother his *parinirvāṇa* is nigh and that he should travel to Kuśinagara to acquire a portion of the relics. Once there, the other claimants resist Utaraseṇa's demands, but he secures a share and brings them back on an elephant to be established in a stupa.[138]

This narrative can perhaps be situated in the early Common Era on the basis of a series of composite reliefs concerning the *Mahāparinirvāṇasūtra* from stupas Butkāra I and Saidu Sharif I, Swat, archaeologically and stylistically dateable to the 1st century CE. Thereon, such events of import as the conflict over relics[139] are depicted, and, if Domenico Faccenna's identification is accurate, Utaraseṇa transporting a portion of the relics atop an elephant.[140] It is quite possible therefore that the Oḍirājas, or Sarvāstivādins[141] likely associated with them, had developed a regionally circumscribed propaganda, narratively interposed between two major pieces of literature to deal with Buddhism's expansion into the Northwest: the *Mahāparinirvāṇasūtra* and its preludial episode retained in the *Mūlasarvāstivādavinaya*, detailing the Buddha's travels along the Northern Route.[142]

It is also in Seṇavarma's inscription that we encounter the third issue, vandalism:

> [12] ye [va]ṇa imo Ekaüḍo thuvo ṇiṭhidao viṇiṭhi[13]tao daheati ite udhu deve va maṇuśe va yakṣe va ṇage va suvaṇi va gadharve va kuvhaḍe va se Aviyamahaṇiraa padeati[143]
> [12] But whoever should burn the Ekaüḍa stupa after it is fully completed, henceforth, whether god, man, *yakṣa*, *nāga*, *suparṇin*, *gandharva* or *kumbhāṇḍa*, may they fall into the great hell Avīci.

Both Seṇavarma's expectation of destruction and his curse that the perpetrator be reborn in Avīci correspond of course to the previously cited doctrinal developments. We thereby know that prohibitive regulations surrounding stupa destruction were current in the Northwest at this time.

That corresponding prescriptive regulations of relic theft were potentially present is evinced by another re-dedicatory inscription, found on the body and upper lid of a spherical schist reliquary from Bajaur, Pakistan (Figure 4.2), that was donated by another Apracarāja figure, Prince Indravarma I, in 63 Azes (=15/16 CE).

[Body] [1] saṃvatsarae treṃṣaṭhimae 20 20 20 1 1 1 maharayasa ayasa atidasa kartiasa masasa divasae ṣoḍaśae imeṇa cetrike kṣeṇ[e][144] idravarma kumare apracarayaputra [2] ime bhagavato śakamuṇisa śarira pradiṭhaveti ṭhiae gabhirae apradiṭhavitaprave [pa]teśe brammapuño prasavadi
[Upper Lid] ime ca śarira muryakaliṇate[145] thubute kiḍapaḍiharia[146] avhiye aheṭhi majimami pradiṭhavaṇami pradiṭha[v]i[d]a[147]
[Body] [1] In the sixty-third 63 year of the Great King Azes past, on the 16th day of the month Kārttika, at this moment of *citrā*,

Figure 4.2 Reliquary inscription of Indravarma I[148]

> Prince Indravarma [I], son of the Apracarāja [Viṣuvarma], establishes [2] this relic of the Fortunate One Śākyamuni at a permanent, deep, previously unestablished location, and produces Brahma-merit
> [Upper Lid] And these relics, having been taken from a Mauryan period stupa, were established in a central location that is without danger, without trouble.

Indravarma I thus appears to directly hearken back to Aśoka's narrative model in another instance of this repeated reception and return. Although the precise location of the Mauryan period stupa is unknown, we may conjecture it stood in the vicinity of Trama, a city of undetermined whereabouts that is named in four other inscribed relic dedications. Of these, two can be firmly associated with the Apracarājas and one inscribed on a Buddha image further details Trama as a 'capital city where a Dharmarājikā was established by Aśoka' ([Tra]matithaṇaṇagaraṃmi Dhamaraïaṃmi Aśorayapraïstavidami).[149]

Akin to sentiments encountered in the dedication of the Apracarāja Vijayamitra quoted earlier, Indravarma I also imparts a concern for the relic's safety. He indicates that the stupa whence the relic was acquired was in some unspecified danger, presumably justifying the excavation of the former and the lawful acquisition and rededication of the latter. Moreover, the ritual practice of rededicating is explicitly designated by a specific formula: 'to establish relics at a previously unestablished location on the earth' (Skt. *pratiṣṭhāpayati apratiṣṭhāpitapūrve pṛthivīpradeśe*). This phrasing is known to nine other epigraphs, several of which are found on twice-inscribed and thus rededicated objects: one donated by a certain Sadaṣaka,[150] one by Patika, son of the satrap of Cukhsa (Chhachh) Liaka,[151] five by the Apracarājas' family members[152] or individuals in their known spheres of governance,[153] and one by the Oḍirāja Ajidaseṇa.[154] The accompanying notion of producing Brahma-merit (*brāhmapuṇya*) is also attested in one further instance.[155]

Scholars have identified this formula in a number of textual passages, in which several other means to produce Brahma-merit are enumerated.[156] Initially these appear to have been limited to reuniting a divided monastic institution,[157] but were subsequently expanded to include several other acts—including activities of institutional concern such as establishing a stupa and a monastic complex—in similar enumerations[158] or isolated instances.[159] The commentaries are united in stating that these acts result in the actor being reborn in heaven, or, more specifically, in the Brahma-world (*brahmaloka*) for a *kalpa*.[160] In this regard, we must note something of a cosmological verticality apropos institutionally directed behaviour. Whilst divisive acts (i.e., destroying a stupa, schisming a monastic community) result in being reborn in Avīci, the lowest stratum of the cosmos in the sense-sphere (*kāmadhātu*),

Table 4.1 Socio-historical analysis of inscribed relics dedications in the Indic Northwest

No	*Title*	*Provenance*	*Date*	*Named donation*	*Ruling group*	*Monastic institution*	*Individuals*		*Ref.*
							Name	*Title*	
1	Reliquary inscription from Menander's reign	Shinkot, Bajaur Pakistan	Unknown year of Menander	relics (*śarīra*)	Indo-Greek				CKI 176 (No. 9)
2	Reliquary inscription of Theodotus	Swat, Pakistan	Unknown	relics (*śarīra*)	—	—	Theodotus	*meridarkh*	CKI 32
3	Copper scroll inscription of unknown Meridarkh	Shahpur, Taxila, Pakistan	Unknown	stupa				*meridarkh*	CKI 33
4	Reliquary inscription of Namipala	Buner, Pakistan	11 [Azes] (=37/36 BCE)	relics (*śarīra*)	Indo-Scythian		Namipala	*mahākṣatrapa*	CKI 827
5	Stone relic-chamber slab inscription of Gomitra	Unknown	12 [Azes] (=36/35 BCE)	relics (*śarīra*)	Indo-Scythian		Gomitra	*maharṣi, dharmakathika*	CKI 464
6	Gold scroll inscription of Tora et al	Haḍḍa, Nangarhar, Afghanistan	39 Azes (=9/8 BCE)	stupa			Tora et al	*sahāya*	CKI 455
7	Reliquary inscription of Loṇa	Charsadda, Pakistan		relics (*śarīra*)	Apracarāja		Loṇa Viṣuvarma	*antaḥpurikā* *kumāra*	CKI 247
8	Reliquary inscription of Naganaṃda	Samarbagh, Pakistan	50 [Azes] (=2/3 CE)	relics (*śarīra*)	Apracarāja	Dharmaguptaka	Naganaṃda Taravia	*bhāryā* *meridarkh*	CKI 454
9	Reliquary inscription of Vijayamitra	Shinkhot, Bajaur Pakistan	5 Vijayamitra (=3/4 CE)	relics (*śarīra*)	Apracarāja		Vijayamitra	*apracarāja*	CKI 176 (No. 1)

(*Continued*)

Table 4.1 (Continued)

No	Title	Provenance	Date	Named donation	Ruling group	Monastic institution	Individuals: Name	Individuals: Title	Ref.
10	Copper plate inscription of Patika	Taxila, Pakistan	78 Maues [=3/4 CE(?)]		Indo-Scythian		Patika Liako Kusuluko Rohinimitra	*putra* *kṣatrapa* *upādhyāya, navakarmika*	CKI 46
11	Reliquary inscription of Sihila et al	Shahpur, Taxila, Pakistan		stupa			Sihila et al		CKI 65
12	Reliquary inscription of Saṃgharakṣita	Unknown	60 [Azes] (=12/13 CE)	relics (*śarīra*)			Saṃgharakṣita		CKI 403
13	Reliquary inscription of Indravarma I	Unknown	63 Azes (=15/16 CE)	relics (*śarīra*)	Apracarāja		Indravarma Viṣuvarma Vijayamitra	*kumāra* *apracarāja* *apracarāja*	CKI 242
14	Silver scroll inscription of Utara	Bajaur, Pakistan		relics (*dhātu*) *śilāstaṃbha*	Apracarāja		Utara Indravarma Dhramasena	*bhāryā* *kumara* *navakarmika*	CKI 265
15	Mathura lion capital	Mathura, India		relics (*śarīra*), stupa	Indo-Scythian	Sarvāstivāda	Yasi Kamui Rajula et al	*agramahiṣī* *mahākṣatrapa*	CKI 48
16	Mathura elephant capital	Mathura, India		*sastaka-dhātu*					CKI 49
17	Reliquary inscription of Rukhuṇa	Bajaur, Pakistan	27 Vijayamitra 73 Azes 201 Yona (=25/26 CE)	stupa	Apracarāja		Rukhuṇa Visuvarma Vijayamitra Indravarma	*bhāryā* *apracarāja* *apracarāja* *stratega*	CKI 405
18	Reliquary inscription of Utara	Unknown		stupa	Apracarāja		Utara Indravarma	*bhāryā* *stratega*	CKI 255
19	Silver Scroll inscription of Mahazada et al	Unknown		relics (*śarīra*), *śīlastambha*			Mahazada et al		CKI 327

20	Gold scroll inscription of Mahazada et al (fake?)	Unknown		relics (*śarīra*), *śīlastambha*					CKI 332
21	Relic-chamber slab inscription of Ramaka	Bajaur, Pakistan	74 Azes (=26/27 CE)	relics (*śarīra*)	Apracarāja		Ramaka Yola. . .	*kṣatrapa*	CKI 251
22	Reliquary inscription of Ramaka and Uḍita	Bajaur, Pakistan		relics (*śarīra*)	Apracarāja		Ramaka Uḍita		CKI 243
23	Gunyar relic chamber slab inscription	Malakand, Pakistan	76 Azes (=28/29 CE)	relics (*śarīra*)					CKI 544
24	Reliquary inscription of Śatruleka	Bajaur Agency, Pakistan	77 Azes (=29/30 CE)	relics (*dhātu*)	Apracarāja	Kāśyapīya	Satruleka Vijayamitra Indravarma et al	*kṣatrapa* *apracarāja* *stratega*, *gandhārasvāmin*	CKI 257
25	Reliquary inscription of Prahodi	Bajaur Agency, Pakistan	32 Vijayamitra (=30/31 CE)	relics (*śarīra*)	Apracarāja		Prahodi Vijayamitra Sirila Aśorakṣida	*antaḥpurikā* *apracarāja* *stūpanavakarmika* *navakarmika*	CKI 359
26	Anonymous inscription Reliquary	Swat, Pakistan	80 Azes(?) (=32/33 CE)	—	—	—	—	—	CKI 828
27	Reliquary inscription of Dhramila's son et al	Aṭhatyi, Unknown	83 Azes (=35/36 CE)	relics (*śarīra*)			Dhramila et al		CKI 266 (No. 33)
28	Reliquary Inscription of Indragivarma	Unknown	—	—	Apracarāja	—	Indragivarma Vijyamitra	*kumara* *apracarāja*	CKI 402
29	Reliquary inscription of Indravarma II	Unknown		relics (*śarīra*)	Apracarāja		Indravarma II Aśpavarma Indravarma I Utara Vijayamitra Indravasu	*kumārastratega* *stratega* *bhāryā* *apracarāja* *apracarāja*	CKI 241

(*Continued*)

Table 4.1 (Continued)

No	Title	Provenance	Date	Named donation	Ruling group	Monastic institution	Individuals: Name	Individuals: Title	Ref.
30	Reliquary inscription of Ariaśrava et al	Dir, Pakistan	98 Azes (=50/51 CE)	relics (*dhātu*)	Apracarāja; Indo-Parthian	Dharmaguptaka	Ariaśrava — Avakaśa Aśpavarma	*gupara* *bhrataputra* *stratega*	CKI 358
31	Reliquary inscription of Śatra	Unknown	—	relics (*dhātu*)	—	—	Śatra	—	CKI 326
32	Copper plate inscription of Helauta	Unknown	121 [Azes] (=73/74 CE)	relics (*dhātu*)		Dharmaguptaka	Helaüta, Tira et al	*kṣatrapa*	CKI 564
33	Reliquary inscription of Kopśakasa(?)	Tramana Unknown	—	relics (*dhātu*)			Kopśakasa	*Mahārāja*	CKI 266 (No. 27)
34	Quoted inscription of Vasusena	Unknown	—	relics (*śarīra*)	Oḍirāja	—	Vasuseṇa Utaraseṇa	*oḍirāja* *oḍirāja*	CKI 249 (No. 37)
35	Gold scroll inscription of Ajidasena	Mata, Swat, Pakistan	4 Oḍi	relics (*dhātu*), *mahāstūpa*	Oḍirāja		Ajidaseṇa	*oḍirāja*	CKI 334
36	Silver scroll inscription of Ayadata	Swat, Pakistan	5 Oḍi	relics (*dhātu*), *dhātustūpa*	Oḍirāja		Ayadata; Varmaseṇa	*kumāra* *oḍirāja*	CKI 401
37	Gold scroll inscription of Seṇavarma	Unknown	14 Oḍi	relics (*dhātu*); *ekaüḍastūpa*	Oḍirāja Kuṣāṇa		Senavarma Kujula Kadphises et al Priamitra	*oḍirāja* *mahārāja, rājātirāja* *stūpapāla*	CKI 249 (No. 34)
38	Reliquary inscription of Śivarakṣidaka	Panr, Swat, Pakistan	—	stupa	—	—	Śivarakṣidaka	—	CKI 267

39	Reliquary inscription of Teyamitra	Swat, Pakistan		relics (*śarīra*), *bodhisatva-gaha*			Teyamitra		CKI 457
40	Reliquary inscription of Priavaśa	Unknown	127 Azes (=78/79 CE)		Kuṣāṇa	Mahīśāsaka	Priavaśa; [Kujula Kadphises]	*śramaṇa yabgu, mahārāja*	CKI 331
41	Reliquary inscription of Priavaśa's wife	Unknown	—	—	—	—	—	*Priavaśabhāryā*	CKI 240
42	Copper plate inscription of Caṃdrabhi et al	Kalawan, Taxila, Pakistan	134 Azes (=86/87 CE)	relics (*śarīra*), *gahastupa*		Sarvāstivāda	Caṃdrabhi	*upāsikā*	CKI 172
43	Silver scroll inscription of Urasaka	Dharmarajika, Taxila, Pakistan	136 Azes (=88/89 CE)	relics (*dhātu*), *bodhisatva-gaha*	Kuṣāṇa		Urasaka [Kujula Kadphises]	*mahārāja rājātirāja, devaputra*	CKI 60
44	Reliquary inscription of Śivarakṣida	Bimaran, Nangarhar, Afghanistan		relics (*śarīra*)			Śivarakṣida		CKI 50
45	Anonymous reliquary inscription	Unknown	139 Azes (=91/92)	relics (*dhātu*)	—	—	—	—	CKI 563
46	Reliquary inscription of Sazaṃduṣa et al	Unknown	144(?) [Azes] (=96/97 CE)	relics (*śarīra*)			Sazamdusa Sroṣa		CKI 466
47	Reliquary inscription of Dhamavadaaṭa	Unknown	147 [Azes] (=99/100 CE)	—	—	—	Dhamavadaata?	*bhaṭṭara*	CKI 536
48	Reliquary inscription of Sadaṣaka et al	Unknown	156 [Azes] (=108/109 CE)	stupa			Sadaṣaka Muṃji		CKI 328 (No. 51)

(*Continued*)

Table 4.1 (Continued)

No	*Title*	*Provenance*	*Date*	*Named donation*	*Ruling group*	*Monastic institution*	*Individuals*		*Ref.*
							Name	*Title*	
49	Reliquary inscription of Khadadata	Unknown	157 [Azes] (=109/110)	stupa	—	—	Khadadata	—	CKI 225
50	Reliquary inscription of Utaraya	Unknown	157 [Azes] (=109/110)	relics (*dhātu*)	—	—	Utaraya	*bhikṣuṇī*	CKI 226
51	Reliquary inscription of Aprakhaha	Unknown	172 [Azes] (=124/125)	relics (*śarīra*)			Aprakhaha		CKI 328 (No. 48)
52	Reliquary inscription of *Macayemana*?	Charsadda, Pakistan	303 [Yona] (=127/128 CE)	relics (*śarīra*), stupa			*Macayemana*? Avakhazada	*kṣatrapa*	CKI 178
53	Reliquary Inscription of Trami	Kula Dheri, Charsadda, Taxila	—	relics (*śarīra*)	—	—	Trami	—	CKI 177
54	Relic-Chamber Slab Inscription of Lala et al	Manikyala, Pakistan	18 Kaniṣka [I] (=144/145 CE)	relics	Kuṣāṇa		Lala Kaniṣka [I] Veśpaśisa Budhila	*daṇḍanāyaka* *mahārāja* *kṣatrapa* *navakarmika* (Mon.)	CKI 149
55	Reliquary Inscription of Ganavhryaka's Son	Manikyala, Pakistan	—	—	—	—	Ganavhryaka	*kāpiśīkṣatrapa kṣatrapa*	CKI 150
56	Reliquary Inscription of Ayabhadra	Sanghol, Punjab, India	—	—	—	—	Ayabhadra	*upāsaka*	CKI 239

57	Reliquary Inscription of Sacabhama	Unknown	—	—	—	—	Sacabhama	*bhāryā*	CKI 400
58	Reliquary Inscription of Śira	Gangu, Taxila, Pakistan	—	relics (*dhātu*)	—	—	Śira	—	CKI 64
59	Anonymous Reliquary	Kabul	—	—	—	—	—	—	CKI 600
60	Anonymous Reliquary Lid	Afghanistan	18 [Kaniṣka I] (=144/145 CE)	relics (*śarīra*)	—	—	—	—	CKI 152
61	Reliquary Inscription of Śveḍavarma	Kurram Valley, Pakistan	20 [Kaniṣka I] (=146/148)	relics (*śarīra*)	—	Sarvāstivāda	Śveḍavarma		CKI 153
62	Reliquary Inscription of Mitravarma	Jalalabad, Nangarhar, Afghanistan	20 [Kaniṣka I] (=146/148)	relics (*dhātu-śarīra*); stupa	—	—	Mitravarma		CKI 368
63	Reliquary Inscription of Saṃghamitra	Haḍḍa, Nangarhar, Afghanistan	28 [Huviṣka] (=154/155 CE)	relics (*śarīra*)	—	—	Saṃghamitra	*navakarmika*	CKI 155
64	Reliquary Inscription of Budhapriya et al	Jalalabad, Nangarhar, Afghanistan					Budhapirya et al		CKI 511
65	Anonymous Relic-Chamber Slab Inscription	Swabi, Pakistan		relics (*śarīra*), *garbha*-stupa					CKI 135
66	Reliquary Inscription of Vagamarega	Wardak, Afghanistan	51 Huviṣka (=177/178 CE)	relics (*śarīra*), stupa	Kuṣāṇa	Mahāsāṃghika	Vagamarega Huviṣka	— *mahārāja, rājātirāja*	CKI 159

(*Continued*)

Table 4.1 (Continued)

No	Title	Provenance	Date	Named donation	Ruling group	Monastic institution	Individuals		Ref.
							Name	Title	
67	Reliquary Inscription of Vagamarega's Daughter	Wardak, Afghanistan	51 Huviṣka (=177/178 CE)	relics (*śarīra*), stupa	Kuṣāṇa	Mahāsāṃghika	— Vagamarega	*kṣudraduhitṛ*	CKI 509
68	Reliquary Inscription of Mahasena et al	Kaniṣkavihāra, Kaniṣkapura Shah-ji-ki-Dheri, Peshwar Pakistan		*gaṇḍakaraṇḍa* (perfume box)	Kuṣāṇa	Sarvāstivāda	Mahasena Saṃgharakṣit a	*āgniśāla-navakarmika*	CKI 145
69	Anonymous Copper Plate Inscription	Rani Dab, Pakistan					Yodamuṇi	*kṣatrapa*	CKI 442
70	Reliquary Inscription of Saṃghilaga et al	Unknown		relics (*śarīra*)			Saṃghilaga et al	—	CKI 975

Source: Compiled by author

their opposites (i.e., establishing a stupa, uniting a monastic community) cause rebirth in the Brahma-world, the first existences considered as beyond the former and now in the form-sphere (*rūpadhātu*).[161]

Matters of institutional integrity and expansion were thus particularly pronounced among the Buddhist institutions of the Indic Northwest around the turn of the Common Era. This, it seems, resulted in the concerted propagation of codified systems of prohibited and prescribed stupa destruction and relic theft in a form sufficiently inspiring to compel regional actors. Although this evidence has afforded a quite different picture of Buddhism in the Indic Northwest, the ramifications extend beyond the region's limits and demand that we reconsider historical models for Buddhism's expansion.

Notes

1 For a recent iteration, see Peter Skilling, 'Relics: The Heart of Buddhist Veneration', in Janice Stargardt and Michael Willis (eds), *Relics and Relic Worship in Early Buddhism: India, Afghanistan, Sri Lanka and Burma*, London: The British Museum, 2018, pp. 4–17 (pp. 4–5).

2 DN 2. 166, *The Dīgha Nikāya II*, eds. T. W. Rhys-Davids and J. Estlin Carpenter, London: Pali Text Society, 1966; Aś-av 34; 51, *The Aśokāvadāna*, ed. Sujitkumar Mukhopadyaya, New Delhi: Sahitya Akademi, 1963.

3 On the notion of relics as the Buddha's presence, see Gregory Schopen, 'Burial "Ad Sanctos" and the Physical Presence of the Buddha in Early Indian Buddhism', *Religion*, 1987, 17(3): 193–225.

4 For some compelling thoughts on this distinction, see Robert H. Sharf, 'On the Allure of Buddhist Relics', *Representations*, 1999, 66: 75–99.

5 Schopen, 'Burial "Ad Sanctos"', p. 206ff.

6 Peter Skilling, 'Ideology and Law: The Three Seals Code on Crimes Related to Relics, Images, and Bodhi-Trees', *Buddhism, Law & Society*, 2015, 1: 69–103 (p. 70ff).

7 Abhidh-k-bh 4. 107, *Abhidharma-Kośabhāṣya of Vasubandhu*, ed. Pralhad Pradhan, Patna: K. P. Jayaswal Research Institute, 1967, p. 107. Yaśomitra's commentary makes a somatic equivalence between destroying a stupa and drawing the blood of a Tathāgata. Abhidh-k-vy 430, *Sphuṭārthā Abhidharmakośavyākhya by Yaśomitra*, ed. Unrai Wogihara, The Publishing Association of Abhidharmakośavyākhya, Tokyo: Sankibo Buddhist Book Store, 1990. For full discussion and further textual references, see Jonathan Silk, 'Good and Evil in Indian Buddhism: The Five Sins of Immediate Retribution', *Journal of Indian Philosophy*, 2007, 35(3): 253–86 (p. 260ff).

8 For this etymology, see *The Pali Text Society's Pali-English Dictionary*, ed. T. W. Rhys-Davids and William Stede, Chipstead: Pali Text Society, 1921, s.v. *avīci*.

9 The *Zengyi ahan jing* 增一阿含經 (**Ekottarikāgama*), said to have been translated by Gautama Saṃghadeva 瞿曇僧伽提婆 in the late 4th century CE, preserves another distinct enumeration of acts that result in being reborn in Avīci 阿鼻地: 'killing [one's] mother and father, destroying a Buddha-stupa, provoking disorder in the monastic community, and holding erroneous and mistaken notions'. 殺害父母，壞佛偷婆，鬪亂衆僧，習邪倒見. T 125. 748a8–11, *Taishō Shinshū Daizōkyō* (大正新脩大藏經), ed. Junjirō Takakusu and Kaigyoku Watanabe, SAT Daizōkyō Text Database 2012 Edition, 1924 [all punctuation of passages in Chinese is my own]. Relatedly, the *Binaye* 鼻奈耶 (**Vinaya*) also states:

'[a monk who] steals the capital of a stupa goes to hell'. 盜塔寺物入地獄. T 1464. 854b25–26. Another enumeration of four 'grave prohibitions' (重禁) is found in two highly expanded 5th century translations of the *Dabanniepan jing* 大般涅槃經 (*Mahāparinirvāṇasūtra*), produced respectively by Dharmakṣema 曇無讖 (d. 433 CE) and Huiyan 慧嚴 (d. 443): 'Disobeying one's mother and father, killing an arhat, breaking a stupa and destroying a monastic community, and causing a Buddha's body to bleed.' 反逆父母，殺阿羅漢，破塔壞僧，出佛身血. T 374. 431a8–9; T 375. 672b12–13. Note that the two acts of institutional import—destruction of a stupa and monastic community—are here classified under one crime.

10 T 1425. Translated by Buddhabhadra佛陀跋陀羅and Faxian法顯, c. 416–418 CE. For details, see Shayne Clarke, 'Vinayas', in Jonathan Silk (ed), *Brill's Encyclopedia of Buddhism*, Leiden: Brill, 2015, pp. 60–87 (p. 64).

11 破塔者，若瞋恚破世尊塔者得偷蘭罪，業行罪報多，若欲治更作好者無罪。T 1425. 444c10–11.

12 See the *Pinimu jing* 毘尼母經 (*Vinayamātṛkā*), dateable to the Qin 秦 Period (351–431 CE) at the latest. T 1463. 843a12–17. For a brief summary of differing definitions of a *sthūlātyaya*, see H. Durt, 'Chūranja', in Sylvain Lévi, 高楠順次郎, Paul Demiéville, Kaigyoku Watanabe (eds), *Hōbōgirin: Dictionnaire encyclopédique du bouddhisme d'après les sources chinoises et japonaises, cinquième fascicule*, Paris and Tokyo: Maison Franco-Japonaise, 1979, pp. 507–22.

13 In the *Sapoduopinipiposha* 薩婆多毘尼毘婆沙 (**Sarvāstivādavinayavibhāṣā*): 'In the case that a powerful [individual] desires to break stupas or destroy images: By using donated gifts they can be fully restored; the flowers and fruits from the grounds of the stupa may be sold; equally, if the stupa has money or other means of support, materials can be obtained—as is suitable to the circumstances'. 若有強力欲破塔壞像，若以贈遺得全濟者，當賣塔地花果，若塔有錢，若餘緣得物，隨宜消息。 T 1440. 524c11–12. The date and translator of this latter text are lost; however, Toru Funayama tentatively places it in the Qin Period and convincingly attributes it to an unknown *lüshi* 律師 (*vinayadhara*) from, or at least highly familiar with, the Indic sphere. Funayama Toru, 'Masquerading as Translation: Examples of Chinese Lectures by Indian Scholar-Monks in the Six Dynasties Period', *Asia Major*, 2006, 19(1–2): 39–55 (pp. 44–6).

14 In one *Mahāparinirvāṇasūtra*: 'If, with desirous intention, [a monastic] destroys a Buddha-stupa, this is to commit a *sthūlātyaya*. One should not be familiar or associated with such a person. If a king or minister sees a stupa old and worn and desires to repair it and make offerings to the relics, here within the stupa they obtain precious substances and thereafter transfer it to the monks'. 若以貪心破壞佛塔犯偷蘭遮，如是之人不應親近。若王大臣見塔朽，為欲修補供養舍利，於是塔中或得珍寶即寄比丘。 T 374. 405c24–28.

15 See André Bareau, 'La construction et le culte des stūpa d'après les Vinayapitaka', *Bulletin de l'École française d'Extrême-Orient*, 1962, 50(2): 229–74; Seishi Karashima, 'Stūpas Described in the Chinese Translations of the Vinayas', *Annual Report of The International Research Institute for Advanced Buddhology*, 2018, 21: 439–69.

16 For some examples of stupa care from *Mūlasarvāstivāda* sources, see Ulrich Pagel, 'Stūpa Festivals in Buddhist Narrative Literature', in Konrad Klaus and Jens-Uwe Hartmann (eds), *Festschrift für Michael Hahn zum 65. Geburtstag von Freunden und Schülern überreicht*, Wien: Arbeitskreis für tibetische und buddhistische Studien Universität Wien, 2007, pp. 369–94 (pp. 389ff).

17 For example, the self-explanatorily entitled 'Avadāna of the Gandhāran King Who Repaired a Stupa to Obtain Longevity' (乾陀衛國王治故塔寺得延命緣) of

the *Zabaozang jing* 雜寶藏經, translated in 472 CE by Kekaya 吉迦夜 and Tan-yao 曇曜, T 203. 1469a6–13.

18 In the *Śrīmatyāvadāna* of the Skt. *Avadānaśataka*, King Ajātaśatru bans the dedication of any gift-worthy objects (*deyadharma*) and removes the taxes (*kāra*) allotted to the hair-and-nail stupa of the Buddha that had been organised by his father King Bimbisāra. A woman of the inner court named Śrīmatī transgresses the ruler's diktat and makes offerings to the stupa. Av-ś 54. 307–308, *Avadānaśataka: A Century of Edifying Tales Belonging to the Hīnayāna*, ed. J. S. Speyer, The Hague: Mouton & Co, 1958, pp. 307–8.

19 The *Śroṇakoṭīkarṇāvadāna* relates that the caravan leader Śroṇakoṭīkarṇa in a past life used the surplus wealth he had garnered whilst trading on the Northern Road (*uttarāpatha*) to repair the breaks and cracks (*khaṇḍasphuṭa*) on Buddha Kāśyapa's stupa. This was necessary because King Sujāta had removed the dedicated taxes and tolls (*karapratyāya*) from the eastern gate of Varanasi previously allotted by his father King Kṛkin. MSV 4. 190–193, *Gilgit Manuscripts,* vol. IV, ed. Nalinaksha Dutt, Calcutta: Calcutta Oriental Press, 1959, pp. 190–3; Divy 1. 22–23, *The Divyāvadāna: A Collection of Buddhist Legends. Now First Edited from the Nepalese Mss in Cambridge and Paris*, eds. E. B. Cowell and R. A. Neil, Cambridge: Cambridge University Press, 1886, pp. 22–3.

20 Kevin Trainor, 'When Is a Theft Not a Theft? Relic Theft and the Cult of the Buddha's Relics in Sri Lanka', *Numen*, 1992, 39(1): 1–26.

21 Vin 3. 41–67, *The Vinaya Piṭakaṃ: One of the Principal Buddhist Holy Scriptures in the Pāli Language. Vol III. The Suttavibhaṅga*, ed. Hermann Oldenberg, London: Williams and Norgate, 1881, pp. 41–67.

22 Trainor, 'Relic Theft', p. 9ff. Monika Zin gives another case of circumvention regarding the 1st century BCE establishment of the Kanaganahalli stupa by King Chimukha, founder of the Satavāhanas. One inscription at the site implies he was gifted a portion of relics by the *nāga* king, which, she suggests, was perhaps inspired by a certain version of the *Aśokāvadāna* found in the *Za ahan jing* 雜阿含經 (*Saṃyuktāgama*), in which the *nāgas* of Rāmagrāma gift the relics to Aśoka, T 99. 165. 16–17. Monika Zin, *The Kanaganahalli Stūpa: An Analysis of the 60 Massive Slabs Covering the Dome*, New Delhi: Aryan Books International, 2018, pp. 132–4.

23 Similar passages occur in the *Sifen lu* 四分律 (**Dharmaguptakavinaya*), T 1428. 766c3–23; *'The Discipline in Four Parts': Rules for the Nuns According to the Dharmaguptakavinaya. Part II. Translation*, trans. Ann Heirman, New Delhi: Motilal Banarsidass, 2002, pp. 879–80; and in the *Mūlasarvāstivādavinayakṣudrakavastu*, Derge 'dul ba Da 172b2–174b5; see Gregory Schopen, 'The Suppression of Nuns and the Ritual Murder of Their Special Dead in Two Buddhist Monastic Texts', *Journal of Indian Philosophy*, 1996, 24(6): 563–92 (pp. 562ff).

24 Vin 4. 308–309, *The Vinaya Piṭakaṃ: One of the Principal Buddhist Holy Scriptures in the Pāli Language. Vol IV. The Suttavibhaṅga*, ed. Hermann Oldenberg, London: Williams and Norgate, 1882.

25 T 1435. Translated in the Latter Qin Period 後秦 (385–417 CE) by Kumārajīva 鳩摩羅什, Puṇyatāra 弗若多羅 and Dharmaruci 曇摩流支, and revised by Vimalākṣa 卑摩羅叉. For details, see Clarke, 'Vinayas', pp. 70–2.

26 See also, T 1440. 517a12.

27 又問：若盗佛舍利得何罪。答曰：偷蘭遮。若尊敬心作是念，佛亦我師，清淨心取無罪。T 1435. 380a2–4. The commentary of Daoxuan 道宣 (d. 667 CE), the *Sifen lu shanfan buque xingshi cao* 四分律刪繁補闕行事鈔 ('The **Dharmaguptakavinaya*: An Abbreviated and Amended Summary of Observances'), preserves a punned version of the reading: 'Stealing relics in the **Sarvāstivādavinaya*:

"With a pure intention to perform worship, one thinks, saying: "You are indeed the teacher, I am indeed the teacher"'. Thinking in this manner there is no crime'. 十誦中偸舍利。並淨心供養自作念言：彼亦是師，我亦是師。如是意者無犯。T 1804. 55c6–8. A commentary on the same passage in the *Bonmō kaihon sho nichishushō* 梵網戒本疏日珠鈔 of Gyōnen 凝然 (d. 1321) agrees with the **Sarvāstivādavinaya* and adds that the relics should not have an owner. T 2246. 86b3–4.

28 T 1441. Translated in 435 CE by Saṃghavarma 僧伽跋摩. For details, see Clarke, 'Vinayas', p. 81.

29 'Full' (滿) is an abbreviation for 'full five *māṣa*' (滿五錢), see T 1441. 613a28; T 1425. 430b29—c3.

30 *Qian* 钱 ('coin'). The *māṣa* (P. *masa*), literally meaning 'bean', is a unit of weight found in all *Vinayas* concerning matters of wealth and transactions. Regulations are variable and oftentimes complex, dependent, for instance, on the nature of the capital (e.g., items belonging to an individual, stupa, or monastery, or tolls issued by monasteries on merchants). Specifically in the case of theft, several *Vinayas* state that if one steals an item valuing five or more *māṣa* it is a *pārājika*, if less than five it is a *sthūlātyaya*, and if one or less it is a *duṣkṛta*. In addition to an object's value, questions of ownership, the intentionality of the thief, and whether the stolen goods were separated from their original location are all factored into the equation when determining the appropriate punishment. See, for instance, T 1440. 517a11–20. This matter needs further research; for a brief discussion, see *The Book of Discipline (Vinaya-Piṭaka) Vol. I (Suttavibhaṅga)*, trans. I. B. Horner, London: Luzac and Company, 1949, p. xxii. That the unit is common to all *Vinayas* from distinct periods and geographies indicates it derives from an early period of textual composition. Originally, the value of a *māṣa* was attached to currency—19 or 20 *māṣa* were equal to one *kārṣāpaṇa* (P. *kahāpaṇa*, Ch. *jilishapan* 罽利沙槃)—and systems of civil law and punishment regarding theft. T 1425. 242c22–23; *The Vinaya Piṭakaṃ, Vol. III*, ed. Oldenberg, p. 45. However, the value eventually became purely emblematic and was transmitted without being adjusted to contextual metrological or economic standards.

31 Daoxuan comments: The *Sarvāstivāda[vinayavibhāṣā]* [see T 1440. 517a10–12] says, 'this means to sell them on.' 薩婆多云：謂轉賣者。T 1804. 55c8–9.

32 Three prints (as well as Gyōnen's commentary) read 僧惡取 ('monk takes with unwholesomeness'); another has 憎惡取 ('taking with hostility').

33 取佛舍利有主，若爲自活偸，滿，波羅夷，不滿，偸羅遮。若增惡取彼我俱無偸羅遮。若爲供養故，　佛是我師，我應供養，滿五錢，突吉羅。T 1441. 612b5–9.

34 In the lines preceding the regulation on relic theft (see fn. 26), the **Sarvāstivādavinayavibhāṣā* also discusses the theft of Buddha-images and sutras in such terms, whereby the severity of the theft is again calculated according to whether the object is stolen for the sake of worship, to make money, and how much it was sold for. T 1440. 517a9–12. On stealing a Buddha-image with relics, see fn. 35.

35 A related case concerning the specific matter of stealing a Buddha image that has relics also arises in the *Mūlasarvāstivādavinaya* preserved in Chinese and Tibetan. I quote a passage from the *Genben shuo yiqieyoubu pinaiye* 根本說一切有部毘奈耶 (**Mūlasarvāstivādanikayavinayavibhaṅga*), translated by Yijing 義淨 (d. 713 CE): If an image has relics, and [one] takes it, it is a *pātayantika* ('offence causing one to fall'); without relics it is a *duskṛta*. If [one] produces a thought of the Great Teacher, taking is not a crime. 若像有舍利，　執得墮罪；

無舍利者惡作。若作大師想，持者無犯。T 1442. 847a2–3. See also, T 1443. 988c6–7. The Tibetan reads: If a monk steals a statue together with relics, he incurs a *pātayantika*. If the statue is without relics, it is a *duṣkṛta*. dge slong gis sku gzugs len na sku gdung dang bcas pa len na ltung byed du 'gyur la | sku gdung med pa len na ñes byas su 'gyur ro || sDe dge'i bka' 'gyur, 'Dul ba Ja 241a1.

In these cases, stealing a Buddha image with relics is deemed a *pātayantika*, an offence which, in line with former prohibitions of destruction and theft, 'cause one to fall' into hell if not expiated before the monastic community. A verse summary in the *Genben shuo yiqieyoubu pinaiye song* 根本說一切有部毘奈耶頌 (**Mūlasarvāstivādanikayavinayakārika*) clarifies: '[Taking] an image etc., which has a relic, at the time of contact produces a base crime (Skt. *mūlāpatti*). If there are no bones, at the moment of contact it is a *duṣkṛta*.' 像等有舍利，觸時得本罪。若無身骨者，觸時便惡作。T 1459. 641a18–19. The commentary, *Genbensapoduo bu lu she*根本薩婆多部律攝 (**Mūlasarvāstivādanikāyavinayas aṃgraha*), attributed to Viśeṣamitra 勝友 (c. 7th century CE) and translated by Yijing 義淨, states: 'Someone who steals relics of the Fortunate One to protect [them], intending to perform worship and producing a thought of the Great Teacher commits a *duṣkṛta*.' 盜設利羅，世尊駄都，有人守護意欲供養。作大師想者。犯惡作罪。T 1458. 535b17–18. One conceivable context for which this regulation may have been devised is the case of Buddha images from the Indic Northwest or China, many of which have small recesses under the *uṣṇīṣa* that are conjectured by some to have contained relics. For further discussion, see Juhyung Rhi, 'Images, Relics, and Jewels: The Assimilation of Images in the Buddhist Relic Cult of Gandhāra: Or Vice Versa', *Artibus Asiae*, 2005, 65(2): 169–211.

36 T 1476. Translated by Guṇavarman 求那跋摩during the reign of Emperor Songwen 宋文帝 (424–453 CE) in the Liusong 劉宋 Period.

37 *Hui* 悔 (lit. 'remorse'). Potentially in the etymological sense of 'misdeed', see Franklin Edgerton, *Buddhist Hybrid Sanskrit Grammar and Dictionary*, New Haven: Yale University Press, 1977, s.v. *kaukṛtya*.

38 若有居士以盜心偷舍利，犯中可悔。若以恭敬心而作是念，　　佛亦我師，清淨心取者無犯。T 1476. 942a29—b2.

39 T 1435. 445c11–447a11. For a synopsis and comparative analysis of this and other major witnesses of the *Mahāparinirvāṇasūtra* in Chinese, Pali and Sanskrit, see Ernst Waldschmidt, *Die Überlieferung vom Lebensende des Buddha. Eine vergleichende Analyse des Mahāparinirvāṇasūtra und seiner Textentsprechungen, zweite Teil, Vorgangsgruppe V-VI*, Göttingen: Vandenhoeck & Ruprecht, 1948, pp. 289ff.

40 On these proceedings, see John Strong, 'The Buddha's Funeral', in Bryan J. Cuevas and Jacquelin I. Stone (eds), *The Buddhist Dead: Practices, Discourses, Representations*, Honolulu: Kuroda Institute University of Hawaii Press, 2007, pp. 32–59.

41 On the potentially collective nature of relic dedications, see Matthew Milligan, 'Corporate Bodies in Early South Asian Buddhism: Some Relics and Their Sponsors According to Epigraphy', *Religions*, 2019, 10(4).

42 爾時阿闍世王勅其大臣婆羅門婆利沙迦羅言：汝往到拘尸城諸力士所。持我言致問無量：氣力安隱身心樂不。又語諸人：佛亦我師，我之所尊。今於汝國般涅槃。請分舍利，欲於王舍城中起塔供養。與我者善。若不見與，當舉兵衆以力奪汝。受勅即嚴四種兵直至拘尸城。T 1453. 446b17–25.

43 On the 'war of the relics' as a narrative trope, see John Strong, *Relics of the Buddha*, New Delhi: Motilal Banarsidass, 2004, pp. 116–21.

44 佛初般涅槃後，起十塔，自是已後，起無量塔。T 1435. 447a11.

45 A synopsis and comparative analysis of the major witnesses can be found at Jean Przyluski, *La légende de l'Empéreur Açoka (Aćoka-Avadāna) dans les textes Indiens et Chinois*, Paris: Paul Geuthner, 1923. For a study and translation of the Skt., see John Strong, *The Legend of King Aśoka. A Study and Translation of the Aśokāvadāna*, Princeton: Princeton University Press, 1983.

46 See also Strong, *Relics of the Buddha*, pp. 132–6.

47 The various versions of the *Aśokāvadāna* are broadly similar in their recount of the episode, although their language regarding the matter of destruction and theft ranges from the gentle to the brutal, cf. Aś-av 52; T 99. 165a13–16; T 2043. 135a3–7.

48 A quality made explicit in another witness of the *Mahāparinirvāṇasūtra* extant in the *Genben shuo yiqieyou bu pinaiye zashi*根本說一切有部毘奈耶雜事 (**Mūlasa rvāstivādanikāyavinayakṣudrakavastu*), whose close anticipates Aśoka's destruction of the Droṇa-stupas and acquisition of the relics. T 1451. 400b24–402c4.

49 For recent discussion, cf. Harry Falk, 'The Fate of Aśoka's Donations at Lumbinī', in Patrick Olivelle, Janice Leoschko, and Himanshu Prabha Ray (eds), *Reimagining Aśoka: Memory and History*, New Delhi: Oxford University Press, 2012, pp. 204–16; Skilling, 'Relics: The Heart of Buddhist Veneration', p. 11ff.

50 Sraman Mukherjee, 'Between Religion and History: Afterlives of Buddhist Relics', *The Newsletter*, International Institute for Asian Studies, 2013, 66: 54. For analyses of relic distribution and commodification during the colonial period, see Himanshu Prabha Ray, 'Narratives of Faith: Buddhism and Colonial Archaeology in Monsoon Asia', *Asia Research Institute Working Paper Series*, 2007, 99: 1–42 (pp. 29–35); Frederik M. Asher, 'Travels of a Reliquary, Its Contents Separated at Birth', *South Asian Studies*, 2012, 28(2): 147–56.

51 In a letter composed in 1899, a year after the relics unearthed at Piprawah Kot were transferred to the king of Siam, W. Hoey, the Officiating Commissioner to the Government of the North-Western Provinces and Oudh, reflects: 'On this occasion we cannot but recall the gathering of rival kings who were prepared to fight at Kusinara for the cremated body of the great preacher of peace. . . . Reflecting on these bygone days we are entitled to congratulate ourselves that we live in an age of toleration and of wide sympathy with the faiths which others profess. As a practical illustration of this sympathy the present memorable occasion [i.e., the transfer of relics] loses none of its significance.' Fully quoted in Ray, 'Narratives of Faith', p. 33. Parentheses are my own.

52 E. Zürcher, *The Buddhist Conquest of China: The Spread and Adaptation of Buddhism in Early Medieval China*, 3rd edn., Leiden: Brill, 2007, pp. 277–80. Ensuing periods saw this pattern repeated by several Chinese emperors. For instance, Wendi 文帝 of the Sui 隨 also exercised this strategy to secure unity across his empire, engineering it so that a total of 30 relic stupas were established on the day of his birthday in 601 CE. Kenneth Ch'en, *Buddhism in China: A Historical Survey*, Princeton: Princeton University Press, 1964, pp. 199–201. Several later attempts were also made at stealing relics from sites associated with Aśoka, see Bernard Faure, 'Relics and Flesh Bodies: The Creation of Ch'an Pilgrimage Sites', in Susan Naquin and Chun-fang Yü (eds), *Pilgrimage and Sacred Sites in China*, Berkeley: University of California Press, 1992, pp. 150–89 (pp. 174ff). For further examples, see Max Deeg, 'From the Iron Wheel to Bodhisatvahood', in Patrick Olivelle (ed), *Aśoka in History and Historical Memory*, New Delhi: Motilal Banarsidass, 2009, pp. 109–44 (pp. 19ff).

53 For a catalogue of reliquaries and associated objects, see David Jongeward, 'Survey of Gandhāran Reliquaries', in David Jongeward et al. (eds), *Gandharan*

Buddhist Reliquaries, Seattle: Early Buddhist Manuscripts Project, 2012, pp. 39–110.

54 Table 4.1: No. 9, 33, 37, 50, 51. See fn. 55 for details.

55 All inscriptions are numbered (No. 1–70) chronologically, as far as possible, and analysed socio-historically in Tab One. Note the proposed chronology is not absolute. Cf. Stefan Baums, 'A Framework for Gandhāran Chronology Based on Relic Inscriptions', in Rienjang Wannaporn and Peter Stewart (eds), *Problems of Chronology in Gandhāran Art: Proceedings of the First International Workshop of the Gandhāra Connections Project, University of Oxford, 23rd—24th March, 2017*, Oxford: Archaeopress Archaeology, 2018, pp. 53–70. References to inscriptions are given according to the 'Catalog of Kharoṣṭhī Inscriptions' (CKI) at Stefan Baums and Andrew Glass, 'Catalog of Gāndhārī Texts', 2002–2019, https://gandhari.org/catalog.

56 For an overview of relevant relief art, see David Jongeward, 'The Buddha's Last Days as Portrayed in Gandharan Sculpture', in David Jongeward et al. (eds), *Gandharan Buddhist Reliquaries*, Seattle: Early Buddhist Manuscripts Project, 2012, pp. 9–38.

57 Mahmood ul-Hasan, 'Depiction of Asoka Raja in the Buddhist Art of Gandhara', *Journal of the Research Society of Pakistan*, 2017, 54(2): 155–62.

58 For instance, two verse addenda to the Skt. *Mahāparinirvāṇasūtra* and P. *Mahāparinibbānasutta*, locate one eye-tooth relic (*daṃṣṭracatuṣka*) in a town in Gandhāra. MPS 51.24, *Das Mahāparinirvāṇa-sūtra: Text in Sanskrit und Tibetisch, verglichen mit dem Pāli; nebst einer Übersetzung der chinesischen Entsprechung im Vinaya der Mūlasarvāstivādins. Teil I-III*, ed. Ernst Waldschmidt, Berlin, 1950; DN 2. 167–168.

59 Aś-av 54–55.

60 John Marshall dates the stupa to the Mauryan Period purely on architectural form, admitting the conclusion is not founded on any firm material evidence. John Marshall, *Taxila. An Illustrated Account of Archaeological Excavations Carried Out at Taxila Under the Orders of the Government in India Between the Years 1913 and 1934, vol. 1., Structural Remains*, Cambridge: Cambridge University Press, 1951, p. 236.

61 Robert Göbl, *A Catalogue of Coins from Butkara I (Swāt, Pakistan)*, ed. Domenico Faccenna, Rome: Instituto italiano per il medio ed estremo oriente and Centro studi e scavi archeologici in Asia, 1976, p. 11 no. 3, Pl. 1.

62 Elizabeth Errington, 'Numismatic Evidence for Dating the Buddhist Remains of Gandhāra', *Silk Road Art and Archaeology*, 1999, 6: 191–216 (pp. 191–2). In the case of Butkara I, Domenico Faccenna maintains that the earliest stratum (GSt. 1) is to be dated to the Mauryan Period. Domenico Faccenna, 'At the Origin of Gandharan Art. The Contribution of the IsIAO Italian Archaeological Mission in the Swat Valley Pakistan', *Ancient Civilisations*, 2003, 9(3/4): 277–380 (p. 279).

63 See Appendix 1 in Errington, 'Numismatic Evidence', pp. 211–13.

64 Three mention the Dharmarājikā at Taxila: CKI 218, 60 and 68. Another is mentioned at Aüdiya, CKI 465, as well as one at Thulabrayaa, CKI 556, and one at Trama, CKI 256. A. Dharmarājikā is also referred to in one Kharoṣṭhī manuscript dated to the early Common Era. Timothy Lenz, 'Ephemeral Dharma: Magical Hope', *Bulletin of the Asia Institute*, 2009, 23: 135–42 (p. 138ff).

65 A. Dharmarājikā is recorded in an inscription at Mathurā, dated 34 Huviṣka (=161/162 CE). Harry Falk, 'A New Kuṣāṇa Bodhisattva from the Time of Huviṣka [2 Figures]', *Annual Report of The International Research Institute for Advanced Buddhology*, 2012, 15: 13–18 (p. 13).

66 Strong, *The Legend of King Aśoka*, pp. 26ff; Deeg, 'From the Iron Wheel to Bodhisatvahood', p. 4.

67 Av[L4] 223–230r; a parallel is to be found in the *Da zhuangyan lun jing* 大莊嚴論經 (**Kalpanāmaṇḍitikā*), attributed to Aśvaghoṣa馬鳴 (c. 2nd century CE) and translated by Kumārajīva 鳩摩羅什 (d. 416 CE), T 201. 285c6–287, see Timothy Lenz, 'The British Library Kharoṣṭhī Fragments: Behind the Birch Bark Curtain', in Alice Collett (ed), *Women in Early Indian Buddhism: Comparative Textual Studies*, Oxford: Oxford University Press, 2014, pp. 46–61.

68 Aśoka occurs in one narrative, T 204. 501a1–15. For a complete translation of this work, see Akira Sadakata (定方晟), '『雑譬喩経』訳注 (Japanese Translation of Tsa-p'i-yü-ching)', 東海大学紀要. 文学部 (Bulletin of the Faculty of Letters of Tokai University), 1989, 51: 47–55. According to Karashima Seishi the attested translator is incorrect and the work is more likely a product of the 3rd century. 'The Avadāna Anthology from Merv, Turkmenistan', in Seishi Karashima and M. I. Vorobyova-Desyatovskaya (eds), *The St. Petersburg Sanskrit Fragments*, Tokyo: The Institute of Oriental Manuscripts of the Russian Academy of Sciences and The International Research Institute for Advanced Buddhology, 2015, pp. 145–524 (p. 343).

69 Aśoka occurs in *avadānas* five, six, and seven, T 205. 503a19—c20. The seventh dates Aśoka to 100 years after the Buddha's *parinirvāṇa*, which indicates perhaps it stems from a Sarvāstivāda institutional context. T 205. 503b17.

70 T 204. 501a6–9. For art-historical witnesses, see Fig. 110–111, Harald Ingholt, *Gandharan Art in Pakistan*, New York: Pantheon Books, 1957; Fig. 351–359, I. Kurita, *Gandhāran Art. I: The Buddha's Life Story*, Tokyo: Nigensha, 2003. It is possible these reliefs depict the Kuṣāṇa ruler Kaniṣka I, whose own narrative cycle includes this episode in the Buddha's journey along the Northern Road in the *Bhaiṣajyavastu* of the *Mūlasarvāstivādavinaya*, see MSV 1. 2, *Gilgit Manuscripts*, vol. III, part I-IV, ed. Nalinaksha Dutt, Srinigar: Calcutta Oriental Press, 1942.

71 T 205. 503b4.

72 T 205. 503b2–16; summarised in Przyluski, *La Légende de l'Empereur Açoka*, pp. 189–90. There is only one possible depiction of Aśoka's engagement with the *nāgas* to acquire relics and it is not patent as to whether he was successful or not. See Fig. 530, Kurita, *Gandhāran Art*; ul-Hasan, 'Depiction of Asoka Raja', pp. 163–5.

73 T 205. 503a19—b1. Although Aśoka's Dharmarājikās have not been identified in art, other related events, such as his collection of the relics and political subjugation of the Mallas, are present. *Ibid*, pp. 162–3.

74 Cf. Aś-av 134–135; T 99. 181b17—c8; T 2042. 111b28—c26; T 2043. 149a15–29.

75 T 2042. 126c1–7. *Ayu wang zhuan* 阿育王傳, translated by Anfaqin 安法欽 in 306 CE. The attested date of this work has been questioned and it is now regarded as being a post-4th century composition. Antonello Palumbo, 'From Constantine the Great to Emperor Wu of the Liang: The Rhetoric of Imperial Conversion and the Divisive Emergence of Religious Identities in Late Antique Eurasia', in Arietta Papaconstantinou, Neil McLynn, and Daniel L. Schwartz (eds), *Conversion in Late Antiquity: Christianity, Islam, and Beyond, Papers from the Andrew W. Mellon Foundation Sawyer Seminar, University of Oxford, 2009–2010*, Farnham: Ashgate, 2015, pp. 95–122 (pp. 111–12).

76 T 99. 177c10–16, *Za ahan jing* 雜阿含經, translated by Guṇabhadra 求那跋陀 in 502 CE.

77 Jan Nattier, *Once Upon a Future Time: Studies in a Buddhist Prophecy of Decline*, Berkeley: Asian Humanities Press, 1991, pp. 224–7.

78 *Ibid*, pp. 155ff.

79 See Av[L1] 182; Av[L7] 9v, Timothy Lenz, *Gandhāran Avadānas: British Library Kharoṣṭhī Fragments 1–3 and 21 and Supplementary Fragments A—C*, Seattle: University of Washington Press, 2010; Av[L6] 53–54, *idem*, *A New Version of the Gāndhārī Dharmapada and a Collection of Previous-Birth Stories: British Library Kharoṣṭhī Fragments 16 + 25*, Seattle: University of Washington Press, 2003, p. 183. Summarised in *idem*, 'Ephemeral Dharma; Magical Hope'. For related sentiments in the Gāndhārī Mahāyānasūtra, see MSū[B] 7r9–11, Ingo Strauch, 'More Missing Pieces of Early Pure Land Buddhism: New Evidence for Akṣobhya and Abhirati in an Early Mahayana Sutra from Gandhāra', *The Eastern Buddhist*, 2010, 41(1): 23–66 (p. 28).

80 Examples of structural development and destruction at several stupa sites are given in Errington, 'Numismatic Evidence'. On the destruction of sites for later periods, see also Giovanni Verardi, 'Buddhism in North-Western India and Eastern Afghanistan, Sixth to Ninth Century AD', *ZINBUN*, 2012, 43: 146–83.

81 For instance, a deposit of 44 coins (dated post-4th century CE) was found in niche Q1 of Butkara I. Domenico Faccenna, Robert Göbl, and Mohammad Ashraf Khan, 'A Report on the Recent Discovery of a Deposit of Coins in the Sacred Area of Butkara I (Swat, Pakistan)', *East and West*, 1993, 43(1/4): 95–114.

82 See, however, destruction by lightning in a following note.

83 One pertinent example arises in John Marshall's analysis of a 'great conflagration' in the procession path at the Dharmarājikā, Taxila, which he dates to the 1st–2nd century CE. He reports the fire did not affect the main stupa (a sign it was accidental) but that it did cause the 'scorched, calcined, and shattered condition of the stonework on the inner faces of these early shrines' which 'can only be explained on the hypothesis that timber and other inflammables were piled up against the sides of the structure'. However, he ultimately discards the possibility of political vandalism on the largely unfounded premise that 'we know of no anti-Buddhist foes at Taxila during this period'. Marshall, *Structural Remains*, p. 250. In another potential case of vandalism, Kurt Behrendt identifies three phases of 'sculptural recontextualisation' in which fragments of sculpture were used to repair stupa sites. In the first phases he observes that following the destruction of schist sculpture in the c. 1st–3rd centuries CE, stucco was introduced as the medium. Despite correlations between the usage of new sculptural technologies and the formation of political power, he attributes *all* such processes of reuse to earthquakes, discounting intentional iconoclasm. Kurt Behrendt, 'The Ancient Reuse and Recontextualisation of Gandharan Images: Second to Seventh Centuries CE', *Gandhāran Studies*, 2010, 2: 17–38.

84 I refer the reader to my doctoral thesis, Henry Albery, 'Buddhism and Society in the Indic North and Northwest, c. 2nd Century BCE—3rd Century CE' (Ludwig-Maximilians-Universität, München, forthcoming).

85 No. 1–3 (No. 1 discussed in a following section).

86 No. 4–24.

87 No. 25–31.

88 No. 32–70.

89 Two possess the general monk's title *śramaṇa*, No. 40, and nun's title *bhikṣuṇī*, No. 50.

90 These include a 'great seer' (*maharṣi*) and 'narrator of the Dharma (*dharmakathika*), No. 5; and 'instructor' (*upadhyāya*), No. 10.

91 One unique title, 'protector of the stupa' (*stūpapāla*), occurs, No. 37. More common are the 'overseer of new constructions' (*navakarmika*) No. 10, 14, 25, 54, 63; 'overseer of new stupa constructions' (*stūpanavakarmika*), No. 25;

and 'overseer of new fire hall constructions' (*agniśāla-navakarmika*), No. 68. In these cases, it is not clear whether the individual is a monastic. In texts, the monastic *navakarmika* is allocated responsibility over the financial affairs and general upkeep of a monastic complex and stupa. Jonathan Silk, *Managing Monks: Administrators and Administrative Roles in Indian Buddhist Monasticism*, Oxford: Oxford University Press, 2008, pp. 27–30, 87.

92 No. 24.

93 No. 40.

94 No. 66–67.

95 No. 8, 30, 32.

96 No. 15, 42, 61, 68.

97 Cf. No. 30. This inscription, found on a circular steatite bowl, stipulates that it was dedicated in the reign of the Indo-Parthian suzerain Avakaśa (Gk. Αβδαγασις) and the Apracarāja 'general' (*stratega*; Gk. *στρατηγός*) Aśpavarma (see fn. 115). Some regard this section of the inscription on the inside of the bowl to be a fake. Akira Sadakata, 'Inscriptions kharoṣṭhī provenant du marché aux antiquités de Peshawar', *Journal asiatique*, 1996, 284: 301–24 (p. 308ff).

98 No. No. 2–3, 8, 14, 37.

99 No. 4, 10, 15, 21, 24, 29, 32, 52, 54, 69.

100 Jihoṇika (Gk. gen. Ζειονισου) issued a series of bilingual Kharoṣṭhī and Greek coinage in silver as satrap (Gk. gen. *Σατραπου*) as well as in copper as great satrap. See Typ. 879–886, Michael Mitchiner, *Indo-Greek and Indo-Scythian Coinage*, London: Hawkins Publications, 1976; Typ. 973–974, Osmund Bopearachchi and Aman Rahman ur, *Pre-Kushana Coins in Pakistan*, Paris: Iftikhar Rasul IRM Associates, 1995.

101 CKI 63. For the excavation report, see Marshall, *Structural Remains*, pp. 150–7.

102 Av^{L2} 1–7. Lenz, *Gandhāran Avadānas*, pp. 96ff.

103 *Ibid*, p. 98.

104 No. 37, [40], [43].

105 No. 54, [68].

106 No. 66.

107 Joe Cribb, 'Kaniṣka's Buddha Coins—The Official Iconography of Śākyamuni and Maitreya', *Journal of the International Association of Buddhist Studies*, 1980, 3(2): 79–88.

108 Max Deeg, 'Aśoka—Model Ruler without Name?' in Patrick Olivelle, Janice Leoschko, and Himanshu Prabha Ray (eds), *Reimagining Aśoka: Memory and History*, New Delhi: Oxford University Press, 2012, pp. 362–79 (p. 359ff); Deeg, 'From the Iron Wheel to Bodhisatvahood', pp. 13–14.

109 See MSV 1. 2–3. Two Chinese travel accounts of Faxian 法顯 (d. 418–423 CE), the *Gaoseng faxian zhuan* 高僧法顯傳, and Xuanzang 玄奘 (d. 664 CE), the *Da tang xiyu jing* 大唐西域記, place Kaniṣka I's stupa in Peshawar. T 2085. 858b9–17; T 2087. 379c. The Shah-ji-ki-Dheri Stupa is often associated with the stupa built by Kaniṣka I, although no such evidence has been found. Cf. No. 68; D. B. Spooner, 'Excavations at Shāh-Jī-Kī-Dhērī', in *Annual Report 1908–9, Archaeological Survey of India*, Calcutta: Superintendent Government Printing, India, 1912, pp. 38–59. For associated relief-art, see fn. 70.

110 'Fierce Kaniṣka'. Parallel to Caṇḍāśoka ('Fierce Aśoka') in the Aś-av prior to his establishing the Dharmarājikās. On this term, see Deeg, 'Aśoka—Model Ruler without Name?' p. 362.

111 See the *Maming pusa zhuan* 馬鳴菩薩傳, T 2046. 183c17–184a; and *Fufazang yinyuan zhuan* 付法藏因緣傳, T 2058. 315b10–11. For a discussion and translation of the relevant passages, see Shoshin Kuwayama, *Across the Hindukush*

of the First Millenium. A Collection of the Papers, Kyoto: Institute for Research in Humanities, Kyoto University, 2002, pp. 32–3.
112 No. 7–9, 13–14, 17–18, 21–22, 24–25, 28–30.
113 No. 34–37.
114 A lack of provenance for objects associated with the Apracarājas and Oḍirājas hinders determining their precise spheres of governance. Richard Salomon, 'Dynastic and Institutional Connections in the Pre- and Early Kuṣāṇa, 'Period: New Manuscript and Epigraphic Evidence', in Doris Meth Srinivasan (ed), *On the Cusp of an Era: Art in the Pre-Kuṣāṇa World*, Leiden: Brill, 2007, pp. 267–86.
115 One Kharoṣṭhī manuscript mentions the Apracarāja *stratega* Aśpavarma (see fn. 97) in a 'Second Avadāna of Zadamitra' in connection with constructing a 'rain residence' (Skt. *varṣakara*). Av^{L1} v185–204, Lenz, *Gandhāran Avadānas*. For the Oḍirājas, see the following section.
116 On this issue, see Richard Salomon, 'Gandharan Reliquary Inscriptions', in David Jongeward et al. (eds), *Gandharan Buddhist Reliquaries*, Seattle: Early Buddhist Manuscripts Project, 2012, pp. 164–99 (p. 170).
117 This is characteristic of later finds from Afghanistan, dateable to no earlier than the Kuṣāṇa Period. Elizabeth Errington, *Charles Masson and the Buddhist Sites of Afghanistan: Explorations, Excavations, Collections 1832–1835*, London: The British Museum, 2017, pp. 148–9; 192; 208. An alternative explanation for animal bone is that these were regarded as relics of the Bodhisatva from his previous existences as an animal. Elizabeth Errington, 'The Buddhist Remains of Passani and Bimaran and Related Relic Deposits from South-Eastern Afghanistan in the Masson Collection of the British Library', in Janice Stargardt and Michael Willis (eds), *Relics and Relic Worship in Early Buddhism: India, Afghanistan, Sri Lanka and Burma*, London: The British Museum, 2018, pp. 31–46 (p. 37).
118 Wannaporn Rienjang, 'Honouring the Body: Relic Cult Practice in Eastern Afghanistan with Comparison to Dharmarajika Pakistan' (University of Cambridge, 2017), pp. 307ff.
119 David W. Mac Dowall, 'The Chronological Evidence of Coins in Stūpa Deposits', in Maurizio Taddei and Pierfrancesco Callieri (eds), *South Asian Archaeology 1987. Proceedings of the Ninth International Conference of the Association of South Asian Archaeologists in Western Europe, Held in the Fondazione Giorgio Cini, Island of San Giorgio, Venice. Part 2*, Roma: Instituto italiano per il medio ed estremo oriente, 1990, pp. 727–35. For specific cases, see Marshall, *Structural Remains*, pp. 271–3; Elizabeth Errington, 'Gandhara Stupa Deposits', *Arts of Asia*, 1998, 28: 80–7 (p. 87); Errington, 'The Buddhist Remains of Passani and Bimaran', p. 44.
120 No. [1] 9, [27] 33, [48] 51.
121 No. 13, [34], 37.
122 No. 31, 52. Richard Salomon, 'The Rededication of Buddhist Reliquaries: A Clue to the Interpretation of Problematic Kharoṣṭhī Inscriptions', in Raymond Allchin and Bridget Allchin (eds), *South Asian Archaeology 1995: Proceedings of the 13th Conference of the European Association of South Asian Archaeologists, Cambridge, 5–9 July, 1995*, New Delhi: Science Publishers, 1997, pp. 365–76.
123 For details, see N. G. Majumdar, 'The Bajaur Casket of the Reign of Menander', *Epigraphica Indica*, 1937, 24: 1–8.
124 Much of the discussion regarding periodisation is contingent on highly debatable palaeographic evidence. This has produced significant fluctuations in

opinion, in some cases from the very same editor. Cf. Majumdar, 'The Bajaur Casket'; Sten Konow, 'New Traces of the Greeks in India', *New Indian Antiquary*, 1939, 2: 639–48; Richard Salomon, 'The "Avaca" Inscription and the Origin of the Vikrama Era', *Journal of the American Oriental Society*, 1982, 102: 59–68 (pp. 63–4); Richard Salomon, 'The Indo-Greek Era of 186/5 B.C. in a Buddhist Reliquary Inscription', in O. Bopearachchi and M. F. Boussac (eds), *Afghanistan : ancien carrefour entre l'Est et l'Ouest : actes du colloque international organisé par Christian Landes & Osmund Bopearachchi au Musée archéologique Henri-Prades-Lattes du 5 au 7 mai 2003*, Brepols: Turnhout, 2005, pp. 359–401 (p. 382); Stefan Baums, 'Catalog and Revised Texts and Translations of Gandharan Reliquary Inscriptions', in David Jongeward et al. (eds), *Gandharan Buddhist Reliquaries*, Seattle: Early Buddhist Manuscripts Project, 2012, pp. 200–51 (pp. 202–3). Harry Falk takes an altogether different view and regards several parts of both inscriptions to be forgeries. Harry Falk, 'The Introduction of Stūpa-Worship in Bajaur', in O. Bopearachchi and M. F. Boussac (eds), *Afghanistan, Ancient Carrefour Entre l'Est et l'Ouest*, pp. 347–57 (pp. 349–53). Salomon has refuted Falk's arguments at several levels and contends the inscriptions are genuine. Richard Salomon, 'The Fine of Art of Forgery in India', in Gérard Colas and Gerdi Gerschheimer (eds), *Écrire et transmettre en Inde classique*, Paris: École française d'Extrême-Orient, 2009, pp. 107–34 (p. 128ff).

125 No. 1.

126 No. 9.

127 No. 47. For a full edition and translation, see Baums, 'Catalog', p. 202.

128 On the potential association between dividing relics into balls and the *śrāddhā* ritual, see Strong, 'The Buddha's Funeral', p. 47. For associated depictions in relief art from the Northwest, see Fig. 516–520, Kurita, *Gandhāran Art*.

129 Image from *Epigraphia Indica* vol. 24, Wikimedia Commons.

130 The inscription (now lost) and associated objects lack any provenance. For details, see Richard Salomon, 'The Inscription of Senavarma, King of Oḍi', *Indo-Iranian Journal*, 1986, 29: 261–93.

131 No. 34.

132 Skt. *utkṣipta* ('raised up') apparently denotes a ritual action of 'excavating' as opposed to 'depositing' (*pra-√kṣip*) relics, this latter act being referred to in several relevant textual passages concerning relic dedication. Divy 22. 327; Aś-av 53–54.

133 See Otto Böhtlingk and Rudolp Roth, *Sanskrit-Wörterbuch: Siebenter Teil* श-ह *Nebst den Verbessesrungen und Nachträgen zum ganzen Werke*, St. Petersburg: Buchdrukerei der Kaiserlichen Akadamie der Wissenschaften, 1886, s.v. *ava-√śā* ('wegnehmen').

134 No. 37. Cf. Baums, 'Catalog', pp. 227–33; Oskar von Hinüber, *Beiträge zur Erklärung der Senavarma-Inschrift*, Stuttgart: Franz Steiner Verlag, 2003, pp. 17–20.

135 Whilst visiting the Kaniṣka Stupa in the 6th century CE, Sung Yun 宋雲 states it was repaired, having been thrice burnt by lightning. T 2092. 1021a27—b15. See fn. 70, 109.

136 Richard Salomon and Stefan Baums, 'Sanskrit Ikṣvāku, Pali Okkāka, and Gāndhārī Iṣmaho', *Journal of the Pali Text Society*, 2007, 29: 201–27.

137 This story is known from several Mūlasarvāstivāda works, MSV 1. 1–2, *Gilgit Manuscripts*, vol. III, Part I-IV, ed. Dutt; T 1448. 41c6; Aś-av 2.

138 T 2087. 884a19–25. For a recent translation and discussion of this and associated passages, see Max Deeg, 'Secular Buddhist Lineages: The Śākyas and

Their Royal Descendants in Local Buddhist Legitimation Strategies', *Religions of South Asia*, 2011, 5(1/2): 189–207 (esp. pp. 194–7).

139 See relief B 1217, Domenico Faccenna, *Sculptures from the Sacred Area of Butkara I (Swat, W. Pakistan)*, Rome: Istituto italiano per il Medio ed Estremo Oriente, 1964), Tav. CDLXX; S 708, Domenico Faccenna, *Il fregio figurato dello stūpa principale nell'area sacra buddhista di Saidu Sharif I (Swat, Pakistan)*, Rome: Istituto italiano per il Medio ed Estremo Oriente, 2001, Tav. 36. For others, see fig. 518–519, Kurita, *Gandhāran Art.*

140 Fragment S 241, Faccenna, *Il fregio figurato dello stūpa principale nell'area sacra buddhista di Saidu Sharif I (Swat, Pakistan)*, pp. 227–9, Tav. 20; Faccenna, 'At the Origin of Gandharan Art', p. 336.

141 On inscriptions evincing the presence of the Sarvāstivādins in Swat, see Harry Falk, '"Buddhist" Metalware from Gandhāra', *Bulletin of the Asia Institute*, 2012, 26: 33–60.

142 See fn. 70.

143 No. 37. Baums, 'Catalog', pp. 227–333.

144 The moon on the 16th day of the month Kārttika in a *pūrṇimānta* ('full moon') reckoning corresponds to the new moon in conjunction with the constellation *citrā*, to which the *vṛddhi* form *cetrika* ('of *citrā*') may pertain. For an alternative explanation, cf. *ibid*, pp. 207–8.

145 Falk, 'The Introduction of Stūpa-Worship in Bajaur', pp. 348–9. Previous editions read: *muryaka-liṇate thubute* ('from the Muryaka cave stupa'), see e.g., Richard Salomon and Gregory Schopen, 'The Indravarman Avaca Casket Inscription Reconsidered: Further Evidence for Canonical Passages in Buddhist Inscriptions', *Journal of the International Association of Buddhist Studies*, 1984, 7(1): 107–24 (pp. 108–9).

146 This term is a *bahuvrīhi* governed by *śarīra*; however, interpretations of its purport have varied wildly. Drawing on potential parallels in textual sources, Richard Salomon and Gregory Schopen suggested Skt. *kṛtaparihārika* ('for which the ritual procession has been done'). *Ibid*, pp. 112–13. Harry Falk read Skt. *kṛtaprātihārya* ('effected transfiguration', that is, by which a transfiguration was effected), associating the term with the Buddha's *yamakapāṭihārya* ('duplicate miracle'), performed by relics in the *Mahāvaṃsa*, whereby 'the relics transform themselves visibly into a form of the Buddha and demonstrate his corporeal and spiritual presence', Harry Falk, 'Another Reliquary Vase from Wardak and Consecrating Fire Rites in Gandhāra', in Claudine Bautze-Picron (ed), *Religion and Art: New Issues in Indian Iconography and Iconology*, London: The British Association for South Asian Studies, 2008, pp. 63–80 (pp. 76–7). Baums opts for the same reading but differs in his understanding of the compound, translating 'on which a miracle has been performed', Baums, 'Catalog', p. 208. Falk's interpretation is undoubtedly possible, and indeed perhaps more favourable than the one I suggest; although it is hindered by the c. 5th century CE Sri Lankan *Mahāvaṃsa* being contextually divorced from the Indic Northwest. I suggest therefore that the latter element of the compound could be interpreted as deriving from Skt. *pari-√hṛ* or *prati-√hṛ* ('to take'), producing *kṛtapārihārya, kṛtapārihārika* or *kṛtaprātihārika* ('having taken', lit. 'on which taking has been performed'), thereby construing it syntactically with the abl. *muryaka-liṇate thubute*. A possible alternative meaning of *prati-√hṛ* is 'protect' ('having protected', lit. 'on which protection was performed').

147 No. 13. Based on the full edition found in *ibid*, pp. 207–78.

148 Image courtesy of The Metropolitan Museum of Art, New York, No. 1987. 142.70a, b.

149 The Aśoraya Buddha, CKI 256. The city Trama (or Tramaṇa) is mentioned in another four inscribed relic dedications, No. 14, 19–20, 33. See Salomon, 'Dynastic and Institutional Connections in the Pre- and Early Kuṣāṇa Period', pp. 272–3.
150 No. 48 [51].
151 No. 10.
152 No. 14, 21, 24, 28.
153 No. 27 [33].
154 No. 35.
155 No. 32.
156 Cf. Salomon and Schopen, 'The Indravarman Avaca Casket Inscription Reconsidered', p. 115ff; Antonello Palumbo, *An Early Chinese Commentary on the Ekottarika-āgama: The Fenbie Gongde Lun 分别功德論 and the History of the Translation of the Zengyi Ahan Jing 增一阿含經*, Taipei: Dharma Drum Publishing Corporation, 2013, p. 286ff; Elsa Legittimo, 'Relics, Relic Worship and Stūpas in the Chinese Translation of the Ekottarika-Āgama', *Journal of Indian and Buddhist Studies*, 2009, 57(3): 1199–205. For full discussion see Albery, *Betwixt Two Empires*.
157 AN 5. 76–77, *The Aṅguttara-Nikāya Part V*, ed. E. Hardy, London: Pali Text Society, 1900; Vin 2. 199, 205, *The Vinaya Piṭakaṃ: One of the Principal Buddhist Holy Scriptures in the Pāli Language. Vol II. The Cullavagga*, ed. Hermann Oldenberg, London: Williams and Norgate, 1880.
158 Groups of four acts are given. In the **Ekottarikāgama*: 1 establishing a stupa where none was previously established, 2 repairing an old monastic complex, 3 uniting a divided monastic community, and 4 the Buddha being persuaded to turn the Wheel of Dharma, T 125. 656b1–9. In the *Saṅghabhedavastu* of the *Mūlasarvāstivādavinaya*: 1 establishing a relic stupa or 2 monastic complex at a previously unestablished location, 3 uniting a divided monastic community, and 4 practising the four 'immeasurable' (*apramāṇa*) meditations, Sbh-v 2. 207, *The Gilgit Manuscript of the Saṅghabhedavastu. Being the 17th and Last Section of the Vinaya of the Mūlasarvāstivādin. Part I-II.*, ed. Raniero Gnoli, Roma: Istituto italiano per il Medio ed Estremo Oriente, 1977. A similar formulation is found at Abhidh-k-vy 4. 128.
159 In one passage of the *Ayu wang jing* 阿育王經, an artisan is compelled by Upagupta to build a *si* 寺 ('stupa' or 'monastic complex') to produce Brahma-merit. T 2043. 164c19–20. This has been shown to correspond to a Sanskrit fragment of the Schøyen Collection (SC), written in Gilgit-Bamiyan Type 1 script (c. 6th century CE), SC 2379/50, Klaus Wille, 'Fragments from the Aśoka Legend', in *Manuscripts in the Schøyen Collection I*, Oslo: Hermes Academic Publishing, 2000, pp. 218–32 (pp. 228–9); Palumbo, *An Early Chinese Commentary on the Ekottarika-āgama*, pp. 291–5.
160 For a summary of alternate views regarding the purport and nature of this rebirth, see Abhidh-k-bh 124a—c; Abhidh-k-vy 128.
161 On the cosmological aspects of causality with respect to the 'five actions whose results are without interval' (see fn. 4–7) in Theravāda and Sarvāstivāda commentarial literature, see Rupert Gethin, 'Cosmology and Meditation: From the Agañña Sutta to the Mahāyāna', *History of Religions*, 1997, 36(3): 183–217 (pp. 196ff).

5

NAMING RITUALS AND SHARING POWER IN THE TIME AND SPACE OF THE TAMIL TEMPLE

Leslie C. Orr

Introduction

The stone walls of the medieval temples of Tamilnadu are covered with inscriptions that record gifts made to the temple by a variety of different kinds of patrons. In some cases, these endowments have as their object the sponsorship of a ritual or of a structure—for example, a *maṇḍapa* (pavilion) or a *gopura* (entrance gate)—that was named for the donor or for someone whom the donor wished to honour. In this chapter, I focus on two types of named rituals whose establishment is recorded in Tamil inscriptions of the 13th to 16th century at temples dedicated to Śiva and Viṣṇu: 1) daily worship services (*canti* Skt *sandhi*), named after donors or rulers, and 2) monthly or yearly birthday celebrations observed on the birth star (*nakṣatra*, or 'lunar mansion') of the person to be honoured, which were often coordinated with temple festivals. Such named rituals seem to have proliferated especially in the far south of Tamilnadu, around Tirunelveli and to its east (the erstwhile Srivaikuntham and Tiruchendur taluks) and south (Nanguneri taluk) and westward through Ambasamudram taluk to Tenkasi and Srivilliputtur taluks on the eastern slopes of the Ghats. This is a region studded with temples—many of which grew during the period under review into large and impressive temple complexes—whose inscriptions I will be surveying here. Pandya kings were prominent in this region, with Tirunelveli as a secondary capital; these rulers appear fairly often as temple patrons, but there were many non-royal donors as well, including some who established the kinds of named rituals that are the object of our interest here.[1]

The sponsorship of such services was a means of forging a relationship between the deity and the donor (or the person honoured by being named), and evoking that (absent) person's presence in the home of the god and his presence in the sequence of daily, monthly or annual ritual observances in which the god participated. Such endowments also brought the donor into relationship with a variety of other actors, including local authorities, temple servants and royal officials. Among the earliest of references to such endowments in the region surveyed here are three inscriptions of the late 12th century, at the Nellaiyappar temple in Tirunelveli, dated in the reign of Jatilavarman Kulasekhara (all engraved on the exterior of the second prakara wall on the west side).[2] These record the king's command to the temple authorities concerning gifts of land for food supplies and for a Brahmin to carry out special monthly services in the temple on the day of Visakha, the birth star (*nakṣatra*) of the king; the name of the donor is not mentioned, but the arrangements are said to have been made at the request of Aiyan Malavarayan.[3] This last figure, likely a member of the king's entourage or a high court official, is represented as the initiator of these arrangements, but other agents are involved as well, including a named Brahmin to take charge of the conduct of the service in honour of the king, and the anonymous groups of temple authorities to whom the royal order is directed.

In what follows, I propose to undertake a series of case studies, focusing on seven specific figures—royal and non-royal—who were honourees or patrons of named services and birthday celebrations in temples. My selection of these figures—among many possible candidates—is based on the fact that we have good epigraphical documentation in multiple cases for the establishment of temple rituals in their names. For each of these figures, I will be paying particular attention to the variety of agents involved in the arrangement of special services and the ways in which the inscriptional records are physically situated within the space of the temple where the rituals were to be performed. These case studies are presented in roughly chronological order, although as we proceed we will be shifting from one part of the region to another, and will need to take into account how local contexts and changing political circumstances had an impact on these endowments and the nature of these rituals.

Maravarman Sundara Pandya I

The Pandya ruler Maravarman Sundara I made his mark on the ritual life of temples as far north as Jambukeshvara, near Trichy, where, in 1223, an annual birthday celebration was instituted in his honour and a daily *canti* service established in his name.[4] In the same year, in the far south of the Pandya region, the focus of our attention, arrangements for the royal birthday were made at the Virapandyeshvara temple at Kattarimangalam, 30 kilometres east of Tirunelveli. Two inscriptions,[5] engraved in prominent positions on the western and northern walls of the central shrine of this modest-sized temple, record the order of Sundara Pandya, issued at the request of a certain Isanadeva—whose name suggests that he was a teacher or member of a

Śaiva initiation lineage. The king commanded that taxes due to him should be retained by the temple for the purpose of conducting annually special worship for the god and goddess on the day of his birth star, Avittam.[6]

The following year, 1224, is the date of two inscriptions at Tiruvalisvaram, to the west of Tirunelveli;[7] these are royal orders to the temple authorities, made by the king from his palace at Madurai, granting land to the temple. The land grant was for the purpose of an annual celebration on the king's birth star day and was made at the request of Malavarayan—a person bearing a courtly title frequently met with in connection with the Pandya rulers.[8] At the Tiruvalisvaram temple, the royal birthday celebration seems to have been coordinated with a pre-existing festival. Arrangements, including provisions for food offerings, were to be made for the god's bath (*tīrttam*) 'on Avittam, the day of our birth, in Purattasi month at the processional festival [established by] Oruvarunartan Tamilappallavaraiyan'.[9] The bathing ceremony would have taken place at the conclusion of the festival. Fourteen years later, a similar celebration was established at the Vaiṣṇava temple of Tirukkolur, east of Tirunelveli, according to a lengthy inscription that covers the whole west wall of the central shrine (Figure 5.1).[10] Maravarman Sundara Pandya, from his throne and at the request of Malavarayan, gave his command to the temple authorities concerning a land grant made to support the ceremony of the god's bath on Avittam, the king's

Figure 5.1 Vaittamanidhi Perumal temple, Tirukkolur, west wall of the central shrine
Source: Author

birth star day, concluding the festival in the month of Pankuni. The fact that we see a variation among temples in which month the king's birth star day would be recognised—Purattasi at Tiruvalisvaram, Pankuni at Tirukkolur—suggests that these new birthday rituals were instituted in accordance with an already established local festival calendar. Also noteworthy is the physical prominence at Kattarimangalam and Tirukkolur of the inscriptions transcribing the royal orders concerning the establishment of temple observances on the occasion of the king's birthday.

Kunramoli Cinkapperuman Kurukulattariyan

In the 16th year of the reign of Maravarman Sundara Pandya I—that is, in 1232—an inscription was engraved on the walls of the Mayakkutta-Perumal temple, dedicated to Viṣṇu, at Perungulam, across the Tamraparni River and 7 kilometres to the northeast of Tirukkolur.[11] Consisting of 11 long lines, the inscription wraps around the north and west walls of the central shrine. Addressed to the temple authorities, it begins with the record of a donation of land made by one Kunramoli Cinkapperuman Kurukulattaraiyan, of the village of Ceyanam, for the expenses of a daily *canti* service in the temple and of a monthly festival on the day of Makha, his birth star. Details of the land boundaries and the taxes due on the land follow, and it is only halfway through this lengthy inscription that we realise that this is a royal order granting remission of the taxes. This tax remission is said to have been given at the request to the king by Annan Tamilapallavaraiyar, evidently a royal official and the same person whom we have already met (as Oruvarunartan Tamilappallavaraiyan) as the sponsor of a festival at Tiruvalisvaram.[12] It is striking that Kurukulattaraiyan, rather than the king, is the dominant presence in the text of the inscription and that it is his birthday, celebrated every month, that is introduced into the ritual program of this important Vaiṣṇava temple.[13]

Further east along the Tamraparni River, 15 kilometres from Perungulam, is the Śiva temple at Attur (Authoor), where Kurukulattaraiyan is again honoured—according to a series of inscriptions dated 23 years later, in 1255.[14] Found amid a plethora of other inscriptions engraved on the central shrine and surrounding walls of this small temple, are two sets of three records, all of the same date. The first set[15] includes the order of King Maravarman Vikrama Pandya II remitting taxes on a land grant, the communication of the order to the temple authorities and a record of the village assembly from whom the land had been purchased. The king ordered the tax remission while he was stationed at Alliyur (a place some 55 kilometres to the southwest) and at the request of his brother-in-law, the Kongu king Vikrama Choladeva. The land had been granted by Kunramoli Cinkapperuman Kurukulattaraiyan for a daily *canti* service instituted in his name and for the celebration of a temple festival in the month of Avani, on the day of his birth star Makha. The second set[16] of inscriptions concerns a portion of the land granted which was assigned to a temple woman for a dance performance during the festival and includes a record of the oral order of the king, its conveyance to the temple authorities and the temple authorities' establishment of the temple woman's rights to the land. In this case, the establishment of the celebration of a non-royal patron's birthday as an annual temple festival is framed by the actions of a king and his relatives and of local temple and village authorities. The royal order[17] is a substantial inscription on the north wall of the temple, of which almost half is given over to the king's *meykkīrtti* (eulogy). Although the donor's name and place of origin is repeated throughout all of the six records, and the celebration in Avani is described as 'his festival', it is only in the record of the village assembly[18] that it is mentioned that the occasion is his birth star day, Makha. But Kurukulattaraiyan's festival is an entirely new one at the temple; he is not building on pre-existing ritual. And the idea that the festival is to be celebrated for years to come is reinforced by the mention that the temple woman's land, granted to her for performing festival dance, is to be enjoyed also by her daughter and her daughter's daughter.[19]

Maravarman Kulusekhara Pandya

King Maravarman Kulasekhara's birthday was celebrated at two of the nine *divyadeśas* of southernmost Tamilnadu, the sacred sites hymned by the Vaiṣṇava poet-saints: at the Vanamamalai temple of Nanguneri and at the Kallappiran temple of Srivaikuntham.[20] At Nanguneri, the records that document the establishment of the observances on the king's birth star (Mula) appear prominently on the south and north walls of the central shrine (Figure 5.2). The two inscriptions on the south wall,[21] dated in the ruler's sixth regnal year (1274), are in the first-person voice of the king and record that, at the request of Kalingarayan, taxes were exempted from donated land. The land had been given by one Tiruvaykkulam Utaiyan Vanamamalai Picchan to provide for special offerings and worship, concluding with the god's bath (*tīrttam*) on the king's natal star day.[22] Two inscriptions on the north wall, dated in the same year,[23] concern the same matter, one being the king's royal order directed to the temple authorities (the *śrīvaiṣṇavas*) while seated on the throne called Kalingarayan.[24]

It is noteworthy that Maravarman Kulasekhara was not the first figure whose birthday was celebrated at this important Vaiṣṇava temple of Vanamamalai. Almost 40 years earlier, in 1236, a festival was established for a man of Malai-mandalam (Kerala) named Cenpakapperanayan on his birthday Puram in the month of Adi. It is not clear from the unfinished inscription[25] who had sponsored this birthday celebration, but the observances included food offerings and a sacred bath for the deity. The inscription is engraved in the same prominent location, on the south wall of the central

Figure 5.2 Vanamamalai temple, Nanguneri, south wall of the central shrine
Source: Author

shrine, as the records of Maravarman Kulasekhara. Another non-royal birthday celebration was established in 1312 at this temple,[26] for a certain Vira Kotai Keralan. The annual observances were fixed for Uttiram day in the month of Chittirai and were supported by a land endowment. Again, it is not clear who the donor of the land was, given the fragmentary nature of the inscription, but the record concludes with the signatures of several local officials, suggesting their assent to a land transfer; it seems likely that Vira Kotai Keralan himself was the sponsor of the festival in his own honour. It is striking that the records of the two non-royal birthday observances at Nanguneri make no reference to royal authority or royal officials and scarcely mention other figures. In contrast, the four records of Maravarman Kulasekhara, dated at the mid-point between these two, bring into play a host of actors—the royal official Kalingarayan, the sponsor of the birthday services Vanamamalai Pichchan, the members of the local Brahman assembly and the temple authorities, in addition to local authorities.

A similar nexus of relationships is apparent in the inscription at Srivaikuntham (Figure 5.3), dated 1304, that records the establishment by Maravarman Kulasekhara of an annual festival in the month of Maci on the day of his birth star, Mula.[27] The king issued his order to the *śrīvaiṣṇavas* of the temple, allocating land to provide for the offerings and services,

Figure 5.3 Kallappiran temple, Srivaikuntham, east wall of the mandapa, left of entrance
Source: Author

concluding with the god's sacred bath, and the record ends with the signature of an important landowner of the region (who bears the title Kalingarayan). These arrangements were made at the request of Tevappiran Tatar, who is evidently someone associated with a *maṭha* ('monastery') at Srivaikuntham.[28] The inscription records the speech of the king: 'Tevappiran Tatar came to see us in Gangaikontacolappuram in Colamantalam'. This record has a very similar format to two others, engraved in immediate proximity—on the east wall of the *maṇḍapa* in front of the shrine of Kallappiran, to the left of the entrance—in which Tevappiran Tatar is said to have visited Kulasekhara's two sons to request land to be granted for the establishment of a Vira Pandya *canti* (dated 1301)[29] and a Sundara Pandya *canti* (dated 1305),[30] which the two kings ordered.[31] In inscriptions engraved continuously with these and preceding them, we find royal commands by Kulasekhara assigning land so that Tevappiran Tatar can make a garden 'in our name' (dated 1300)[32] and can build a Kulasekhara *maṇḍapa* (dated 1305),[33] and commands by Sundara Pandya concerning Tevappiran Tatar's building of a *gopura* and an enclosing wall in the name of this king (dated 1310 and 1316).[34] Each of the records concludes with the signature of one or more local 'chiefs' allied with the king.[35] This group of inscriptions, covering a whole wall as one approaches the entrance to the main shrine and focusing on the establishment and naming of temple structures and services, provides an account of the linkages of the Pandya royal family with regional notables and with local temple and institutional authorities—including the peripatetic Tevappiran Tatar, who journeyed from Srivaikuntham in the far south of the Tamil country to the Chola country, where the Pandyas exerted territorial control. Also, this wall of inscriptions would have borne witness to the services whose establishment they record, including the annual celebration of Kulasekhara's birthday and the daily *cantis* named for his two sons. Priests would have passed before the wall as they entered the *maṇḍapa* with their offerings for the god within the central shrine and circumambulated the *maṇḍapa* and central shrine to make *śrībali* offerings during *canti* services, and the bathing of the deity's processional image at the annual festival would have taken place in the area in front of the *maṇḍapa* entrance.

Tirunelveli Perumal Virapandya

Engraved on the wall to the right of the *maṇḍapa* entrance at Srivaikuntham are more inscriptions, including one which is a record dated 1439 and issued by Tirunelveli Perumal Virapandya, one of the so-called Tenkasi Pandyas.[36] The king instructs the *śrīvaiṣṇavas* of the temple to arrange for the celebration of the festival in the month of Vaikaci, which had apparently not been observed for some time, the festival 'beginning on the day of Cataiyam and concluding with the god's bath (*tīrttam*) on Tiruvatirai, the day of our birth'.[37] Tax-free land was allocated for this purpose, and reference is made to a previous land grant made to support a Virapandya *canti* at dawn every day established 'in our name'. Here the annual festival purports to be a revival of a pre-existing temple observance in the month of Vaikaci, whose culmination in the ritual bath of the deity is coordinated with the king's birthday. Again—as in the case of the inscriptions of Tirunelveli Perumal Virapandya's predecessors on the same mandapa wall, to the left of the entrance—the record of 1439 to the right would have served as a witness to the festival bathing ritual as well as the daily *canti*. And Tirunelveli Perumal Virapandya's record ties him to the locality, with its details of tax exemptions on a piece of temple land acquired from a particular individual.

At the nearby Vaittamanidhiperumal temple of Tirukkolur, another of the Vaiṣṇava *divyadeśas*, Tirunelveli Perumal Virapandya appears again.[38] The inscription,[39] dated in his 30th regnal year (1450), is engraved in a prominent position, on the east wall of the *maṇḍapa* to the right of the entrance to the inner shrine—in precisely the same location as the king's record at Srivaikuntham. In this case, however, it is an order issued by the god of the temple, as he was seated in state together with his two consorts.[40] The deity refers to the king as 'our son (*kumāra*)' and mentions the donation of land by the ruler together with a certain Pandipperumal, with the object of establishing a midday Virapandya *canti*. The god's command concerns the distribution of food offered during the *śrībali* ritual of the daily observance; evidently the donor Pandipperumal was the recipient of this consecrated food. The distribution of this *prasadam* would have taken place just in front of where the inscription is engraved.

From his title Tirunelveli Perumal ('lord of Tirunelveli'), and his visibility at the Vaiṣṇava temples just to the east of this city, one of the capitals of the early Pandyas, we may presume that this king was primarily based in this region. He was co-regent with Arikecari Parakrama Pandya, who is credited with building the Kasi Visvanatha temple in Tenkasi in 1446—and thus establishing Tenkasi as a royal centre for these latter-day Pandyas.[41] But Tirunelveli Perumal Virapandya is scarcely mentioned in the inscriptions of the Tenkasi area. Engraved on the gopura of the Kasi Visvanatha temple are some verses praising a ruler named Virapandyan Abhiraman Viramaran Seliyan, who conquered Villavan (the Chera king) and captured Vallam;[42] it is suggested by the government epigraphist that this inscription refers to Tirunelveli Perumal Virapandya.[43] There is no other evidence of the recognition of this king in the Tenkasi region.[44]

Sankaranarayana Venrumankonda Bhutalavira Viramarttandavarman

A ruler who is very much present in the Tenkasi region, a century later, is Sankaranaryana Venrumankonda Bhutalavira Viramarttandavarman of Kerala. On the south wall of the *maṇḍapa* attached to the central shrine of Kasi Visvanatha in Tenkasi is an inscription dated 1547[45] recording that Sankaranarayana Venrumankonda Bhutalavira Viramarttandavarman made a gift of land for the expenses of a service called Cenpakaraman *canti*, named for one of his titles. In fact, in an inscription of 1525,[46] some 20 years earlier, this same Kerala king claims—or has the deity announce, as a divine command—to have reconsecrated the Kasi Visvanatha temple, it having become dilapidated, and to have revived rituals that were no longer being conducted. Acknowledging that it had been founded by Arikecari Parakrama Pandya, Bhutalavira Viramarttandavarman evidently wanted to establish himself as the inheritor of the Pandya legacy.[47]

In the 16th century, the Tenkasi Pandyas were somewhat beseiged by the Kerala rulers, who established themselves in parts of Ambasamudram and Nanguneri districts to the east of the Western Ghats and south of Tenkasi. Srivilliputtur, 90 kilometres to the north, was 'occupied' by the Kerala king in 1534, until he was 'driven out' by the Pandya king Srivallabha.[48] This surmise is based on the presence of two virtually identical inscriptions prominently positioned in the Perumal (Vatapatrasayi) and Antal temples in Srivilliputtur (Figure 5.4), on the central shrines' south and north walls respectively.[49] The inscriptions are from 1534 and record the gift of land by Bhutalavira Viramarttandavarman to support services in the Antal temple: a

Figure 5.4 Antal temple, Srivilliputtur, north wall of the central shrine
Source: Author

daily Viramattandan *canti* and monthly observances on the Asvati *nakṣatra*. The endowment was also meant to support the feeding of Brahmins in a *maṭha* named Viramarttandan, after the king.[50]

Indeed, it does seem that Bhutalavira Viramarttandavarman and other members of the Kerala ruling family were 'driven out' of this region, since we do not find any inscriptional references to them after this time around Srivilliputtur or Tenkasi, with the exception of the record of 1547 establishing a Cenpakaraman *canti* at the Kasi Visvanatha temple. But Bhutalavira Viramarttandavarman's presence was definitely felt in the erstwhile Pandya heartland. At the old Śiva temple at Manaippadaividu, just to the north of Tirunelveli, an inscription dated 1544[51] records the Kerala king's gifts of land to several temples in the locality (one dedicated to Viṣṇu and three to Śiva). a century earlier, this temple had been the focus of patronage by the Pandya ruler Kulasekhara, who established daily, monthly and annual festivals, including on his birth star day (dated 1467).[52] In the 1530s and 1540s, Bhutalavira Viramarttandavarman was active as a donor in a cluster of temple towns around the curve of the Tampiraparni River to the west of Tirunelveli. At one of these, Tiruppudaimarudur in Ambasamudram taluk, there is an inscription dated 1546[53] that records the appointment of a temple accountant by the Kerala king at this famous Śaiva temple.[54] Nearby, at the Śiva temple at Kallidaikkuricci (dated 1531)[55] he and his queen made gifts to support offerings, and at Ambasamudram, he made land grants to several temples, both Śaiva and Vaiṣṇava.[56]

To the south, in Nanguneri taluk, Bhutalavira Viramarttandavarman established a ritual in his name, at the Shasta (Aiyanar) temple in Padmaneri, donating land so that a Viramarttandan *canti* service could be conducted daily (dated 1545).[57] This endowment adds to the impression we have that this ruler inclined toward eclectic habits of patronage. Here at Padmaneri, we have a ritual established in his name for the god Shasta; at Srivilliputtur the rituals in his name were in honour of Antal, the consort of Viṣṇu, and at Tenkasi, they were for Śiva. We also see in this king's donative activity attention being paid to both older temples, especially those with earlier Pandya patronage, and new ones. In the latter category is the Jagannatha Perumal temple at Shenbagaramanallur, dedicated to Viṣṇu. This seems to be something of a 'dynastic' temple for the 16th-century Kerala kings—a marker of their emplacement in Pandya territory and perhaps a response to the presence of the Vanamamalai temple in nearby Nanguneri, a *divyadeśa* patronised by Pandya kings since the 13th century, as we have seen in the case of Maravarman Kulasekhara Pandya.[58] In 1528 a command by the god Jagannatha Perumal confirmed the order that 'our son' the Kerala king Bhutalavira Viramarttandavarman had given, appointing a certain individual to the position of treasury accountant.[59]

And although Bhutalavira Viramarttandavarman did not establish ceremonies in his name at the Shenbagaramanallur temple, one of his immediate successors did.[60] In 1545, Sankaranarayana Venrumankonda Bhutalavira Ramavarman made a gift of land for a Cenpakaraman *canti*, in his name, and for special observances on his birthday of Asvati in the month of Avani.[61] Some ten years earlier, Bhutalavira Ramavarman's predecessor, Bhutalavira Viramarttandavarman, had also instituted celebrations on Asvati day, on a monthly basis, at the Antal temple in Srivilliputtur. Viramarttandavarman does not claim that this ritual was instituted in his name (although the other observances detailed in the inscription were named for him); might this have been in honour of Ramavarman's birthday, or did it have some other significance?[62] What is even more puzzling, however, is the fact that Bhutalavira Ramavarman's birthday celebrations at the Shenbagaramanallur temple were designed to take place at precisely the same time—on Asvati day in the month of Avani—as those of the Pandya ruler, Jatilavarman Tirunelveli Perumal Kulasekhara, in Tenkasi. Perhaps this was another case of the Kerala rulers' attempts to appropriate the royal persona of the Pandya kings whose territory they wished to lay claim to.

Jatilavarman Tirunelveli Perumal Kulasekhara Pandya

According to an inscription dated 1548, engraved at the Kasi Visvanatha temple in Tenkasi (Figure 5.5), Jatilavarman Tirunelveli Perumal Kulasekhara allowed the temple to retain the taxes due to him in order that they could be used to fund offerings and worship at a daily Viravenpamalai *canti*, named for him, and to support a festival on his birthday, Asvati in the month of Avani.[63] This record is inscribed in the same prominent location, on the south wall of the mandapa in front of the central shrine, as Bhutalavira Viramarttandavarman's record at Tenkasi concerning the establishment of a Cenpakaraman *canti* in his name, and is dated one year later than the Kerala king's record. Four years later, in 1552, an inscription was engraved on the north wall of the mandapa that records that a gift of land was made to the temple by Tirunelveli Perumal Kulasekhara Pandya.[64] The land was given in order to support services on 'our birthday, the Asvati *nakṣatra*' every month, and on the annual occasion, on Vaikaci Vicakam day, when the deity would be brought to the bathing mandapa that had been built by the king.

In addition to his building activities and the ceremonies in his honour that he established at the Kasi Visvanatha temple in Tenkasi, Tirunelveli Perumal Kulasekhara did a great deal to shape temple life in the vicinity of the capital. At the Nagarisvaram temple in Panpuli, 10 kilometres to the northwest of Tenkasi, a temple that was unknown before the 16th century, seven of the ten inscriptions record his activities.[65] Between 1544 and 1550, he was particularly involved in assigning land and privileges to various individuals who were to perform service in the temple, including a native of Tenkasi who was given the right to handle the accounts at several temples in the

Figure 5.5 Kasi Visvanatha temple, Tenkasi, outer gopura
Source: Author

area. The Madhyasthanatha temple at Darukapuram, 40 kilometres north of Tenkasi, was not such a new temple—having inscriptions dating from the 13th century—but it enjoyed the attentions of the Tenkasi Pandyas in the 16th century, including those of Tirunelveli Perumal Kulasekhara. This king is referred to in a divine command as 'our son (*kumāra*)' and aids the deity by arranging that a Brahmin be granteed the duties of recitation and calendrical calculations.[66] At nearby Sankaranarayanakoyil, we see again a series of divine orders giving the king the responsibility of appointing temple servants.[67] And ten kilometres further north, at Karivalamvandanallur, the god Palvannanatha entrusts 'our son' Tirunelveli Perumal Kulasekhara with the duty of assigning the right to serve as temple treasurer.[68] Just as the king implants what is his—'our birthday' celebration—at the Kasi Visvanatha temple, so does he share in the prestige of being claimed as 'ours' by the deities (the Śivas) of the temples newly built in the region; and by acting as the agent of these deities and assigning positions and privileges, he establishes his presence at these sites.

Alakan Perumal Ativirarama Srivallabha Pandya

The last figure whose sponsorship of named temple rituals we will examine is Alakan Perumal Ativirarama Srivallabha.[69] Not only did he establish ritual services, but this king sponsored the building of temples. At Tenkasi, on the north bank of the Chittaru River and to the east of the great Kasi Visvanatha temple, he built in 1567 a grand temple dedicated to Śiva as Kulasekara.[70] At Srivilliputtur, this ruler was responsible for building a Kṛṣṇa temple in 1571.[71] The mixed patronage of Śaiva and Vaiṣṇava temple foundations evident here is also characteristic of the named ceremonies that Ativirarama Srivallabha established. According to an inscription of 1561 at the Perumal temple in Srivilliputtur, engraved on the north wall of the central shrine, he made a gift of land in order to sponsor a Srivallabha *canti* service in the Antal temple next door and for feeding 24 *śrīvaiṣṇavas* in a *maṭha*.[72] Not only was a Srivallabha *canti* instituted at the Vaiṣṇava *divyadeśa* of Srivilliputtur but, 25 years later, one was established at the Kutralam temple, one of the sacred places to which the Śaiva poet-saints dedicated their hymns. This temple, a few kilometres away from Tenkasi, received a land grant from Ativirarama Srivallabha to conduct the service in his name, according to a slab inscription set up on the gifted land in Kalunirkulam, some 25 kilometres to the east of Kutralam (dated 1586).[73]

Ativirarama Srivallabha was recognised at another temple (Figure 5.6) close to Tenkasi, the Alagiyamanavala Perumal temple in Shenkottai. This diminuitive temple may have been built in the time or in honour of Jatilavarman Tirunelveli Perumal Kulasekhara, whom we have discussed in the previous section, since the earliest inscriptions date from the 1540's and the god of the temple is referred to as Kulasekhara Vinnakar Emperuman. An inscription of 1564[74] covers the lower moldings of the west wall of the central shrine and records a gift of land by Tankaccivenrumalaiyitta Perumal. The gift was meant to cover the cost of renovating the temple 'from its base to its pinnacle' and of (re)consecrating the god and goddess and

Figure 5.6 Alagiyamanavala Perumal temple, Shenkottai, west wall of the central shrine

Source: Author

to provide for a daily Srivallabhan-*canti*, with elaborate offerings of food, flowers, lamps and so on. This record seems to have been issued by Ativirarama Srivallabha himself, as it is dated in 'our regnal year' and the god of the temple is referred to as 'our lord'.

Discussion and conclusions

By tracing the manner in which named temple rituals were instituted, their character and the ways in which they were recorded, we see how power and presence were established and shared among patrons; rulers; temple deities and royal, local and religious authorities. My review of the appearance of seven individuals as sponsors or honourees of named rituals, in the particular context of southernmost Tamilnadu from the 13th to the 16th century, clearly cannot yield any broad generalisations but is suggestive of certain political and ritual dynamics.

I have considered three figures of the 13th century: two Pandya kings—Maravarman Sundara I of the first half of the 13th century and Marvarman Kulasekhara whose reign, beginning in 1268, stretched into the early 14th century—and one non-royal figure, Kurukulattaraiyan, active in the mid-13th century. Most of the rituals established in the names of these figures were annual or monthly celebrations marking the day of the honouree's birth star (*nakṣatra*). These observances were instituted at both Śaiva and Vaiṣṇava temples; the Vaiṣṇava temples were all *divyadeśas*—a festival for Sundara at Tirukkolur, for Kurukullattaraiyan at Perungulam and for Kulasekhara at Nanguneri and Srivaikuntham (and not at any Śaiva temples). In all of these 13th-century cases, the inscriptions tell us, the establishment of the rituals involved a 'requester': Maravarman Sundara was asked to grant land or give a tax remission to the temple twice, by the royal official Malavarayan and (at Kattarimangalam) by Isanadeva, evidently a teacher or religious leader; Kurukulattaraiyan's institution of rituals in his name depended on tax remissions granted by the king at the request of a royal official (at Perungulam) or a relative of the king (at Attur); Kulasekhara gave a tax remission on land that had been donated by Vanamamalai Picchan at the request of a royal official and gave land for his own birthday celebration at Srivaikuntham at the request of the head of a *maṭha*. In addition to the 'requesters', temple authorities and regional notables often make an appearance in the arrangements surrounding the institution of these rituals; the records concerning Kurukulattaraiyan's annual birthday celebration at Attur make provisions for the support of a temple woman (and her descendents) appointed to perform dance. Many of the 13th-century inscriptions recording the establishment of named rituals have the form of a royal order, but the king is not always a dominant presence, as we see in the case of the record of Kurukulattaraiyan's institution of monthly celebrations of his birth star day at Perungulam.

For the 15th century, we have considered the latter-day Pandya ruler Tirunelveli Perumal Virapandya, who at Srivaikuntham established a daily Virapandya *canti* at dawn and an annual festival on the day of his *nakṣatra*, and at Tirukkolur, a midday Virapandya *canti*. In the choice of these two temples—both Vaiṣṇava *divyadeśas*—Virapandya replicates the institution of named services made by his 13th-century Pandya predecessors. But a novel feature of the inscription recording the establishment of the *canti* service at Tirukkolur is that it is not a royal order, but rather a command made by the temple deity who refers to Virapandya as 'our son'. Such divine commands become a feature of inscriptions in the 15th and 16th centuries in the regions to the east and south of Tirunelveli, and in Tenkasi and Srivilliputtur and the area between these two centres. Usually such records do not concern the establishment of named rituals but involve the granting of privileges or positions, including the appointment of temple functionaries and administrators (often 'accountants').[75] Indeed, the inscription informing us of the Virapandya *canti* at Tirukkolur has as its main purpose the granting by the deity of the right to receive consecrated food, offered during the daily ritual, to a figure who seems to have been responsible for sponsoring the *canti*. In this case, as in other divine commands, the person whom the god designates as 'our son'—Virapandya—serves as the god's agent or as the 'requester' of the divine decree. Meanwhile, the figure of the 'requester' as we know him from 13th-century inscriptions—the royal official or religious leader who initiates or advances the establishment of named temple rituals—is no longer found in the records of the 15th and 16th centuries that I have examined here.

The three 16th-century figures for whom named rituals were instituted, considered previously, were all kings—the Kerala ruler Bhutalavira Viramarttandavarman and two members of the Tenkasi Pandya dynasty, Tirunelveli Perumal Kulasekhara and Ativirarama Srivallabha. Many of the rituals established were daily *cantis*, and the temples where the services were conducted were either the Antal temple in Srivilliputtur or temples in or around Tenkasi; the only exception is Bhutalavira Viramarttandavarman's sponsorship of a *canti* in his name at the Shasta temple in Padmaneri, 60 kilometres to the southeast of Tenkasi. Bhutalavira Viramarttandavarman's and Tirunelveli Perumal Kulasekhara's gifts intersect with one another, being made in the middle of the 16th century, and include monthly or annual observances as well as *cantis*; rituals in honour of Ativirarama Srivallabha were established a decade or more later. The rulers themselves were directly responsible for establishing services in their names, with land grants or tax remissions, except for the Srivallabhan *canti* instituted at Shenkottai by a non-royal patron, who also sponsored the complete renovation of the temple. In contrast to many of the 13th-century records we have considered, the 16th-century inscriptions instituting named rituals rarely reference agents or actors other than the patron-ruler. Even when there is the mention of a *maṭha*, as we see in the Srivilliputtur inscriptions of both Bhutalavira Viramarttandavarman and Tirunelveli Perumal Kulasekhara, no *maṭha* official is named. The central relationship emphasised in these 16th-century records is that between the king and the temple deity—and, indirectly, as I will discuss later, relationships among kings.

The placement of the inscriptions on temple walls seems significant, as virtually all of the records of the establishment of named rituals—for all seven figures considered here—are positioned prominently. They are on the walls of the central shrine or of the *maṇḍapa* that is attached to the central shrine on the east side, often commanding a good deal of space. Thus, these inscriptions would have borne witness to the daily *canti* services whose establishment they recorded, as the *maṇḍapa* and central shrine were circumambulated in the course of the ritual; the name of the ritual—that is, of the honouree—perhaps pronounced by the priests as well as present in engraved stone. The placement of such inscriptions on the east wall of the *maṇḍapa*, on either side of the entrance to the inner shrine, seems particularly apt, in the cases of the 13th-century inscriptions of Maravarman Kulasekhara at Srivaikuntham and of the 15th-century inscriptions of Tirunelveli Perumal Virapandya at Srivaikuntham and Tirukkolur. The space before this wall would have been the site of a good deal of ritual activity, whether in daily, monthly or annual observances, including the bathing (*tīrttam*) of the deity at the conclusion of a festival, which is specifically mentioned in several inscriptions. The placement of these records also suggests a reiterative or competitive display.[76] For example, the 15th-century Tirunelveli Perumal Virapandya's royal order concerning the annual observance of his birthday at Srivaikuntham is engraved just on the other side of the *maṇḍapa* entrance from that of his 13th-century Pandya predecessor. And the inscription (dated in 1548) at the Kasi Visvanatha temple recording Tirunelveli Perumal Kulasekhara's establishment of a *canti* and a birthday celebration in his name is engraved on exactly the same wall (the south wall of the mandapa) as the record of Bhutalavira Viramarttandavarman's insitution of a *canti* in his name, one year earlier. Similarly, the engraving (in 1561), on the north wall of the Perumal temple at Srivilliputtur, of a record concerning Ativirarama Srivallabha's establishment of a *canti* in his name and arrangements for feeding *śrīvaiṣṇavas* in a *maṭha* is anticipated in 1534 by Bhutalavira Viramarttandavarman's inscription on the other side of the same temple (the south wall) recording the institution of a *canti* in his name, feeding of Brahmins in a *maṭha* named for him and celebration of monthly festivals on the Asvati *nakṣatra*.

In terms of time instead of space, however, we may see imitation working in the opposite direction, with the Kerala kings appropriating something belonging to the Tenkasi Pandyas. It cannot be a coincidence that (in 1534) Bhutalavira Viramarttandavarman established monthly observances of the Asvati *nakṣatra* at Srivilliputtur, that (in 1545) his successor Bhutalavira Ramavarman arranged for for a festival on his birthday of Asvati in the month of Avani at Shenbagaramanallur, and that (in 1548) at the Kasi Visvanatha temple in Tenkasi, the Pandya ruler Tirunelveli Perumal Kulasekhara instituted a festival on *his* birthday, precisely the same day, as well as establishing monthly Asvati services at this temple several years later. Although the Kerala kings seem to have chronological precedence, in fact there was a Pandya ruler who was a contemporary of Bhutalavira Viramarttandavarman's—Jatilavarman Srivallabha Tirunelveli Perumal 'who revived the past'—whose *nakṣatra* was Asvati. This Pandya king was active as a temple patron in Tenkasi and Srivilliputtur in the 1530's, and the Kerala ruler may have 'borrowed' the Asvati *nakṣatra* in his institution of services at Srivilliputtur.[77] In the following decade, Bhutalavira Ramavarman's establishment of an Asvati festival in Avani month and claiming it as a birthday celebration—in the new Kerala stronghold in Pandya territory, at Shenbagaramanallur—seems to mirror, or boldly anticipate, what was happening in the royal temple of the Tenkasi Pandyas in the observance of Tirunelveli Perumal Kulasekhara's birthday.

To continue with a consideration of the timing of monthly and annual named festivals, and to conclude with some observations on the significance of this timing in channeling power and establishing presence, we need to look more closely at temple birthday celebrations. While a 'birthday' might seem of minor significance, the *nakṣatra* of the day of one's birth has profound and personal meaning. From early times associated with the moment of conception as well as birth, and with the granting of one's first name, it has until today been regarded as a key element in astrological calculations.[78] Thus, the birth *nakṣatra* is linked to an individual's very origins and his or her destiny. The institution of temple services to mark ones *nakṣatra* on a monthly or annual basis would have been a way to assure well-being and to forge a personal relationship between the individual and the temple deity being offered worship in the ritual. As we have seen, such observances were established by both royal and non-royal figures throughout the period under review. Also, it is striking how often we find references to the coordination of the *nakṣatra* observance with the final purifying *tirttam* of the god at the conclusion of a festival, particularly in the case of the 13th-century Pandya kings we have considered.[79] To have a temple festival culminate on the day of ones *nakṣatra* with the sacred bath of the body of the god would be extraordinarily auspicious and would create an especially intimate connection between god and honouree. And ultimately—in the case of all of the named rituals considered here—this kind of connection was the aim of establishing these observances, a shared co-presence in the time and space of the temple.

Notes

1 In a survey of more than 3000 inscriptions dating from the 8th to 13th centuries, in study areas both in the heartland of the Pandya rulers, around Tirunelveli and Madurai and in the Chola territories near Tiruchirappalli and Thanjavur, I found only four referring to temple celebrations named for the Chola king or marking his birthday but close to 30 inscriptions describing special services established in honour of a Pandya ruler. More than half of these 30 appeared in inscriptions in the Tirunelveli region, but the Pandya rulers' names were also

attached to newly instituted rituals in temples in the Chola country, especially during the 13th century. Leslie C. Orr, 'Cholas, Pandyas, and "Imperial Temple Culture" in Medieval Tamilnadu', in Adam Hardy (ed), *The Temple in South Asia*, London: British Academy, 2007, pp. 109–30. For temple celebrations in honour of Chola rulers, see also N. Sethuraman, 'Date of Birth, Date of Coronation and Last Day of Raja Raja Chola', in K. K. A. Venkatachari (ed), *Rājā Rājā—The Great (Seminar Proceedings)*, Bombay: Ananthacharya Indological Research Institute, 1987.

2 SII 5.428, ARE 1927/34, ARE 1927/40.

3 The earliest inscriptional reference to special birthday celebrations that I have found in the southern part of Tamil Nadu dates from 1134 and is engraved at the temple of Tirukkottiyur, near Madurai (SII 14.234). It is an order issued by the Pandya king Srivallabha granting land for a nine day festival in the month of Aippaci, that would conclude with the god's bath (*tīrttam*) on the birth star day (Cittirai) of the king; the land grant was made at the request of one Tennavan Mangalatarajan.

4 ARE 1937–38/21. On inscriptions providing information about this ruler, see N. Sethuraman, *The Imperial Pandyas: Mathematics Reconstructs the Chronology*, Kumbhakonam: Author, 1978, pp. 26–34. I follow Sethuraman in the dating of inscriptions of this king. The Pandya king's birth star was Avittam.

5 ARE 1929–30/369 and 370.

6 In this same period, early in the rule of Maravarman Sundara I, the king's birthday was marked by festivals at two Śaiva temples located to the east of the Pandya capital of Madurai: an annual celebration at Tiruppattur, established in 1226 at the request of the king's brother-in-law (ARE 1935–36/183), and a monthly observance on the king's birth star in the temple at Chaturvedimangalam, instituted in 1227 at the request of Malavarayan (ARE 1927–28/303 and 304).

7 ARE 1916/338 = ESITA 36 and ARE 1916/340.

8 The throne on which the king was seated when giving this order was also named Malavarayan.

9 ARE 1916/338. K. D. Swaminathan suggests that an inscription of several years earlier (ARE 1916/344 = ESITA 24), referring to a temple procession on the day of Avittam in the month of Karttikai, indicates that there were other occasions when Maravarman Sundara was honoured at this temple, although there is no mention of the king in this record. *Early South Indian Temple Architecture: Study of Tiruvāliśvaram Inscriptions*, Trivandrum: CBH Publications, 1990, p. 63.

10 ARE 1962–63/717. An abbreviated copy of this inscription is engraved on the south wall of the central shrine (ARE 1962–63/718). The very long *meykkīrtti* (royal eulogy) of ARE 1962–63/717 is published in S. Krishnaswami Aiyangar, *South India and Her Muhammadan Invaders*, New Delhi: S. Chand, 1971 [1921], pp. 208–16.

11 ARE 1932–33/243. Sethuraman, *The Imperial Pandyas*, p. 82, identifies the ruler and provides the date of this inscription.

12 This figure also appears in inscriptions from the Madurai area (at the Madurai Minaksi temple ARE 1943–44/187 and at Tirupparankunram ARE 1941–42/248), at Tirunelveli (ARE 1940–41/292), at Kilacceval (in Ambasamudram taluk ARE 1911/523–525), and at Singikulam (in Nanguneri taluk ARE 1940–41/269)—often paired with Aiyyan Malavarayan and identified as the person who instigated or requested an endowment to be made, but sometimes acting as a donor himself, as he seems to be at Tiruvalisvaram.

13 The Mayakkutta Perumal temple at Perungulam is one of the nine *divyadeśas* of southernmost Tamilnadu, famed as one of the sites to which the Vaiṣṇava

poet-saints dedicated hymns. Others of these nine temples include Tirukkolur, encountered earlier in the text, and Nanguneri and Srivaikuntham, to be discussed in the following section. Further north—to the southwest of Madurai—is the *divyadeśa* Srivilliputtur to which we also refer in the following section.

14 Sethuraman, *The Imperial Pandyas*, p. 67.
15 ARE 1929–30/427, 428 and 451.
16 ARE 1929–30/444–446.
17 ARE 1929–30/427.
18 ARE 1929–30/451.
19 ARE 1929–30/444 and 446.
20 For information about this king, and his two sons Jatilavarman Vira Pandya (acc. 1297) and Jatilavarman Sundara Pandya (acc. 1303), see N. Sethuraman, 'Two Jatavarman Sundara Pandyas of Accession 1303 and 1304 A.D.', *Journal of the Epigraphical Society of India*, 1983, 10: 15–29.
21 ARE 1927–28/250 and 251.
22 The sponsor of the royal birthday celebration, Vanamamalai Pichchan, may possibly have been a Vaiṣṇava religious leader; more likely, he was simply a wealthy patron in the region. In either case, he was later recognised in the temple by having a sacred canopy named for him. According to an inscription of 1589 (ARE 1927–28/258), the deity issued an order while enthroned beneath the 'Vanamamalai Pichchan pantal'. See Leslie C. Orr 'Making and Marking Place in the Temples of Medieval Tamilnadu', paper presented at the Annual South Asia Conference, Madison, Wisconsin, 2018.
23 ARE 1927–28/254 and 255.
24 Far to the north, at a Śiva temple in Tirukkadaiyur, east of Thanjavur, according to an inscription dated 1280 (ARE 1925/247), Kalingarayan again requested Maravarman Kulasekhara to establish observances in his name: the celebration of a daily Kulasekhara *canti* and an annual festival on the king's birth star day (Mula) in the month of Ani. Some years later, in 1312, at a small Śiva temple in Tirumalugandankottai, to the northeast of Tirunelveli near the coast, Jatilavarman Sundara Pandya arranged for monthly offerings to be made on the day of Mula, the natal star of his father Maravarman Kulasekhara (ARE 1931–32/51). It is possible that this gift was made in the year of Kulasekhara's death.
25 ARE 1927–28/252.
26 ARE 1927–28/259.
27 (ARE 1959–60/379.
28 According to one of the inscriptions engraved nearby (SII 5.741), dating from 1304, Tevappiran Tatar was given land for a *maṭha*, which the king (Kulasekhara) had made tax exempt. For a discussion of the character of *maṭhas* in this region and period—as feeding houses, schools, monasteries, and administrative centres—and of the related matter of the functions of temple accountants and treasury officials, see Leslie C. Orr, 'Maṭhas in the History of Southernmost India: Temple, Guru, God and Patron in the 14th to 17th Centuries', in Sarah Pierce Taylor and Caleb Simmons (eds), *Beyond the Monastery: The Entangled Institutional History of the South Asian Maṭha*, New York: Oxford University Press, forthcoming.
29 ARE 1959–60/378.
30 ARE 1959–60/377.
31 All three kings, Maravarman Kulasekhara and his two sons, were ruling simultaneously, which was typical among the Pandya rulers.
32 ARE 1959–60/374.
33 ARE 1959–60/380.
34 ARE 1959–60/381 and 373.

35 Among these signatories are those bearing the dynastic name Vanarayan or Vanatarayan. See Leslie C. Orr, 'The Bhakti of the Bāṇas', in Manu V. Devadevan (ed), *Clio and Her Descendants: Essays for Kesavan Veluthat*, New Delhi: Primus Publications, 2018, pp. 347–86.

36 ARE 1960–61/342 cf. SII 5.742. See N. Sethuraman, 'The Later Pandyas (1371–1750)', *Journal of the Epigraphical Society of India*, 1994, 20: 96–116, 98–9 and 112 for this ruler in particular.

37 One of the inscriptions to the left of the entrance to the mandapa, dating from the early 14th century, records a gift of land—probably made by King Maravarman Kulasekhara—to provide for 'the old (*palaiya*) Vaikaci festival' (ARE 1959–60/376). The festival in Vaikaci month continues to be of significance at the Srivaikuntham Kallappiran temple, as the occasion for the Garuda *sevai* celebration, but we cannot be at all sure that the modern festival is of the same character or takes place on precisely the same dates as those observed in medieval times.

38 We remember that, as discussed previously, the 13th-century Maravarman Sundara Pandya had instituted an annual festival timed to coincide with his birth star at Tirukkolur—as is recorded in a very lengthy and prominent inscription at the temple.

39 ARE 1962–63/725.

40 On divine commands, see Orr, 'Making and Marking Place'.

41 N. Sethuraman, 'Tenkasi Parakrama and His Successors', *Journal of the Epigraphical Society of India*, 1982, 9: 58–67; Leslie C. Orr, 'Making Place in a Small Space: The Sacred Worlds of the Tenkasi Pandyas', paper presented at the Association for Asian Studies annual meeting, Chicago, 2015. On the Kasi Visvanatha temple, see Crispin Branfoot, *Gods on the Move: Architecture and Ritual in the South Indian Temple*, London: Society for South Asian Studies, 2007, pp. 19–21.

42 ARE 1909/516 = SII 26.546.

43 Another inscription at the Kasi Visvanatha temple, dated 1462, refers to a donation made by prince Venrumalaiyitta Perumal Virapandyadevar (ARE 1909/526 = SII 26.556); the government epigraphist takes this to refer to Tirunelveli Perumal Virapandya, but the date seems too late for this identification. It is worth noting that in the 15th century, in the area around Tenkasi, there are scarcely any temple services that were named for rulers or patrons. As we shall soon see, this was all to change in the 16th century. I have found only a single 15th-century inscription—engraved in a prominent position on the walls of the central shrine of the Kasi Visvanatha—that records the establishment of a Parakrama Pandya *canti* on the occasion of the ruler's birth star of Mrgasirsa (ARE 1912/5, dated 1450); this service was instituted to honour the temple's builder Arikecari Parakrama.

44 I have found only a single inscription in the Tenkasi area in which Tirunelveli Perumal Virapandya is cited as the ruler in the date portion of the record. This is at the Kutralam temple, five kilometres distant from Tenkasi (ARE 1917/452).

45 ARE 1917/528.

46 ARE 1917/576.

47 The old temple at Kutralam, five kilometres from Tenkasi, bears an inscription of uncertain date in which Bhutalavira Viramarttandavarman even adopts the name of his 15th-century Pandya predecessor. The record (ARE 1917/423) is a divine command issued by the Lord of Kutralam confirming that 'our son' Viramarttanda Parakrama Pandya had renovated the temple and appointed new personnel.

48 Sethuraman, 'The Later Pandyas', p. 111. See also N. Nagam Aiya, *The Travancore State Manual*, vol. 1, Trivandrum: Travancore Government Press, 1906, pp. 295–7; R. Kannan, *Tiruppudaimarudur Murals and Woodcarvings*, Chennai: Government Museum, 2014, p. 32.
49 ARE 1926/540 = SITI 163 and ARE 1926/576.
50 See Orr, 'Maṭhas in the History of Southernmost India.' On the temples of Srivilliputtur, see Archana Venkatesan and Crispin Branfoot, *In Andal's Garden: Art, Ornament and Devotion in Srivilliputtur*, Mumbai: Marg, 2015.
51 ARE 1909/444 = SII 26.467.
52 ARE 1909/450.
53 ARE 1916/420.
54 Anna Seastrand, in her study of the murals inside the gopura of the temple at Tiruppudaimarudur, has suggested that they were painted in the early 16th century. The high visibility of Bhutalavira Viramarttandavarman and others of his family in Nanguneri and Ambasamudram taluks in the first half of the 16th century may indicate that the Kerala kings had some role in sponsoring this artistic production. Anna Lise Seastrand, 'Praise, Politics, and Language: South Indian Murals, 1500–1800' (unpublished Ph.D. dissertation, Columbia University, 2013).
55 ARE 1916/321 and 322.
56 ARE 1916/303.
57 ARE 1929–30/366.
58 The Kerala rulers themselves also turned their attention to Vanamamalai, as attested by an inscription dated 1545, recording King Bhutalavira Ramavarman's order, issued from Shenbagaramanallur, according the rights of temple accountant to a certain Ramanuja Jiyan (ARE 1927–28/261).
59 ARE 1928–29/13 = 1976–77/238.
60 Frequently two or more Kerala kings ruled concurrently, and they shared many of the same names and titles. Here I am distinguishing between Bhutalavira Viramarttandavarman and the slightly later ruler Bhutalavira Ramavarman. See Nagam Aiya, *The Travancore State Manual*, vol. 1, pp. 276, 295–9.
61 ARE 1928–29/14 = 1976–77/239.
62 Sethuraman suggests that particular *nakṣatras* might be recognised, and even referred to as birth stars, when they were the date of a Pandya king's coronation—Sethuraman, 'Tenkasi Parakrama Pandya', p. 59.
63 ARE 1917/531.
64 ARE 1917/513.
65 ARE 1917/657–660, 662–663, and 666. Sethuraman attributes some of these inscriptions at Panpuli to Jatilavarman Srivallabha Tirunelveli Perumal 'who revived the past', who reigned from 1534 to 1545. This king was also called Kulasekhara in certain inscriptions and his birth star was Asvati. Sethuraman, 'Later Pandyas', pp. 103, 113.
66 ARE 1915/567 = SII 30.216. According to Sethuraman (*ibid*: 103 and 113), the king referred to in the Darukapuram inscription is Jatilavarman Srivallabha Tirunelveli Perumal 'who revived the past'.
67 ARE 1944–45/57–59.
68 ARE 1908/277 = SII 25.277. The earliest inscription at Karivalamvandanallur dates from 1402; this site seems to have been a focus of devotion for the later Pandya ruler Abhirama Varatungarama, whose birthday celebration here was established in 1587 (ARE 1908/272 = SII 25.272; Orr, 'Making Place in a Small Space'). This king was the older brother of Ativirarama Srivallabha, whom we will soon meet, and was an author; his works include verses in praise of the

god Palvannanatha of Karivalamvandanallur (David Shulman, *More Than Real: A History of the Imagination in South India*, Cambridge: Harvard University Press, 2012, chapter 7). The history of the Sankaranarayanakoyil temple is quite obscure, but no inscriptions earlier than the mid-15th century have been reported here. Thus, it too is a 'new' temple at the time of the Tenkasi Pandyas, although there is no indication that the temples discussed here—with the exception of the Kasi Visvanatha temple—were built by these rulers.

69 Sethuraman, 'The Later Pandyas', pp. 106–7. On Ativirarama Srivallabha as a literary figure, see Shulman, *More Than Real*, chapter 8. Although we do not find birthday celebrations instituted in his honour, the inscriptions routinely identify him as having been born on the *nakṣatra* Punarvasu.

70 In the previous year, 1566, Ativirarama Srivallabha's younger brother, who bore the same name, had built the Vinnakaram Perumal temple, dedicated to Viṣṇu, virtually next door to the site of the Kulasekhara temple (Sethuraman, 'Later Pandyas', pp. 106–7; ARE 1917/ 498 and 501). The king's building of the Kulasekhara temple and the consecration therein of the god and his consort Kulalvaymolimangai, as well as arrangements for festivals and daily worship, are recorded in inscriptions on the walls of the central shrine (ARE 1909/534 = SII 26.564; ARE 1909/ 535 = SII 26.565; ARE 1917/490). One of these inscriptions (ARE 1909/535) is a divine command issued by the god Kasi Visvanatha, referring to Ativirarama Srivallabha as 'our son'. This king was also referred to as 'our son' by the god of Sankaranayanarkoyil, in an inscription of 1562 (ARE 1944–45/61), in which he was involved in the appointment of temple servants, just as was his predecessor in the 1540's, Tirunelveli Perumal Kulasekhara (ARE 1944–45/57–59). On the Kulasekhara temple in Tenkasi, see Branfoot, *Gods on the Move*, pp. 111–13.

71 ARE 1926/592. It is said that Ativirarama Srivallabha built the Krishna temple for the merit of Virappa-Nayaka, one of the Madurai Nayakas. This is one of the very few references to these Madurai rulers that we encounter in this region. For the architecture of the Krishna temple, see Branfoot, *Gods on the Move*, pp. 110–12.

72 ARE 1926/531. The arrangements here—for a service in the ruler's name in the Antal temple and for providing food in a *maṭha*—are very similar to those made by the Kerala king Bhutalavira Viramarttandavarman in 1534, according to the inscriptions engraved on the south wall of the Perumal temple and the north wall of the Antal temple (ARE 1926/540 = SITI 163 and ARE 1926/576).

73 ARE 1918/325.

74 ARE 1980–81/260.

75 Orr, 'Making and Marking Place'.

76 On this phenomenon among kings and 'chiefs' at Kanchipuram, Srirangam, and Tiruvannamalai, see Leslie C. Orr, 'Chiefly Queens: Local Royal Women as Temple Patrons in the Late Chola Period', in Emmanuel Francis and Charlotte Schmid (eds), *The Archaeology of Bhakti: Royal Bhakti, Local Bhakti*, Pondichéry: Institut Français de Pondichéry / Ecole française d'Extrême-Orient, 2016, pp. 413–16.

77 Bhutalavira Viramarttandavarman's gift at Srivilliputtur was made to provide for a daily Viramattandan *canti* and monthly observances on the Asvati *nakṣatra* in the Antal temple, and for feeding Brahmins in a *maṭha* (ARE 1926/540 and 576). Jatilavarman Srivallabha Tirunelveli Perumal 'who revived the past' granted land to temple servants at the Kasi Visvanatha temple in Tenkasi, in 1535 (ARE 1909/525 = SII26.555) and built an enclosing wall at the Perumal temple in Srivilliputtur in 1536 (ARE 1926/561).

78 See Harry Falk, 'The Early Use of *Nakṣatras*', in David Brown et al. (ed), *The Interactions of Ancient Astral Science*, Bremen: Hempen Verlag, 2018, pp. 527–32.

79 Previously, I have referred in passing to the fact that two non-royal birthdays were celebrated at Nanguneri in the 13th and early 14th centuries. Although the 16th-century kings we have considered do not have *nakṣatra* observances timed to coincide with bathing rituals, we see in the case of Tirunelveli Perumal Kulasekhara's gift of 1552 at the Kasi Visvanatha temple a concern with the god's ritual bath at an annual festival, as the king provided for services when the deity would be brought to the bathing mandapa that he had built.

6

POWER, PROCESSIONS AND THE FESTIVAL ARCHITECTURE OF THE TAMIL TEMPLE

Crispin Branfoot

Alongside the road leading north from Madurai to the great Tamil Vaiṣṇava temple and pilgrimage site at Alagarkoyil is a small pavilion. The unremarkable exterior of this flat-roofed *maṇḍapa* contrasts with the wide aisle and high ceiling of the spacious interior before a raised enclosed platform at the south end. Facing into this space are four life-size sculpted figures of men, all elegantly dressed and bejewelled, with their hands placed together before their chests in a gesture of greeting or devotion (Figure 6.1). Both the location and the iconography of these early 17th-century images suggest the absent presence of the object of their devotion, the temple's deity, who would periodically take up residence in this columned hall when brought in procession to sit upon the raised platform. Until recently, this modest hall was in a dilapidated condition and remains unused for temporary festivals at this otherwise active site of pilgrimage. Yet the remains of disused buildings such as this illustrate a wider pattern of architectural transformation in the south Indian temple since the 11th century, with increasing numbers of buildings and spaces designed to frame processions and accommodate the temporary residence of deities.

Many historians have understood India's historic temples built across south Asia from the 5th–6th centuries CE as archaeological sites, focussing on the materiality of their richly ornamented built form and the animated programme of figural imagery that transforms the sculpted surfaces. In Tamil Nadu, some of the oldest temples—such as Narttamalai or Kodumbalur—are archaeological sites. However, many South Indian temples have long ritual and religious histories and many are very large indeed, with additions extending over centuries to create the temple cities that the region is famous for. As a result, no study of the Tamil temple that addresses the history of the form and ornament of the main shrine alone may be considered complete. This chapter examines how the study of the architecture and material

Figure 6.1 Interior of Tirumala Maṇḍapa, Alagarkoyil

Source: Author

culture of the Tamil temple procession—the mobile images and the modes of transport, the routes they take and their destinations—may contribute to the understanding of the ritual dynamics and expression of power within the Tamil temple. This will emphasise that processions and ritual movement are an essential factor to understanding the transformation of scale, layout and design of temples.

Architecture, sacred space and experience

The use of ritual as an analytic and conceptual tool across the range of material-cultural disciplines—archaeology, architectural history, the history of art—has seen a remarkable increase since the 1990s, as Elsner has remarked. 'The question of architecture is a special case of the theme of ritual and art, since it is about the orchestration of (performative) space—the frames within which people were constructed as ritual subjects—as opposed to the specific artifacts used by people within ritual.'[1] Although architecture is necessarily static and site-specific, it may shape human actions—the routes towards and through a building, the lines of sight and destinations—and by framing topography and shaping space establish the conditions for religious ritual.[2] Scholars interested in the archaeology of ritual performance and dynamics, such as in ancient Greece, Rome or Egypt, have had to rely on texts and archaeological data. Amid the burgeoning literature from the 1990s onward on ritual, living images, sacrifice, pilgrimage, sacred landscape and processions in the ancient Greek and Roman Mediterranean, several scholars have turned to contemporary South Asia for cross-cultural comparison of ethnographic practice.[3] Religious processions and festivals are such a prominent spectacle of modern South Asia that they have been subject to extensive examination, especially their social and political dimensions.[4] The rich traditions of South Indian temple processions are often among such studies, though less attention has been paid to their impact upon the performative interpretation of temple architecture and urban space.[5]

In South India, festivals are a part of every temple's ritual calendar, both minor ones that occur each month and major annual ones lasting ten days or more. Festivals occur as part of the lunar calendar in common with other similarly dedicated temples, often on the first day of the month or the new moon, and as local events, dramatising the myths of a particular deity and temple site. A marriage festival (*kalyāṇotsavam*) of the god and goddess is commonly held, for example, at temples throughout South India. A central feature of most festivals is the procession (*puṟappāṭu*, 'going forth' or *eḻuntaruḷ*, 'to graciously appear'). Contemporary ritual practices offer the opportunity to understand temples and cities as dynamic spaces. In our examination of Srivilliputtur, Archana Venkatesan and I interpreted the Āṇṭāḷ-Vaṭapatrāśāyana temple at the centre of the town as a ritual and processional space, animated by the movement of devotees inward and around the various shrines and by the processions of the deities themselves within the temple walls and out and around town.[6] At other temples, such as the Nampirāyar at Tirukkurunkudi, far fewer processions may take place outside the temple walls. We cannot assume that contemporary practice is the same as the past, whether 50 or 500 years ago, yet such observations highlight the continuing dynamic nature of ritual practice in Tamil temples since the 7th century.

Processions in Tamil literature and epigraphy

In South India there is a deep-rooted tradition of moving deities on procession in and around the temples of the Tamil region, as attested by literature, inscriptions and the buildings themselves. In Sangam literature of the early 1st millennium CE, the processions and pilgrimage of devotees to specific sites is mentioned.[7] Contemporary with the increasing numbers of temples constructed in brick and stone from the 7th century is the outpouring of passionate devotion to deities rooted in the landscape by the Vaiṣṇava and

Śaiva poet-saints. Appar evokes an image of Śiva's 'going forth' during the Tiruvātirai festival at Tiruvarur:

On every street, white flags flutter,
canopies studded with great bright gems
glitter, festooned with strands
of priceless coral and pearl.
Such is the splendour of Ātirai day
Of the Primal Lord in Ārūr. (Appar IV.21 v.3)

The ascetic god goes in procession,
led by the immortal gods
whose heads are bowed to him,
while lovely celestial women
with shoulders graceful as the bamboo
follow behind, and ash-smeared devotees
surround him, singing his praise.
Such is the splendour of Ātirai day
Of the Lord of Ārūr! (v.8)[8]

However evocative of deities in procession, there are far more references in *bhakti* literature to the movement of devotees to temples than the deity's movement.[9]

Although the roots of Tamil temple processions may be traced to the 7th century, more substantive literary and epigraphic evidence indicates that processions had become an important feature of both religious and royal ritual by the 10th to 13th centuries. In *Śaiva Siddhānta* cosmology, a pan-Indian school of Hinduism from the 10th to 13th centuries and the dominant form of Śaivism in Tamilnadu with a rich literature in Sanskrit and Tamil composed from this period, ritual performance re-enacts the oscillation of the universe between moments of creation and destruction, emission and reabsorption, expansion and contraction. The temple is 'an emanated structure, unfolding from its centre, and space within the temple is organised as a concentric hierarchy, with the most exalted areas located at or nearest the centre'.[10] During temple festivals, Śiva's procession is an 'emission outward' (*udbhūtasṛṣṭi*), a visible manifestation of Siva's creative activity (*sṛṣṭi*) according to the *Kāraṇāgama*. Śiva transfers his presence from the immobile, undifferentiated *liṅga* to a variety of portable, differentiated manifestations so that he can proceed from the centre to the outer regions of the ritual space. Furthermore, he also emanates his lordship to those subordinate deities that he visits and extends his grace to the wider community.[11]

Our understanding of Tamil temple processions in this period is enriched by Richard Davis' commentary and translation of the Sanskrit *Mahotsavavidhi*, a Śaiva ritual guidebook of rules or prescriptions for the conduct of a major temple festival, that was composed by the *ācārya* Aghoraśiva in 1157 during the reign of Rājarāja II (r. 1146–72). This presented a 'priest's-eye vision of how an ideal festival should be enacted within a Śaiva temple' and though we cannot know the exact relationship this medieval text bore to existing temple practices, Davis considers this prescriptive work to have played a significant role in institutionalising and disseminating a shared pattern for Śaiva temple festivals in medieval India.[12] Such ritual texts outline the procedures for the range of festivals that take place within Tamil Śaiva temples: the 'daily festival' (*nityotsava*), the periodic festivals that may take place weekly (*varotsava*), fortnightly (*pakṣotsava*), or monthly (*māsotsava*), those that are coordinated with star alignments (*ṛkṣotsava*) or solar transitions (*saṅkrānti*) and the annual great festivals (*mahotsava*) that can last up to fifteen days. Among the complex set of ritual activities, twice-daily processions are an important feature of the *mahotsava*.

In Leslie C. Orr's detailed study of processions drawing upon the inscriptions of the 9th to 14th centuries, she notes the centrality of the deity as actor; these processions are about the deity actively seeing and not just an opportunity for them to be seen by devotees.[13] Though there is some continuity with later practices, Orr notes that the processions of the Chola period do not seem to emerge from the temple into the streets beyond as often as later. 'Conspicuous by their absence are epigraphical references to the god's circular movement outside the temple compound—the type of trajectory that may be interpreted as a demarcation of the Lord's domain, and which seems integral to the character of modern temple processions'.[14] Though the evidence is fragmentary, some inscriptions from before the 14th century suggest that a few contemporary festivals celebrated at some of the most important temples are of great antiquity. After the 14th century, the number of festivals and their duration tended to increase, especially at the Tamil region's major temples.[15]

The Venkaṭeśvara temple at Tirumalai (Tirupati) provides unusually good data for illustrating the changes in festival ritual over the past millennium. Before the 14th century, there were a limited number of festivals celebrated at the temple but after this there was a huge expansion. From 966 only one major festival was celebrated each year but by 1328 there were five, in 1390 seven and 11 by 1583; the duration in days also increased over this period to 13 days each by the late 16th century. Before the late 1330s, there is little clear mention of processional deities, but they do appear in some later records together with other details such as the use of different *vāhana*s. New festivals celebrated from the 15th century at Tirumalai include the recitation festival (*adhyanōtsavam*), a float-festival in the tank and a Vasanta festival.[16] Few temples have such extensive, site-specific evidence for the antiquity or provision of festivals and processions. Inscriptions referring to festivals do not routinely mention processions, instead more commonly referring to food offerings for the deity and devotees, the bathing and adorning of the god's image, and other arrangements such as the provision of lamps, garlands and the singing of hymns.[17] Furthermore, inscriptions only occasionally mention the spaces and buildings of processions or the objects carried.

Material culture of the procession: images and vehicles

When deities travel beyond the main shrine, it is not the stone *mūlamūrti* that is carried but a metal image (*cala-* or *utsava-mūrti*). Until the 1990s discussion of south Indian bronzes concentrated on the classification, identification and chronology of bronze images with less attention to their purpose and function. The material culture turn in religious studies has now focused welcome attention on the reception of bronze images in their temple setting, the role of ornament—such as clothing and jewellery—and the occasions, means and destinations of their transportation.[18] The earliest surviving bronze images from the Tamil region are contemporary with the expanding number of temples built in stone—and brick, though few of these have survived later renovations—in the 8th–9th centuries, though far more may be ascribed to the 10th to 12th centuries when temple processions seem to have become routine. Short of a more detailed survey, attention may be drawn to a few material issues in considering Tamil temple bronzes: just how portable are they? Why were so many made? And should all bronzes be considered mobile, festival images?

The requirement that they are to some degree portable, together with the limitations of the lost-wax casting process, results in many bronze temple images of 40–80 cm high; some of the largest are around 150cm high.[19] The earliest surviving metal images are a fraction of this height at up to 30cm. Few publications of Chola-period bronzes cite the weight, but many would not be easy to shift onto a *vāhana* or be carried by one or two people.[20] Pairs of attached rings on the sides or circular holes in the base are suggestive of their processional function, enabling a separate metal dowel together with rope to fix the image onto a more substantial wooden platform or vehicle.[21] However, some early images made before 950 do not have such a substantive surviving base to ensure stability during a procession that may suggest the gradual adaptation to the processional purpose from the 10th century, though some were separately cast.[22] Furthermore, it would be over-simplistic to attribute all metal images stored within temples to public processional use; not all metal images, such as the very smallest ones used in domestic shrines, are necessarily to be understood as for processions.

There is a variety of bronze images and temples usually have multiple, rather than a single, festival image. Amid the burgeoning scholarly interest in the history of collecting, we have precious little evidence for the number and range of bronzes in an individual temple's possession around the time of its establishment with two notable exceptions. Inscriptions record the collections of images at two Chola temples, both Śaiva.[23] One dated 1018 from the Gomuktiśvara temple at Tiruvaduturai lists 25 bronze images in the temple's possession, including ten different forms of Śiva, six forms of Umā (with and without Śiva), Gaṇeśa, an *astradevar* (trident), a bull, Śiva's favoured devotee Caṇḍeśa and the three most important poet–saints (Appar, Sundarar, Sambandar). The monumental Rājarājeśvara temple at Tanjavur has inscriptions that record the donation of over 60 different metal images upon its consecration in 1010. Although there are a wide range of iconographic types, several of the same deity were also donated, including two images of Naṭarāja and two of Tripuravijaya with their consorts, in addition to nine images of Gaṇeśa of varied dimensions and weight: there are far more than necessary.

The multiplicity of bronze images in a single temple may be partially accounted for by the routine use of five during a Śaiva festival procession: Gaṇeśa leading, Caṇḍeśa bringing up the rear and with Somāskanda, Umā alone and another such as Naṭarāja or Skanda between. Different festivals may require a different form of Śiva but the primary processional form is Somāskanda, explaining the great number of such images in existence; indeed, the *Ajitāgama* states that a Somāskanda image can be used as a substitute for other images if they are not available for specific festivals.[24] Candraśekhara ('moon crowned', Śiva wearing the moon in his crown or hair) may be used during festivals held at the moon's transitions, full or new, and other forms of Śiva may be appropriate for specific days during longer festivals.[25] In contemporary practice in Vaiṣṇava temples Perumāḷ (Viṣṇu) travels alone or with his two consorts, Śrī and Bhū; bronzes of his avatars, such as Bhū-Varāha, Narasiṁha or Kṛṣṇa on Kāliya may be used in specific festival events or at temples where this form of Perumāḷ is enshrined.

As is evident from the many early 19th-century paintings of processions and festivals today, images of deities are carried on three types of vehicle.[26] The smallest are the wooden palanquins (*palakku*) carried by two to four men, often simple platforms between long bamboo poles. More elaborate versions with the deity suspended beneath a sinuous bow-shaped pole were commoner in the 17th–18th centuries. These palanquins are used for daily processions around the temple, such as the twice-daily movement of the god and goddess from separate daytime shrines to spend the night together in their bedchamber (*paḷḷiyaṟai*) or for the subsidiary deities and poet-saints of the temple complex. During annual festivals two larger types of vehicle are used, the *vāhana* and the wheeled mobile temple-chariot (*ratha, tēr*). *Vāhana*s are made from wood and painted or occasionally covered in sheet metal, such as silver; few remain that date earlier than 1900. Contemporary practice and the evidence from medieval *āgama*s indicate that many different *vāhana*s were used for the morning and evening processions during a single festival lasting from ten to 15 days (Figure 6.2). Śaiva *vāhana*s

Figure 6.2 Somaskanda on silver Nandi *vāhana*, Jambukeśvara temple, Srirangam
Source: Author

include a lion, the Sun, Moon, a Bhūta, Hamsa, Nāga, Bull, Swing, Elephant, Horse and Tree of Plenty (*kalpataru*).[27] Many similar *vāhaṇa*s are used in Vaiṣṇava temples, together with ones in the form of Śeṣa, Garuḍa, Hanumān, Kāmadhenu, a *yāḷi* or a peacock.[28] The *tēr*s are constructed with a wooden base in the form of an inverted pyramid with large wheels each side. Elaborate sculpted panels, often fine examples of South Indian woodcarving, may be placed around the base. A temporary wooden pavilion is constructed each year that is covered in coloured appliqué or painted textiles to shelter the throne platform for the processional images.[29] There are reference to *tēr*s in *āgamic* literature in the 12th century together with a few examples of temple *maṇḍapa*s with sculpted horses and wheels.[30] A growing number of inscriptions from the 15th mention them, but surviving examples date to the 19th century at the earliest.

Architecture, space and the procession

Sacred places are often in a state of constant architectural accumulation and modification as structures are added, modified or replaced. Medieval literature and inscriptions, colonial-era paintings and contemporary practice all offer a range of compelling evidence for the significance of temple processions. But how can processions be revealed in the archaeological record? What is the material and spatial context within which these processions took place? Thinking about the processional movement of deities outward also entails a consideration of the movement of devotees inward, and how architectural space conditions, constructs and frames that experience. Broadly speaking, two types of movement may be identified: linear, goal-oriented and circumambulatory movement. The latter is routinely clockwise (*pradakṣiṇa*), a long-established and widespread act of respect to the image, person, building or space. Many of the earliest sacred monuments in the Tamil country, dating to the late 6th to 8th centuries, are rock-cut caves. Their usual layout invites linear movement directly to the central, frontal shrine for there is no provision for circumambulatory movement around the ritual focus, unless the rock or hill in which the cave is excavated was itself circumambulated. The addition of a series of columned halls before some rock-cut caves that have remained the focus of worship in later centuries served to amplify and extend the linear route inward and the procession of the deity directly outward. This is evident at Tirupparankundram near Madurai, for example, the 8th-century Pandya cave now entered via a series of *maṇḍapa*s and a *gopuram* built between the 11th and 17th centuries.[31]

As structural temples began to be built in greater numbers from 700, it became common for the main shrine to be surrounded by an enclosure wall punctuated by one or more gateways usually aligned with the primary axis of access towards the ritual centre. The subsequent millennium-long history of the Tamil temple sees the temples' expansion with longer approaches to the main shrine, often hidden within multiple concentric walled enclosures (*prākāra*) punctuated by a series of pyramidal gateways (*gopuram*). The multiplication of concentric enclosures begins in the 11th century but is primarily a development of the 13th century and later for the largest, most important temples. By the 17th century, many temples in the Tamil region are of vast scale, dominating the urban fabric, the largest with two-four high-walled enclosures—or seven in the exceptional case of the Raṅganātha temple at Srirangam—entered through aligned series of *gopurams*. Temple space is thus organised as a concentric hierarchy around the most powerful, sacred centre, the location of the pre-eminent deity. The hierarchy of sacred space emanating out from the centre that the walls and gateways defined had a social dimension in the gradation of access of both individuals and groups to seeing and being seen by the deity, the important Hindu ritual of *darśana*.

Two distinctions in the ordering of temple space have often been stated: first, that 'caste Hindus' were allowed into temples and 'untouchables' were not, and second, among the former category of caste Hindus, only the priests had access to the deity's shrine itself within the temple.[32] Missing from such accounts are not only the king or lord, but the more elaborate gradations of different classes of devotees, according to caste and initiation, that are elaborated in many medieval *āgamas* used in Śrīvaiṣṇava and Śaiva Siddhānta temples in South India. In some texts, there is an explicit relationship between categories of devotees and the innermost part of the temple that an individual could stand when viewing the deity, from the *garbhagṛha* itself through the series of attached *maṇḍapas* (*antarāla, ardha-, mahā-* and *mukhamaṇḍapas*) to the outer pavilions and the gateway of the *gopuram*.[33] The hierarchy of architectural space is thus both an ordering of emanating divine power outward from the centre and the inward gradation of social access to that divine authority.

The movement of devotees inward and around the temple is shared with the processional movement of deities outward and around. Even quite modest material features of temple design may be understood in terms of deities' processions. Small rectangular plinths, sometimes as little as 30–40 cm long, with usually three or five rounded projections on top are often located around the base of temples or their enclosure walls, either directly adjacent or one or two metres away. These are sacrificial stones related to a larger stone *balipīṭha*, an often-elaborate moulded platform supporting a sculpted lotus, that is normally placed alongside an image of the temple deity's vehicle (*vāhaṇa*), the seated bull Nandi for Śiva or kneeling Garuḍa for Viṣṇu, and the flagpole (*dhvajastambha*) used to mark the beginning and conclusion of a festival (Figure 6.3). The commonest processions within a temple are the daily ones that form part of the *śrībali* ritual that honours the guardians of the directions of space indicated by these stones. It is the larger *balipīṭha* rather than the temple walls or gateways through them that demarcates an important point of ritual transition inward and out, together with the additional smaller altars surrounding the temple. These modest sculpted stones are of significance for they define the boundary of one layer of the site and deity's and temple's sacred power, and processions by priests reinscribe this daily, as is evident from both contemporary practice and

Figure 6.3 Balipīṭha and dhvajastambha of Kaḷḷapirān temple, Srivaikuntam
Source: Author

agamic injunctions. In Chola-period inscriptions, *śrībali* processions are the most common ones mentioned.[34]

Processions are not only concerned with movement but also temporary pauses at certain places: before shrines, at important ritual axes, or for longer periods of rest in structures specifically built for the purpose. The number, scale and elaboration of buildings specifically designed for use during periodic rituals in Tamil temples, especially detached columned halls (*maṇḍapa*) for the temporary display of deities, is evidence for the growing importance of festivals from the 12th century. Earlier festivals may have used temporary wooden structures or not have had an architecturally-defined festival space. These stone *maṇḍapa*s vary enormously in scale, from the ubiquitous small four-columned pavilions to the monumental 1000-column halls at major temples such as Chidambaram and Srirangam, both built in the 13th century, and in the late 16th century at Madurai. Named for their number of columns, such as the largest 100- or 1000-column *maṇḍapa*s (even when the number is slightly less), or the festival that usually takes place there—*vasanta* (Spring), for example—they are perhaps better identified as more simply festival (*utsava*) *maṇḍapa*s if their primary purpose is not known. The construction of multiple specialised *maṇḍapa*s for particular festivals, rather than having just one festival *maṇḍapa* for all celebrations, emphasises the growing significance of festival ritual to an understanding of the layout of the Tamil temple complex built and expanded from the 11th century.

During a festival, deities are brought in procession to the *maṇḍapa*, where they stay for a few hours or many days. Many of these *maṇḍapa*s are located at some distance from the main shrine, so the processions to the buildings and the temporary enthronement are both about the emanation of divine authority outward and the wider social access to the deity. These festival *maṇḍapa*s are often rectangular, with a similar exterior elevation to the other temple structures: a moulded basement (*adhiṣṭhāna*), rows of columns supporting a flat roof with a curved eave all round and brick-and-plaster pavilions above. The interior is based around a single processional aisle leading to a platform for the deity to rest on. Even very large *maṇḍapa*s with dense rows of columns will have a wider central aisle leading to a platform, so though there may be space to move around between columns, the focus is on the approach to the deity. The design principles of festival *maṇḍapa*s are similar to those of the temple complex as a whole: pronounced axiality on a single axis of approach, a lesser emphasis on the four cardinal directions and a concentric layout. These festival *maṇḍapa*s are to be seen as galleries or theatres: they are both a space to move through and a space for display, in this case one or more deities (Figure 6.4). The homology of the royal and the divine, evident in temple ritual, is evident in the architectural design of these audience halls for the temporary residence of deities holding court for their assembled subjects and devotees. The central aisle within the *maṇḍapa* is emphasised by its height and width, especially from the later 16th century,

Figure 6.4 The goddess Āṇṭāḷ enthroned in the maṇḍapa in the garden marking her birthplace in Srivilliputtur

Source: Author

as larger columns enabled greater distances to be spanned, compared with the plainer columns in the rows supporting a lower ceiling. As a result, both grander processional paths towards the raised throne platform upon which the deity was placed could be created and more devotees were able to assemble in rows down each side to worship the enthroned deities as a modest congregation.

Architectural sculpture may similarly inform our understanding of patterns of ritual movement within the sacred space. From the 16th century large two-metre-high sculptures of deities appear within many Tamil temples—especially in the far south—and the locations and concentration of such sculpture at the entrances to and along the aisles within festival *maṇḍapa*s suggests a connection with the major processional routes through the temple to performative spaces. Increasing numbers of standing male figures—often up to life-size and usually richly dressed, ornamented and bejewelled—appear in the corridors and festival-*maṇḍapa*s of Tamil temples in the same period. These human images are routinely shown standing with their hands held in front of their chests (*añjalimudrā*) and are mostly located in corridors, in the gateways of *gopura*s and in festival *maṇḍapa*s. These are all on processional routes or places where deities are normally absent but at certain times crucially present; these images are placed to greet deities when they are moving or temporarily enthroned during festivals. Though the identification of known historic individuals is complex, many of these may be understood as images of royal patrons and donors. It is only when the festival dimension of the temple complex is appreciated that their positioning and iconography as the protector and devoted servant of the deities make sense. They see the deity and the deity sees them, but this is a three-cornered relationship, for not only do the god and king or lord greet each other, but the devotees or worshippers see both the ruler and the deity and the relationship between the two when they are assembled for the festival. Ten such figures, plus male attendants, line the third *prākāra* corridor of the Nellaiyappar temple at Tirunelveli, dating to the middle of the 17th century. During festivals, Nellaiyappar circumambulates the great corridors of the third *prākāra* past these figures before leaving the temple for the streets outside. Their position in the southeast section of the *prākāra* also means that these sculptures will greet deities passing on the more frequent processions within the temple, such as the twice-daily procession taking Nellaiyappar to and from the *paḷḷiyaṟai* (bedchamber) in the Kantimati (Ammaṉ) temple each morning and evening. The height of the plinths on which the figures are placed is explained by the elevation of passing deities being carried in a palanquin or *vāhana*.[35]

The analysis of architectural design and the distribution of sculpture in festival *maṇḍapa*s and corridors is assisted by observations of contemporary practice in which ritual spaces are seen to be periodically animated by the movement and temporary display of bronze images of deities. But even at archaeological sites with no current ritual activities, past temporary festival display may be suggested by the presence and design of such ancillary structures. Furthermore, the routes of processions may also be indicated by the locations of major figural sculpture even at temples where the use of *maṇḍapa*s and the location for certain festival events may have changed or been abandoned. There is little reference to *maṇḍapa*s' functions in *āgama*s, which are more concerned with variations in size and proportion.

Temples are not static buildings: rituals change, the routes of processions may be altered, pilgrim numbers may rise and fall. Architectural additions and modifications may be indicative of such shifting of ritual requirements. For example, at the Nampirāyar temple at Tirukkurunkudi, a 16-column stone *maṇḍapa* dating to the 17th century, indicated on the earliest known plan in 1898, was shortly afterwards relocated 250 feet west to the other end of the same *prākāra*. Disused *maṇḍapa*s may reveal their former purpose through the interpretation of their architectural sculpture and design. This is the case with the ruined *maṇḍapa* at Alagarkoyil with which we began, within which four life-sized portrait images either side and facing toward a rear platform suggest the periodic presence of a now-absent deity (Figs. 6.1, 6.5). From a comparison with other similar images, the pair

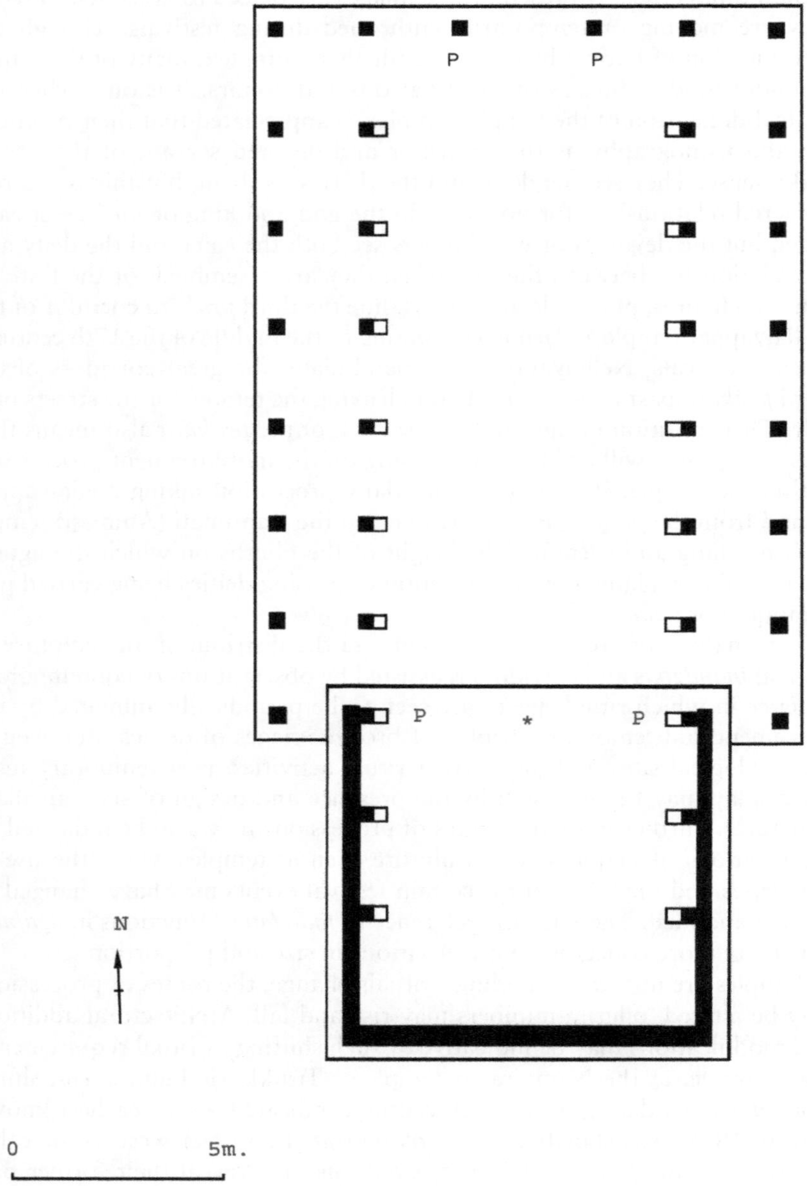

Figure 6.5 Plan of Tirumala Maṇḍapa, Alagarkoyil (* marks the position of the processional image; P portrait images)

Source: Author

either side of the platform may be identified as Tirumala Nayaka (r. 1623–1659) and his brother and predecessor Muttu Vīrappa (r. 1609–1623), each joined by a smaller queen who faces outward. The two facing the platform from the north may be their late 16th century Madurai Nayaka predecessors, Kṛṣṇappa (r. 1564–1572) and his son Vīrappa (r. 1572–1595), establishing a visual genealogy of the Madurai Nayakas within this *maṇḍapa*.[36] A large palace, similar to the Nayaka-period palace at Madurai with multiple domed roofs, was built alongside this *maṇḍapa*, further indicating the legacy of Tirumala and the Madurai Nayakas' patronage of the temple and the architectural display of their authority.[37]

In an archaeology of performance in such structures, considering the mutual visibility and interaction between immanent deity and the varying scale and social inclusiveness of the devotional audience is important. But the emphasis on sight, so critical to Hindu ritual, needs to be joined with the broader sensorium in the understanding of festival *maṇḍapa*s. This might include the acoustics of these flat-roofed buildings used for oral, collective recitation and instruction, music performances and—until the early 20th century—dances by professional women before the deity, or indeed the impact of the smoke from lamps and torches, or the fragrance of flowers and incense.

Beyond the temple walls: tanks, maṇḍapas and routes

Processions periodically venture beyond the temple walls, especially during the most important festivals, though interior processions in the first and second *prākāra*s are far more common. The most visible and prominent of such processions outside the walls are the 'chariot' processions, usually held on the penultimate day of a major festival. The street directly outside the outermost enclosure wall is usually used for the *tērotsavam*, though in some very large and important temples—the Raṅganātha at Srirangam or Mīnākṣī-Sundareśvara in Madurai—it may be further out. The 'Car Street' can usually be identified within the urban plan by the greater width of the roads. The practicalities of moving and especially manoeuvring the *ratha* clockwise around corners necessitate additional streets for the numerous men pulling the ropes at the front to continue moving directly forwards until the *ratha* can be levered 90 degrees right, for the wheels are fixed.[38]

Given the difficulty of turning a *ratha* around corners, it is important to recognise the importance of linear and goal-oriented processions within the urban plans of temple towns. Studies of urban plans in Tamil South India have tended to draw attention to the concentric layers of space around a central major temple and the relationship with the idealised conceptions of space in *maṇḍala*s. Circumambulatory processions seem to redefine these limits of the sacred zone and, though mentioned in the *āgama*s, the presentation of such movement is neither consistent nor precise. Many Tamil towns have continuous histories of occupation over the past millennium, so investigating historic layouts and street patterns is difficult; few medieval towns have remained as archaeological sites to investigate. Gangaikonda-cholapuram was occupied from the early 11th until the 13th century before abandonment and, though archaeological surveys have revealed the outline of the rectangular settlement plan with a central palace and the well-known Śiva temple at its northeast corner, no traces of streets have been found. The long 14th century period of political disruption may not have affected urban fabrics much, despite the historical rhetoric of destruction and iconoclasm towards a few major temples that has suggested otherwise. Maps of cities made by the British and French during the Carnatic Wars of the 1750–1760s and later provide suggestive evidence for pre-modern layouts, but detailed plans of the majority of Tamil temple towns do not exist before the 1890s. Between the 1840s and 1860s, the British transformed many major towns, including Trichy and Madurai, by demolishing their fortifications walls and filling in the moats to create new, wide roads. In spite of the long period of Tamil urban development, the evaluation of some town plans and inscriptions does suggest that linear processions were initially important and circumambulatory processions by the deities were gradually introduced from the 15th century onward. This was when 'new patterns of patronage, new conceptions of divinity, new mobility and militarization, and new demarcations of social and sacred space all had an impact on processions and their meanings'.[39]

The wide 'chariot' streets on all four sides of the Naṭarāja temple at Chidambaram are a prominent part of the urban plan, but festival practice, the earliest inscriptions and the temple's building history suggest that linear processions may have been more important than circular ones before the 13th century or even later. A wide road links the Naṭarāja temple directly west with the Ānantiśvara temple, the site of Patañjali's hermitage, via the Illamaiyakkinar temple, the location of Vyāghrapāda's original *liṅga*s. The earliest inscriptions from Chidambaram dating to the reign of Vijayālaya (c. 850–885) were found not at the Naṭarāja temple but at the Ānantiśvara temple during its wholesale renovation in the 1930s.[40] The western side of town was the earliest to be built up and the initial construction from 1150 of the west *gopuram* before the remaining three gateways on the north, east and south sides, is suggestive of the importance of this east–west processional route linking these temples. One of the earliest known festivals at Chidambaram is the Masi *tīrthayātra*, a procession of Naṭarāja to a *maṇḍapa* by the sea at Killai seven miles east, which underscores the importance of linear, goal-oriented processions at Chidambaram, even if its significance subsequently declined.[41] Inscriptions of Vikrama Cola (r. 1118–1135) mention his patronage to the temple, including a *ratha* to draw Naṭarāja in procession at the 'festival of the great name' (*Perum peyar viḻa*) 'so as to cause prosperity on the great earth and joy to the gods' and the building of a long temple street, though it is unclear which one.[42] The present 'car' streets on the four sides of the temple may have been widened when the 18th-century fortifications were dismantled enabling greater numbers to witness the annual *ter* processions.[43]

Further north, the sack of Vijayanagara in 1565 by the Deccan sultanates has resulted in the surviving archaeological remains giving a good indication of the layout of this great 15th–16th century city without subsequent modification. Though in the northern Deccan, the major temples at the site were built according to the Tamil conception of a temple in both design and layout with multiple concentric enclosures and *gopurams*. All the major temples at the site either significantly expanded or built anew in the early decades of the 16th century—the Virūpākṣa, Viṭṭhala, Kṛṣṇa, Tiruveṅgaḷanātha, Paṭṭābhirāma—include long, straight processional streets extending several hundred metres beyond the main axial entrance (Figure 6.6). Though the geological limitations of the site may also have had an impact, the presence of a platform at one side near the temple gateway for the preparation of the tall *ratha* and *maṇḍapa*s at the termination of the street suggest that these are designed for linear 'chariot' processions rather than having streets on all four sides as is familiar later in Tamilnadu.

Processions may pause at important axes or before other deities and may rest for longer in other buildings designed for their temporary reception.

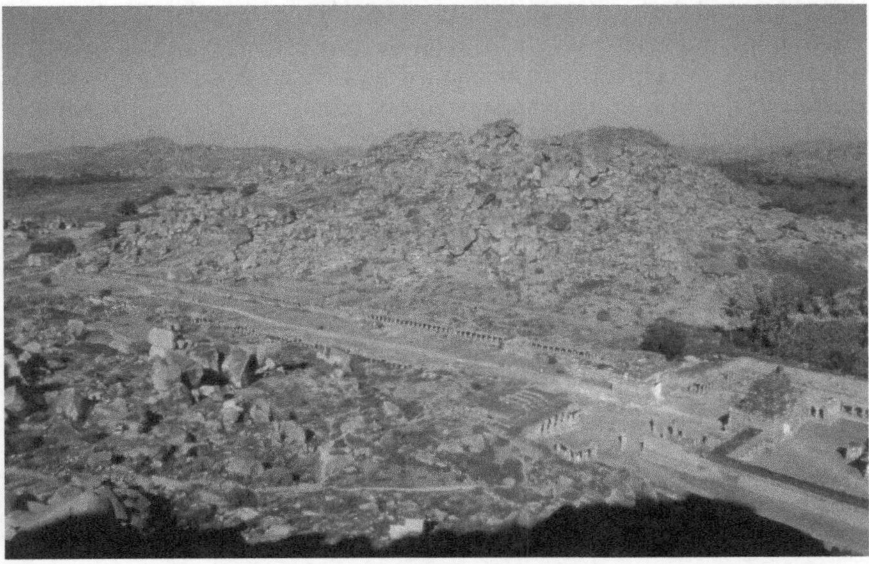

Figure 6.6 Street in front of Tiruvengalanatha temple (1530s), Vijayanagara
Source: Author

Inscriptions record endowments for the construction of *maṇḍapas*—permanent stone and temporary wooden ones—along processional routes and for the ceremonial reception of deities (*maṇṭappaṭi*) offerings at them. Deities may also travel to attend other temples' festivals. Among the deities present each year at the Adi *brahmotsavam* in Sriviliputtur, for example, is Viṣṇu from Tiruttangal, 15 miles away. Further surveys of the landscape between temples may reveal *maṇḍapa*s on processional routes that have fallen out of use in the past century or earlier. A series of *maṇḍapa*s built from the 17th century along the road between Alagarkoyil and Madurai 15 miles south are still in use each year during the Cittirai festival (April–May). Several 17th-century *maṇḍapam*s are located a few miles north of Srivilliputtur on the road to Madurai, suggesting points of rest for deities, or indeed Nayaka rulers, as they travelled between the temple cities. Alongside one *maṇḍapam* are the remains of a small Nayaka-period palace, perhaps for royal viewing or the reception of passing deities.[44]

Water-filled tanks are a notable feature of South Indian temples and the urban fabric, used for ritual bathing and for water storage; temples had a significant influence on the spread of irrigation as part of the medieval agricultural economy. Tanks may feature within the site-myths (*sthalapurāṇa*) of temples: water from the three rivers Gaṅgā, Yamunā and Saraswati filled the tank in Srivilliputtur, for example, in which Viṣṇu cleansed his *cakra* after killing the demon Kālanemi. Tanks are used for the purification of deities (*tīrttavāri, tīrthasnāna*) from the pollution incurred by processions outside the temple and the bathing of deities is routinely mentioned in Chola-period inscriptions. Some festivals focus upon the procession of a deity to a river or sea for a special bath, as mentioned previously. A reference to a procession to the 'sea' at Tiruvannamalai 60 miles from the coast was probably to a nearby tank in the town.[45] A 'Seven Seas Tank' (Ēḻukkaṭalkkulam) was commissioned by the Vijayanagara king Kṛṣṇadeva in 1516 east of the Mīnākṣī-Sundareśvara temple in Madurai, though it is now under a shopping block.[46]

Some temple-tanks are built specifically for the celebration of a festival once per year. Three kilometres south of Alagarkoyil lies a large stepped tank, now dilapidated, just west of the road to Madurai (Figure 6.7). The presence of a central four-columned *maṇḍapa* suggests that this was not constructed primarily for water storage but was formerly a *teppakkulam*, a tank built for the celebration of a *teppotsavam* or float festival. These normally take place on one day only, often in either the month of Tai or Masi. *Teppakkulams* are not routinely located within the temple walls but may be located a significant distance from the temple to which they are associated: the still-functioning Vandiyur *teppakkulam* in Madurai is around 300 metres square and was built in the 1630s, seven kilometres southeast of the Mīnākṣī-Sundareśvara temple. Many were built in the 16th and 17th centuries, when *teppotsavams* became more common. During a float festival

Figure 6.7 Ruined teppakkulam, 3 kilometres south of Alagarkoyil

Source: Author

the deities are placed on a *teppam*, a floating equivalent of a *ter*, and then are either poled around by men on the *teppam* or dragged around the tank clockwise by people on the outer edge holding long ropes. The central island is used primarily for the deities to rest periodically during the festival, but also for a few men to hold ropes attached to the *teppam* to keep it in the middle of the tank's circumambulatory channel or for musicians who perform during the deities' movement round the tank. The central *maṇḍapam* is an important distinguishing feature separating a *teppakkulam* from a mere tank; the design of the columns may suggest a date.

Processions and ritual movement are an essential consideration in understanding the transformation of scale, layout and design of the south Indian temple both as a tradition across over 1400 years and within individual temples. The south Indian temple is a processional space not only for devotees going in to greet the deity, but also for the deities themselves to emerge during festivals. The architectural hierarchy of sacred space excluded some social groups from the temple, while periodic public processions of the deity to peripheral spaces within the temple walls or beyond them into the surrounding streets or countryside enabled broader ritual inclusion. The centrifugal and centripetal ritual circulation of the deities themselves serves to establish the pre-eminence of the processing deity within a ritual hierarchy of subservience. The evidence of literature, inscriptions and ethnography in addition to the architectural fabric can all inform our interpretation of the historical development of the Tamil temple processions from the bronze images carried around, to the gradual construction of festival *maṇḍapa*s and long corridors, the distribution and iconography of architectural sculpture, the planning of the large temple cities, through to the evaluation of the ritual landscape around and between the many temples that dominated the Tamil landscape until the rapid urban expansion of more recent decades.

Notes

The author is very grateful to Himanshu Prabha Ray, Leslie C. Orr, Anna Seastrand, Archana Venkatesan, Ute Hüsken, together with the other participants of the symposium at which this chapter was delivered for their comments and questions.

1 Jaś Elsner, 'Material Culture and Ritual: State of the Question', in Robert G. Ousterhout and Bonna D. Wescoat (eds), *Architecture of the Sacred: Space, Ritual, and Experience from Classical Greece to Byzantium*, Cambridge and New York: Cambridge University Press, 2012, pp. 1–26 (p. 2).
2 Robert G. Ousterhout and Bonna D. Wescoat, *Architecture of the Sacred: Space, Ritual, and Experience from Classical Greece to Byzantium*, Cambridge and New York: Cambridge University Press, 2012, pp. 366–74.
3 For example, Ian Rutherford, 'Theoria and Darśan: Pilgrimage and Vision in Greece and India', *The Classical Quarterly*, 2000, 50(1): 133–46 [Sabarimalai]; Antony Spawforth, *The Complete Greek Temples*, London: Thames and Hudson, 2006 [Jain temple ritual]; Joan B. Connelly, 'Ritual Movement in Sacred Space: Towards an Archaeology of Performance', in *Ritual Dynamics in the Ancient Mediterranean: Agency, Emotion, Gender, Representation*, Stuttgart: Franz Steiner Verlag, 2011, pp. 313–46 [Tamil temples]; Eftychia Stavrianopoulou, 'The Archaeology of Processions', in Rubina Raja and Jörg Rüpke (eds), *A Companion to the Archaeology of Religion in the Ancient World*, Chichester: Wiley Blackwell, 2015, pp. 349–61 [Nepali processions].
4 See Knut A. Jacobsen, South Asian Religions on Display: Religious Processions in South Asia and in the Diaspora, Abingdon: Routledge, 2008.
5 On South India, see: Guy R. Welbon and Glenn E. Yocum (eds), *Religious Festivals in South India and Sri Lanka*, New Delhi: Manohar, 1982; Paul Younger, *Playing Host to Deity: Festival Religion in the South Indian Tradition*, Oxford: Oxford University Press, 2002.
6 Archana Venkatesan and Crispin Branfoot, *In Andal's Garden: Art, Ornament and Devotion in Srivilliputtur*, Mumbai: Marg, 2015. In addition, see Ute Hüsken, 'Gods and Goddesses in the Ritual Landscape of Seventeenth and Eighteenth-Century Kāñcipuram', in Eric Nelson and Jonathan Wright (eds), *Layered Landscapes: Early Modern Religious Space Across Faiths and Cultures*, Abingdon: Routledge, 2017, pp. 63–81.
7 Leslie C. Orr, 'Processions in the Medieval South Indian Temple: Sociology, Sovereignty and Soteriology', in Jean-Luc Chevillard and Eva Wilden (eds), *South Indian Horizons*, Pondicherry: IFP & EFEO, 2004, pp. 437–70.
8 Indira Viswanathan Peterson, *Poems to Siva: The Hymns of the Tamil Saints*, New Delhi: Motilal Banarsidass, 1991, p. 184.
9 Orr, 'Processions', p. 440.

10 Richard H. Davis, *Ritual in an Oscillating Universe: Worshipping Siva in Medieval India*, Princeton: Princeton University Press, 1991, p. 69.
11 *Ibid*, p. 72.
12 Richard H. Davis, *A Priest's Guide for the Great Festival: Aghorasiva's Mahotsavavidhi*, New York and Oxford: Oxford University Press, 2010, p. 17.
13 Orr, 'Processions', pp. 443, 459.
14 *Ibid*, p. 453.
15 On changes in festival provision over time, see *ibid*, p. 477fn12.
16 T. K. T. Viraraghavacharya, *A History of Tirupati*, 2nd edn, 3 vols., Tirupati: Tirumala-Tirupati Devasthanam Religious Publications, 1977 (1st published 1953), vol. I, pp. 69, 362; vol. II, pp. 392–5. The number of festivals and their duration decreased from the late 17th century as the temple's income declined.
17 Orr, 'Processions', p. 448.
18 Joanna Waghorne, 'Dressing the Body of God: South Indian Bronze Sculpture in Its Temple Setting', *Asian Art*, 1992, 5(3): 9–33; Richard H. Davis, *Lives of Indian Images*, Princeton: Princeton University Press, 1997; Vidya Dehejia, *The Sensuous and the Sacred: Chola Bronzes from South India*, New York, Seattle and London: American Federation of Arts and University of Washington Press, 2002; Vidya Dehejia, *Chola: Sacred Bronzes from Southern India*, London: Royal Academy of Arts, 2006.
19 The mid-12th century Naṭarāja in the Rijksmuseum is exceptional for the period, at 153cm high (Rijksmuseum, Amsterdam, accession number AK-MAK-187). The early 11th century Naṭarāja in the Nageśvara temple in Kumbakonam is 156cm high.
20 Exceptions are the Brooklyn Museum's image of Candraśekhara, dated 970, that is 65.4 cm high and weighs 22.91kg (Accession number 2007.2) and the Rijksmuseum's aforementioned Naṭarāja, weighing an extraordinary 255kg for the figure including the dwarf and the lotus-base alone, plus a further 40kg for the rectangular base.
21 The dowel is usually absent in museum collections, but an early-10th-century Naṭarāja in the Victoria & Albert Museum has a single metal dowel still in place (V&A IM.2–1934).
22 For example, a Naṭarāja image in the British Museum (1969,1216.1) is dated c. 930–40, or even as early as 800, according to Sharada Srinivasan, 'Shiva as "Cosmic Dancer": On Pallava Origins for the Nataraja Bronze', *World Archaeology*, 2004, 36(3): 432–50 (p. 440).
23 Dehejia, *The Sensuous and the Sacred*, pp. 82–5.
24 Davis, *A Priest's Guide for the Great Festival*, p. 106fn46.
25 *Ibid*, p. 28.
26 Between the 1780s and 1850s, a significant genre of paintings on paper and mica developed in South India by local artists for mostly British but also French audiences, that depicted festivals and processions—Hindu, Christian and Muslim. Illustrations of these processions are often detached from any sense of spatial context though occasionally temple walls are in the background. Sets of such paintings may demonstrate the range of often animal *vāhanas* on which deities are mounted, as outlined in *āgamic* sources, or the more magnificent annual 'chariot' procession. Though the scenes may seem generic, specific deities and temples are sometimes depicted: Raṅganātha of Srirangam is comparatively common, a consequence of both the great temple's popularity and religious significance, and the presence of European consumers stationed in nearby Trichy. See Crispin Branfoot, 'Painting Processions: The Social and Religious Landscape of Southern India in a "Company" Album', *Orientations*, 2007, 38(8): 73–8;

Anna L. Dallapiccola, *South Indian Paintings: A Catalogue of the British Museum's Collections*, London: British Museum Press, 2010.

27 For a list of processional vehicles and events according to the *Mahotsavavidhi*, *Kāmikāgama* and *Kāraṇāgama*, see Davis, *A Priest's Guide for the Great Festival*, p. 108.

28 On *vāhanas*, see H. Daniel Smith, 'Vāhanas in the Cultic Art of South Indian Temples', in A. Venkatachari (ed), *Proceedings of the Seminar on Symbolism in Temple Art and Architecture*, Bombay: Ananthacharya Indological Research Institute, 1982, pp. 12–29; Joanna Waghorne, 'Vāhanas: Conveyors of the Gods', in George Michell (ed), *Living Wood: Sculptural Traditions of Southern India*, Bombay: Marg, 1992, pp. 15–28.

29 On *tērs*, see Jacques Dumarçay, 'L'architecture des chars processionels du Sud de l'Inde', *Bulletin de l'École française d'Extrême-Orient*, 1975, 62: 192–209; Raju Kalidos, *Temple Cars of Medieval Tamilaham*, Madurai: Madurai Kamaraj University, 1989; Jan Pieper and Margret Thomsen, 'South Indian Ceremonial Chariots', *Art and Archaeology Research Papers*, 1979, 16: 1–10.

30 Gerd J. R. Mevissen, 'The Suggestion of Movement: A Contribution to the Study of Chariot-Shaped Structures in Indian Temple Architecture', in Debala Mitra (ed), *Explorations in Art and Archaeology of South Asia: Essays Dedicated to N.G. Majumdar*, Calcutta: Directorate of Archaeology and Museums, Government of West Bengal, 1996, pp. 477–512.

31 Crispin Branfoot, 'The Madurai Nayakas and the Skanda Temple at Tirupparankundram', *Ars Orientalis*, 2004, 33: 147–79.

32 Ronald Inden, 'The Temple and the Hindu Chain of Being', in Ronald Inden (ed), *Text and Practice: Essays on South Asian History*, New Delhi: Oxford University Press, 2006, p. 201.

33 On social hierarchies and temple access in the *āgamas*, see Davis, *Ritual in an Oscillating Universe*, pp. 69–72; Pierre-Sylvain Filliozat, 'Le droit d'entrer dans les temples de Śiva au XIe siècle', *Journal Asiatique*, 1975, 263: 103–17; Inden, 'The Temple and the Hindu Chain of Being'; Karen Pechliss Prentiss, *The Embodiment of Bhakti*, Oxford: Oxford University Press, 1999, pp. 122–4. From the perspective of epigraphy, Orr questions how restrictive access may have been in practice, for 'the names of donors from a wide range of backgrounds and professions are engraved on the stone walls of *maṇḍapas* in the inner compound and on the central shrine itself—surely the people themselves were admitted to these same places'. *Ibid*, p. 463.

34 *Ibid*, pp. 443–4. Cf. C. J. Fuller, 'Sacrifice (Bali) in the South Indian Temple', in V. Sudarsen, G. Prakash Reddy, and M. Suryanarayana (eds), *Religion and Society in South India*, New Delhi: B. R. Publishing Corporation, 1987, pp. 21–35.

35 Crispin Branfoot, 'Dynastic Genealogies, Portraiture, and the Place of the Past in Early Modern South India', *Artibus Asiae*, 2012, 72: 323–76; Crispin Branfoot, 'Heroic Rulers and Devoted Servants: Performing Kingship in the Tamil Temple', in Crispin Branfoot (ed), *Portraiture in South Asia since the Mughals: Art, Representation, History*, London: I. B. Tauris, 2018, pp. 165–97.

36 See Branfoot, 'Dynastic Genealogies, Portraiture'.

37 There is no surviving trace of the palace at Alagarkoyil, which was dismantled around 1912.

38 These street extensions are indicated in red at the corners of the concentric series of roads around the central shrine in a painting of the Raṅganātha temple at Srirangam dated c. 1830 in the British Museum (1962,1231,0.13.1): see Dallapiccola, *South Indian Paintings*, pp. 74–5.

39 Orr, 'Processions', p. 456.

40 S. R. Balasubrahmanyam, *Early Chola Art: Part One*, Bombay: Asia Publishing House, 1966, p. 100.
41 This festival is mentioned in inscriptions from Kulottunga I's reign (1070–1120) [*South Indian Inscriptions*, vol. 4, No. 225] and in 1259 [*Annual Report on Epigraphy*, No. 297 of 1913]. Two other temples to the north and south of Chidambaram also held processions to the sea (see Orr, 'Processions', p. 449). The Vaiṣṇnava Bhū-Varāha temple 15 miles further inland also conducted a procession to the sea at Killai, more than 20 miles away, in the 19th century (John Henry Garstin, *Manual of the South Arcot District*, Madras: Lawrence Asylum Press, 1955, p. 433).
42 See K. A. Nilakanta Sastri, *The Colas*, 2nd edn, Madras: University of Madras, 1955, pp. 344–5.
43 For a town plan of Chidambaram in the mid-18th century see Robert Orme, *A History of the Military Transactions of the British Nation in Indostan*, 2nd edn, Madras: Pharaoh and Co., 1861, vol. 3, n.p.
44 Venkatesan and Branfoot, *In Andal's Garden*, p. 125.
45 Orr, 'Processions', p. 449.
46 *Annual Report on Epigraphy*, No. 161 of 1937.

Part III

SPACE

7

MONEY FOR RITUALS

Akṣayanīvī and related inscriptions from Āndhradeśa

Ingo Strauch

Introduction

The majority of inscriptions found in Buddhist monastic contexts record donations of buildings, art objects and monastic utensils. This rather straightforward relation between donor and recipient is in contrast to more-complex donations that mention 'permanent endowments' (*akṣayanīvī*) of money or agricultural land in order to maintain or support a particular institution. Texts of this kind are attested all over India from different periods and in different religious contexts. They bear witness to a practice that allows religious institutions to develop into sustainable ritual centres with a strong economic relationship to their respective hinterlands. So far, studies on *akṣayanīvī* inscriptions have focused on the corpus of Sātavāhana and Kṣatrapa epigraphs, where this term is attested for the first time, in the context of Buddhist donative inscriptions in the Western Ghat caves. It has been argued that this institution developed in the context of advanced economic conditions based on a money economy and expanded trade contacts between Western India and other parts of the subcontinent.[1] From there, it quite soon spread north and south, and it also left the boundaries of Buddhist institutions.

Back in 2003, Harry Falk republished a remarkable copper-plate inscription from an equally remarkable archaeological site.[2] The cave Kashmir *smast* has attracted scholars' attention for many years—being a huge natural cave, with artificial structures inside and on the plateau in front of it, overlooking a wild valley that is particularly hard to access. In spite of this, it seems to have attracted in antiquity devotees from far afield who came here in order to venerate the mighty female deity Bhīmā, whose name is even preserved in the *Mahābhārata* and in the reports of Chinese pilgrims. Bhīmā is also mentioned in the copper-plate inscription and is depicted on numerous seals and sealings that were discovered in the surroundings of the site. Although systematic archaeological investigation is still to be carried out, the artefacts that have found their way to collectors and art dealers present a multi-faceted picture of an impressive religious site. The most detailed description of the institutional structure of this site comes from the copper-plate. According to its inscription, the site accommodated several *maṭhas* (temples) that run the financial activities of the goddess Bhīmā. Visitors used to invest money into one of these *maṭhas*, the gain of which was apparently attributed to the deity. For the first time we encounter here the term *akṣayanīvī* in the Northwest of the Indian subcontinent. However, as Falk correctly remarks, it is not the first time the term occurs in a non-Buddhist context. It is also found in an inscription from Mathura dated in the Kuṣāṇa year 28, that is,155 CE.[3] The recipient of this record is a *puṇyaśālā*, 'hall of merit', and the interest of the capital should be used for feeding 100 Brahmins and for food to be given to 'destitute people, hungry and thirsty'.[4] Although there is little doubt about the fact that the institution of *akṣayanīvī* was introduced in the context of Buddhist monasteries,[5] Falk is certainly right, when he subsumes,

> Once the akṣayaṇīvis were invented and installed they seem to have become customary. . . . Once a start was made in northern Deccan, the idea spread from the Kṣatrapas and Sātavāhanas north to Gandhara. . . . The idea spread fast; it involved all religious communities and retained its aspect of providing food, to clerics and public alike.[6]

In my chapter, I investigate many *akṣayanīvī* and related texts that belong to a subsequent phase, namely the period of the Ikṣvākus of Vijayapurī (3rd–4th century CE). By pointing out continuities and discontinuities, my chapter aims to show how the institution of *akṣayanīvī* developed under the changed historical conditions of this period.

The material from Āndhradeśa

The Ikṣvāku dynasty was no doubt one of the most important and successful powers succeeding the mighty Sātavāhanas in the Southern Deccan area. The majority of their inscriptions come from their capital, Vijayapurī, today known as the archaeological site Nagarjunakonda. There are, however, numerous inscriptions from other sites that confirm this dynasty ruled over a rather large territory in present-day Andhra Pradesh and Telangana for at least 150 years, during the 3rd and 4th centuries CE.

The corpus of Ikṣvāku inscriptions was the main object of the joint research project, 'From Vijayapuri to Sriksetra? The Beginnings of Buddhist Exchange across the Bay of Bengal as Witnessed by Inscriptions from Andhra Pradesh and Myanmar', run from 2016 to 2017 and supported by the The Robert H. N. Ho Family Foundation, administered by the American Council of Learned

Societies. The project was led by Arlo Griffiths, and the research group for Indian inscriptions comprised Stefan Baums (Munich), Vincent Tournier (now Paris) and Ingo Strauch (Lausanne). My subsequent discussion is based on the joint edition and translation of Āndhradeśa inscriptions that is now accessible in an online database, the Early Inscriptions of Āndhradeśa (EIAD).[7] If not stated otherwise, text and translation are based on this edition.

Out of the 200 inscriptions that can be attributed or related to the Ikṣvāku dynasty, only five refer to the term *akṣayanīvī*: EIAD 53, 55, 56, 60, and 200. A few others, mainly fragmentary records, can be added to this small group, based on certain formal features that will be discussed in a later section. In the following, I will briefly present these records and their archaeological contexts, as well as the text portion that contains central information regarding the character and conditions of the *akṣayanīvī* transaction. A table at the end of this section subsumes the relevant data (Table 7.1).

EIAD 53

Inscribed object: Octagonal pillar (= *dhvajasthambha*)
Archaeological context: site 34 at Nagarjunakonda, Puṣpabhadrasvāmin temple[8]
Date: reign of Siri-Ehavalacāntamūla, year 16

TEXT:

bhagavato puṣpabhadrasvāminaḥ devakulaṁ kāritaṁ ◊ dhvajastaṁbaś ca pratiṣṭhāpitaḥ grāmaś ca puḍokeḍaṁ °***akṣayanivī*** *dattaḥ ◊*

TRANSLATION:

had (this) temple (*devakula*) of the Bhagavant Puṣpabhadrasvāmin made, established a flagstaff and gave as **permanent endowment**[9] (*akṣayanīvī*) the village Puḍokeḍaṁ

EIAD 55

Inscribed object: Copper plates
Archaeological context: Unclear. Findspot: Patagandigudem (Kallacheruvu)
Date: reign of Siri-Ehavalacāntamūla

TEXT:

*°ettha pithuṁḍe ◊ sābhittāṇehi ◊ mahāvihārasa °avaraddāre ◊ cātusāle °amhehi kāritaṁ ◊ °etassa ya ◊ khaṇḍapullasaṇṭhappasa cātusāle ◊ °āgaṁtukavatthavvāṇa pavvayitāṇaṁ ◊ vissāmaṇatthaṁ ◊ rañ[o] °ehalavatthamāṇavatthavehi ◊ pavvayitehi avaraddāraseliyehi ◊ °aryyayakkhapamuhehi °aṇuṭṭhiya ◊ sāsanaṁ kāritaṁ sāsanaṁ kāritaṁ ◊ °**akkhayanivviṁ** ◊ kātūṇaṁ ◊ raño °appaṇo puṇṇappāya-ṇāyubalavaddhaṇatthaṁ °ayandatāraka « ṁ » kātūṇa ◊ pithuṇḍe ◊mahāvi-hārasa ◊ nagarassa ◊ °uttaradisāye ◊ mahāsetīye ◊ mahācelakasa °eṭṭhassa ◊ k[ū]latthapaddaggāmapatthe ◊halaṁkkhettasa niyattāṇā bat[t] ī(sa) 30 2 nidejaṁ ◊ nipoli || pithuṇḍassa ◊ °uttaradisāye va hatthivārī ◊ pachimadisāye ◊ pupphakalase halaṁkkhettasa niyattaṇacatusaṭṭhi 60 4 ◊ nidejaṁ nippoli °avaraddārī ◊cātusālassa ◊ halo bhikhubhogaṁ ◊ kātūṇa samyadattaṁ*

TRANSLATION:

Here in Pithuṇḍa we had a quadrangular compound made by *sābhittāna*s (?) at the western gate of the Great Monastery. For its repair of broken and shattered (parts), for the repose of renunciants who (will) arrive and who (presently) reside in the quadrangular compound, the (following) royal order was issued, to be carried out (*anuṣṭheya* ?) by the Avaraddāraseliya renunciants residing in the plot of King Ehala, headed by Aryayakkha (Āryayakṣa): Having made **a permanent endowment**, having made (it permanent) as long as moon and stars, in order to expand the king's own merit and to increase his lifespan and power, to the Great Monastery in Pithuṇḍa 32 *nivartana*s of plowable land are to be given (*nideya*) (and) registered (?), in the northern direction of the town, at the Great Shrine of the *mahācelaka* Eṭṭha, at the road (leading to) the village Kulatthapadda. North of Pithuṇḍa, west of the elephant grove, in Pupphakalasa, sixty-four—64—*nivartana*s of plowable land are to be given (and) registered (?). Having made (this) plowable land (*hala*) the revenue of the monks of the quadrangular compound at the western gate, the gift is completed (*samyagdattam*).

EIAD 56

Inscribed object: Pillar
Origin: site 126 at Nagarjunakonda, facing a shrine chamber at the 'Royal burning ghāṭ'[10]
Date: reign of Siri-Ehavalacāntamūla

TEXT:

*bhagavato [noḍhagī]saras[ā]misa ◊ devakulaṁ thali[ṁ] [ca] [kāri]tā °**akhayanīvi[ṁ]** ca kat[ū]ṇa mas[anu]mas[ika]sa [vi]dhi ? ? ? ? ? ? ? ? ? ? ? ? dh[i]kaseni[ya] [dināri] ? ? ? ? ? ? ? ? ? ? [dinā]ri dasa 10 panikaseniye dināri dasa 10 ◊ puvikasen[i]ye dināri dasa 10 ◊ °eva[ṁ] senis[u] catusu ? ? ? ◊ dinarisa[ta] (. . .) [°ā]gaṁ[tu]k[a]vathavehi ? ? g. ? [ka] ma[ra]t[e]h[i] ◊ ca ? ? ? seṭhipamukha ? ? ? ? ni ? ? no[ḍha] ? [de]va[sa] [te]thikanakhati[k]āpa[hā]raḍhikā ◊ bhagaphulasa[ṁ]ṭhapa ◊ °apanā ca ◊ citanaṁ ◊ katavaṁ ◊*

TRANSLATION:

. . . had a temple and a platform (*thali*) made for the Bhagavant Noḍhagīsarasāmi. And having made **a permanent endowment** . . . month after month . . . dināris (are to be deposited ?) in the . . . dhika guild, ten—10—dināris . . . ten—10—dināris in the betel-leaf guild, ten—10—dināris in the betel-nut guild. Thus, in four guilds . . . hundred dināris . . . by those devoted to ritual acts, who (will) arrive and who (presently) reside . . . headed by the guilds . . . the *taithika*, *nākṣatrika* as well as *prāharika* rites and so forth (are to be performed) for the god Noḍha. . .; the repair of what is damaged and dilapidated and the embellishment are to be made by themselves.

EIAD 60

Inscribed object: Pillar
Origin: site 17 at Nagarjunakonda, so-called 'Hāritī temple'[11]
Date: reign of Siri-Ehavalacāntamūla

TEXT:

*+ + + /// ? ? [ca] tethika[na] + + ? ? kā + ? + + /// lasa ca bhaḍaphulasaṁṭhapasa [°ā]gaṁtukavathave[h]i + ///bhuṁjitavasa °**akhayanivikā** datā gāma[ṁ] pa + + /// ? haṁ kakolūraṁ nelācava[saṁ] /// + + + + + + /// ? ? ya ca °apara[ma] /// + + + + + + + ? s[a] ca °a[khaya]n[i]-v[i] dīnārimāsak[ā] divaḍhaṁ sataṁ ? supayuta[ṁ] °esā ca °**akhayanivī** ku(l)[ī]-kapamukhāya[ṁ] ? °anutheya ci[t]i ? yaṁ .i*

TRANSLATION:

. . . (for) the *taithika*, the *nā*(*kṣatrika* ?), and for the repair of what was damaged and dilapidated; it should be enjoyed by those who (will) arrive and who (presently) reside. **As permanent endowment**, the village(s) of . . . Kakolūra (and) Nelācavasa . . . and *aparama* . . . **a permanent endowment**, (consisting in) one and a half hundred of *dīnārimāṣaka*s, is duly invested[12] to. . . . And this permanent endowment is to be executed by . . . headed by the *kulika*s.

EIAD 200

Inscribed object: Pillar
Origin: Alluru, 'from a small mound not far off from Alluru',[13] Buddhist stūpa site[14]
Date: not dated, paleographically assignable to the 2nd century CE

TEXT:

*? [lasa]maḍavasac[eti] (ya) + + + + + + sarāmo vihāro deyadhamaparicā(ko) + + + + nigalasimāya vetarakuḷo na ? + + + + tikheta sorasa pāpikalasimāya + + + + [n]ivatanāni rājadatini cā raṭhe macha + + + + paḍasimāya batisa nivatanāni rā(jadatāni) ? [ra] purasīmāya catuvisa nivatanān(i) + + + + ḍalasa gāvina pacasatāni coyaṭhībaliva ? + + + sakaḍāni pesarupāni dāsidāsasa catāl(i-) [sa] + kubhikaḍāhasa catari lohiyo be kaḍāhāni kaṁsa{sa}bhāyanāni catāri vadālābhikāro karoḍiyo yo[na]kadivikāyo ca °ataragiriya picapāke taḷāka kāhāpanāna ca purānasahasa °**akhayaniv(i)** °esa mahātalavarasa deyadhamaparicāko °atape °utarapase bāpana*

nivatanāni °eta sabhāriyasa saputakasa sanatukasa °ayirāna puvaseliyāna nigāyasa

TRANSLATION:

. . . a monastery with a pavilion, with a shrine (hall), . . . with a garden as the giving away as a pious gift . . . At the border to . . . *nigala* a reed cluster (*vetrakula*) . . . a field, 16 (**nivartana*s). At the border to Pāpikala. . . *nivartana*s and . . . given by the king in the district Maccha . . . At the border to. . . *paḍa* 32 *nivartana*s, (given by the) king. At the border to ?[ra]pura 24 *nivartana*s.

Of. . . ḍala 500 cows, four-poled (*caturyaṣṭi*) bullock . . . carts, as servants (*preṣyarūpa*) 24 female and male slaves, four jar-shaped cauldrons (*kumbhikaṭāha*), two iron cauldrons, four brass vessels (*bhājana*), a eddy-shaped (? *abhikāra*) bowl and "Greek" lamps, a tank behind the Antaragiri, and one thousand old Kāhāpanas **as permanent endowment**. This is the Great Talavara's giving away as a pious gift. In Atapa, at the northern side, 52 (?) *nivartana*s. This (of the Great Talavara) together with his wife, sons, and grandsons. To the *nikāya* of the noble Puvvaseliyas.

Inscription EIAD 200 is exceptional, since it seems to report rather a list of several donations made by an unnamed official without giving any details about the specific circumstances. It is not entirely clear whether the final designation of the gift as 'permanent endowment' relates to the entire list or only to its last item, the amount of 1,000 *kāhāpana*s.

If taken together, these five inscriptions confirm the development described earlier; namely, that the institution of *akṣayanīvī* came to be adopted by other religious currents. Out of the five epigraphs, only two are affiliated to Buddhist sites (EIAD 55 and 200); the remaining three belong to non-Buddhist institutions (EIAD 53, 56, and 60). On a formal level, Buddhist and non-Buddhist texts share some common features. The formula that refers to the 'repair of broken and shattered (parts), for the repose of renunciants who (will) arrive and who (presently) reside' is found in both types (EIAD 55, 56, 60). Since its wording is typical for the language of the Buddhist *Vinaya*,[15] it can be assumed that it was taken over by non-Buddhist traditions. These non-Buddhist traditions added another formula that remained restricted to them. It refers to a series of rituals that were to be supported from the income of the *akṣayanīvī*; namely, the *taithika*, *nākṣatrika* as well as *prāharika* rites,[16] apparently rituals that had to be conducted on certain lunar days (*tithi*), in conjunction with certain lunar constellations (*nakṣatra*) and at certain hours (*prahara*).

If we consider these phrases as characteristic for *akṣayanīvī* inscriptions, there is at least one other text that can be safely related to our small corpus. The Phanigiri pillar (or doorjamb) inscription (EIAD 105) reports the establishment (of buildings and pillars?) as an eternal pious gift and adds a series of further benefits that are granted to the monastic community on an annual basis. Although the preserved text does not contain the term *akṣayanīvī*, Oskar von Hinüber is certainly right when he says: 'The wording *deyadhamma sasatakālika* seems to correspond to the expression *akṣayanīvi* also used in Ikṣvāku inscriptions and particularly by the Kṣatrapas'.[17]

This characterisation is further strengthened by the use of the typical phrase *bhadaphulasaṁṭhapasa*. Moreover, the text contains a rather detailed description of the conditions that accompany the donation. Based on all these features, EIAD 105 can safely be included in the corpus of Āndhradeśa *akṣayanīvī* inscriptions. Since the fragmentary text of EIAD 106 (also a pillar fragment from Phanigiri) corresponds in its preserved portions nearly literally to EIAD 105, it seems safe to add this text too, although the small fragment shows none of the typical phrases nor the term *akṣayanīvī*.

Less clear is the last case, EIAD 139, the earliest preserved inscription issued by a member of the Pallava family and paleographically datable to the second half of the 3rd century CE. It was discovered near the village Manchikallu, in the Guntur District of Andhra Pradesh. Although it contains two of the characteristic phrases (highlighted in bold in the text and translation that follows), its overall context does not allow for a clear attribution to the group of *akṣayanīvī* texts. The text, as read and translated by Arlo Griffiths, Emanuel Francis and Vincent Tournier, runs as follows:

> *siddha[ṁ] ‖ — bhāradāya[sa]go[ttena] + + + + [dha]reṇa palavāṇaṁ sī[ha]vaṁmaṇa ◊ °ap[p]aṇo vejayike ? + + + [lava]dhaṁṇīke saṁntisathiyāyaṇaṁ kātūṇa ◊ bhaga[va](to) (siri)[jīvaś]ivasāmisa* ***tethikanak[kh]attik[ā]pahārakādi*** *kātaṁ kapa ? devakulasa* ***bhag[ga]****/// ? + + + + + + + + ? + + + + + [sa] pāda[m](ū)le /// + + + +*
>
> Success! By (king) Sīhavamma of the Pallavas, with a view to his own victoriousness and for increasing his . . . and power, *śānti* and *svastyayana* were carried out and the *taithika*, *nākṣatrika* as well as *prāharika* and so forth were performed for Lord Siri-Jīvaśivasāmi. . . (the repair of) what was damaged (and dilapidated) of the temple of Kapa . . . at the base of. . .

The inscription is heavily damaged. As read and interpreted in the translation, it seems to refer to former accomplishments of the Pallava ruler Sīhavamma. This interpretation is mainly based on the assumed ppp. *kātaṃ* ('performed'). The somewhat ambiguous shape of the letters *na* and *ta* would, however, also make possible a different interpretation:[18] ***tethikanak[kh] attik[ā]pahārakādikānaṁ*** *kapa(naṃ?)* 'the performance of the *taithika*, *nākṣatrika*, *prāharika* and other (rites)'. Thus, this phrase, along with the following phrase beginning with *bhag[ga]*, would indicate the donative purpose of the present inscription, rather than specific rituals that were carried out by this Pallava king. Because of the bad state of preservation, it is not possible to favour any of the suggested interpretations and it cannot be excluded that both formulae were used here in a different context. EIAD 139 will therefore not be included in our corpus. The text confirms, however, two important observations. First, the *taithika*, *nākṣatrika*, and *prāhārika* rites are associated with a Śaiva context, and second, both formulae occur side by side in a non-Buddhist context.

The relevant portions of EIAD 105 and 106 are given here:

EIAD 105

Inscribed object: Pillar or doorjamb
Origin: Phanigiri Buddhist monastic complex, exact location unknown
Date: not dated, on palaeographical grounds datable between 300 and 350 CE

. . . [pa](ti)ṭhāpitā . . . ṭhāpitaṁ ***sasatakālikaṁ °imaṁ deyadhaṁmaṁ*** *bhadaphulasaṁṭhapasa [va] °anuvasikaṁ ca pavāraṇāmahe puphachatanasa kāraṇāya gāvīnaṁ diyaḍhasataṁ tariḍelāna 100 50 saṁpadattaṁ tato °anu[va]sikaṁ bhikhusaṁghena dātavā puphamolaṁ kāhāpaṇa cha 6 dīvatelasa ca sāṇi[k](i)yo [ca]tāri ⟨⟨4⟩⟩ dātava °etaṁ °avisaṁvadaṁtena °a[n]uvaṭetavaṁ*

. . . are established. . ., (they) established **this pious gift as eternal**. For the repair of broken and shattered (parts) and for the preparation of a flower canopy, annually at the Pavāraṇā festival, one hundred fifty—150—*tariḍela* cows are given. Moreover, the monks' order must give annually six—6—*kāhāpaṇas* as price for flowers, and four—4—*sāṇikis* (*śāṇikā*) of lamp oil. This has to be carried without raising any objections.

EIAD 106

Inscribed object: Fragment (of a pillar/doorjamb)
Origin: Phanigiri Buddhist monastic complex, exact location unknown
Date: not dated, palaeographically assignable to the 3rd–4th century CE

+ [ma]titatho bhikhu[sa] (ṁ) /// (ghena) (°a)nuvasikaṁ dātavaṁ pavāraṇām[a] he puphamolaṁ kāhāpaṇa cha 6 gaṁthanasutasa palāni paṁca [5] divatelasa [ca] kuḍo °e[ko] /// (1) + + + + [dh]. ? ? + + +

. . . the monks' order must give at the (occasion of the) Pavāraṇā festival, as price for flowers six—6—*kāhāpaṇa*s, for the string for tying (flowers) 5—five—*pala*s, one—(1)—*kūḍa* of lamp oil. . .

Both texts add an important aspect to the character of *akṣayanīvī* inscriptions in the Ikṣvāku period. They refer to the Pravāraṇā festival and thus indicate a clear ritual function of the donation. Beside the maintenance of the buildings, the donations are also used for the provision of ritual implements on the occasion of this festival.[19] This largely corresponds to the non-Buddhist rites discussed earlier.

They further contain another, at the first sight disturbing, regulation: both texts prescribe that the respective provisions are to be given by the monastic community (Skt. *bhikṣusaṃghena dātavya-*). Apparently, the donation was administered by the monastery itself and not by an external agent. We will come back to this feature in the concluding part of this chapter.

In subsuming the data for *akṣayanīvī* inscriptions in Āndhradeśa discussed previously, we can highlight the following features. Out of the 200 inscriptions published so far by the project 'Early inscriptions of Āndhradeśa', seven can be attributed to the institution of *akṣayanīvī*. Among these, three belong to a Buddhist context and four to a non-Buddhist environment. Some of the Buddhist and non-Buddhist texts share a common terminology, with the exception of certain formulae that refer to religious festivals that are peculiar to the respective religious context:

	Common formulae	*Specific formulae*
Buddhist inscriptions		
55	*etassa ya ◊ khaṇḍapullasaṇṭhappasa cātusāle ◊ °āgaṁtukavatthavvāṇa pavvayitāṇaṁ ◊ vissāmaṇatthaṁ*	
200	—	—
105	*bhadaphulasaṁṭhapasa*	*pavāraṇāmahe*
106	*bhag[ga]/// ?*	*pavāraṇām[a]he*

	Common formulae	Specific formulae
Non-Buddhist inscriptions		
54	—	—
56	*[°ā]gaṁ[tu]k[a]vathavehi ? g. ? [ka]ma[ra]t[e]h[i] ◊ . . . ◊ bhagaphulasa[ṁ]ṭhapa °apanā ca ◊ citanaṁ ◊ katavaṁ*	*[te]thikanakhati[k]āpa[hā]raḍhikā*
60	*bhaḍaphulasaṁṭhapasa [°ā]gaṁtukavathave[h]i*	*[ca] tethika[na] + + ?*
*139	—	*tethikanak[kh]attik[ā]pahārakādi*

With regard to other features, the inscriptions offer a rather heterogeneous picture. Donors function not only as members of the royal family or high officials, but also as members of the monastic hierarchy, such as the *vinayadhara* of EIAD 105. Although the gifts are generally connected to certain buildings or entire institutions, the *akṣayanīvī* is granted in different forms:[20]

- Villages (2) or agricultural land (2): 53, 55, 60, *200
- Animals (2): 105, *200
- Human servants (1): *200
- Money (5): 56, 60, 200, 105, 106

Only one inscription mention guilds as intermediaries of the financial transaction (60).

In some epigraphs, the *akṣayanīvī* is explicitly destined for certain ritual purposes, such as the Buddhist Pravāraṇā festival (105, 106) or the non-Buddhist *taithika*, *nākṣatrika* and *prāharika* rites (56, 60).

The earliest *Akṣayanīvī* texts from the Western Deccan

As stated previously, the beginnings of *akṣayanīvī* donations have to be looked for in the context of early Sātavāhana and Kṣatrapa epigraphs from Western India. Although it cannot be stated with certainty, perhaps the earliest donation of this kind is represented by the well-known inscription of the Kṣaharāta ruler Uṣavadāta from Nasik, dated to the years 42 and 45 of a still-disputed era. This record mentions a permanent endowment to be invested in guilds and to be used for clothing and other expenses of the Buddhist monks.[21] Few other texts from Nasik testify to the continuation of this practice at the site (e.g., Nasik no. 3,[22] no. 15,[23] no. 17)[24].

The perhaps largest concentration of *akṣayanīvī* texts, however, hails from Kanheri, where about 100 caves were carved into the natural rock to form a huge monastic complex. Out of the 58 recorded inscriptions there, 14 refer to the donation of a permanent endowment that usually accompanies

Table 7.1 Akṣayanīvī (AN) inscriptions from Āndhradeśa

EIAD	*Donor*	*Donee*	*Object*	*Conditions/purpose*
53	The Great Crown-Prince, Great General Hāritīputra Śrī-Vīrapuruṣadatta of the Ikṣvākus	Bhagavant Puṣpabhadrasvāmi	*Devakulaṁ* and village	—
55	King Siri-Ehavalacāntamūlavamma of the Ikṣvākus	The Avaraddāraseliya renunciants residing in the plot of King Ehala, headed by Aryayakkha (Āryayakṣa):	(?) A quadrangular compound at the western gate of the Great Monastery and agricultural land as revenue of the monks (*bhikhubhoga*)	For its repair of broken and shattered (parts), for the repose of renunciants who (will) arrive and who (presently) reside in the quadrangular compound
56	Bhagava . . ., wife of the chamberlain of the female appartments; Ratavisā, daughter of the Guild's Chief; Viḍā . . .	Bhagavant Noḍhagīsarasāmi	*Devakula* and platform, and AN, endowment to guilds, monthly revenue	By those devoted to ritual acts, who (will) arrive and who (presently) reside . . . headed by the guilds . . . the *taithika*, *nākṣatrika* as well as *prāharika* rites and so forth (are to be performed) for the god Noḍha . . .; the repair of what is damaged and dilapidated and the embellishment are to be made by themselves.

60	?	Hāritī temple?	(Buildings?) and two Villages and money, endowment to guilds	And this permanent endowment is to be executed by . . . headed by the *kulikas* . . . . . . (for) the *taithika*, the *nā(kṣatrika* ?), and for the repair of what was damaged and dilapidated; it should be enjoyed by those who (will) arrive and who (presently) reside.
200	Great Talavara Talavara and family	To the *nikāya* of the noble Puvvaseliyas	A) . . . a monastery with buildings and agricultural land, animals, servants, instruments and a tank B) money as AN C) agricultural land	—
105	Vinayadhara and family	Buddhist institution	Building (?) and cows and money (?by the order)	For the repair of broken and shattered (parts) and for the preparation of a flower canopy, annually at the Pavāraṇā festival Money for flowers, lamp oil
106	?	Buddhist institution	? And Money (? by the order)	Money for flowers, strings, lamp oil at the Pavāraṇā festival

Table 7.2 Akṣayanīvī (AN) inscriptions from Kanheri (after Gokhale 1991)

No.	*Donor*	*Donee*	*Object*	*Conditions/ purpose*
6	?	Buddhist institution	Several buildings (cells) with unspecified AN	—
24	Lay merchant with family	Buddhist institution	Field as AN	—
25	Lay merchant with family	*cātudisa bhikhusaṃgha*	Cave and hall and money as AN, given to the community, and a field as AN	Cloth money (to be given by the Order)
28	Merchant	*cātudisa bhikhusaṃgha*	A) Cave and cistern, etc., and money as AN B) house and dining hall, and a house as AN	A) Money for cloth, alms bowls, shoes, repair of cave B) Rent of the house for buildings, cloth
30	Monk (*pavajita*) with relatives	*saṃgha*	Cave and money as AN	Cloth money
33	?	Bhādrayanīya school	Cave and money	Interest (*vaḍhi*), unclear
34	Nun (*therī*)	*cātudisa bhikhusaṃgha*	Cave and cistern, and money as AN	Interest for cloth money
35	Monk (*thera*)	*saṃgha*	Cave and cistern, and money as AN	Interest for cloth money
38	Nun (*pavaïtikā*) and relatives	*cātudisa bhikhusaṃgha*	Cave and cistern, and unspecified AN	Interest for cloth money
40	Merchant and family	Buddhist institution	Cave and cistern, and field as AN	Cloth money and repair of porch and windows
43	Housewife, wife of layman and merchant	*cātudisa bhikhusaṃgha*	Cave, cistern, tanks, and money as AN	—
44	Merchant together with his mother, a nun (*pavacātikā*)	Buddhist institution	Cave, and unspecified AN	—

No.	Donor	Donee	Object	Conditions/ purpose
51	Monk (*pavajita*)	*cātudisa bhikhusaṃgha*	Cave and cistern, and unspecified AN	—
57	Layman (*upāsaka*)	*cātudisa bhikhusaṃgha*	AN to a cave	Cloth money

the donation of the structure. The site was occupied for many centuries, from the 1st century CE up to the 9th century CE. The table 7.2 above provides an overview of the main characteristics of the *akṣayanīvī* inscriptions that belong to the earliest phase of occupation; that is, the Sātavāhana and Kṣatrapa period.[25]

The evidence from Kanheri confirms that the practice of *akṣayanīvī* quickly became firmly rooted in Buddhist donative activities shortly after its introduction at the end of the 1st century CE. At the same time, the Kanheri records show that this process was accompanied by a rather remarkable diversification with regard to the donors and the objects donated. It is possible—as suggested by Visvanathan and others—that *akṣayanīvī* donations were initially restricted to the investment of money with certain guilds and thus reflected the changing socio-economic conditions in Western India during the first centuries of the Common Era.[26] But the evidence from Kanheri shows that this restriction—if it ever existed—was very soon given up: If the inscriptions specify the character of the endowment, it is in at least four cases a real estate (field, house). The same is true for the important inscription no. 3 from Nasik cave 3.[27] This text, dated in the 19th regnal year of the Sātavāhana king Pulumāyi, refers to the donation of a village (*gāma*) and of land (*bhikhuhalaparihāra*) as forms of permanent endowment. This leads us to assume that if the *akṣayanīvī* indeed began as a deposit of money, it rather quickly absorbed the character of other types of permanent donations, in particular those of villages and land. The latter type is deeply rooted in Indian Brahmanical culture, and it is certainly not without significance that the *akṣayanīvī* donation from Nasik cave 3 borrowed heavily from the terminology of these customary land donations, including the long list of immunities and tax privileges that usually accompany the donation of real estate. At the same time, we observe in later inscriptions that the terms of perpetuity typical for Brahmanical land grants came to be applied in *akṣayanīvī* records, such as *śāśvatkāla-* (Phanigiri, EIAD 105) or *ācandratāraka-* (EIAD 55). It is therefore highly probable that both types of permanent donations—land grants and money investments—did not develop independently from each other and were subject to certain mutual influences.

Contrary to Nasik, with its strong support of royal donors, the *akṣayanīvī*s at Kanheri were donated by merchants or monastics. Not a single inscription at Kanheri refers to guilds or similar institutions that would administer the endowed money. The interest was to be used either for the daily needs of the order, such as clothing, or for the maintenance of the structures that were in many cases donated alongside the *akṣayanīvī*. There is no reference to any ritual actions that would have to be conducted by the use of the donated endowment.

Conclusion: the *Akṣayanīvī*s from Āndhradeśa in context

If we compare the later texts from Āndhradeśa with the evidence from the Western Ghat caves, certain differences become obvious that probably reflect developments within the administrative organisation of religious institutions and of their socio-economic contexts: although in the early period *akṣayanīvī* donations were clearly restricted to Buddhist institutions, the material from Āndhradeśa confirms the development referred to earlier, that within the first centuries after its introduction, the institution *akṣayanīvī* was adapted by other religious communities such as Śaivas. Perhaps the earliest evidence for this development is the aforementioned inscription from Mathura dated in the Kuṣāṇa year 28, or 154–155 CE. As Harry Falk suggested, the use of the Macedonian month name *gurppiya* (Gorpaios) shows that the inscription was composed by someone from the Northwest.[28] At first glance this is surprising, since the use of this term seems to be restricted in this period to the Deccan area. On the other hand, it is possible that the adaptation of an otherwise exclusively Buddhist term into a different religious context is much easier in an environment where this term has no concrete religious connotation. This was the case in the Northwest, but also in other regions of the Indian subcontinent.

Although in the earliest inscriptions the permanent endowment was firmly linked to the constructive maintenance of the building to which it was attached, as well as to certain daily requisites of the Buddhist community, the Āndhra material indicates that the purpose of *akṣayanīvī*s was extended to certain ritual activities conducted at the respective places. This development did not really affect the character of the endowment, it still remaining a requisite that was meant to guarantee the long term functioning of the religious site.

In other instances, we observe a remarkable continuity. Thus, the corpus from Āndhradeśa shares the diversity of objects that are typical for *akṣayanīvī* donations. Although it is highly probable that this type of endowment was indeed initially restricted to money transactions,[29] it very soon became common for other types of objects, such as villages or agricultural land. The predominance of money investment, however, is still clearly visible in early Āndhradeśa, where five of the seven inscriptions refer to financial transactions.

Continuity is also found in the way in which these transactions are administered. As noted earlier, Oskar von Hinüber was quite astonished by the fact that the two Phanigiri records stipulate that the money was to be given *by* the Order, and not *to* it:

> Most interesting is the third part, because here money is demanded by the donor from the Saṃgha which seems to be unique. The text is straightforward, because the instrumental case *bhikhusaṃghena* leaves no room for a different interpretation: The monks have to provide six Kāhāpaṇas yearly to buy flowers.[30]

Both texts give no indication where the money was to be invested. Thus, it cannot be excluded that the endowment was directly given to and administered by the monastic community who took care of the investment. Such a procedure seems indeed to be described by some of the earlier *akṣayanīvī* inscriptions. Thus, the Nasik inscription no. 17 (cave 12) says,

> . . . *leṇaṃ deyadhaṃmaṃ catudisasa bhikhusaṃghasa niyātitaṃ data ca ṇeṇa akhayanivi kāhāpaṇasata 100* ***saghasa hathe*** *eto vasavuthasa pavaïtasa civarikaṃ dātavaṃ bārasakaṃ*
>
> This cave, a pious gift . . . bestowed on the universal *Saṃgha* of monks generally; and by the same have been given as a perpetual endowment one-hundred—100—*kāhāpaṇas* **in the hands of the *Saṃgha*.** Out of this the cloth money of twelve *kāhāpaṇa*s is to be given to the ascetic who keeps the *vassa* (here).[31]

In nearly identical wording, a record from Kanheri (no. 25) describes the transaction:

> . . . *pava(te) Kaṇhasele leṇam koḍhi ca deyadhāmaṃ cātudise bhikhusaghe paḍiṭhāpita savasatāṇaṃ hitasughatha etasa ca akhayanivi data kāhāpaṇāna satāni*
>
> *be 200* ***saghasa yeva haṭhe*** *paḷike sate eṭha ca ādhapanakhetiyasa kheta gāme Magalathāne bhojākapati eto* ***saṃgheṇa dātava civarika*** *solasaka paliko ca māse utukāle*[32]
>
> . . . On the Kaṇhasela mountain, a cave and a cistern were established as pious gift for the universal community of monks, for the welfare and happiness of all beings. And for this two hundred, 200, *kāhāpaṇas* were given as permanent **endowment in the hand of this very community** (at the interest of) one *paḷika* (= *kāhāpaṇa*) per hundred, and a field of half-share ownership

> in the village of Magalathāna for being enjoyed. Out of this **the community should give as cloth money** (to the monks) sixteen (*paḷika* = *kāhāpaṇa*) and one *paḷika* (= *kāhāpaṇa*) per month in the rainy season.[33]

Both texts make it clear that the Phanigiri records are not as unique as Oskar von Hinüber suggested. In fact, the already widely quoted *Mūlasarvāstivādavinaya* text introduced and discussed by Gregory Schopen quite explicitly refers to the possibility that a permanent endowment of money could be administered by the monastery itself. The relevant passage runs (in Schopen's translation):

> (. . .) the donors thought: 'If even the *vihāras* of those who are still living, abiding, continuing, and alive fall thus into ruin, how it be for the *vihāras* of those who are dead? We should give a perpetuity (*akṣaya*) to the monastic Community for building purposes'.
>
> Having thought thus, and taking a perpetuity, they went to the monks. Having arrived, they said this to them: 'Noble Ones, please accept this perpetuity for building purposes'!
>
> The monks said: 'Gentlemen, since the Blessed One has promulgated a rule of training in this regard, we do not accept them'.
>
> The monks reported this matter to the Blessed One.
>
> The Blessed One said: 'For the sake of the Community a perpetuity for building purposes is to be accepted'.
>
> The monks, having heard the Blessed One, having accepted the perpetuity, put it into the community's depository (*koṣṭhikā*) and left it there.
>
> The donors came 'Noble Ones, why is there no building being done along and said: on the *vihāra*'?
>
> 'There is no money (*kārṣāpaṇa*)'.
>
> 'But did we not give you perpetuities'?
>
> **The monks said**: 'Did you think we would consume the perpetuities? They remain in the Community's depository'.
>
> 'But of course, Noble Ones, they would not be perpetuities if they could be exhausted, but why do you think we did not keep them in our own houses? Why do you not have them lent out on interest (*prayojayati*)'?
>
> The monks said: 'Since the Blessed One has promulgated a rule of training in this regard, we do not have them lent on interest'.
>
> The monks reported this matter to the Blessed One.
>
> The Blessed One said: 'For the sake of the Community a perpetuity for building purposes must be lent on interest'.
>
> Devout brahmins and householders having in the same way given perpetuities for the sake of the Buddha, the Dharma and the

Community, the Blessed One said: 'Perpetuities for the sake of the Buddha, the Dharma and the Community are to be lent on interest. What is generated from that, with that accrued revenue (*siddha*) worship is to performed for the Buddha, the Dharma and the Community'.[34]

The text goes on to explain how exactly the money has to be invested and it makes one fact sufficiently clear: The monks themselves took care of the investment, they installed the money and they drafted and signed the contract in this regard. But the text contains another piece of important information: Permanent endowments might have been started as an instrument for providing maintenance of buildings, but they could also be meant for ritual purposes, such as the worship of the three jewels.

The *Vinaya* passage thus confirms what the epigraphical evidence has already suggested: the term *akṣayanīvī* comprises a rather complex institution that has in common the notion of perpetuity on the one side and the purpose of maintaining the functioning of a religious institution on the other side. The permanent character of the donation was either granted by the investment of money or by the donation of land or villages.

By comparing the Āndhradeśa evidence to both earlier and contemporary *akṣayanīvī* texts, it can now be argued that the institution of permanent endowments was initially introduced to guarantee the maintenance of donated buildings, but soon—if not even at the same time—acquired a multi-faceted character that involved various kinds of donated objects and different aspects of ritual activities at the respective religious sites.

Notes

1 See in particular, and with references to earlier scholarship, Meera Visvanathan, 'Akhayanivi: The Eternal Endowment in the Early Historic Deccan', *Journal of the International Association of Buddhist Studies*, 2018, 42: 509–35.

2 See Harry Falk, 'A Copper Plate Donation Record and some Seals from the Kashmir Smast', *Beiträge zur Allgemeinen und Vergleichenden Archäologie*, 2003, 23: 1–19 (reprinted in Harry Falk, *Hariśyenalekhapañcāśikā: Fifty Selected Papers on Indian Epigraphy and Chronology*, Britta Schneider and Ingo Strauch (eds), Bremen: Hempen Verlag, 2013, pp. 333–51). For further objects from this site, and a discussion of the *akṣayanīvī* donation, see Harry Falk, 'Money Can Buy Me Heaven: Religious Donations in Late and Post-Kushan India', *Archäologische Mitteilungen aus Iran und Turan*, 2008, 40: 137–48 (reprinted in Falk, *Hariśyenalekhapañcāśikā*, pp. 406–17).

3 Falk, 'A Copper Plate Donation Record', p. 11.

4 Sten Konow, 'Mathura Brahmi Inscription of the Year 29', *Epigraphia Indica*, 1931–32, 21: 55–61 (p. 61).

5 Gregory Schopen, 'Art, Beauty, and the Business of Running a Buddhist Monstery in Early Northwest India', in D. Meth Srinivasan (ed), *On the Cusp of an Era—Art in the Pre-Kuṣāṇa World*, Leiden and Boston: Brill, 2007, pp. 287–317 (p. 305); Falk, 'Money Can Buy Me Heaven', p. 145.

6 *Ibid*, p. 145.

7 http://hisoma.huma-num.fr/exist/apps/EIAD/index2.html. Further bibliographical references on previous editions and discussions can be found on the website. I want to thank Vincent Tournier for his valuable comments on an earlier version of this paper.

8 See K. V. Soundara Rajan, *Nagarjunakonda (1954–60): The Historical Period*. Memoirs of the Archaeological Survey of India, 75. New Delhi: Archaeological Survey of India, 2006, pp. 228–9.

9 For the sake of consistency, I changed 'perpetual' to 'permanent'.

10 *Ibid*, pp. 242–3.

11 *Ibid*, pp. 174–8. The identification of the statue of a female deity found in situ in the interior of the temple as Hāritī is at least doubtful.

12 The online edition has "firmly attributed to . . ." for *supayuta[ṁ]*. Based on the terminological use of *pra-yuj* "to invest" as attested in epigraphical and literary sources, I propose the given translation. For the use of *pra-yuj* in Buddhist and Dharmaśāstra texts, see Gregory Schopen, 'Doing Business for the Lord: Lending on Interest and Written Loan Contracts in the *Mūlasarvāstivāda-vinaya*', in *Indian Monastic Buddhism: Collected Papers on Textual, Inscriptional and Archaeological Evidence, Vol. II*: Buddhist Monks and Business Matters, New Delhi: Motilal Banarsidass, [1994] 2010, pp. 45–90 (pp. 56–7). For its use in contemporary inscriptions, see e.g. Uṣavadāta's Nasik inscription: *ete ca kāhāpaṇā prayutā* in Emile Senart, 'The Inscriptions in the Caves at Nasik', *Epigraphia Indica*, 1905–06, 8: 59–96 (p. 82, No. 12), and Nasik inscription No. 15: *akṣayanivī prayuktā* in *ibid*, p. 88).

13 See the Hirananda Sastri, 'Epigraphy', *Annual Report of the Archaeological Survey of India*, 1925–26: 131–51 (pp. 139–40). Calcutta and New Delhi: Archaeological Survey of India.

14 Muhammad Hamid Kuraishi, 'Trial Excavations at Alluru, Gummadidurru and Nagarjunikonda', *Annual Report of the Archaeological Survey of India*, 1926–1927: 150–61 (pp. 150–2). According to M. H. Kuraishi, who in 1926 conducted trial excavations at the site, the inscribed pillar was one of the *stūpa*'s *āyaka* pillars. According to his report, he discovered the fragments of three other pillars, two of them apparently inscribed. Another inscribed fragment belonged to the reliefs. *Ibid*, pp. 151–2.

15 For this expression and its variants in literary and epigraphic records, see in particular Oskar von Hinüber, 'Behind the Scenes: The Struggle of Political Groups for Influence as Reflected in Inscriptions', *Indo-Iranian Journal*, 2013, 56: 365–79. See also Oskar von Hinüber, 'Again on the Donation Made by the Vinayadhara Dhammasena and on Other Inscriptions from Phanigiri', *Annual Report of the International Research Institute for Advanced Buddhology at Soka University for the Academic Year 2012*, 2013, 16: 3–12 (in particular pp. 225–6).

16 The formula was misread and misinterpreted in D. C. Sircar, 'Two Inscriptions from Guntur District: 1. Velpūru Inscription of Aira Mā[na]sada; 2. Mañchikallu Inscription of Pallava Siṁhavarman', *Epigraphia Indica*, 1957–58, 32: 82–90 (p. 88).

17 von Hinüber, 'Behind the Scenes', p. 8.

18 Both letters—and the related akṣara *ṇa*—are sometimes written with and sometimes without a loop. The space between *-ādi* and *kā-* is apparently due to a fissure on the surface of the rock.

19 For this festival and further references, see Oskar von Hinüber, 'A Second Inscription from Phanigiri (Andhrapradesh): Dhaṃmasena's Donation', *Annual Report of the International Research Institute for Advanced Buddhology at Soka University for the Academic Year 2011*, 2012, 15: 3–10 (p. 7f).

20 In the case of EIAD 200 it is not clear whether the term *akhayanivi* is related to the entirety of the donated items or only to the money mentioned last in the list. Therefore, these items are marked here by an asterisk.
21 For an exhaustive discussion of this text and further references, see now Visvanathan, 'Akhayanivi'.
22 Senart, 'The Inscriptions in the Caves', pp. 65–71.
23 *Ibid*, pp. 88–9.
24 *Ibid*, p. 90.
25 Later inscriptions as No. 21 (dated Śaka 775) and No. 22 (Śaka 765) testify to the continuation of the *akṣayanīvī* practice at Kanheri. Although they provide important and interesting data, they will not be considered in the present discussion.
26 See Visvanathan, 'Akhayanivi', p. 532: "an analysis of the inscriptional record suggests that the *akhayanivi* began as a monetary endowment and it is only subsequently that the term became applied to the gift or grant of land. . . . It arose in an urban world of commerce and trade, a world marked by political dynamism, socio-cultural accommodation and religious networks of remarkable complexity'. See also also Annette Schmiedchen, 'Art. 19. Inventionen, Innovationen und Imitationen im interkulturellen Kontakt: 19.6. Die indologische Perspektive', in Michael Borgolte (ed), *Enzyklopädie des Stiftungswesens in mittelalterlichen Gesellschaften*, Bd. 3, Berlin: Stiftung und Gesellschaft, pp. 477–88 (p. 479): 'Dass indische Stiftungskonzepte ursprünglich in enger Verbindung mit dem Instrument des Gelddepositums entwickelt worden waren, spiegelt sich aber noch in terminologischen Reminiszenzen. So wurde z.B. der Begriff *akṣayanīvī*, "unvergängliches Kapital", der seit den ersten Jahrhunderten u.Z. eine typische Bezeichnung für Geldstiftungen zu religiösen Zwecken war, später zum Teil auch für Landverleihungen benutzt'. In her investigation of *akṣayanīvī* inscriptions, Njammasch comes to the more cautious conclusion: 'Gelddeposita waren nur eine, doch zugleich die verbreiteteste Form des *akhayanivi* unter den Sātavāhanas'. Marlene Njammasch, 'Akhayanivi-Schenkungen an Klöster und Tempel im Dekhan unter den Sātvāhanas', *Acta Orientalia Academiae Scientarum Hungaricae*, 1971, 24: 203–15 (p. 206).
27 See for this inscription also Shimada Akira, 'Royal and Non-Royal Buddhist Patronage in the Early Deccan', *Journal of the International Association of Buddhist Studies*, 2018, 42: 473–507 (pp. 488–90).
28 Falk, 'A Copper Plate Donation Record', p. 11.
29 As noticed already by numerous other scholars, the term *nīvī*, a 'piece of cloth wrapped around the waist; capital', indicates the initial character of these endowments. On the etymology of this term that points to the habit of carrying valuables or money in a piece of cloth, see Manfred Mayrhofer, *Etymologisches Wörterbuch des Altindoarischen*, Bd. 2, Heidelberg: Universitätsverlag Winter, 1996, s.v. See also Falk, 'Money Can Buy Me Heaven', p. 147. A similar semantic development is attested in the much later Gujarati-Sanskrit term *potta/pottaka/potaka* 'cloth, cloth-bag -> treasury, treasure', see Ingo Strauch, *Die Lekhapaddhati-Lekhapancāśikā: Briefe und Urkunden im mittelalterlichen Gujarat. Text, Übersetzung, Kommentar, Glossar (Sanskrit-Deutsch-Englisch)*, Monographien zur Indischen Archäologie, Kunst und Philologie, Berlin: Dietrich Reimer, 2002, p. 86f.
30 von Hinüber, 'Again on the Donation Made by the Vinayadhara Dhammasena', p. 8.
31 Senart, 'The Inscriptions in the Caves', p. 90.

32 After Shobhana Gokhale, *Kanheri Inscriptions*, Pune: Deccan College Post Graduate and Research Institute, 1991, p. 75.

33 The translation is partially based on Vasudev Vishnu Mirashi, *The History and Inscriptions of the Sātavāhanas and the Western Kshatrapas*, Bombay: Maharashtra State Board for Literature and Culture, 1981, p. 73; as quoted by Visvanathan, 'Akhayanivi', pp. 529–30.

34 Schopen, 'Doing Business for the Lord', p. 48.

8

NEITHER CAVE NOR TEMPLE

Creating and commemorating 'place' in the ritual landscapes at Badami

Lisa N. Owen

The rock-cut caves and structural monuments at the site of Badami in Karnataka are among India's most well-known examples of temple architecture. With many monuments dating from the 6th through 8th centuries, the site clearly served as an important place of worship for members of the Early Chalukya court as well as for residents within the capital city. Although art historians have recognised the importance of Badami's temples for understanding early architectural developments in Southern India,[1] there are other monuments at the site that have *not* been examined as they defy easy classification as 'caves' or 'temples.' These are 'rock-reliefs'—natural rock formations that have sculptures of temples and deities carved across their surfaces. As Badami's rock-reliefs do not exhibit interior spaces for worship, like a cave and structural temple; they are typically excluded from art historical studies of the site. Indeed, if mentioned at all, they are dismissed as a mere repository of well-known subjects in Hindu sculpture. I contend that this is misguided, as these carvings can prompt us to ask new questions about the nature of, and the use for, such imagery. Importantly, Badami's rock-reliefs allow us to consider how they might create a power of place and contribute to this site's ritual landscape. Moreover, if we look closely at the evidence of these reliefs, we discover that they reveal much about how the site was conceived—especially by those who lived, worked, and worshipped there. In contrast to other scholarly approaches to Badami which tend to focus on the roles of the political elite, I am interested in highlighting the choices made by others at Badami, including artists, visitors, pilgrims, and local residents. I argue that the rock-reliefs form a dialogue with other monuments and imagery at the site and that this dialogue reveals sophisticated and diverse acts of commemoration performed by these communities.

Numerous rock-reliefs are carved on a colossal boulder located at the eastern end of the site's water tank (Figure 8.1). Known today as Agastya

Figure 8.1 View of the colossal boulder and Bhutanatha temple complex
Source: Author

Teertha, this manmade reservoir still serves as the primary water source for Badami village. The boulder is a prominent feature in the landscape as it can be viewed both in isolation as a unique natural formation and as an integral part of the site's rocky environment. The visual appeal of the boulder likely contributed to the site location for the c.-8th century Bhutanatha temple. Both the water tank and the natural boulder are essential elements in the design and conception of the Bhutanatha temple and for the smaller, later shrines that were built around it. Like the cliffs, caves, and structural temples that demarcate the northern and southern edges of the site, the boulder and Bhutanatha complex serve to delineate its eastern periphery.

The rock-reliefs are carved along the northern and northeastern surfaces of the boulder (Figs. 8.2–4). In general, there are two types of carvings: 1) reliefs of structural temples and 2) deities in figural form carved within rectangular niches. The few scholars that have addressed these carvings typically date the temple-reliefs to the mid-6th or 7th century based on their stylistic and architectural features that align more or less with structural temples at the site. They exhibit the Dravida architectural system employed at Badami and elsewhere. However, it is worth pointing out that while these temple-reliefs are similar in style, they are not identical in their architectural elements. In fact, in the *Encyclopaedia of Indian Temple Architecture*, Meister and Dhaky identify at least four different variations of the Dravida temple on this boulder.[2] They see these reliefs as 'temple-models' and examine them in order to construct typologies for the Dravida temple tower.

K V Soundararajan and R K Rajarajan also view these carvings as models or designs for structural temples.[3] They see them as either representing a transitional phase from rock-cut excavation to structural temple building or as some sort of practical exercise undertaken by artists. In his assessment of both the temple-reliefs and the figural deities, Soundararajan writes:

> The details [of the temple-reliefs] would seem to suggest an age approximately contemporary with the structural temples of Bādāmi. At the same time, if one were to compare stylistically the relief carvings of divinities shown on the same boulders, these would tend to push the date a little forward, probably towards the close of the seventh century A.D.[4]

Figure 8.2 View of rock-reliefs on the northeastern side of the boulder
Source: Author

The late 7th or early 8th century attribution for the figural deities supported by Soundararajan and other scholars rests primarily on iconographic and stylistic analyses. The figures are typically compared to sculpted deities found on dated structural temples at Badami and at other neighbouring sites in the Malaprabha valley.

As I also agree that the boulder's temple-reliefs predate the figural deities (with one exception, discussed later), I begin my examination of Badami's rock-reliefs with these temple forms. Carved along one section of the northeastern surface of the colossal boulder are the following reliefs from left to right (Figure 8.3): a small *liṅga* and square *pīṭha* enshrined within a plain niche (approximately 12.7 cm in height); a small, four-armed Viṣṇu within a plain niche (approximately 15.2 cm in height); a shrine and superstructure housing a *liṅga* and square *pīṭha* (approximately 1 m in height); a large, four-armed Viṣṇu in a plain niche (just under 1 m in height); and two roughly carved shrines with superstructures (approximately 1 m in height). All but one of the reliefs are carved high up on the boulder—at least seven feet above ground level.

The northern surface of the boulder also exhibits numerous carvings of temples (Figure 8.4). The largest and most elaborate ones are three *liṅga*

Figure 8.3 Detail of rock-reliefs on the northeastern side of the boulder
Source: Author

Figure 8.4 View of rock-reliefs on the northern side of the boulder
Source: Author

shrines with tall superstructures preceded by smaller, flat-roofed *maṇḍapas* for Śiva's bull, Nandi. The *liṅga* shrines measure between 1 and 1.7 m in height. Other carvings on the boulder include a four-armed Viṣṇu in a plain niche, a *liṅga* and square *pīṭha* in a plain niche, and a barely discernable carving of Gaṇeśa. All of these reliefs are accessible to the human touch, they face the Bhutanatha temple complex, and are carved in close proximity to the tank.

Given their powerful visual presence and potential ritual roles, how do these temple-reliefs add (or build upon) the larger artistic and ritual landscape of Badami? Do they represent a more economically efficient means of creating a temple and what might this tell us about their patrons and audience? Do they serve as an abbreviated referent to the most important part of a temple complex—namely the temple's tower—thereby indicating the location of the sanctum and the divine presence within? Are the temple-reliefs worshipped directly or do they serve as visual reminders of devotional practice—inviting us to visit neighbouring structural and rock-cut temples that we can actually enter? Or might such imagery creatively suggest that the gods can be housed anywhere and everywhere, in both manmade and natural forms?

In her recent work on early monuments in the Deccan region, Subhashini Kaligotla explores the meanings of temple-images found on the exterior of temples as well as those carved on the overdoor (lintel) to temple sanctums.[5] For example, she analyses the temple-reliefs carved above the main shrines in Badami's caves and on select temples at other early sites. She notes that temple-images function in different ways depending on their location on the temple's plan. When located over liminal spaces—such as doorways, thresholds, and juncture walls—the temple form appears to serve apotropaic and/or auspicious functions, much like other motifs found in these areas (such as door guardians, loving couples, and female imagery). When temple-reliefs enshrine an image, the sacred environment is amplified as the relief simultaneously references the temple itself while remaining a distinct motif. In her overall assessment of the deployment of temple-images on early monuments in the Deccan, Kaligotla highlights their multivalency stating that they can serve 'as architectural frame, as ornament, as discursive sign, and as an independently signifying and functioning entity'.[6]

Building from Kaligotla's work, I think it is important to consider the location and context of the boulder's temple-reliefs as they are *not* carved on or within a temple. They are carved on a *boulder* and we need to ask what it means to carve a temple on a boulder. Moreover, when we look at the boulder from across the site, we realise that it not only exhibits rock-reliefs, but it also serves as a support for actual built temples. In a ground-breaking study of Badami, Srikumar M. Menon was able to climb up on top of this boulder, and what he found further adds to the ways that we can understand these temple-reliefs.[7] On top of the boulder are two c.-11th-century-built shrines. It appears that these shrines were constructed from rock excavated directly from the boulder itself. Although this would obviously serve a practical function (as it eliminates the need to haul stone blocks to the top of the boulder), it also clearly enacts the transformation of stone from a natural to manmade visual form.

One of the shrines faces west and carved beside it is a small, rock-cut *liṅga*. Housed inside the structure is a loose slab carved with four *liṅgas*.[8] Similar slabs with multiple *liṅgas* have been found elsewhere in the Malaprabha valley. Menon, and other scholars, have suggested that these sculptures and their associated shrines likely functioned as memorials erected for the deceased. Evidence of such practices is found at Mahakuta and at sites near Aihole and Pattadakal.[9] In many ways, these practices continue a much earlier established tradition of commemoration, as seen in the numerous surviving megalithic monuments in the valley.[10]

Further evidence for what Menon calls 'a zone of commemoration' around this boulder is found within the neighbouring cluster of structural temples comprising the Bhutanatha complex. Significantly, one of the smaller shrines is built a few meters away from the boulder and it contains a relief carving of a seated devotee on its interior southern wall (Figure 8.5).

Figure 8.5 Relief carving of a male figure inside a memorial shrine near the boulder
Source: Author

The figure holds an offering in his cupped hands and a *kalaśa* is situated nearby. He wears his sacred thread looped over his proper right shoulder (rather than his left), which appears to indicate that he is in the act of performing post-death rituals.

Given the evidence of this later material, Menon suggests that the boulder's rock-reliefs also functioned to commemorate the deceased. Depending on the sectarian affiliation of the deceased person, a relief of a *liṅga* temple or an image of Viṣṇu was carved. Menon's interpretation of these rock-reliefs as memorials is made all the more convincing through his analyses of other monuments across Badami. These include Jain *pādukās* (commemorating deceased monks), hero stones, and a laudatory (and possibly memorial) inscription to an Early Chalukya hero known as Kappearabhata. This inscription is carved in the cliffs to the northwest of the boulder where there are a few scattered rock-reliefs depicting *liṅga*-shrines and images of Viṣṇu. A prominent example (Figure 8.6) is found on a rock formation opposite the Archaeological Survey of India site museum. Although the *liṅga* in this case is enshrined in a plain, rectangular niche, the visual pairing of the *liṅga* and Viṣṇu resonates with imagery carved on the boulder. Given the range of

Figure 8.6 View of rock-reliefs near the Archaeological Survey of India site museum
Source: Author

material at the site, it is clear that Badami served as an important place for practices of commemoration and remembrance.

Menon also mentions the fact that the area near the Bhutanatha temple served as a locale for performing *śrāddha* rituals up until a recent prohibition by the Archaeological Survey of India (ASI).[11] Can these acts be viewed as a continuation of long-standing practices? While it is difficult to reconstruct practices that might have occurred at Badami in the 6th through the 8th centuries, we can consider the name of the temple, Bhutanatha. This appellation is based on an inscription inside the temple that identifies Śiva as 'Lord of the *bhūta*s' or 'ghosts' that can be found in liminal worlds. As *śrāddha* rituals are performed to honour and propitiate deceased ancestors, we can consider how the Bhutanatha temple and the boulder might have contributed to the efficacy of these acts. According to Mary McGee and her work on contemporary post-death rituals,

> Memorial rites are performed annually, but the *śrāddha* ceremony immediately following a death has special significance and purpose as it helps transform the newly deceased into a revered ancestor

> (*pitṛ*). Without these rites, a soul would wander aimlessly in the intermediate world, threatening the order and well being of the family.[12]

Thus, the transformative aspects of *śrāddha* rituals in guiding the deceased's bodiless spirit to the realm of the ancestors might have been heightened and linked to the nearby temple dedicated to Śiva in this particular form.

Moreover, we can acknowledge the potential role of the tank in post-death ritual performances. According to McGee:

> Offerings of water to cool the dead after the cremation process are accompanied by *mantras*. Water is also used to purify family relatives of the deceased who have become temporarily polluted by death. Within three days of the cremation, the remaining bones and ashes are collected by the chief mourner and are either buried in an urn and commended to Mother Earth or are cast into the flowing waters of a river. Following this rite, the chief mourners undergo yet another purification rite with ablutions.[13]

The eastern edge of the tank at Badami as well as the banks of the Malaprabha River could have served as powerful places for such activities.

The rock-reliefs carved on the boulder not only appear to commemorate individual deceased people (thus contributing to rituals of remembrance) but they also literally demarcate this area near the tank as the physical space or place for these activities. Collectively, the rock-reliefs create a visual field or backdrop for such performances. However, by the 11th century, it clearly became more popular to construct three-dimensional shrines to articulate the performative aspects of this space. Evidence of the status and function of the Bhutanatha's smaller shrines as memorial temples is not only demonstrated by the carving of the male figure performing post-death rituals discussed earlier, but also by the very fact that shrines were constructed on top of—and out of—the boulder itself. Thus, the transformative properties of the rituals are also expressed visually through the transformation of the boulder from a natural form to one that is manmade.

In understanding the visual power of Badami's memorial temple-reliefs, I think it is also important to consider the different *ways* that they are presented to us on this boulder. A close examination of their forms suggests a greater multivalency in their meanings. For example, some of the *liṅgas* and Nandis are enshrined in simple structures or niches while others are crowned by elaborate superstructures. Some of the temple-images are finely articulated while others are barely incised into the rock. What could these variations mean? Are the artists consciously playing with their roles as makers—makers of rock-reliefs, caves, and built temples? Could the barely incised temples be conceived of as *svayambhu* (self-manifesting), thereby further complicating the maker's role? Or, when viewed specifically as memorial monuments, could these variations of form connote aspects of time and its effect on memory and remembrance? In other words, could the shallowly incised reliefs allude to decreased abilities in recalling/remembering the past and/or in performing commemorative acts? Furthermore, how is the memorial/commemorative nature of the temple-reliefs further defined through their visual juxtaposition with the main series of figural deities that is also carved on this boulder? I would like to suggest that in addition to serving as part of a memorial landscape, these rock-reliefs also commemorate *place*.

I would like to now turn to an examination of the main series of deities carved on this boulder (Figure 8.7). The upper register (from left to right) depicts the following gods: Varāha, Gaṇeśa, the *trimūrti* (Brahmā, Śiva, and Viṣṇu), Durgā Mahiṣāsuramardinī, and Narasiṃha (followed by another temple-relief discussed in a following section). The register measures over 4.5 meters in length with each figure approximately 76 cm tall. Carved beneath these figures is a series of *nāgas* in semi-human form. They are seated in the lotus posture with their palms placed together in homage.

Figure 8.7 Detail of main series of gods on the northeastern side of the boulder
Source: Author

Although these gods have played an instrumental role in Hindu devotional and artistic activities beginning as early as the 1st century CE, their inclusion here, I contend, is site-specific. When we stand in front of the boulder, gazing at the deities, we are simultaneously facing the direction of Badami's four rock-cut caves. Although there are still debates about the relative chronology of these caves, there is consensus that they were completed by the end of the 6th century.[14] Cave 3 is an imperial commission and contains a lengthy inscription that tells us that Mangalesha, a son of the dynasty's founder Pulekeshin I, commissioned and dedicated the cave for the merit of his older brother, King Kirtivarman.[15] The installation of an image of Viṣṇu and the accompanying festivities and performances of gift-giving took place in the year 578 CE. In the inscription, the cave is described as 'surpassing all things divine and human' and that it was 'constructed by most marvelous labour'.[16] Importantly, the inscription is carved on a pilaster next to an over-life-sized relief of Varāha that is carved on the northeastern wall of the veranda. This sculpted panel of Varāha clearly makes a visual connection to the main series of deities on the boulder which begins with Varāha and ends with Narasiṃha. Completing this visual connection is the large relief of Narasiṃha that is carved on the southern (or opposite) end of Cave 3's veranda. Thus, we can consider the selection and arrangement of deities on the boulder to be a quotation from this very prominent cave.

The remaining deities on the boulder also correspond to specific sculptures found across the site. These include large-scale sculptures of Gaṇeśa and Durgā Mahiṣāsuramardinī in Cave 1 and imagery found in the structural Jambulinga temple. Cave 1 at Badami is dedicated to Śiva and features a small rock-cut shrine at the west (right) end of its façade. The rear wall of the shrine features a large, four-armed Durgā Mahiṣāsuramardinī. Her voluptuous form contrasts with the slenderer body of the eight-armed Durgā carved on the boulder. In addition, the cave relief depicts the vanquished demon in his buffalo form while the boulder relief presents him as a crowned, male figure. Such stylistic and iconographic differences align with the likely dates for these carvings—c. 6th and early 8th century, respectively. The Gaṇeśa sculpture, also carved within the façade shrine of Cave 1, has a greater visual correlation with the boulder relief. However, in the cave, he is presented with a more corpulent body and with two arms rather than four.

A more dramatic connection between the main series of figural forms on the boulder and other sculpted images at Badami is, however, found in the context of the Jambulinga temple. Carved on one of the porch pillars of the temple is an inscription dated to the early years of the reign of Vijayaditya (699–700 CE).[17] The content of the inscription informs us that Vijayaditya's mother, Vinayavati, installed images of the gods Brahmā, Viṣṇu, and Maheśvara (Śiva) in the temple and provided other gifts for their worship. The temple currently has three shrines, but only a solitary Śiva-*liṅga* remains extant. The *liṅga* is housed in the western shrine which is on axis to the temple entrance. Images of Brahmā, Śiva, and Viṣṇu, are carved in high relief on the ceiling of the main hall.[18] Given the temple's location in the western sector of Badami (i.e., across the tank from the boulder), the rock-relief can be seen as a counterpoint or balance to this temple and its imagery—one that literally brings the *trimūrti* and its worship across the capital city of Badami. Its inclusion on the boulder as the central panel in the series of deities, as well as the primacy given to Śiva who forms the centre of the triad, reflects a conscious choice by the artists and seems to promote this particular expression of divinity at Badami.

Moreover, a later carving of the *trimūrti* appears inside a structural stone shrine that abuts the southeastern side of the boulder. This shrine shelters a c. 7th or 8th century rock-relief of Viṣṇu Anantaśayana discussed later. The *trimūrti* is carved on the shrine's left wall and depicts Śiva in the centre as in the rock-relief. The triad is also presented within a temple-relief, thereby combining the two types of imagery found on the surfaces of the boulder itself. The presence and articulation of the *trimūrti* at Badami is all the more notable as representations of this triad do not appear to have gained popularity in other temples and imagery in the Malaprabha valley. This suggests that it had a special significance for Badami's patrons and audiences.

Supporting the upper register of deities on the boulder is a series of *nāgas* and they too appear to serve as external referents to images across the site. For example, in the cliffs to the north, *nāgas* are depicted in pure serpent form and are found along the pathways connecting the tank to the North Fort area and Badami's structural temples. *Nāgas* are also commonly depicted in loose sculpture that has been relocated to some of the 11th century shrines surrounding the Bhutanatha temple and to other monuments across the site. The *nāgas* carved on the boulder also clearly make connections to the impressive relief-carving of Viṣṇu Anantaśayana sheltered by the structural stone temple that also contains the *trimūrti* relief.

Although the Viṣṇu Anantaśayana relief is now enclosed within a built shrine, it may have once received ablutions from the water-filled tank. The sculpture, carved directly from the boulder, measures approximately 2 m long and nearly 1 m in height. Viṣṇu's head (and the canopy of serpent hoods) is oriented towards the tank. At the god's feet are Lakṣmī and Garuḍa. Emerging from Viṣṇu's navel is a curving stalk capped by a large open lotus that supports the god Brahmā. Brahmā forms the centre of a series of divinities that hover over the body of Viṣṇu. These include Viṣṇu's ten avatars beginning on the left with the fish (*matsya*) avatar and ending with a figure on a horse (Kalki).

As many scholars have noted, the subject of Viṣṇu Anantaśayana denotes the beginning of time as it centres on the birth of the god Brahmā from the navel of Viṣṇu as he dreams about the cosmos. As Brahmā is often considered to be the creator of the universe, his own birth signifies the very beginning of that point of cosmic origination and the role of Viṣṇu as the supporter and sustainer of cosmic time. In his description of a similar relief sculpture at the site of Udayagiri in Madhya Pradesh, Michael Willis states:

> There he [Viṣṇu] is shown on the serpent Ananta, resting and regenerating after the *kalpānta*, the end of the previous aeon. Ananta—the 'endless-one'—combines both time and water: he is not just ordinary time but endless time, the infinite itself; he is not just ordinary water but the unmeasured cosmic waters. On him and out of him a whole new creation will be manufactured by Brahmā the creator. This is why Ananta is named Śeṣa, the 'remainder'—he is the residue of the previous age, the sole survivor of a vanished world who will provide the seed for a new universe.[19]

Although the Viṣṇu relief carved on the boulder at Badami can be seen as a referent to other Viṣṇu Anantaśayana sculptures at the site—specifically in Caves 2 and 3—the significance of this subject on the boulder is made even more meaningful when we consider its juxtaposition with the tank and with the commemorative/memorial rock-reliefs. Collectively, these images allude to conceptions of time, states of transformation, and residual matter that play pivotal roles in performances of post-death rituals.

In their general visual form, however, the *nāgas* on the boulder seem to best correlate with an innovative image of Viṣṇu found in the imperial Cave 3. In this sculpture, Viṣṇu is not reclining but seated on the coils of Ananta and protected by his serpent hoods. The panel is quite large in size and presents Viṣṇu seated in royal ease and holding his identifying attributes of the conch and discus. Lakṣmī and Garuḍa are seated in attendance at the base of Ananta's coils and two female *nāginī*s with fly-whisks stand on either side of the god. In this representation, Viṣṇu is alert, sitting upright and facing the viewer. Might this panel represent the first few moments of Viṣṇu's wakefulness from his cosmic slumber? Does it represent a period of time prior to his manifestation in the form of ten *avatāra*s, especially since these figures are not included in the relief?[20] Although the *daśāvatāra* are not included in the Cave 3 sculpture of Viṣṇu, the panel itself is carved adjacent to the Varāha relief and royal inscription discussed earlier. In many ways, these panels blend into one another, as demonstrated by the *nāginī* who is shared by both sculptures.[21] The sheer number of *nāginī* attendants in these two panels, combined with the innovative presentation of Ananta and the series of *nāga*s on the boulder (coincidently, ten *nāga*s), suggest that these serpent forms serve as more than just the supports of deities. They represent—or are a part of—local water bodies (such as the tank at Badami) and the 'unmeasured cosmic waters'.

In the boulder's rock-reliefs, the *nāgas* are presented in worshipful gestures towards us and invite us to engage with them. As we know from the work of Julia Shaw and Robert DeCaroli, *nāgas* are often connected with local agricultural production.[22] If propitiated properly, they protect and/or sustain manmade water management systems and, as a result, ensure economic success. Thus, their inclusion on the boulder invites us to consider their roles in association with the tank and the diverse social and economic base within the Chalukya capital. Moreover, as Himanshu Prabha Ray has argued, access to water-bodies served as one of the major deciding factors for the location of temples and/or sacred sites within the Malaprabha valley.[23] Water was critical not only for ritual purposes but for sustaining the communities that continued to engage with and maintain temple sites. With this in mind, we can easily see why this particular boulder was selected for the rock-reliefs given its proximity to the tank and its visual connections to the site's other sacred monuments and imagery.

The roles of the boulder in creating a power of place for ritual activities is further attested to in the modifications that are made into the rock. At some point after the initial creation of the deities, mortise holes were carved into the surface of the boulder to support a wooden structure or canopy. Although it is impossible today to tell whether or not a structural canopy extended further outward to provide shelter and shade for worshippers, evidence from early medieval Jain rock-reliefs in Tamil Nadu suggest that these additional structures could be quite elaborate.[24] What is clear is that such an addition would provide shelter for the deities and perhaps facilitate some activities, such as the hanging of garlands and other ritual items. An external structure would articulate a more defined ritual space as well as present the deities within a similar ritual visual vocabulary as the adjacent temple-images and the nearby structural temples. The fact that the figural deities are individually framed by pilasters clearly shows that the artists conceived of them in such a setting. And, perhaps to further foster this connection, a temple-relief was subsequently added to the series of figural forms. It is clear that this relief (seen to the right of the figures) was added later given the matrix of rock that was left for the artists to work with. The artists had to carve as closely as they could next to the culminating pilaster framing Narasiṃha, while trying to avoid a friable section of the rock at the far right. Ultimately this section cleaved off as can be seen in the temple-relief's present condition. The addition of this relief is significant as it indicates the continued importance of commemorating the deceased (through images of temple-reliefs) while linking them to other forms of commemorative practice (such as valorising the site of Badami through images of select deities). Moreover, the inclusion of mortise holes above some of the site's memorial reliefs (such as those on the rock near the ASI site museum) indicates similar types of ritual activities for both types of commemorative imagery.

If Badami's main series of figural deities served devotional as well as site-commemorative purposes, it is important to note that these practices must have primarily involved *darśan* as the registers are too high up on the rock to include other forms of *pūjā*, such as lustration, touching the images, and/

or placing physical offerings directly on them. At the same time, circumambulation of the rock may have been possible. The rock formation has a deep crevice that was further excavated to allow passage to the tank. Although the ASI has filled this crevice in with concrete, it appears that one was once able to walk around this section of the rock. Moreover, steps were likely cut into the side of the boulder to allow access to the structural shrines on top.[25] Thus, we can speculate that worship activities could have involved relatively large groups of worshippers and practices that highlight sight, recitation, and physical movement. These acts could be performed in front of (and around) the figural forms and the numerous temple-reliefs adjacent to the tank. The boulder and the rock-reliefs create a power of place where one could worship the gods and one's ancestors. They serve to integrate multiple audiences and practices and allow for introspection of one's past, present, and future.

A final, but critical, connection in thinking about the ways that the rock-reliefs at Badami create and commemorate place is found in the sequential processes of carving. The rock-reliefs literally cut into earlier inscriptions that once covered the surfaces of this boulder. This can be seen around the mortise holes above the figures and where the rock was removed to form a triangular canopy over each deity. Srinivas Padigar has published 11 fragmentary records from this boulder.[26] According to his assessment, they are written in an early Kannada script and record the personal names and epithets of Badami's artists. In one case, an epithet is used to identify the artist as 'one devoted to stone sculpting'.[27]

The inclusion of these epigraphs on the boulder mirrors the nearly 200 Kannada and Sanskrit inscriptions found throughout the site, particularly those among the sandstone cliffs surrounding the caves.[28] The vast majority of these inscriptions date to the 6th and 7th centuries and are carved in Telugu-Kannada characters. However, a few inscriptions surrounding Cave 3, also include names in Sanskrit written in early Nāgarī (or Siddhamātrikā) characters. The use of different languages and scripts in recording personal names (and those primarily of artists) certainly points to the diversity of Badami's artists, supporters, and worshippers.

In the case of the boulder, the names were recorded before both the carving of the temple-reliefs and the figural deities, thereby adding another layer to our understanding of commemorative forms and their functions. We can therefore look at the visual and rhetorical ways that the rock-reliefs serve to commemorate. The rock-reliefs on this boulder present a layering of imagery—forms carved over earlier forms. As such, the subtractive process can be thought of as an additive one. The superimposition of imagery not only assists us in understanding creative processes but invites us to consider how meaning might be made through their collective traces. The inscriptions and rock-reliefs trace the development of the site as seen and made by the artists and experienced by residents and worshippers. Rather than being peripheral to a site long recognised for its architectural achievements, these rock-reliefs reinforce the multi-faceted identities of Badami as a thriving center for artists, as a memorial landscape for the deceased, and as a sacred site for the worship of gods.

As many scholars have noted, Badami was indeed a sophisticated, early urban centre. Its cosmopolitanism is reflected in the art historical and epigraphical material that points to diverse audiences and makers. The employment of multiple languages and scripts, along with multiple architectural systems and ways to create ritual space, suggest a vibrancy and dynamism that remains to be studied further. Of significance, the boulder with its rock-reliefs and the two small shrines on top replicate (on a miniature scale) the main features of Badami itself—rock, temple, and sculpted form.[29] This iteration brings together the seemingly disparate forms of the 'cave' and 'temple' and reminds us that there are many ways to express and experience our place in this world and beyond it.

Notes

1 Seminal works include Mulk Raj Anand (ed), *In Praise of Aihole, Badami, Mahakuta, Pattadakal*, Bombay: Marg, 1978; Henry Cousens, *The Chalukyan Architecture of the Kanarese Districts*, Calcutta: Government of India, 1926; Adam Hardy, *Indian Temple Architecture: Form and Transformation, the Karnata Drāviḍa Tradition, Seventh to Thirteenth Centuries*, New Delhi: Indira Gandhi National Centre for the Arts and Abhinava Publications, 1995; Subhashini Kaligotla, 'Beyond Borderland: Claiming a Conceptual Space for Early Deccan Buildings', *Getty Research Journal*, 2016, 8: 1–16; George Michell, *Temple Architecture and Art of the Early Chalukyas: Badami, Mahakuta, Aihole, Pattadakal*, New Delhi: Niyogi Books, 2014; K. V. Soundararajan, *Early Temple Architecture in Karnataka and Its Ramifications*, Dharwar: Kannada Research Institute, 1969; Gary Tartakov, 'The Beginnings of Dravidian Temple Architecture in Stone', *Artibus Asiae*, 1980, 42(1): 39–99.

2 Michael Meister and M. A. Dhaky (eds), *Encyclopaedia of Indian Temple Architecture*, vol. 1, Part 2, South India: Upper Drāviḍadesa, Early Phase, A.D. 550–1075, Philadelphia: University of Pennsylvania Press, 1986, pp. 14–17.

3 K. V. Soundararajan, *Cave Temples of the Deccan*, New Delhi: Archaeological Survey of India, 1981, pp. 159–60; R. K. Rajarajan, *Rock-Cut Model Shrines in Early Medieval Indian Art*, New Delhi: Sharada Publishing House, 2012, pp. 41–2.

4 Soundararajan, *Cave Temples of the Deccan*, p. 159.

5 Subhashini Kaligotla, 'Shiva's Waterfront Temples: Reimagining the Sacred Architecture of India's Deccan Region' (unpublished Ph.D. dissertation, Columbia University, 2015).

6 *Ibid*, p. 114.

7 Srikumar M. Menon, 'Temples of Memory: The Bhutnath Temple Environs at Badami as a Commemorative Landscape', *Heritage: Journal of Multidisciplinary Studies in Archaeology*, 2017, 5: 576–605.

8 According to Sheelakant Pattar, who was also able to climb to the top of this boulder, the sculpture with four *liṅga*s may have originally had a fifth which gave rise to the local name of this small temple (and hence the boulder) as

Panchalinganaphadi. Sheelakant Pattar, *The Singing Rocks of Badami*, Badami: Shilpa Publication, 1979, p. 109.

9 For in-depth studies of the temples and practices in this region see K. V. Ramesh, *Chalukyas of Vatapi*, New Delhi: Agam Kala Prakashan, 1984; Himanshu Prabha Ray, 'Creating Religious Identity: Archaeology of Early Temples in the Malaprabha Valley', in Himanshu Prabha Ray (ed), *Archaeology and Text: The Temple in South Asia*, New Delhi: Oxford University Press, 2010, pp. 15–37; Hemanth Kadambi, 'Sacred Landscapes in Early Medieval South India: The Chalukya State and Society ca. AD 550–750' (unpublished Ph.D. dissertation, University of Michigan, 2011); Meena M. Mohite, *Early Chalukya Art at Mahakuta*, New Delhi: B. R. Publishing Corporation, 2012.

10 Kathleen D. Morrison, *Daroji Valley: Landscape History, Place, and the Making of a Dryland Reservoir System*, New Delhi: Manohar Publishers, 2009; Srikumar M. Menon, 'The Curious Case of the Galaganatha Dolmen: Possible Links Between Megalithic Monuments and Early Temples at Aihole', *Heritage: Journal of Multidisciplinary Studies in Archaeology*, 2014, 2: 54–73.

11 Menon, 'Temples of Memory', p. 594.

12 Mary McGee, 'Saṃskāra', in Sushil Mittal and Gene Thursby (eds), *The Hindu World*, New York: Routledge, 2007, p. 354.

13 *Ibid*, p. 353.

14 See, for example, the discussion in Gary Tartakov (Tarr), 'Chronology and Development of the Chāḷukya Cave Temples', *Ars Orientalis*, 1970, 8: 155–84.

15 J. Eggeling, 'An Inscription from Badami', *The Indian Antiquary*, 1874, 3: 305–6.

16 *Ibid*, p. 306.

17 Srinivas V. Padigar, *Inscriptions of the Calukyas of Bādāmi*, Bangalore: Indian Council of Historical Research, 2010, pp. 155–6.

18 George Michell, *Badami, Aihole, Pattadakal*, Mumbai: Pictor Publishing Pvt. Ltd., 2011, p. 57.

19 Michael Willis, *The Archaeology of Hindu Ritual: Temples and the Establishment of the Gods*, New York: Cambridge University Press, 2009, p. 37.

20 This is suggested by Michael Willis. He identifies the seated figure as Viṣṇu Vaikuntha and that this representation depicts him 'in his first days of wakefulness, that is, between the *utthānaikādaśī* and the *kārttikapaurṇamāsa*'. Willis, *The Archaeology of Hindu Ritual*, p. 45.

21 The carving and seated position of the *nāginī* that allows her to be in both panels simultaneously is noted by Gary Tartakov (Tarr) in his essay, 'Chronology and Development of the Chāḷukya Cave Temples', p. 164.

22 Julia Shaw, 'Nāga Sculptures in Sanchi's Archeological Landscape: Buddhism, Vaiṣṇavism, and Local Agricultural Cults in Central India, First Century BCE to Fifth Century CE', *Artibus Asiae*, 2004, 64(1): 5–59; Robert DeCaroli, '"The Abode of the Nāga King": Questions of Art, Audience, and Local Deities at the Ajanta Caves', *Ars Orientalis*, 2011, 40: 142–61.

23 Ray, 'Creating Religious Identity', pp. 23–4.

24 At some Jain rock-cut sites near Madurai, post holes have been carved in the rock floor preceding boulders and/or rock shelters to support additional wooden structures. See Lisa N. Owen, 'Local Bhakti or Monastic Advertising? The Functions of Medieval Jain Rock-Reliefs in Tamil Nadu', in Emmanuel Francis and Charlotte Schmid (eds), *The Archaeology of Bhakti II: Royal Bhakti, Local Bhakti*, Pondicherry: École française d'Extrême-Orient, 2016, pp. 423–42. As the rock floor in front of Badami's boulder has been recently repaved with stone walkways, the extent of such features cannot be determined.

25 According to Menon, these steps are blocked by the concrete. See Menon, 'Temples of Memory', p. 581.
26 Padigar, *Inscriptions of the Calukyas of Bādāmi*, pp. 317–19.
27 *Ibid*, p. 318.
28 Srinivas V. Padigar, 'Craftsmen's Inscriptions from Bādāmi: Their Significance', in Ratan Parimoo, Deepak Kannal, and Shivaji Panikkar (eds), *Ellora Caves: Sculptures and Architecture*, New Delhi: Books & Books, 1988, pp. 398–405.
29 I would like to thank Nachiket Chanchani for this observation and for his suggestion to pursue this idea further.

9

RITUALISING LAND AND CULTIVATING DISTINCTIONS

Medieval period donative practices and a political ecology of the Raichur doab

Andrew M. Bauer

Introduction

For many good reasons, archaeologists of Southern India have questioned the utility of imposing binary distinctions between 'profane' and 'sacred' or 'prosaic' and 'ritual' on interpretations of past social practices and cultural spaces. On the medieval Deccan, for instance, it has been noted that basic agricultural production practices, such as rice irrigation, might simultaneously have been oriented toward performing merit, devotional practices, and subsistence ends for many inhabitants.[1] Moreover, during the Iron Age the production of pastoral herding resources, such as stock pools constructed on many of the region's granitic hills, was often linked with commemorative mortuary practices, challenging the degree to which either could be accurately partitioned as constitutive of a sacred landscape that was distinct from a realm of quotidian economic activities.[2] Thus, it is worth noting at the outset of this chapter that I am sympathetic to Ray and Hartmann's prefatory questioning of whether 'rituals are always focused on divinity' or other entities that are frequently associated with 'religion' in post-Enlightenment, secular, social science paradigms.[3]

At the same time, however, I am reluctant to entirely elide the analytical utility of identifying practices as religious or ritual. Doing so would be to eschew the usefulness of analytical and comparative categories for the sake of ontology. During the Medieval Period, institutionalised patronage of temples with land grants and other donative gifts to support maintenance and regular offerings to the god often occurred at prescribed auspicious times and was accompanied with formalised practices and *praśasti* (praise) for donors, the latter of which was frequently engraved in stone. Such donative practices and the worship they supported were by most definitions 'religious'—if by religious practice one means 'ritualised venerations' of some form of other-than-human power—though their effects, and perhaps even the motivations of patrons, were hardly confined to a clearly bounded domain of religious activities.[4] Analyses of donative inscriptions have allowed scholars to suggest that these practices both perpetuated hierarchical social relationships, bestowing distinctions upon donors, and incorporated a variety of people differentiated by status or occupation into shared communities of patronage; of course, land donations also had the effect of redistributing agricultural holdings and arrangements between temple management, lease rights to land, and obligations for payment in cultigens.[5]

This chapter examines evidence for Medieval Period practices of ritualised land donations in the context of archaeological evidence for land use around the site of Maski, Raichur District, Karnataka. In doing so, it calls attention to how donative practices, when set within the unique geography of the Raichur *doab*, articulated with the production of a new value-laden geography of social differences during a period of significant agricultural expansion. Although many scholars have called attention to the social and political significance of the extension of irrigation in Medieval South India, few have stressed other properties of agricultural land, such as colour or texture, that appear significant to ritual donations on the Raichur doab.[6] An assessment of the content of donative inscriptions—and specifically concerns for emic distinctions related to soil texture, colour, irrigation conditions, and cultigens—in the context of material evidence for land use suggests that many inhabitants became reliant on cultivating the region's more marginal agricultural spaces. This may appear as a counterintuitive conclusion, given the existence of a substantial historiography that speaks of the Raichur doab's significance to Medieval Period empires and polities because of its extensive 'fertile' and well-watered soils. My concerns in this chapter are largely with how both social and material environments concurrently came into being during the period, and in that sense, they articulate with a variety of scholarships identified as *political ecology*.[7]

In this chapter, I draw from political ecology an emphasis on how the production of social inequalities was coupled with the materialities of environmental conditions, as well as a concern for how environmental discourses powerfully shape both historical processes and historiographies. I will suggest that conceptions of the Raichur doab as a space of rich agricultural fertility in the historiography about the Deccan's Medieval Period have tended to obscure the region's variegated ecological characteristics and the historical production of an agricultural landscape of differentially valued soils and cultigens. Beginning around the start of the 11th century at Maski, this newly generated landscape contributed to shaping forms of social inequalities as agriculture and ritualised land grants to temples were extended. To make this argument, I begin by briefly reviewing historical scholarship on the significance of the Raichur doab to South Asian social history.

The Raichur doab and the cultivation of empire

The site of Maski is situated in the western portion of Raichur District, northern Karnataka (Figure 9.1). It is well known in Indian archaeology for a Brāhmī inscription at the base of a granitic inselberg ('island mountain') that names the Mauryan emperor Asoka (c. 268–232 BCE) as a 'follower of the Buddha', allowing scholars to identify him as the 'author' of a number of other minor rock edits that attest to interactions across the subcontinent during the Early Historic Period (c. 300 BCE—500 CE).[8] Excavations by the Archaeological Survey of India in the 1950s revealed a history of occupation of substantial depth near the outcrop, including materials associated with all canonical archaeographic periods of Southern India (e.g., Neolithic, Iron Age, Early Historic, and Medieval). This chapter focuses on renewed research at the site since 2010 by the Maski Archaeological Research Project (MARP), focusing on new evidence for spatial practices during the Medieval Period (c. 500–1550 CE).[9]

The Raichur doab—a semi-arid expanse of peneplain soils, alluvial deposits, and punctuated rocky hills between the Krishna and Tungabhadra

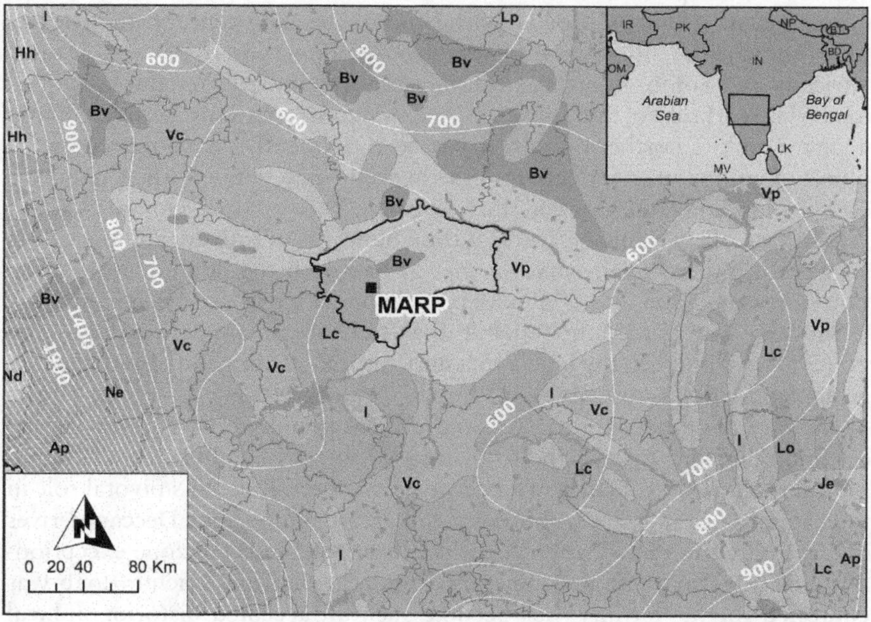

Figure 9.1 Location map of the Maski Archaeological Research Project in Raichur District, Karnataka (black outline), overlain on generalised FAO soil series and 100 mm isohyets of the region. Isohyets were interpolated from district-level annual precipitation averages, 2013–2017, available from the Stanford Geospatial Center

Rivers—has been well established as a region of particular significance during the Medieval Period and consequently to the broader social history of South Asia. A number of scholars have stressed that the Medieval Deccan is a paradigmatic example of India's unique multicultural history, often considered an exemplar of a medieval 'frontier' in which cultural and political practices rooted in South India intersected, fused, and came into tension with others from Southwest Asia, Central Asia, and Africa.[10] Within the Deccan the Raichur doab was the epicenter of this interaction. It was consistently contested as a space of territorial control during the Medieval and Early Modern Periods (c. 1550–1850 CE), rarely within the core territories of any of the region's multiple polities for long. Eaton and Wagoner, for instance, have aptly characterised it as an 'extremely unstable' area, having 'changed hands' four times in the 16th century alone.[11] Indeed, between 1362 and 1565 Vijayanagara and various Deccan sultanates would wage at least 15 military campaigns against each other in the region.[12] It was in this 'frontier' space, or 'contested border region between prevalent powers in the Deccan', where claims of sovereignty by Muslims, Śaivaites, and Vaiṣṇavaites overlapped, rulers erected innovative defensive architecture and moved troops, and varied populations of military personnel, agriculturalists, and merchants settled.[13] By the end of the 16th century, the Deccan likely showed the influence of a more diverse population of Persians, Arabs, Africans and South Asians than did even north India.[14] Yet the history of medieval warfare on the doab far predates confrontations between Vijayanagara and its northern rivals. It has been frequently characterised as the object of competition for early polities as well—first between the Chalukyas and Cholas, and later between the Kakatiyas, Yadavas, and Hoysalas. Careful scrutiny of epigraphic records of the Chalukyas of Kalyani and the Chola suggest that these rival dynasties met in battle on the doab at least seven times between 1005 and 1068 alone, including a battle at Maski in 1021.[15]

Most have attributed the Raichur doab's history of competing claims and political instability to the land's rich agricultural fertility and essential value as an economic resource base for imperial rulers, leading to regular efforts of military conquest, innovation, and diverse populations of newly settled communities that gave shape to distinctive forms of multiculturalism and pluralism. Stated explicitly by Eaton and Wagoner: 'Raichur's pivotal role in the evolution of military technology and architecture in the Deccan derives in large part from its location . . . in the heart of a coveted zone exceptionally rich in agriculture and minerals'.[16] Indeed, that the Raichur doab was contested for its 'fertility' has become such an accepted historiographical trope that it often requires little substantiation. Histories of the Deccan's medieval dynasties describe 12th-century confrontations between the Hoysalas and Yadavas, for instance, as occurring in locations 'of well-known fertility, being in fact the south-west portion of that famous Raichur doab for which dynasties contended until the collapse of the Maratha Empire'[!][17]

Thus it has been easy for some scholars to further naturalise the logic of confrontation in this context, noting that the fertility of the doab itself was the cause of warfare.[18]

That the Raichur doab was frequently the location of competing claims of sovereign territory throughout the 11th and 16th centuries is well founded. However, it is important to recognise that the region is far from inherently 'fertile' as an agricultural resource. It falls in the rain shadow of the Western Ghats and as a whole receives the lowest precipitation totals in southern India, collecting only 550–650 mm annually (Figure 9.1). Moreover, the region's soil series are by no means uniformly arable. Generalised soil maps generated by the Food and Agricultural Organization of the United Nations (FAO) indicate that Raichur District is comprised primary of chromic luvisols (strong brown to red argillic B horizons) and pellic vertisols (very dark clay-rich soils), though remote sensing analyses and field observations indicate that significant local variation exists within these broad classes.[19] For instance, soils that are more accurately characterised as lithosols, in which the underlying bedrock is within 10–20 cm of the surface, are widely distributed on the region's residual hills and in relatively large tracts on the peneplain of the western portion of the district, such as around Maski. The surface textures of these red soils are coarse with relatively high concentrations of gravel. In contrast, the region's vertisols show fine textures with markedly high concentration of clay, shrink and swell features, and often are very dark in colour. These latter soils have historically been referred to as *regur*, or 'black cotton soil', and because of their clay-rich moisture retention have remarkably different agricultural production capabilities in the semi-arid context of the region.[20]

Taking the precipitation and soil conditions of the doab together, it becomes evident that 'fertility' in this context had to be *produced*—culturally in terms of how it was imagined and valued and materially through assembling irrigation technologies with some cultigens (e.g., rice and sugarcane) and clay-rich, water-retentive soils (i.e., *regur*) with others that are more drought tolerant (e.g., cotton, millets). To that point it is worth adding that few archaeological projects have hitherto addressed material evidence (e.g., soils, sediments, botanical remains, and agricultural features) that attest to the history of Medieval Period land use on the doab.[21] Thus, whether the region was a rich agricultural resource base that stocked the coffers of dynastic courts and empires for nearly the entirety of the Medieval Period remains a much more open question than what is frequently stated.

In the following sections, I offer one approach to begin to address the history of land use on the Raichur doab by bringing the archaeological record for agricultural activities and settlement around the site of Maski to bear on the inscriptional record for Medieval Period donative practices in the region. Synthesised summaries by the Karnataka Directorate of Archaeology and Museums of 523 historical inscriptions recorded in modern Raichur

District, many of which are also fully transcribed in other sources, provide a rich corpus with which to assess aspects of the material practice and socio-political significance of land use throughout the Medieval Period.[22] Detailed assessments of the inscriptions specifically associated with Maski, for instance, imply that inhabitants differentiated particular soil series that held disparate productive capabilities and symbolic significance. Further contextualising the inscriptional sources for ritual donative practices with the archaeological record will allow me to make several substantive points about the socio-politics of land use in the region, stemming from a basic demonstration that the Raichur doab should *not* be considered a homogenous tract of rich agricultural resources for imperial appropriation. Indeed, to talk about the doab as a uniform whole overshadows its differentiated material characteristics as well as its fractured political history, even in simplified dynastic terms that are common to the historiography of the region.[23]

The inscriptional record and the dynastic contours of the Raichur doab

Inscriptional compilations indicate that there are 116 towns or villages in contemporary Raichur District from which inscriptions indicative of construction activities, memorialisation (e.g., hero stones), donative practices or temple patronage have been recorded.[24] Of this total, most are in small villages with only one or two epigraphic records. The statistical distribution is strongly skewed positively, having a mean of 3.7 records, a median of 2, and a mode of 1. Only seven locations (Ballatigi, Gabbur, Kuradi, Manvi, Maski, Mudgal, Raichur) in the entire district have more than ten reported inscriptions, and the forts at the two locations of Mudgal (105) and Raichur (73) provide approximately one-third of the district's total records. Notwithstanding potential biases in the data,[25] statistical and spatial examinations of the distribution of dated Medieval Period inscriptions from the region indicate that there were two primary periods of intense donative practices, temple patronage, and monumental construction: one during the 11th and 12th centuries while the Chalukyas of Kalyani claimed sovereignty of the region and a second during the 16th century, when the Raichur region ostensibly 'changed hands' multiple times between Vijayanagara and the sultanates to the north (Figure 9.2). The intervening centuries, when the Hoysalas, Yadavas, and Kakatiyas competed for control of the Deccan, evidence relatively few inscriptions in the dataset.[26]

The spatial distribution of inscriptions during this 'intermediate' period shows an interesting relationship to the centres of patronage and intense construction of both earlier and later periods. During the 11th and 12th centuries, for instance, the primary patronage sites do not occur in the eastern portions of the doab near the fluvial confluence of the Tungabhadra and Krishan Rivers; rather, they are more broadly spread across the central

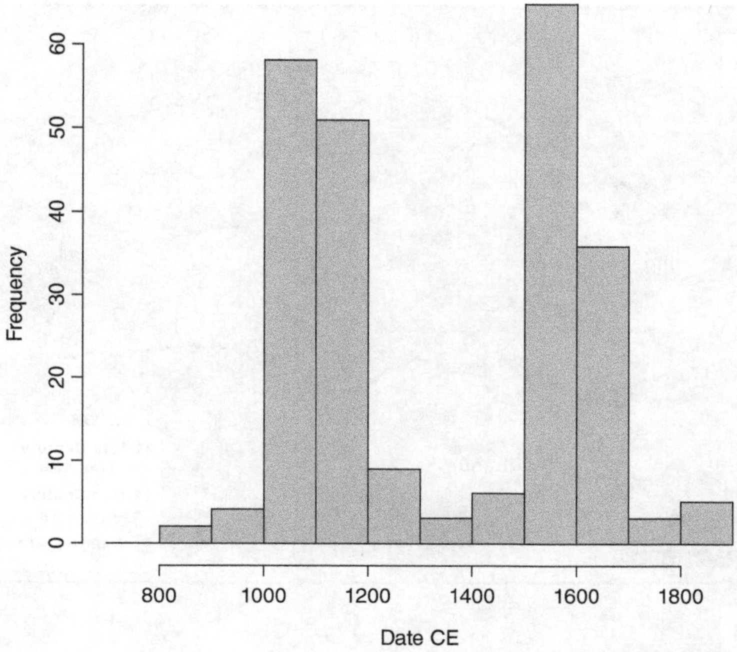

Figure 9.2 Frequency distribution of dated and published Medieval to Early Modern Period inscriptions from Raichur District

Source: KUES vol. VII

and western portions of the district, where there are larger tracts of red lithosols. Successors of the fragmented Chalukya Empire in the late 12th century patronised many of the same places, ostensibly to maintain some of the same feudatory relationships as their predecessors (see further). Yet it is clear that they also invested heavily in establishing new centres of building activity that would persist as such throughout the later centuries of the Medieval Period. Raichur, a fort initially constructed by a feudatory of the Kakatiyas in 1294 and in the eastern portion of the doab, would be heavily patronised, refortified, and remodelled over the next several centuries.[27] In the westernmost portion of the district the same can be said for the fort at Mudgal, which appears to have served as an administrative centre of the region under the Yadavas during the late 12th and 13th centuries and that would similarly became a locus of intense imperial investment and remodelling in the subsequent centuries (Figure 9.3).[28]

Maski is one of the few locations that shows a significant number of inscriptions during both the earlier and later medieval periods (Figure 9.4). Relatively numerous 11th and 12th century stone inscriptions from the

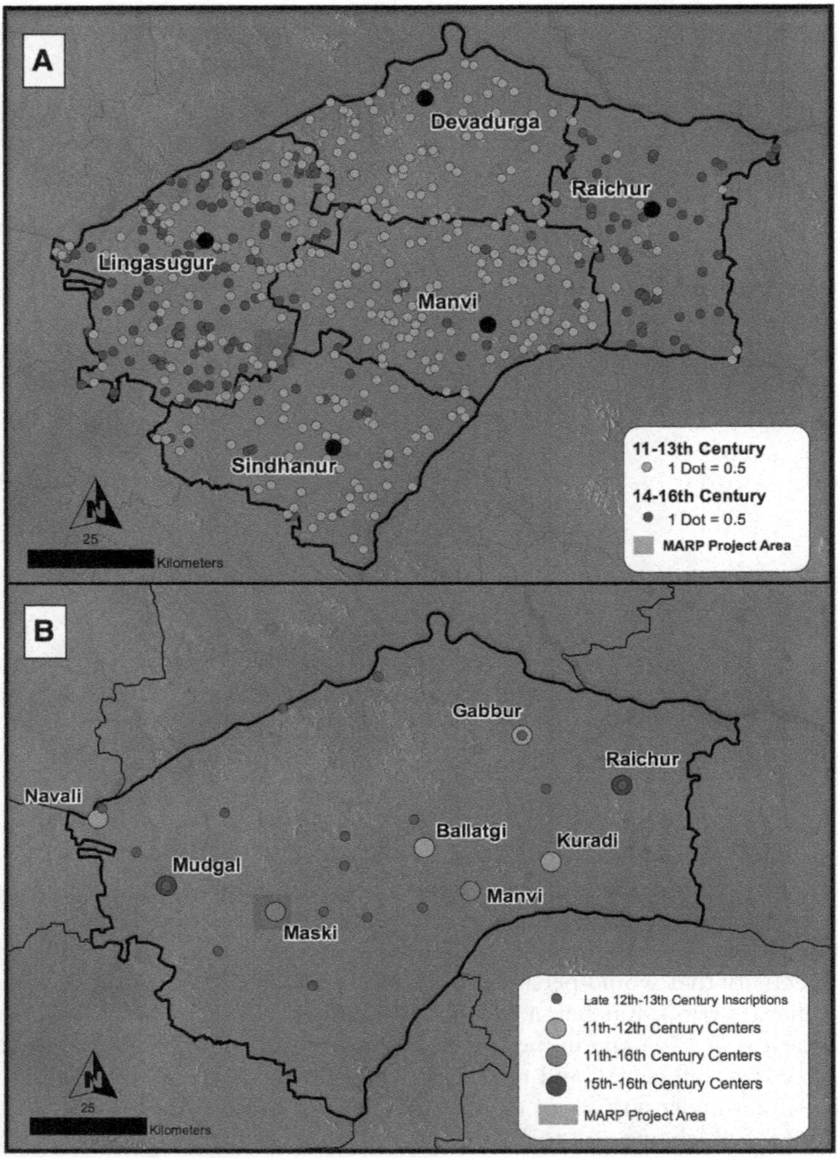

Figure 9.3 Spatial distribution of inscriptions in Raichur doab: A) generalised dot-density distribution according to period and district taluk (source: KUES vol. VII), and B) village-based distribution of 12th- and 13th-century inscriptions in relationship to earlier and later centers of patronage

Source: IK vol. 3–4

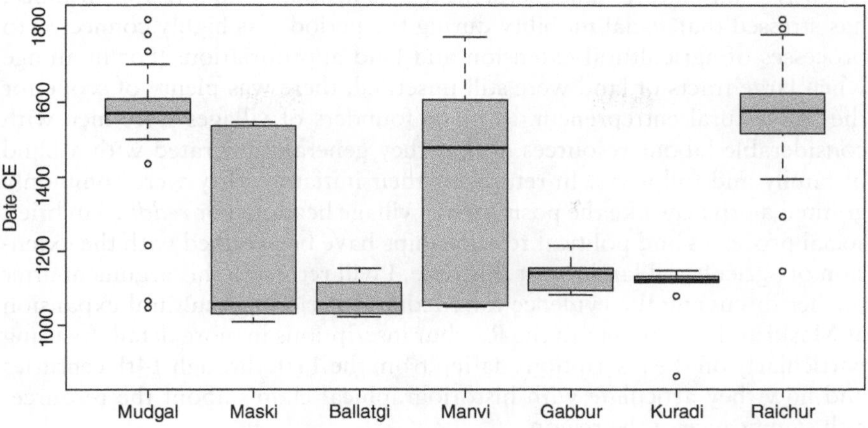

Figure 9.4 Box plot showing the chronological distributions of inscriptions at Raichur District locations that have more than 10 dated Medieval Period inscriptions

Source: IK vol. 3–4

vicinity of the largest medieval site in the area suggest that the Chalukyas of Kalyani (c. 973–1163 CE), who were seated until the mid-11th century at Malkheda (Gulbarga District, Karnataka) and then subsequently at Basavakalyana (Bidar District, Karnataka) some 150 and 200 km to the north of Maski, respectively, made strong imperial claims to the place. Patil and Patil's synthesis of inscriptional data led them to conclude that Maski was a Chalukyan regional capital during their imperial dominance of the Deccan.[29] Although this claim requires further evaluation, the archaeological and inscriptional records make clear that Maski was a significant place at the time, and that temple patronage, settlement and agricultural activities probably expanded there during the period. Moreover, these activities likely continued after the dissolution of the Chalukyan Empire with the ascendance of their successors, the Yadavas to the north and the Kakatiyas to the east. During the periods of Yadava and Kakatiya control of the Deccan, rulers seated at Daulatabad (Aurangabad District, Maharashtra) and Warangal (Telangana) and their local subservient 'chiefs' would continue to invest heavily in their claims to the doab. The inscriptional record of the Yadavas, for instance, suggests that they administered at least the western portion of the region via a local subsidiary at Mudgal. Yet it is clear that feudatories of the Kakatiyas also made strong claims to the area around Raichur, defending it militarily in at least several battles.[30]

Historians have often portrayed the period of Kakatiya (c. 1163–1323 CE) control of the eastern Deccan as one of great social mobility and extensive agricultural and settlement expansion.[31] Talbot, for instance, has stressed that social mobility during the period was highly connected to processes of agricultural extension and land appropriation: 'For in an age when large tracts of land were still unsettled, there was plenty of scope for the agricultural entrepreneur. . . . The founders of villages were men with considerable labour resources in that they generally migrated with a band of family and followers. In return for their initiative, they were commonly granted a privilege like the position of a village headman or *reddi*'.[32] In brief, social processes and political relationships have been linked with the extension of agricultural land use at this time. I will return to this argument after further discussing the evidence for Medieval Period agricultural expansion at Maski and the content of the Raichur inscriptions in more detail, focusing particularly on the inscriptions dating from the 11th through 14th centuries and how they articulate with historiographical claims about the resource-rich significance of the region.

Donative practices and the cultivation of social relationships on the Raichur doab

Links between devotional ritual practices and the sociology of agricultural land use on the medieval Deccan have been well established by historians relying on a rich inscriptional corpus of temple donations, land grants, infrastructural investments, tax remissions, and other deeds. Donative inscriptions dating between the 10th and 16th centuries evidence a range of social differences that often include rank, status, or the occupation of donors and simultaneously attest to temples' roles as centers of patronage and mediators in the constitution of social affiliations and distinctions, as well as in the distribution of agrarian production.[33] It is rather telling that sponsoring the construction of irrigation reservoirs has been noted in some historical sources as 'one of the seven' canonical 'meritorious acts' that a person should perform during the course of their life.[34] In short, land improvement and the expansion of agricultural infrastructure was deeply embedded in ideologies that drew relationships between cosmologies, status distinctions, and even the legitimacy of rulers during the period. As a paradigmatic example from Raichur District, the opening *praśasti* (praise) of a local feudatory of Vikramaditya VI (c. 1076–1127 CE) in a donative temple inscription dated to 1121 at Idapanuru celebrates the *nāyaka* for his great efforts at building temples, wells, and tanks. The charter itself details the construction of a temple and several land grants for the service of a god and to supply for the maintenance of the temple and its students and festivals.[35]

The Idapanuru grant is not uncommon in establishing close links between agricultural improvements, such as the construction of irrigation features, and temple patronage during the reign of the Chalukyas of Kalyani on the Deccan, of which Vikramaditya's was arguably the apogee. For instance, a similarly commissioned inscription at a Śiva temple in Munirabad, just upstream from Raichur along the Tungabhadra River, proclaims that a land grant received from the king was donated by a village headman and his wife, along with accompanying donations of 50 *mahājanas*, for the construction and maintenance of the temple. The deed is careful to detail their familial accomplishments in building an irrigation channel from the Tungabhadra River and further specifies the characteristics and area of granted lands, including roughly 850 *kamma* (a measuring unit) that was predominately considered to be 'irrigated garden' and 'paddy' land and 'twenty *mattar* of red-loamy land'. In addition, the deed states: 'The fifty men of the assembly of Mahajanas, at the time of the consecration, (also) gave to the glorious god Somesvara free of all encumbrances two hundred *kamma* of garden . . .; four *mattar* of cultivable land in the proximity of the field called Devaraykeyyi and one flower garden south of the temple'.[36] The proclamation assiduously indicates how 'the money realized on these lands of the god' will meet the expenses of the temple and its staff, including the daily supply of one '*kolaga* of superior rice for the food-offering of the god; one *mana* of green-pulse; one *mana* of ghee; one *vileya* (consisting) of twelve areca nuts and twenty-four betel leaves and one perpetual lamp'.[37]

The prevalence of such donative inscriptions on the Medieval Deccan has been the subject of extensive scholarship, the corpus of which I cannot do full justice to here. Most conventionally these inscriptions have served as the basis for reconstructing the political-dynastic history of the region reviewed previously, as they provide a record of dynastic lineages, local feudatory relationships, marriage alliances, and claims of sovereignty.[38] More importantly to the present context, scholars have also stressed how such donative practices and their associated rituals were also critical to legitimating the authority of medieval rulers and local elites or 'chiefs'.[39] These scholars point out that ritual donations were opportunities to perform personal and familial 'merit' while simultaneously having it inscribed and legitimated through ritual specialists who had unique abilities to heighten the donor's status. As Kulke summarises: 'This happened in different ways. One way was for Brahmins to create genealogies which traced the origin of the new local ruling "dynasty" back to a mythical progenitor of remote epic antiquity or even directly to a god. Further, Brahmins vested the new rulers with the paraphernalia of Hindu royalty', such as the royal umbrella and the construction of temples themselves.[40] In this way incipient rulers were constituted as legitimate through the ideological symbolism of particular artefacts as well as narratives of their origins and associations with divinities. In the specific case of the Chalukyas of Kalyani such genealogies often established them as *kṣatriyas* with historical links to Ayodhya and associations with the avatar Rama.[41] Thus, as Chattopadhyaya has argued more generally for early medieval India, the institutionalisation of political authority and ritual specialists was highly 'interdependent'.[42]

To be clear, donative practices were not limited to dynastic royals in their efforts to realise local or trans-regional claims to sovereignty. The majority of the donative inscriptions on the Deccan between the 11th and 14th centuries do *not* appear to have been commissioned by imperial kings and queens; rather, they record the meritorious actions of a diverse suite of temple patrons, ranging from local feudatories, administrators, village headmen, merchant and craft guilds, temple staff, and even confederations of smaller land owners. Talbot, for instance, has documented that the 'minor' temples of interior Andhra Pradesh commonly received land grants from *nāyakas* (local military leaders and administrators) and non-royal elite landowners between the 12th and early 14th centuries. Contrary to notions of fixed status or caste in pre-colonial India, Talbot stresses that this was a period of great social mobility on the Deccan. The inscriptional archive suggests that local land-controlling elites (e.g., *nāyakas, reddis*) who were likely newly enabled through the appropriation of agricultural spaces made most gifts to local temples, and would subsequently become political intermediaries between kingly rulers and local populations.[43] For these reasons, the interior Deccan of this period has been characterised as a space of opportunity.[44]

Yet it should be noted that Pariti's analysis of a selection of Chalukyan inscriptions has arrived at a fairly similar conclusion for the preceding period between the 11th and 12th centuries. Although she does not stress aspects of social mobility to the same degree, according to Pariti, later Chalukyan donative inscriptions show a substantially more diverse range of donors than those of earlier centuries when royalty represented the predominant donor class.[45] Thus, it would appear that status distinctions as mediated through donative practices were also fluid prior to the sublimation of the Kakatiyas on the Deccan.[46] Furthermore, an expansion of donors by the 11th century illustrates that ritual activities also served to integrate a community of differentiated inhabitants through a shared suite of practices and beliefs.[47] Changes to the content of Chalukyan land donations ostensibly also occurred during the 11th and 12th centuries. Parati documents a shift away from commonly ceding the revenues of entire villages or groups of villages to temples in earlier periods and toward granting smaller, individual land parcels that were frequently detailed as to size, location, and physical attributes.[48]

The large corpus of donative inscriptions thus also provides insight into how agricultural lands were distinguished and potentially valued during the Medieval Period. Indeed, innovative efforts by scholars to systematically quantify medieval inscriptions from a number of South Indian sources of present day Andhra Pradesh, northern Karnataka, and Telangana, indicate that emic distinctions were made between specific assemblages of soil, water and cultigens during the period.[49] In the context of the semi-arid interior of the southern Deccan and the cultural associations between meritorious action and water management noted previously, it is unsurprising that much of this scholarship has rightly emphasised the expansion of irrigation and the distinctions between 'wet-land' and 'dry-land' that are evident in the donative record.

However, the inscriptional corpus also indicates that inhabitants recognised distinctions among other land attributes, going far beyond the differences between wet-land and dry-land. Many inscriptions note properties related to soil texture and colour and the various cultigens they could support. 11th and 12th century Chalukyan inscriptions qualify 'black soil land', 'red soil land', 'red and black soil land', 'gravel soil land', and 'wasteland', as well as references to cultigens (e.g., rice, betel nut, etc.) and irrigation features.[50] Other historical sources that specifically detail the practice of agriculture during the period include considerable commentary on soil, even describing the proper way to manure fields for specific crops.[51] Thus, it should perhaps be unsurprising that soil properties of gifted lands were specified in ritual donations. That soil colour or texture were attributes worthy of distinction in some donative inscriptions of the period suggests that even in the absence of infrastructural improvements, such as the expansion of irrigation, not all dry-land was equivalent for the production of culturally valuable cultigens for temples, deities or donors alike. Indeed, this appears true in the context of Maski, where there is little evidence for widespread irrigation during the Medieval Period (see further).

The inscriptional corpus of the Raichur doab and that specifically associated with Maski largely substantiates many of the general conclusions of prior scholarship noted earlier. At Maski, all but two of the 12 (83%) dateable and published medieval inscriptions are specific land donations, the majority of which are to temples and indicate attributes related to the size and qualities of soil, water, and cultigens. The two exceptions are a grant of an entire village in the Maski district for maintaining the offerings to a local deity and a tax remission to barbers, both dating to a period of Vijayanagara administration during the 16th century. Consistent with other observations noted previously, the inscriptional record at Maski includes donations by local elites and administrators as well as those of imperial dynastic rulers. In the present context, it is particularly noteworthy that the limited numbers of records from royal donors in which the details are preserved all indicate the soil colour (e.g., black) or irrigation conditions of the donated land.[52] For example, in 1032 the Chalukyan king Jagadekamalla (Jayasimha II) granted '100 *mattars* of black soil, two *mattars* of wetland in fields of Piriya Mosangi, an oil mill and lamp'.[53] Indeed, other instances in the Maski corpus suggest that 'black land' was a common royal gift to temples in the region.[54] A broader view across Raichur District further suggests that in specific geographical situations such differences between soil types were especially significant to inhabitants, donors and temples. For instance, donative records from a number of locations on the doab show distinctions in land types according to soil colour where, like at Maski, the surrounding areas are dominated by both large tracts of clay-rich, water-retentive, dark soils and less water-retentive red sandy soils.[55]

As a result of such donations temples became important mediators in the distribution of agrarian resources while also shaping the symbolic significance of particular consumption practices and assemblages of soils and cultigens. The increasingly large landholdings of temples allowed them to lease out production activities to labourers who subsequently provided revenue to support a range of staff, including smiths, masons, dancers, and musicians, among others.[56] Inscriptional records that specify these details allow further insight into how distinguishable soils and cultigens were culturally significant. It is worth reiterating, for instance, that the Munirabad inscription noted earlier details how donated lands were to fund particular staff and activities, such as the payment of priest fees, maintaining temple stone work, feeding temple Brahmins, and, critically, for the daily food offering of 'superior rice' to the god.[57] Indeed, the minutiae of some such grants imply remarkable disparities in the relative value of particular land types to temples, and presumably donors. For instance, an inscription dating to the reign of Chalukyan Jayasimha II (c. 1015–1044 CE) from Kuluner (Dharwar District) stipulates how a royal land grant inclusive of black, red, and black-and-red soil types should be divided, indicating that '30 *kamma* paddy-field [and] 25 *kamma* black-loam land, are to go to the god; 30 *kamma* paddy-field, 25 *kamma* black-loam land, 1 *mattar* red-black land, to the monastery for giving instruction, 20 *kamma* paddy-field, 25 *kamma* black-loam land, 1 *mattar* red-black land, to the flute-players, . . . and 1 *mattar* red land are to be for the use of the stone-mason'.[58] It is noteworthy in this case that the god received only 'paddy land' and 'black soil land', while the mason received only 'red land'. Such associations between gods and paddy land or black soil land in Raichur District have already been noted. Yet it is worth stressing that the presence of such details, especially in the context of archaeological evidence for the expansion of agriculture across different soil series in the region (see further), suggests that scribes did not merely specify land types for the sake of cadastral legibility, but rather that different configurations of hydrological conditions and soil types held especially significant symbolic and material implications. It appears that donations of black land and red land were not always equal as gifts, nor were they likely equal in their abilities to cultivate crops in the semi-arid context of the interior Deccan. At the same time, in some contexts there is an explicit preference for the consumption of rice among gods, Brahmins, and temple staff in the inscriptional record of the Chalukyas of Kalyani. Thus, it is probable that not all landowners and labourers had equal abilities to produce such 'superior' foods—and this appears particularly true in large areas of the Raichur doab, such as around Maski.

The Maski Archaeological Research Project: intersecting history and archaeology

The Maski Archaeological Research Project (MARP) began in 2010 as a collaboration between the project co-directors and the Karnataka Department of Archaeology, Museums, and Heritage to evaluate the recursive relationships between social and environmental production throughout the Neolithic, Iron Age, Early Historic, and Medieval Periods around the multicomponent site of Maski, in northern Karnataka. Here I draw on its first phase of research, which consisted of an intensive pedestrian survey of more than 50% of a 64 km² study region and several test excavations to date specific features and contexts through radiometric evaluations.[59] The study region was divided into 160 survey blocks (40 km² each), of which more than half were systematically surveyed at 20 m pedestrian spacing. Archaeological sites were identified by dense concentrations of artefacts or features, and most frequently included settlements with extant architecture, occupied rock shelters, rock art panels, and agricultural infrastructure, such as wells and abandoned milling stones (e.g., Figure 9.5). Most important to the present discussion, results indicate that settlement in the region expanded considerably during the Medieval Period, which is marked by

Figure 9.5 Example of Medieval Period archaeological sites and features recorded by MARP include A) step wells, B) temple elements, C) room blocks and D) defensive walls

an increase in the number of habitation sites, the total occupied area, and multiple agricultural installations across the region (e.g., retention walls and wells). Multiple radiocarbon assays from two of the Medieval Period settlements documented hitherto suggest that the region was occupied by at least the start of the 13th century, largely corroborating expectations based on the associated inscriptions from Maski.

In addition to recording such sites, MARP also recorded low-density background artefact scatters across much of the study region's broad peneplain. Most of these were ceramics that were diagnostic of Medieval Period occupation or of Iron Age to Early Historic period occupation. These low-density artefact scatters were recorded and coded according to artefact type and period with handheld GPS devices from which densities and distributions were evaluated.

Given the context of the inscriptional evidence presented in the previous section, here I underscore the distribution of more than 9,000 off-settlement artefacts documented by MARP as a means to assess Medieval Period land use. Scholars working on a variety of archaeological contexts have convincingly argued that broad low-density artefact distributions are often the result of past agro-pastoral land-use activities, and specifically manuring and fertilisation practices associated with agriculture.[60] Thus, they represent an important record of agricultural activities. The MARP data also indicate that low-density artefacts (typically fewer than 40 sherds per hectare) generally correspond to the extent of past agricultural activities that can be inferred through other archaeological means, such as the presence of infrastructural check-dams, milling stones, and sites identified as agro-pastoral field stations by discrete concentrations of artefacts, including occasional sickle blades. The interpretation of low-density ceramic scatters as the results of manuring activities or dispersed field stations thus appears to be the most probable interpretation in the Maski context, too. Temporally controlled analyses of low-density artefact distributions according to geomorphological context is therefore likely to shed important light on how past inhabitants constituted agricultural spaces and cultural tasks in relation to particular assemblages of soil and other landscape features.

Spatial analyses of different artefact classes in relation to soil maps generated through remote sensing classifications yielded several distributional patterns worth highlighting here.[61] First, low-density ceramics that are characteristic of the Iron Age and Early Historic period (c. 1200–300 BCE, 300 BCE–CE 500) are primarily confined to areas of the study region that are predominately composed of dark clay loams, or *regur*. Second, Medieval Period low-density ceramics are much more broadly distributed across the study region, occurring on both dark clay loams and red, sandier soils in more equal proportions. In this way, the artifact distributions suggest spatial differences between Iron Age or Early Historic land-use practices that produce low-density artifact scatters and those of the Medieval Period. It appears that medieval agricultural land-use practices were extended across the study region, such that both dark, clay-rich vertisols and the red, sandy lithosols were constituted as agricultural production spaces to a degree not seen in the earlier periods. Third, low-density concentrations of iron slag, reflective of dispersed metalworking or smithing, rarely appear in survey blocks dominated by darker, clay soils, suggesting that the dark soils were preferentially used for agricultural production (Figure 9.6).

The archaeological analyses and soil mapping just summarised have important implications for historiographical framings of Medieval Period land use on this portion of the Deccan. The archaeological record around Maski corroborates the expansion of agriculture on the Raichur doab during

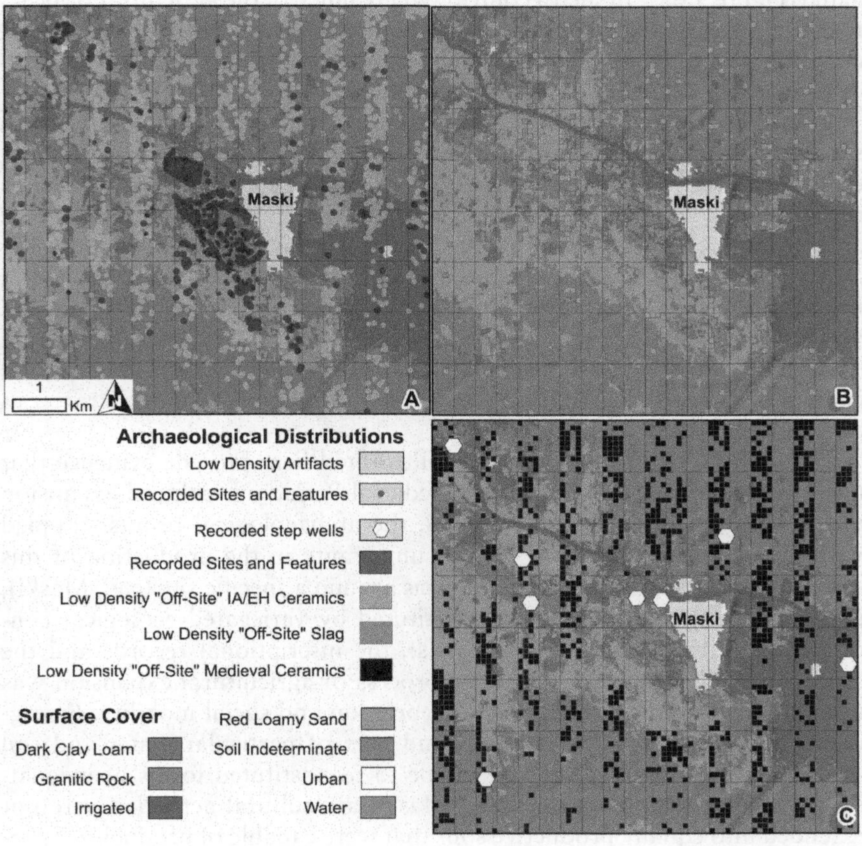

Figure 9.6 MARP distribution of all recorded sites and low-density artifacts (A), distribution of slag and Iron Age-Early Historic period ceramics (B), and distribution of Medieval Period ceramics and wells (C) (Figure modified from Bauer, 'Remote Sensing Soils'.)

the period; however, it also adds important detail about how we might understand this social process in ways that complement what has been stressed through the historical record. For instance, as noted earlier, the process of agricultural expansion has generally been characterised as enabling significant social mobility during the 12th through 14th centuries. And indeed, there can be little doubt about the rearticulation of social relationships associated with this period of agricultural expansion, as some inhabitants had new access to land holdings. However, soil on the Raichur doab is highly variable. As the data at Maski attest, not all agricultural expansion occurred onto equally water-retentive or irrigated soils. In fact, the distribution of Medieval Period wells and irrigation features in the MARP study region demonstrate that much of the area cultivated during the period was *not* irrigated (Figure 9.6).[62] In such a context, where much of the agriculture appears to have been non-irrigated, the distinction between moisture-retentive, clay-rich soils and less-retentive sandy red soils was probably highly significant for the production of culturally valued cultigens.

Archaeological evidence for the extension of agriculture to dry, red, sandier soils on the Raichur doab adds important contextual detail to why donors and scribes may have distinguished some landed gifts according to their assemblages of water, soil colour and cultigens in the interior Deccan: agricultural soils and their associated crops were neither equal nor equally accessible. On the Raichur doab black soil appears to be distinguished in inscriptions from geographical contexts where there was significant soil variability and perhaps, as was the case around Maski, where different soil series were simultaneously under dry agricultural production. In short, the content of donative inscriptions was likely highly contextual in character as agriculture expanded.

The archaeological and soils data illustrated here provide evidence that goes beyond merely substantiating Medieval Period agricultural expansion on the Raichur doab. More critically, the archaeological results, coupled with soil maps, highlight the lack of uniformity in the production of this social landscape. By focusing an analysis around a specific site (e.g., Maski), and a landscape context partly constituted by variegated ecological conditions (e.g., red soils and black soils), the inscriptional records and the archaeological data suggest that the process of agricultural expansion was not one of straightforward land appropriation and social mobility. Emerging differences in the social values and uses of particular water and soil assemblages simultaneously gave shape to reconstituted forms of inequality and social distinctions. Around Maski, agricultural activities were not extended into equally productive soils that were capable of producing 'superior rice', or even dry farmed millets and pulses. In short, some inhabitants practised agriculture in social and environmental contexts that were potentially marginalising, given that they had unequal productive capabilities in the semi-arid and rainfall-dependent context of the interior Deccan to generate culturally valued crops (e.g., cotton and rice) that had well attested relationships to a variety of different ritual and economic uses. In short, along with the extension of agriculture into new ecological contexts comes evidence for differentiated abilities to cultivate culturally desirable cultigens and to patronize temples with valuable donations, such as the apparent preference for "black soil land" in the royal inscriptions at Maski. Thus, it appears that social distinctions related to different production and donative practices were also developing during the period of agricultural expansion and land devolution suggested by the inscriptions.

Published inscriptions from Maski and radiometrically dated occupational contexts suggest that these developments occurred prior to the 14th century. While I am not disputing that significant social transformations occurred in association with the extension of agricultural land use, such as during the reign of the Kakatiyas highlighted previously, treating this process as one of uniform status improvement as inhabitants newly appropriated agricultural resources would elide significant social and material variation. To begin with, the distribution of Iron Age/Early Historic sherd scatters suggests that some black-soil lands were likely already being cultivated in the region around Maski by the onset of the Medieval Period and, more important to the present argument, cultural distinctions were made between desirable soil conditions (i.e., red soils and black soils) even in the absence of irrigation improvements. As the archaeology of Maski implies, there would probably have been new symbolic associations of specific assemblages of water, soil, and cultigens as less-productive red, sandy soils came into non-irrigated production along side moisture-retentive regur on the Raichur doab. Some of these production environments would have been highly *marginal* both in the ecological and social senses of the term.[63] In a cultural and historical context in which one can reasonably expect there to be significant social distinctions associated with diet and consumption practices, such as the consumption of 'superior rice' or a geographically specific *gastro-politics*, it is not difficult to see how a careful analysis of the spatial organisation of agricultural activities across differentially valued and productive soils series might contribute to new understandings of modes of social differentiation during the period.[64] Historical knowledge of this social landscape derived solely from the region's Medieval Period donative inscriptions might fail to account for how cultural values associated with particular soil and hydrological conditions were linked with a reconfigured material landscape of agricultural and social practices.

Future research notwithstanding, it appears that agricultural land use between the 11th and 14th centuries recast meaningful differences in soil distinctions, as dark, clay-rich soils and red, sandier soils both became used to raise crops for a variety of ritual and subsistence ends around Maski. The activities of ploughing, seeding, and harvesting these soils and their various associated cultigens probably further highlighted the different water-retention and consequent soil-fertility properties of the distinctive soils in non-irrigated contexts. Archaeological evidence suggests that regional inhabitants already recognised some of these differences by at least the Early Historic period, but as agriculture expanded they became more saliently integrated in processes through which both ecological and social conditions were concurrently produced in the Medieval Period.[65] Spatialised differences in access to valued-laden land types likely reinforced newly emerging social distinctions associated with agricultural expansion and potentially with distinctive consumption, production, and ritual activities.

Conclusion: archaeology and a political ecology of donative rituals on the Raichur doab

By way of conclusion, I would like to stress two fundamental points from the review of historical scholarship on Medieval Period ritualised donative practices, inscriptional records from the Raichur doab, and the archaeology around Maski. The first is methodological and addresses the significance of archaeology to an understanding of the inscriptional archive of ritualised land grants and temple patronage during the period. Archaeological evidence for the extension of agriculture to red, sandier soils during the Medieval Period adds important contextual detail to why donors and scribes may have distinguished some landed gifts according to their assemblages of water, soil colour, and cultigens on the Raichur doab. On the Raichur doab, black soil appears to be distinguished in inscriptions from geographical contexts where there was significant soil variability and probably, as is the case around Maski, different soil series were simultaneously under agricultural production at times. Thus, inscriptional analyses that generalise to the state (e.g., Karnataka) or the administrative district (e.g., in Raichur District) might fail to appreciate contextual details of geographical and spatial variation that are important to understanding the social and cultural significance of inscriptional content. In that sense, a detailed archaeological survey does much more than simply identify new archaeological sites, such as forts, temples, reservoirs, or wells, where scholars might locate ritual practices and donative inscriptions; it provides important socio-material context for their interpretation and the historiographies that they enable.

My second point is more substantive with regard to the fertility and social history of the Raichur doab. The archaeology of Maski provides information on politicised social processes that are less visible using the inscriptional record of ritual activities and monumental building practices alone. The artefact distributional data indicate that as agriculture was extended in the region some inhabitants cultivated assemblages of cultivars, soils, and water that held both significantly different cultural value and significantly different productive capabilities in the semi-arid context of the region. In short, some inhabitants had newfound access to valued agricultural lands—and equally important, high-status temple gifts among a shared community of patronage—while, as suggested by archaeological evidence, others appear to have become reliant on less moisture-retentive, red-sandy soils in the rainfall-dependent contexts of the interior Deccan. Insightful previous scholarship on medieval Deccan land use has thus rightly focused on the social and political significance of irrigation during the period and inscriptional references to hydrological conditions. As a complement to those analyses, however, data from Maski—and the Raichur doab more generally—attest that Medieval Period inhabitants made significant distinctions among land types even in the absence of widespread irrigation improvements. Archaeological evidence for non-irrigated agricultural production across various soil series at Maski implies that any donative preferences for black soil land during the Medieval Period probably would have contributed to the cultivation of elite distinctions in the process of marginalising other inhabitants who depended on less culturally valuable lands in this region, which was hardly an homogenous plain of black, well-watered, or inherently fertile agricultural space.

Notes

1 K. D. Morrison, *Daroji Valley: Landscape History, Place, and the Making of a Dryland Reservoir System*, New Delhi: Manohar, 2009; K. D. Morrison, 'Doorways to the Divine: Vijayanagara Reservoirs and Rural Devotional Landscapes', *South Asian Studies*, 2012, 28(2): 157–69.

2 A. M. Bauer, *Before Vijayanagara: Prehistoric Landscapes and Politics in the Tungahbadra Basin*. New Delhi: Manohar and American Institute of Indian Studies, New Delhi, 2015

3 H. P. Ray and J-U. Hartmann's initial call for the "Rituals for Power: Rituals for Prosperity" conference at LMU–Munchen that engendered this chapter asked participants to consider rituals in ways that went beyond a concern for religion. For notable anthropological scholarship on the utility of religion as an analytical concept, see T. Asad, *Formations of the Secular: Christianity, Islam, Modernity*, Stanford: Stanford University Press, 2003; S. Fowles, *An Archaeology of Doings: Secularism and the Study of Pueblo Religion*, Santa Fe, NM: School for Advanced Research Press, 2013.

4 This definition of 'religion' comes from T. R. Pauketat, *An Archaeology of the Cosmos: Rethinking Agency and Religion in Ancient America*, New York: Routledge, 2013. See also L. Fogelin, 'The Archaeology of Religious Ritual', *Annual Review of Anthropology*, 2007, 36: 55–71, on the dialectical relationships between been religion and ritual.

5 See, for example, H. Kulke (ed), The State in India: 1000–1700, New Delhi: Oxford University Press, 1995; A. Pariti, Genealogy, Time and Identity: Historical Consciousness in the Deccan, Sixth Century CE-Twelfth Century CE, New Delhi: Primus, 2015; C. Talbot, 'Temples, Donors, and Gifts: Patterns of Patronage in Thirteenth Century South India', Journal of Asian Studies, 1991, 50(2): 308–40; C. Talbot, Precolonial India in Practice: Society, Region, and Identity in Medieval Andhra, New York: Oxford University Press, 2001.

6 The social significance for the expansion of irrigation has been discussed by many scholars. See, for instance, D. Ludden, *Peasant History in South India*,

Princeton: Princeton University Press, 1987; Morrison, *Daroji Valley*; Talbot, *Precolonial India in Practice*.

7 As a corpus of scholarship, *political ecology* has generally called attention to how power-laden social relationships mediate the use, construction, and historical production of environmental conditions. Over the course of the past 50 years, its emphases have ranged from Marxist concerns for the social relationships of production to postmodern framings of the discursive construction of Nature, and even more recently to 'posthumanist' frameworks that de-privilege humans in giving shape to conjoined socio-environmental histories. See recent reviews in A. M. Bauer, 'Questioning a Posthumanist Political Ecology: Ontologies, Environmental Materialities, and the Political', *Archaeological Papers of the American Anthropological Association*, 2018, 29: 157–74; C. T. Morehart, J. K. Millhauser, and S. Juarez, 'Archaeologies of Political Ecology—Genealogies, Problems, and Orientations', *Archaeological Papers of the American Anthropological Association*, 2018, 29: 5–29; A. Biersack and J. B. Greenberg (eds), *Reimagining Political Ecology*, Durham, NC: Duke University Press, 2006.

8 The Ashoka inscription at Maski was originally published in the first issue of the *Hyderabad Archaeological Series (HAS)* in 1915. For extensive discussion of some of the historical and social processes related to the spread of Buddhism and the patronage of its monasteries in the Early Historic Period, see the expansive work of H. P. Ray, most recently *Archaeology and Buddhism in South Asia*, London: Routledge, 2018.

9 The Maski Archaeological Research Project is a collaboration between the Karnataka Department of Archaeology Museums and Heritage, Peter G. Johansen (McGill University), and Andrew M. Bauer (Stanford University). Previous excavations of the site were carried out by Archaeological Survey of India in the 1950s, e.g., B. K. Thapar, 'Maski 1954: A Chalcolithic Site of the Southern Deccan', *Ancient India*, 1957, 13: 4–142.

10 C. B. Asher and C. Talbot, *India Before Europe*, Cambridge: Cambridge University Press, 2006; R. M. Eaton, *A Social History of the Deccan, 1300–1761: Eight Indian Lives*, Cambridge: Cambridge University Press, 2005; R. M. Eaton and P. B. Wagoner, *Power, Memory, Architecture*, Oxford: Oxford University Press, 2014.

11 Eaton and Wagoner, *Power, Memory, Architecture*, pp. 272–3.

12 This figure is compiled from multiple sources, including the summaries of Eaton and Wagoner, *Power, Memory, Architecture*; A. A. Kadiri, 'Bahmani Inscriptions from Raichur District,' *Epigraphia Indica: Arabic & Persian Supplement*, 1962: 53–66; K. A. Nilakanta Sastri, *A History of South India*, Madras: Oxford University Press, 1958.

13 Eaton, *A Social History of the Deccan* discusses this context as a 'frontier', p. 16; J. J. Gommans, 'The Silent Frontier of South Asia, c. AD 1100–1800', *Journal of World History*, 1998, 9(1): 1–23 (p. 6), speaks of competing powers.

14 Asher and Talbot, *India Before Europe*, pp. 163–6.

15 This figure comes from compiling the campaigns substantiated by both Chalukyan and Chola sources discussed by K. Murari, *The Calukyas of Kalyani*, New Delhi: Concept Publishing House, 1976.

16 Eaton and Wagoner, *Power Memory, Architecture*, p. 242.

17 J. D. M. Derrett, *The Hoysalas: A Medieval Indian Royal Family*, London: Oxford University Press, 1957, p. 59.

18 Deccan architectural historian H. Philon, for example, has stressed that the 'fertile black soils' and 'the well watered territory that lay between the Bhima and Tungabhadra rivers' led to 'constant warfare between Vijayanagara and the

Bahmanis over the mineral-rich Raichur doab', *Gulbarga, Bidar, Bijapur*, London: Jaico, pp. 13–15.

19 See discussion in A. Bauer, 'Remote Sensing Soils and Social Geographies of Difference: The Landscape Archaeology of Regur from Iron Age through Medieval Period, Northern Karnataka, Southern India', *Journal of Field Archaeology*, 2018, 43(1): 31–43.

20 B. P. Radhakrishna and R. Vaidyanadhan, *Geology of Karnataka*, Bangalore: Geological Society of India, 1997.

21 Historical ecological fieldwork on the Raichur doab largely has been limited to areas of its southwestern portion in modern day Koppal District, Karnataka, where several projects have extended field investigations slightly north (< 10 km) from the Tungabhadra River; e.g., Bauer, *Before Vijayanagara*; C. M. Sinopoli and K. D. Morrison, *The Vijayanagara Metropolitan Survey: Volume 1*, Museum of Anthropology, University of Michigan Memoirs, No. 41, Ann Arbor: University of Michigan, 2007; K. D. Morrison, *Fields of Victory: Vijayanagara and the Course of Intensification*, Contributions of the University of California Archaeological Research Facility, No. 53, Berkeley: University of California, 1995.

22 C. S. Patil and V. C. Patil have synthesised these records in *Inscriptions of Karnataka: Inscriptions of Raichur District*, vol. 4, Mysore: Directorate of Archaeology and Museums, 1998; *Inscriptions of Karnataka: Inscriptions of Koppal District*, vol. 3, Mysore: Directorate of Archaeology and Museums, 1998 (IK). Some of these records have been fully transcribed in the *Kannada University Epigraphical Series* (KUES), *Epigraphia Indica* (EI) and the *Hyderabad Archaeological Series* (HAS).

23 Murari, *Calukyas of Kalyani*; Nilakanta Sastri, *History of South India*; O. P. Verma, *The Yadavas and Their Times*, Nagpur: Vidarbha Samshodhan Mandal, 1970, exemplify such dynastic histories.

24 To be clear, many of the compiled inscriptions are fragmentary and the practice of commissioning donations or inscriptions was not restricted to temple patronage. See IK vols. 3–4.

25 K. D. Morrison and M. Lycett provide a lucid discussion and demonstration of how the content of Vijayanagara Period inscriptions are related to the context of their recovery, and equally importantly, how biases in recovery contexts have been related to different research practices. See 'Inscriptions as Artifacts: Precolonial South India and the Analysis of Texts', *Journal of Archaeological Method and Theory*, 1997, 4(3–4): 215–37.

26 See, for instance, Nilakanta Sastri, *History of South India*, for a discussion of these dynasties.

27 The inscriptional sources make this abundantly clear, IK vol. 4, pp. 124–45.

28 E.g., *ibid*, pp. 23, 124.

29 *Ibid*, p. xix.

30 *Ibid*, p. 124.

31 See discussions in Eaton, *A Social History of the Deccan*, pp. 12–16; Talbot, 'Temples, Donors, and Gifts'.

32 Talbot, *Precolonial India in Practice*, p. 77.

33 Scholarship on inscriptional records as a source of social history and the effects of medieval temples in mediating social relationships and political and economic practices is rather extensive. Examples pertinent to the present context include Kulke, *The State in India*; IK vols. 3–4; Morrison, *Fields of Victory*; Morrison and Lycett, 'Inscriptions as Artifacts'; Pariti, *Genealogy Time and Identity*; Talbot, *Precolonial India in Practice*; Talbot, 'Temples, Donors, and Gifts'.

34 Verma, *The Yadavas*, p. 273.

35 KUES vol. VII, p. 1.
36 HAS 1922, No. 5, pp. 10–11.
37 *Ibid*, p. 12.
38 E.g., Murari, *Calukyas of Kalyani*; Nilakanta Sastri, *History of South India*; Verma, *The Yadavas*.
39 E.g., B. D. Chattopadhyaya, 'Political Processes and Structure of Polity in Early Medieval India: Problems of Perspective', *Social Scientist*, 1985, 13(6): 3–34; H. Kulke, 'The Early and Imperial Kingdom: A Processural Model of Integrative State Formation in Early Medieval India', in H. Kulke (ed), *The State in India: 1000–1700*, New Delhi: Oxford University Press, 1995, pp. 233–62 (p. 237); Pariti, *Genealogy, Time, and Identity*, pp. 74–81; R. Thapar, *Ancient Indian Social History*, Hyderabad: Orient Longman, 1978, pp. 131–2.
40 Kulke, 'The Early and Imperial Kingdom', p. 238.
41 Eaton and Wagoner, *Power, Memory, Architecture*, p. 10; Pariti, *Genealogy, Time and Identity*, pp. 78–80, 227–32.
42 Chattopadhyaya, 'Political Processes', p. 8.
43 Talbot, *Precolonial India in Practice*; Talbot, 'Temples, Donors, and Gifts'; C. Talbot, 'Political Intermediaries in Kakatiya Andhra, 1175–1325', *Indian Economic and Social History Review*, 1994, 31: 261–89.
44 Eaton, *A Social History of the Deccan*, p. 16.
45 E.g., Pariti, *Genealogy, Times, and Identity*, pp. 166, 169.
46 For a lucid treatment of the Early Historic period and the fluidity of social distinctions in relationship to the patronage of Buddhist monastic institutions, see H. P. Ray, *Monastery and Guild: Commerce Under the Satavahanas*, New Delhi: Oxford University Press, 1986.
47 See also Talbot, 'Temples, Donors, and Gifts'.
48 Pariti, *Genealogy, Times, and Identity*, pp. 180–1.
49 Examples include Morrison, *Fields of Victory*; Morrison and Lycett, 'Inscriptions as Artifacts'; Talbot, *Precolonial India in Practice*, p. 100; Talbot, 'Temples, Donors, and Gifts'.
50 Pariti, *Genealogy, Time, and Identity*, p. 184.
51 D. Ali, 'Botanical Technology and Garden Culture in Somesvara's *Manasollasa*', in D. Ali and E. J. Flatt (eds), *Garden and Landscape Practices in Pre-colonial India: Histories from the Deccan*, London: Routledge, 2012, pp. 39–53; G. Wojtilla, *History of Krsisastra: A History of Indian Literature on Traditional Agriculture*, Wiesbaden: Harrassowitz Verlag, 2006.
52 IK vol. 4, pp. 3–36; KUES vol. VII, pp. 161–79.
53 KUES vol. VII, p. 166.
54 *Ibid*, pp. 163–4, 178–9.
55 Although this is not a complete list, other examples record black land donations to gods in the vicinity of Devasuguru, (*ibid*, p. 41), and Raudakunde (*ibid*, p. 41).
56 Pariti, *Genealogy, Time, and Identity*, p. 168.
57 HAS 1922, No. 5, p. 12.
58 EI 15, pp. 329–34.
59 Systematic pedestrian survey was an appropriate strategy to assess the occupational history of the region because peneplain erosional processes have produced feature and artifact visibility at or very near ground level for materials dating as far back as the Palaeolithic period. Here I summarise results of MARP previously reported in Bauer, 'Remote Sensing Soils', A.M. Bauer and P.G. Johansen, 'The Maski Archaeological Research Project (2010–18): Initial Results from a Multi-Period Interdisciplinary Project on the Raichur Doab, Karnataka, India',

Current Research, 2019, 117(1): 46–56; A. M. Bauer and P. G. Johansen, 'Prehistoric Mortuary Practices and the Constitution of Social Relationships: Implications of the First Radiocarbon Dates From Maski on the Occupational History of a South Indian "Type Site"', *Radiocarbon*, 2015, 57(4): 795–806; P. G. Johansen and A. M. Bauer, 'Beyond Culture History at Maski: Land Use, Settlement and Social Differences in Neolithic Through Medieval South India', *Archaeological Research in Asia*, 2015, 1: 6–16.

60 E.g., J. Bintliff, 'Human Impact, Land-Use History, and the Surface Archaeological Record: A Case Study From Greece', *Geoarchaeology*, 2005, 20(2): 135–47; J. Bintliff and A. Snodgrass, 'Off-Site Pottery Distributions: A Regional and Interregional Perspective', *Current Anthropology*, 1988, 29(3): 506–13; T. J. Wilkinson, 'Extensive Sherd Scatters and Land-Use Intensity: Some Recent Results', *Journal of Field Archaeology*, 1989, 16: 31–46.

61 For methodology, statistics, and tests of significance, see Bauer, 'Remote Sensing Soils'.

62 Note that the distribution of step wells appears restricted to locations very near to the Maski River, where ground water could more easily be tapped.

63 The political ecology of P. Blaikie and H. Brookfield (*Land Degradation and Society*, London: Methuen, 1987, pp. 19–23) is concerned with the spatial convergence of an ecological concept of 'marginal' as an 'area or zone within which there is expected killing stress, but over which a plant or plant association can expand when that stress is absent' with economic and political-economic concepts of marginality. Here I am less concerned with formalised economic concepts of 'margin' but do intend to highlight a convergence between an ecological 'marginality' of producing crops on red-soils in the drought-prone conditions around Maski and social abilities to generate culturally valuable crops that are related to status differences, consumption practices, temples gifts, and merit in the historical context of the Medieval Deccan.

64 A. Appadurai, 'Gastro-Politics in Hindu South Asia', *American Ethnologist*, 1981, 8: 494–511.

65 E.g., D. Harvey, *Justice, Nature and the Geography of Difference*, Oxford: Blackwell, 1996.

10

SACRED FRAMES

Knowledge, culture and ritual agency in ancient *tālukas* of Karnataka (late 10th–12th centuries)

Nupur Dasgupta

Located centrally in the mineral-rich zone of Karnataka, along with the adjacent districts of Dharwar and Bellary, the modern Gadag district housed numerous ancient administrative units and temple centres since the time of the Western Chalukya rule, followed by those of the Seuṇa Yādavas and Hoysalas. Evidence from three different nodal settlements within this zone illustrate how the local administrative, civic and mercantile agency led to the creation of certain distinctive rituals and cultural traditions with the temples and religious institutions as sites of cultural activity, creativity and socio-cultural negotiations. The present chapter explores these traditions and ideas with reference to a few select late 10th–12th century CE epigraphic records from the sub-region. These records reflect the burgeoning of cultural and intellectual notions and practices indicating the creation of newer matrices of cultural signifiers with specificities typifying the micro-level history.

The main focus in this chapter is on teasing out the various shades of philosophical and intellectual developments reflecting absorptions of ideas and practices both from the classical traditions and the transformed or recreated regional or local idioms. Nuances of these aesthetes radiated a culture of the sacred, especially through myriad ritual practices which was finally manifest in the creation of a sacred space around the given sphere of such activity. The material base of these developments was rooted in the regional and local sites with control over resource accession. The records bear evidence of these processes, as well as the hint of a culturally nuanced engagement with the regional space. We note the gradual emergence of notions of the local geography invested with moral excellence and religious sanctity, built in with diverse philanthropic programmes, moral and intellectual paradigms and liturgical practices.

Looking at the regional space: sites of culture and agents of power

The sub-region under review is located to the north of the Tungabhadra valley, where the river runs in its eastern course leading to its confluence with the Krishna. Traditionally it falls in the southern periphery of the Kuntala region, which covered the Western Deccan and Karnataka. Following the overarching control of the Rāṣṭrakūṭas since the 9th century, the area fell under the domain of the Western Chalukyas from the late 10th century onward to the late 12th, when the sub-region came under the Seuṇa Yādava governors, who were followed by the independent Hoysala kings. The Western Chalukyas have been described in their epigraphs as lords of the Kuntala region, a region well-known since the time of the Vākāṭakas, and its historical significance may have been projected further during the rule of the Western Chalukyas as they repeatedly claimed the territory as their own. Fleet mentions the principal divisions of Kuntala to comprise of the Banavāse Twelve-Thousand, Pānuṅgal Five-Hundred, Puligere Three-Hundred, Beḷvola Three-Hundred, Kūṇḍi Three-Thousand, Toragale Six-Thousand, Kelavāḍi Three-Hundred, Kisukāḍ-Seventy, Bagadage Seventy and Tardavāḍi Thousand.[1]

Of these provinces, we are especially focusing on the Beḷvola Three-Hundred and the Kisukāḍ-Seventy, where the old Gadag and Ron *tālukas* were located, now comprising the modern District of Gadag (Figure 10.1). Within this

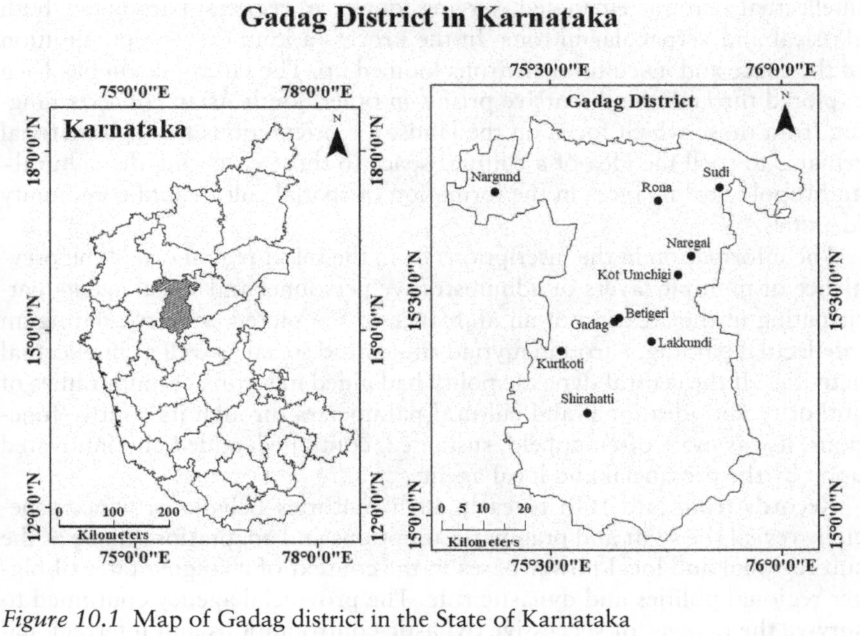

Figure 10.1 Map of Gadag district in the State of Karnataka

zone, we shall note cultural developments in the three emerging centres of Kratuka/Kradugu, Lokkiguṇḍi, Sūṇḍi and adjacent areas. Closely situated, all three gained some prominence in the 11th–12th centuries. Lokkiguṇḍi (or the modern village of Lakkundi, as it is presently known) lay 11 km southeast of Kradugu, which is now the modern town of Gadag. Sūṇḍi or modern hamlet of Sudi lay 55 km to the northeast of Gadag. The three sites also seem to have emerged as different functional zones. Sudi grew as an administrative town and the capital of the ancient province of Kisukāḍ-Seventy. Kradugu, or Gadag, was a small *agrahāra*, which grew to be a religious and administrative unit in Beḷvola province. Lakkundi, in the same province, was evidently a commercially important *mahāgrahāra* and a mint centre, favoured by multiple religious sects, as indicated in epigraphic evidence (Figs. 10.2–4.). We note a concentration of religious edifices in these areas, marked by very distinctive architectural attributes, especially from the middle of the 11th century (Figure 10.5). The temples of Gadag and Ron *tālukas* would emerge as distinct regional models[2] and sub-regional seats of culture which could also be linked to the rising Kannaḍa literary genres. It is also significant that most of the epigraphic records, which constitute the most important and richest repository of evidence for the history of the sub-region, were found in the precincts of temples in the ancient Beḷvola and Kisukāḍ provinces in general and at these three select centres in particular. There is no doubt that these shrines, often with step-wells and tanks in their precincts constituted the core of the sub-regional cultural setting from where complex religious, ritual and intellectual patterns emanated, forging long-term regional paradigms, both classical and vernacular in tone. In the process a kind of conceptualisation of the space and its cultural environs loomed up. The phenomenon has been explored through the discursive prisms in other South Asian contexts ranging from those which focus on the landscape orientations through material remains to spell the idea of a cultural space to those exploring the cultural–anthropological nuances in the formation of spatial culture and community identities.[3]

The information in the inscriptions from the select region reveal the prevalence of multiple layers of administrative personnel and social agents participating in the creation of an ambiance of the sacred and articulating an intellectual paradigm around myriad rituals and social as well as intellectual activities. If the central dynastic polity had aided in setting certain frames of authority and ideational and cultural parameters through its courtly functions, it was more often upheld, sustained, continued, added and innovated upon by the provincial and local agents.

Records from late 10th to early 11th centuries Beḷvola province especially reveal the swift and pragmatic adoptions and adaptations made at the sub-regional and local power bases in the context of changing fates of bigger regional polities and dynastic rule. The provincial agency continued to survive the ravages of successive dynastic confrontations and interregional

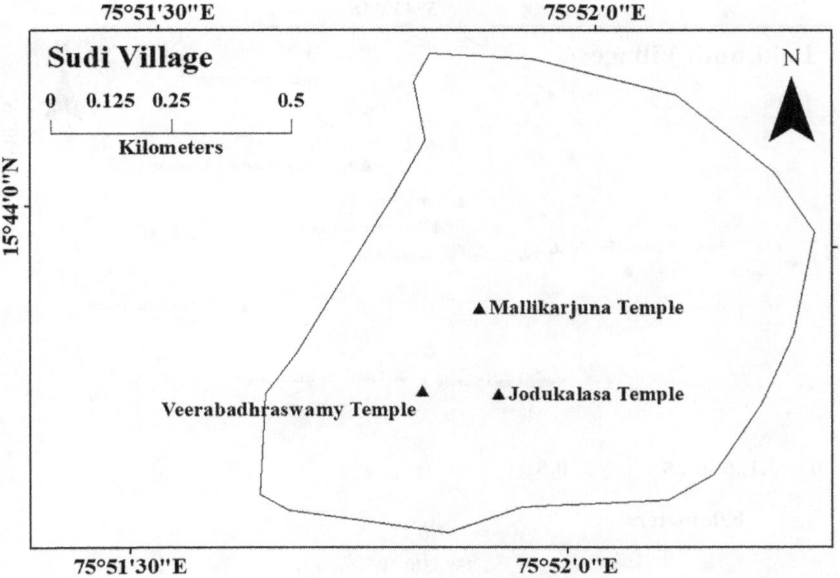

Figure 10.2 Map of Sudi Village and major temples

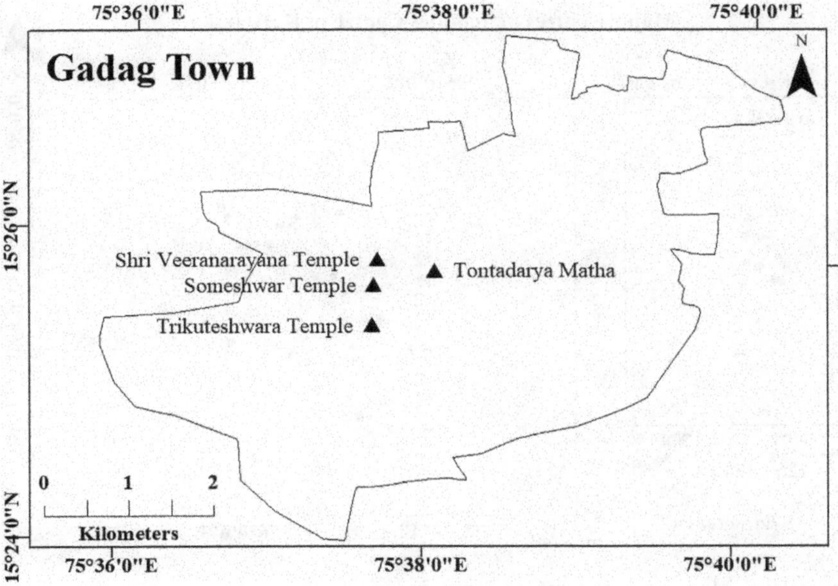

Figure 10.3 Map of Gadag Town showing major temples

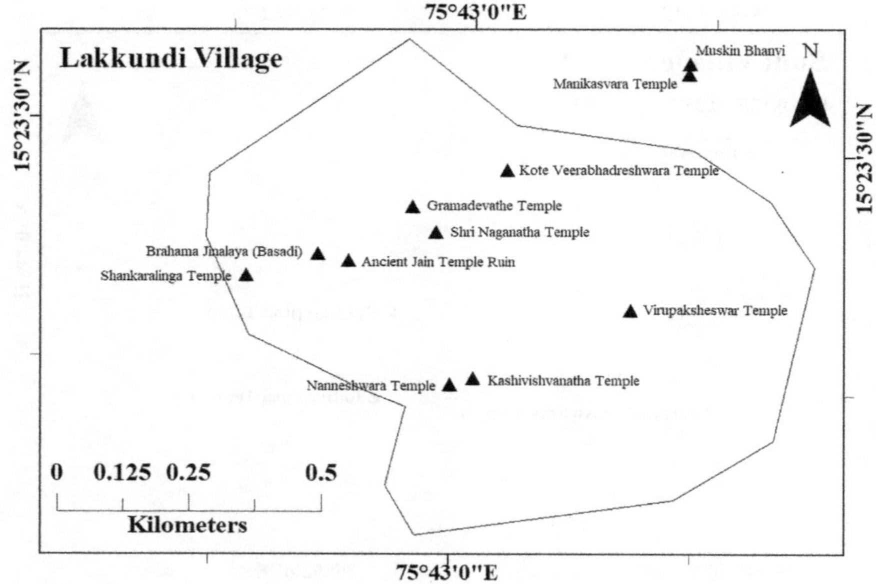

Figure 10.4 Map of Lakkundi Village with major temple sites

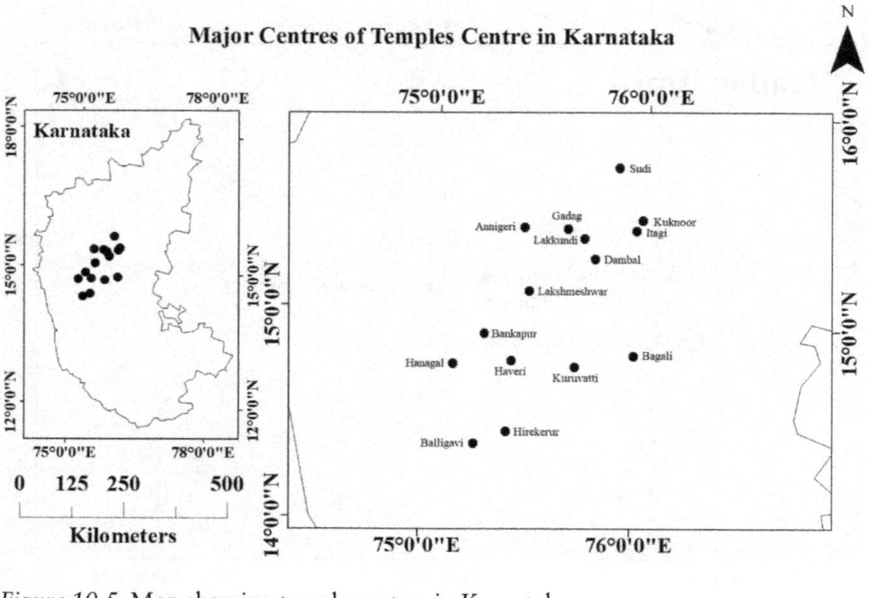

Figure 10.5 Map showing temple centres in Karnataka

Source: Author

combats and responded in strategic manoeuvres, manifest in the form of rapidly shifting power dynamics. We note the gradual shift in political allegiances of the provincial governors and local ruling families from the erstwhile ruling Rāṣṭrakūṭas to the rising Western Chalukyas from the late 10th century records found, for example, in the Navalgund and Ron *tālukas*.[4] At the same time, these shifts in political balance were possibly sought to be counterpoised with deep-seated religio-cultural moorings through temples and associated ritual and cultural activities. We note the continued trend of religious patronage manifest in the form of ritual and cultural benefactions and heightened cultural activities at the sub-regional and local levels. These carried deeper significance to the populace amidst changing power dynamics at the regional and supra-regional levels. The provincial *sāmantas*, *mahāmaṇḍaleśvaras* and *mahādaṇḍanāyakas* made major contribution in creating this cultural ethos, designative of the rising local-sub-regional idiom which invested the regional space with marks of cultural excellence and sacred attributes in the perception of the community. A clear indication of the historical process is apparent when we note the cultural landscape of the sub-region getting resplendent from the 11th to the 13th centuries with the growing concentration of beautifully commissioned religious monuments and the myriad epigraphic records posted around them, disseminating temporal and sacerdotal communions (Figure 10.5).

Provincial and local administrative centres were getting crystallised into centres of busy activity in the Beḷvola and Kisukāḍ provinces, with settlements of commercial communities on the rise, as is apparent from the rich epigraphic evidence. Temples and associated institutional appendages related to Śaivism are encountered in this zone along with Jain *basaḍis* and Vaiṣṇava temples from the early 10th century. The tradition of temples and endowments and the related activities sustained the reverses of the dynastic rule and change in the line of monarchs, just as we note the shifts in allegiances of the provincial and local potentates. However, that is not to deny the overarching role of the central hegemony of the kingdom in creating the ambiance for these cultural activities. But the important point is that the local and provincial institutions, including the temples and *maṭhas*, emerged at the initiative and patronage of the provincial agencies irrespective of the changes in the central ruling dynasties. Lakshmeswar, Gadag and Ron respectively in the provinces of Puligere Three-Hundred, Beḷvola Three-Hundred[5] and Kisukāḍ-Seventy, saw this phenomenon in a most crucial way from the Rāṣṭrakūṭa days onward. In 929 CE during the rule of Rāṣṭrakūṭa Govinda IV and Krishna III, a temple and its monastery are referred to be flourishing in the *agrahāra* Ereyana-Kāḍiyūr within the provincial orbit of Puligere-Laksmeswar, now in the Kūṇḍgol *tāluka* of Dharwad District.[6] A 10th century (933 CE) inscription from the Ron *tāluka* mentions the *gavuṇḍa* Ballajja, the village headman of Kovujagere, who is said to have constructed five temples and *maṭhas* in Kovujagere, Belvanige and Evamgal.[7] The Kurtakoti inscription of 949 CE[8] and the Soratur inscription of 951 CE[9] from the Gadag *tāluka* and the Naregal inscription of 950 CE[10] from Ron *tāluka* indicate the trend in patronage extended to multiple religious sects, including Śaivism and Jainism by local potentates under the Gaṅga Mahāmaṇḍalika Būtuga, ruling the Beḷvola Three-Hundred and Puligere Three-Hundred in the reign of Rāṣṭrakūṭa Krishna III.[11] The donations emanated from a variety of personages ranging from the Gaṅga governor's queen to local *perggaḍe* and *gavunḍa*.

The continued trend under the Western Chalukya rulers is evident from the early records of Taila II in the Navalgund *tāluka* in Belvola country. The Kurhatti inscription of 980 CE[12] refers to a family of local chiefs, *gavuṇḍas* who built a Śiva temple and a [Jai]na-sāla. It mentions also a host of Vedic scholars some of whom were versed in the *Lakulasiddhānta*. The inscription records gifts of land and money by Taila II and his subordinate Sobhanarasa to Guṇanidhi. A concentrated thrust in temple building, a surge in multiple faiths and sects as well as bestowal of patronage and gifts to these from various local elites appear to emerge as common features in the Beḷvola Three-Hundred, Kisukāḍ-Seventy and adjacent areas through the 10th–11th centuries (Figure 10.5).

Sites of multiple religions: early stir of activity

Located within the modern Ron *tāluka*, Sūṇḍi/Sudi was growing into an important town and capital of the ancient division of Kisukāḍ-Seventy since the early 10th century CE. Probable emergence of a power base for local heroes is noted from a Viragal of the time. Multiple temples and religious establishments would emerge at Sudi from the early 11th century onward (Figure 10.2). The beginnings of a tradition of devotion to Śiva and the prevalence of the *ācāryas* over rituals and grants connected to shrines as well as institutional organisation of ascetic congregations may be noted in early inscriptions. One such record (n.d.), assumed by L. D. Barnett to be dated to the 10th century CE,[13] may have belonged before the rule of the Western Chalukyas had set in. More importantly, we already note the emerging trend of making donations on auspicious days or *tithi*, for example, on *Uttarāyan saṁkrānti* or *Makara saṁkrānti*. The present grant refers especially to the settlement of a religious endowment in perpetuity on a shrine of the god Baddegīśvara, possibly Śiva, and the feeding of a thousand ascetics on the said auspicious occasion. The ritual of bestowing the grant was performed in the presence of a *śaivācārya*, Murtiśivācāryya and the 'Seventy', indicating possibly the elite or head Brahmins of the locality in Kisukāḍ-Seventy. The rising prominence of the Brahmin *Mahājanas* was evidently regularised through local administrative supervision, which is observed from the next record that we come across at Sudi in the reign of Vikramāditya V dated in 1010 CE (Saka 932), discovered on the left-hand side of the Jodukalasa temple at Sudi.[14] The record belonged to the time when Akkādevi, the sister of Vikramāditya V, was running the administration of Kisukāḍ-Seventy. The subject of this record was a transaction by which six *gavuṇḍas* and eight *seṭṭis* of Sudi leased out certain specified estates to the *Mahājanas* or heads of the Brahmin community residing in the local Brahmapuri or Brahmin quarter. Barnett considered the *gavuṇḍas* and *seṭṭis* to represent the secular administration in the area. This record suggests their extended supervision over the sacerdotal administration.

At Gadag in the heart of the Beḷvola nāḍu (Figure 10.3), beginnings of the two most eminent establishments of Śaivism and Vaiṣṇavism are noted in the early decades of the 11th century. This is indicated in two early records located in temple precincts in the town of Gadag. The first was found in the *prākāra* of the Trikūṭeśvara temple, dating to the reign of Irivabeḍeṅga Satyāśraya in 1002 CE.[15] It records a grant endowed for the temple of Svayambhūdeva, bearing the hint for the initial roots of the Śaiva establishment at the place. This has been cited as having laid the foundation of the Trikūṭeśvara tradition.[16] The second, a record of 1037 CE, found in the precincts of the temple of Veeranarayana, belongs to the reign of Jagadekamalla Jayasiṁhadeva II.[17] It registers a gift of land made by one Dāmodara-Seṭṭi after he purchased it from Maddimayya-Nāyaka, the *ūr-oḍeya* of Lokkiguṇḍi. The gift was made to the two temples of Traipuruṣadeva and Bāraha-Nārāyaṇadeva (Twelve Nārāyaṇas). It is worthwhile to note that both these establishments were founded and maintained by the members of one local family through generations. The father of Dāmodara, Perggaḍe Dhoyipayya is stated to have constructed these temples and set up the *garuḍastambha* therein. It is in these institutions that the incipient roots of the two major religions and associated establishments may be tracked, flourishing as the Trikūṭeśvara and the Veeranarayana temples. Although there is no available evidence so far for the origin of the former temple, it is generally held that the edifice of the latter temple was either founded or, more probably, restored by the Hoysala ruler Biṭṭideva, the latter being credited with temple building projects in numerous epigraphic records.[18] The *garuḍastambha* that still graces the Veeranrayana temple yard may have been related to the evidence in this record. The record also indicates that the present Gadag town was till then under the *agrahāra* of Lokkiguṇḍi and mentions the eminent *Mahājanas* as well as points to the significance of the community as major patrons of religious establishments.[19]

So far as Lakkundi is concerned, we can locate the instances of Jain *basaḍi* in the early 11th century, which we shall discuss later. Epigraphic records dwelling on temple building activity and patronage to Śaivism is available only from the late 11th century on. The earliest instance comes from an inscription of 1064 CE (ruler Someśvara I)[20] describing a gift of land made by the Mahāmaṇḍaleśvara Mārarasa, governing Beḷvola Three-Hundred, to the temple of Someśvara in Lokkiguṇḍi, entrusting the fund to *ācārya*

Tatpuruṣajīya. That would put the temple itself to be in existence much before 1064 CE.

It is mostly at Sudi that a continued trend of patronage to Śaiva establishments is noted throughout the 11th century, marked by the involvement of diverse social groups and emergent ritual patterns. Epigraphic records, most of which were located in temple precincts, indicate a huge development in the administrative structure and hierarchy, which was associated with administering religious grants. We have already encountered the *gavuṇḍas* and *seṭṭis* as the force behind the provincial administration at the local level who had empowered the religious elites, in their various administrative and economic capacities.[21] They continued supervising the religious endowments and establishments till the middle of the 11th century. Thereafter we find the *mahāmaṇḍaleśvaras* stepping into the business of managing religious affairs and munificence for education and charity. They were also associated with the creation and maintenance of the ritual space, in which the figure of the *ācārya* was gradually gaining prominence.

It was around the time of Someśvara I Āhavamalla that religious establishments started to get more organised under the supervision of provincial and local officials at Sudi. An inscription of the time, when Akkādevi was still acting as the governor of Kisukāḍ-Seventy, sets about recording the rules for the funds granted for a temple. Dated in 1054 CE, it was discovered on a stone standing in the Mallikārjuna temple.[22] We come to know about the drawing up, sanctioning and implementing of a statutory constitution for the temple of god Akkeśvara in Sudi, a temple most probably founded by Akkādevi and running already. The statute was issued by the administrative officials, headed by all the ministers of state including the *nāḍa pergaḍe*, the Commissioner of the County, Nāgadevayya as well as the Secretary and the Chief Justice from the standing camp or the *nele-viḍu* of Vikrampura, modern Arasibīḍī. The constitution would regulate the disposal of lands and also ensure the due performance of its rituals. We get names of various beneficiaries. The principal figure among them was the Paṇḍit Viśva Śivācārya, followed by a troupe of temple dancers and musicians and a manager, *pergaḍe*. The tone in this record is extremely significant, for it implies that every such grant had to be worked out within a stipulated pattern of dispensation or regulation. Four years later, an inscription of 1058 CE[23] records another grant towards the establishment of the god Akkeśvara and the 1,000 persons of that establishment, along with the staff and attendants. The continued patronage of the religious institution indicates crystallisation of the sect and the establishment and its popularity or growing appeal and prominence in the local society. Moreover, this effaced inscription contains lines which hint at the prevalence and upkeep of the statutory constitution established four years earlier by Akkādevi.

Although evidence from Sudi in the Ron *tāluka* reveals rapid rise in administrative and religious institutions, not much epigraphic record comes from the *agrahāra* of Gadag in between 1064 and the chronologically next record of 1101 CE.[24] However, one may assume the religious institutions, particularly the Śaiva and the Vaiṣṇava establishments noted earlier, to have been flourishing, as later records would substantiate. The patronage of local elites and officials seem to have been disposed not only towards temple construction and upkeep of worship and rituals as well as maintenance of preceptors and priests, but also towards promoting learning in an institutional frame. We hear of two specific kinds of gifts similar to *vidyādāna*, which were *bhaṭṭavritti* and *chhātravritti* mentioned[25] in many records since the 11th century. The root of this philanthropy for intellectual pursuit goes far back in time to the days of the Rāṣṭrakūṭas and the provincial governors under them ruling in the region.

Patronage for learning: Vidyādāna

One of the major themes in this sub-regional cultural pattern was the philanthropic orientation centred round dissemination of knowledge and education, which was possibly imbued with a sense of glory not only for the benefactor but imparted a sense of excellence at the local level. Such anchors could have been felt to be significant in the regional political frame within which the local elites were functioning. The term *vidyādāna* is often encountered in epigraphic records of the context listing benevolence. In this regard, the earlier-mentioned inscription from Soratur in Gadag tāluka dated 951 CE provides significant and one of the early instances for a *vidyādāna*.[26] Dating from the Rāṣṭrakūṭa times, it involves the role of the local *mahājanas* and the revenue officer—*ūraḍeya*. The grant came in the form of both land and cash and was bestowed on the *maṭha* attached to a temple at Saratavura, present Soratura. The *vidyādāna* came from the local *pergaḍe* and the *gavuṇḍa*. Again, in 969 CE, land was donated by a local chief and a subordinate of the Gaṅga governor Mārasiṁha II for imparting education at the *maṭha* as well as for maintaining a feeding house attached to the Śaiva temple of Rameśvara at Nagavi in the Gadag *tāluka*.[27] These activities register a local level social and ritual function with the management and participation of the community, which would continue to prevail irrespective of changes in dynastic rule at the central and even provincial levels.

The late 10th and early 11th century records from Western Chalukya rule mention such acts of benevolence on the part of local elites like *gavuṇḍas* and *mahāsāmantas* in connection with established temples and associated *maṭhas* at Hosur and Gadag, in Gadag *tāluka*. The first belongs to the time of Nurmādi Taila II in 995 CE, which states about a *vidyādāna* in the form of land donation endowed by a local *gavuṇḍa* to the temple of Mulasthānadeva at the village of Eleya-Posavuru (modern Hosur).[28] The second record has already been cited. Dating to the reign of Irivabeḍeṅga Satyāśraya in 1002 CE,[29] it records a grant made by the great Mahāsāmanta Sobhanarasa as *vidyādāna* to Kālajñānī Vakkhāni-Jiya, the disciple of Koppina-Vakkhāni-Jiya, who was the student (*vidyāśiṣya*) of Puliya-Paṇḍita, of the temple of Svayambhūdeva at Kradugu (modern Gadag), and we come to know from this record that Gadag was an *agrahāra* in the Belvoḷa-nāḍu. Tradition of religious/sectarian schools and doctrines and lines of priest novices associated with such temples sets the mark of a new stage in the development of the most eminent Śaiva establishment at Trikūṭeśvara temple at the beginning of the 11th century. In fact, the possibility of the later-evolved Traipuruṣadeva temple serving as a *ghaṭikāsthāna* has also been suggested, based on its twin, the temple of Saraswati, which in fact constitutes one of the distinctly beautiful examples of the Western Chalukya architectural style.[30]

Several categories of establishments for general and higher education associated with religion or general kinds had been prevalent in ancient Karnataka, as noted by R. S. Mugali. He points out that *maṭhas* of the Buddhists and *basaḍis* of the Jains, as well as the *brahmapuri* and *ghaṭikā* of the Brahmanical, Śaiva and Vaiṣṇava sects, were the main centres of education where general education and religious studies in both Sanskrit and Kannada were imparted.[31] Early records from Sudi in Ron *tāluka* mention the existence of *brahmapuris* in the locality, preservation of which was evidently the responsibility of the local administrators. The residents of the local *brahmapuri* were endowed with land from which they derived *bhaṭṭa bhāga*.[32] Such patronage to communities of *bhaṭṭas* or teacher-scholars, reflect institutional developments at the local level.

A most significant record in this connection is available from the village of Koṭavumachigi, now Kotumachagi, within the Gadag *tāluka*, about 22 kms northeast of the town of Gadag.[33] This inscription of the time of Vikramāditya V (1012 CE) mentions the grant bestowed by the Daṇḍanāyaka Kesavayya, who was ruling over Beḷvola and Puligere provinces. Kesavayya made over the village of Ummachige to Maunara Śridharabhaṭṭa of Roṇā, Ron *tāluka*. This noble priest had entrusted the administration of the endowment to the One Hundred and Four *Mahājanas*, specifying certain conditions to be observed by them. The specifications included that the grant be spent on maintenance of the temples and temple servants, for emoluments of the *bhaṭṭa* and the *akkariga*[34] (a man skilled in the alphabet), the stipends of students and the feeding of the *eḷkoṭi* ascetics. *Akkariga* is derivative from *akkara* and it also meant knowledge according to the 11th century CE grammar text *Karnāṭaka Bhāṣābhūṣaṇa* of the Jain writer Nāgavarma, cited by R. S. Panchamukhi.[35] The term *eḷkoṭi* has been suggested by Panchamuki as possibly indicating devotees of Śiva.[36] We also come to know that a group of *Naiṣṭhika* ascetics belonging to a distinct school were residing at the spot.[37] The *bhaṭṭavṛtti* was granted to scholars for imparting knowledge associated with Prabhākara and Nyāsa schools of thought. The latter possibly refers to *Nyāsa*, an 8th-century commentary on Vāmana-Jayāditya's *Kāśikāvṛtti*, itself a commentary on the grammar of Pāṇini.[38] The regional tradition of deep scholarship in Vedic learning including Purva-Mīmāṁsā, along with Nyāya-Vaiśeṣika and Vyākaraṇa, was ongoing within the high intellectual circuit of Karnataka and the last few disciplines were initially considered foundational for Śaiva *āgama*.[39] The *akkariga vṛtti* was provided for the scholar Nāgadesiga, who was stated to be a master in mathematics, astronomy, prosody, poetics and grammar. It seems that he was also responsible for feeding the students once a day besides teaching them, as he received benefactions for both besides his own upkeep. He was also to supply his pupils with clothes every year. The *bhaṭṭa*, the *akkariga* and the students received separate allotments from the grant. The curriculum seems to have been clearly divided into two streams: A) general and B) particular knowledge of classical philosophy and grammar. We also note the distinctions made between the *akkariga* and the *bhaṭṭa* in terms of the emolument, placing the latter at a higher level of academics. Apart from these grants further endowments were specified to be spent towards the expenses of *abhiṣeka* of the god, and for maintenance of several retinues including barbers and drummers and for feeding the personnel who were responsible for maintaining the *guṇaśāsana*. Besides these *guṇaśāsana* holdings, other grants of land were made for general charity houses, feeding houses and auxiliary gifts.

The village of Koṭavumachgi continued to flourish as a temple and educational centre, as we note from another inscription on a slab set on the Someśvara temple at the village more than 80 years later, dated to 1099 CE. This was during the reign of Vikramāditya VI Tribhuvanamalladeva. It records the eulogy of the king's subordinate, Mahāsāmantādhipati, Mahapradhāna, Banasavergaḍe, Anantapālarasa mentioning especially the large bounties made by this governor of Beḷvola Three-Hundred and Puligere Three-Hundred for feeding and educational purposes.[40]

Jain institutions, literary culture and other associations

At a different level, the vernacular Kannaḍa literary culture was closely associated especially with Jainism in the early days of late 10th to early 11th centuries. Patronage to Jainism, in the form of construction of edifices of *basaḍi* and endowments, continued since the earlier Rāṣṭrakūṭa times and we note prevalent lines of Jain scholars and preceptors. It should be pointed out here that already the locality of Mulgund in Gadag *tāluka* had become a centre of the eminent Sena *anvaya* of Jain Mūlasaṅgha with Kumārasena (860 CE) residing in the place and thus literary and scholarly associations were ripe. Ajitasena (960 CE) was the most famous personage of this *anvaya* or *gaṇa* and was also the preceptor of the Gaṅga princes Mārasiṁha, Rāchamalla and the general Cāvuṇḍarāya. His hagiography would be composed half a century later by the famous Kannaḍa poet Ranna at the behest of Attimabbe, a pious Jain aristocratic lady from the sub-region.[41]

We know of material munificence extended to Jain establishments in the earlier Rāṣṭrakūṭa days in the form of the famous endowments of a tank and a *dāna sale* (charity house) attached to the Naregal *basaḍi*, all built by Padmabbarasi, the wife of the Gaṅga Chief Butayya in the Ron *tāluka*, in 950 CE.[42] Half a century later, we note two charters from Lakkundi recording large-scale endowments in the form of land made by the earlier-mentioned aristocratic lady, Attimabbe/Attiyabbe, to her preceptor Arcanandi-paṇḍita of the Surāṣṭa-gaṇa and the Kaurur-gaccha attached to a Jain *basaḍi* at Lakkundi in 1007 CE. The *agrahāra* was shortly to grow into a Jain centre and a site of multiple faiths.[43]

The tradition of Jain literary culture continued during the rules of Taila II and Irivabeḍaṅga Satyāśraya, both of whom were described as patrons of the great Kannaḍa poet Ranna.[44] But it was the legend of Attimabbe's benevolence and devotion which loomed large in the epigraphic records and in the works of Ranna. She was the wife of the chief Nāgadevayya, who was described as the *nāḍa pergaḍe* of Kisukāḍ-Seventy,[45] while her son *paḍevala* or General Taila is described as governing the Māsavaḍi country.[46] Thus she commanded the resources and power over the locality to patronise the Jain monastic and intellectual tradition. The example of Attimabbe grew to legendary proportions. In his hagiographic *campū* work *Ajitapurāṇa*, the Kannaḍa poet extols the lady as a generous, dutiful and devout Jain. But more importantly, we come to know from the poet himself how the inspiration provided by her had facilitated the writing of this wonderful and distinctive literary composition. In this context there appears to be another legend of great significance, propagating the story that Attimabbe got made 1,000 copies of Ponna's *Śāntipurāṇa* and 1,500 hundred images of Jina and distributed them freely among the devotees.[47] Patronage and dissemination of Jain literary compositions marked a growing cultural ambiance in and around the place, along with great artistic creations in the form of richly curved and embellished Jain temples, initiating the creation of the sacred space at Lakkundi. In the legends of Ranna we hear that Attimabbe built as many as 1,501 *basaḍis* in the Kalyāna Chalukya kingdom, among which the Brahma Jinalaya at Lakkundi stands as the most beautiful example with its distinctive architectural style. The other *basaḍis* built during the period included the Pārśvanātha *basaḍi*, now known as Naganātha temple at Lakkundi. Continued patronage from Chalukya rulers enhanced the trend. The Lakkundi inscription states that after the conquest of Gujara country, the Chalukya monarch Satāśraya himself made some endowments to the Brahma Jīnālaya which had been constructed by Attimabbe.[48]

Religion, charity and the culture of knowledge

Looking at the present-day contours of the Gadag district, which covers both the Beḷvola Three-Hundred and Kisukāḍ-Seventy, one notes that the three centres, Sudi, Gadag and Lakkundi, witnessed steady development of religious edifices and associated ritual and cultural practices. In fact, these zones saw a concentration of temple-building activities throughout the period with which we are concerned. (Figure 10.2) The beginnings of these trends may be traced to the days of the Rāṣṭrakūṭas and yet, with the Western Chalukyas and the diverse successive provincial governing forces, whether from stocks of older dynastic lineages or local leaders, the thrust of administration and political–economic programmes were more and more focused on these parts of north-central Karnataka, a zone that emerged fast as a culturally endowed orbit.

The records from the mid-11th century indicate closer ties between intellectual and charitable activities in *maṭhas* and temple rituals under the supervision of the preceptors attached to the religious institutions. We often come across evidence of lineages of *ācāryas* and *śiṣyas* and their prominent role in the creation of networks of religious and intellectual activities. Epigraphic records indicate the emergence of classes of chief preceptors who probably enjoyed eminence at supra-regional levels, revealing certain itinerant and sojourning patterns too. An example may be cited from Mulgund in Gadag *tāluka*. An inscription dated to the 1028 CE[49] of the reign of Jayasiṁhadeva (II) introduces us to Bhavaśivadeva, who was the spiritual head of several temples, including that of the temple of Jagadekamalleśvara constructed by Kundarāja at Muchchundi in Bānavāsi-nāḍu as well as the temple of Sobhaneśvara built at Mulugunda by Sobhanarasa, the governor of the two Six-Hundreds under Taila II. The two institutions were located in two wide-apart locales, Banavāsi-nāḍu and Beḷvola-nāḍu. Such officiating horizons reveal extensive networks between temple institutions. Moreover, the inscription mentions that his chosen pupil Nāgasvāmin made a gift of gold, land and house-site for certain charities before he started on his pilgrimage to fulfill certain *vratas* at Gayā, Vārānasī (Benares), and so on. Thus, regional and supra-regional connections were emerging. This is also reflected in the way that intellectual and cultural practices were getting garnered.

Some of the religious establishments and their heads grew influential in eminence and attracted the philanthropic spirit of the local elites. This is quite evident at Sudi, now the administrative capital of the Kisukāḍ *tāluka*,[50] where a highly structured and well-supervised religious centre appears to have emerged on the scene with the continued development of Śaiva establishments. These activities were still connected to wider intellectual pursuits. But the sectarian ritualistic orientation related especially to the Kālāmukha practices were on the horizon. This is especially clarified if we look at the provisions made in a grant of a village made in 1060 CE[51] by the Mahāmaṇḍalādhipati Daṇḍanāyaka Nāgadeva to Someśvara Paṇḍita Deva, a Śaiva scholar-preceptor attached to the temple of Nagareśvara. The estate was primarily given as a *tālavṛtti* for expenses of worship, public works and maintenance of ascetics. Distinct provisions were made for the upkeep of professors for lecturing to the ascetics, separately for teachers and students attached to the monastery, a substantial amount for four youths associated to the assembly hall, for Brahmins offering oblations, and various categories of public women in different kinds of services, artisans and the like. This throws light on intellectual pursuits at many levels. Patronage came to the entire community associated with the establishment. Interestingly enough the inscription also refers to the sect of Kālāmukhas and mentions the typical sectarian practices on a curiously regulatory note. It comes as a strong directive from the royal agent and the temple supervisors, the old group of six *gavuṇḍas* and eight *seṭṭis*, that the *Goravas* or Śaiva ascetic-mendicants of the monastery,[52] who were Kālāmukhas, should be devout and not be neglectful in respect to their assigned duties. What these duties exactly specified remains in doubt. More importantly for our present concern, there were strong directives regulating the conduct of general students, '*viśva Vidyārtthirga*'. They were instructed to be mindful of studies and were to be supervised properly so that, should they fail to study actively, they would not be allowed to stay in the monastic establishment. The wording and the tone of the record were categorical.[53]

Continued philanthropy for disseminating knowledge associated with Śaiva establishments is noted in the Sudi inscription of 1075 CE[54] which mentions one Someśvara paṇḍita deva who, officiating in his capacity as the chief priest of Sudi, had received a grant from Someśvara Bhuvanaikamalla, the Chalukya ruler. The grant was for the maintenance of the cult of Pañca-liṅga deva and for disseminating knowledge and dispensation of food for local learned men and ascetics. Patronage to these institutions and the preceptor continued which is evident from another grant coming from Vikramāditya VI Tribhuvanamalla's wife Lakṣmā-devi in 1084 CE[55] while she was reigning in Kisukāḍ-Seventy. The town of Poṁgari was made over as a *sarva namasya* grant to Someśvaradeva, who is now described as the chief priest of the temple of Acaleśvara. The grant would go towards bearing the expenses for dispensation of food—*āhāra dānakkaṁ*, for facilitating the imparting of knowledge to the local ascetics—*vidyā dānakkaṁ*. Grant was also extended for the personal enjoyment of the god—*devar aṅga bhogakkam endu*, and for maintaining local cults and charities.

At the same time, the Jain tradition of knowledge and doctrinal learning had also been brought under the patrons' attention during Someśvara II Bhūvanaikamalla's times and this is evident from the Gawariwad records in the Gadag *tāluka*. Two inscriptions in consecutive years in 1071 and 1072 CE mention that after the Chola ravages the Mahāmaṇḍaleśvara Lakṣmarasa, governing Beḷvola and Puligere provinces, had revived the Jain establishments in the area and promoted the welfare of the doctrine in honour of the memory of the Gaṅga prince Būtuga, who had ruled the sub-regions more than 100 years earlier. A historical survey of the state of Jainism under the previous Gaṅga provincial lord was described in the inscription, which reveals a long line of Jain preceptors and scholars having graced the seat of Jainism for long at these centres in Beḷvola and Puligere countries. The whole process of this revival of Jain faith and restoration of the Jain establishments was stated to be attained as a part of the ushering in of the Śaka era with its glory in reviving qualities, attainments and apertures of the best kind on the auspicious *tithi* of Vishuvat *saṁkrānti* in the month of Chaitra. It was on this auspicious occasion that the provincial governors bestowed great favours on the religious establishments of the province, including practices such as quit-rent, festival expenses, free allotments of lands, properties, etc. The management of this grant was invested with 30 merchants of the locality, all mentioned by name in the record and hailed as '*manuṣya-deva-putra*'.[56] The inscription reveals continuation of religious traditions, attempts at revival after political disturbances especially initiated by the provincial governors and their local officials and elite community. Epigraphic evidence thus reveals convergence of rituals, patronage and philanthropy, which went towards nurturing distinct cultural traditions. Such trends, taken together with the general rise in institutionalised religion and cultural activities, substantiate our argument about local initiative in the efflorescence of a cultural paradigm at the sub-regional level.

The late 11th century scene at the *agrahāra* of Kardugu (Gadag town) witnessed the efflorescence of a different kind of intellectual culture. Evidence comes from an important inscription of 1098 CE issued in the reign of the Western Chalukya monarch Vikramāditya VI Tribhuvanamalla associated with religious endowments issuing from his Minister, the Dharmādhikarī-Mahādaṇḍanāyaka-Mahāpradhāna Someśvara Bhaṭṭa.[57] The minister bestowed endowments for the establishment of neither a temple nor a *maṭha*, but a lecture hall, '*byākhyāna śāle*',[58] for practising and teaching the Prabhākara doctrine of the Pūrva-Mīmāṁsā School of Philosophy. It is specifically highlighted in the record that Someśvara Bhaṭṭa in his great wisdom chose to establish a lecture hall for the purpose and made full provision for a teacher and a company of students attending the institution from distant parts. This lecture hall and associated educational establishment were chosen to be installed not in Kradugu but in the nearby *mahāgrahāra* of Lokkiguṇḍi under the diligent supervision of its Thousand *Mahājanas*. The tradition of the Mīmāṁsā School is therefore seen to be continuing in the provincial orbit. More importantly, the present inscription hints at the growing invocation of Sanskritic modes in the local cultural ambiance with a prominent orientation for imbibing Vedic rituals and intellectual practices. The tone of the inscription reveals an underlying effort to glorify the sub-region and build a sense of cultural hierarchy. It also indicates the close administrative as well as socio-cultural contiguity of Gadag-Betegeri and Lokkkigundi, the significance of which would be apparent in other records from Lakkundi in terms of religio-cultural transactions.

Emergent paradigm of culture

A climate of intellectual pursuits evolved on the scene under the Western Chalukya rulers, whose court was graced by several noted scholars, litterateurs and teachers. Most importantly, the royal patronage went toward encouragement of literary pursuits both within and outside the circuit of religious institutions. Again, both classical Sanskrit and the vernacular projects and composers received recognition. We have seen how patronage to religion and literature went hand-in-hand in the instances of Taila II and Satyāśraya's patronage to the greatest poet of the time, Ranna, who was a devout Jain and was bestowed with the title of Kavichakravarti.[59] Appreciation for learning in general and the pursuit of the vernacular specifically among the royal circuit is evident when we note how Chalukya King Jagadhekamalla II (1138–1150) bestowed honours on Nāgavarma II, the noted grammarian and composer of the Kannaḍa grammar, the *Karṇāṭaka Bhāṣābhuṣaṇa*, endowing him with the titles of 'Kaṭakācharya' and 'Kaṭakopādhyāya'.[60] The great Sanskrit litterateur Bilhaṇa, the composer of the classic *Vikramāṅkadevacarita* graced the court of Vikramāditya VI Tribhuvanamalla along with the great Jain scholar and Nyāya expert, Vaḍirāja and the notable *smṛti* commentator Vijñāneśvara.[61] Some of the royal figures have themselves been associated with literary achievements like Someśvara III who possibly composed the lexicon text, *Mānasollāsa*, while Jagadhekamalla II has been credited with composing the *Saṅgītacūḍāmaṇi*, a work on music. These trends during the time of the Western Chalukya rule had actually been initiated since the Rāṣṭrakuṭa-Gaṅga times with the famous poets Pampa and the great work on literary criticism, the *Kavirājamārga*, on which Sheldon Pollock has thrown critical light.[62] He has cited the linkages between cultural texts and state inspiration for the Kannaḍa language in the contexts of the Rāṣṭrakuṭa, Western Chalukya and Hoysala courtly interventions and patronage. Much earlier, we have an illuminating comment on the *Kavirājamārga* from R. S. Mugali, who hailed it as a composition on poetics focused especially on facilitating aspirant litterateurs in the Kannaḍa language to attain a distinctive 'critical credo' enabling composers to imbibe the classical style and yet strike their own path in the vernacular.[63] At the same time we note the rise of the distinctive regional *campū* literature with the vibrant compositions like Ranna's *Gadāyuddha* as well as the vernacular devotional *vacana* verses of the Vīraśaiva mystic devotees representing the other facet. This cultural efflorescence was thus a combination of the classical and the vernacular, drawing inspiration from both the courtly elite and the courtly as well as the religious ideations at the local grassroots.

Reflection of the high and elite courtly culture is available in the classic overtones one encounters in the local epigraphic record from provincial circuit of Gadag-Betegeri-Lokkigundi as discussed earlier. The record of 1098 CE eulogising the Western Chalukya dynasty had set an elite cultural tone, which may be situated within this provincial setup. The main protagonist in this inscription, *daṇḍanāyakam* and *mahāpradhāna*, the great master-*ayya*, Someśvara Bhaṭṭa, is credited with high skill in Vedic learning. Comparative attributes were ascribed to the High Minister, citing established legendary figures who were traditionally known experts in different disciplines or epistemic categories indicating the growing awareness of the pedagogic and literary tradition in the pan-Indian context. We see the minister Someśvara Bhaṭṭa being equated with a Śākalya in Vedic studies, identified as Guha (Kumāra) in the sequence of grammar, a Śaṅkara in the six courses of logic, a Vālmīki in his discriminating sense of poetry, a Vyāsa in knowledge of the *Purāṇa* and Manu in religious Law. He is described as performing the Vedic chants in august gatherings, in the heart of the *sabhā* which is then imbibed by accomplished men. Furthermore, Someśvara is also described as surrounded by a troop of good poets and sages.[64] This hints at some kind of an aspiration and association with classical brahmanical learning at the provincial, even local *mahāgrahāra* level, spilling out from the courtly circuit. Taking cue from Daud Ali's proposed discourse on courtly culture,[65] it is possible to observe an extended sphere of cultural activity here. Instances of the invocation of classical cultural parameters are found in epigraphic records associated with the provincial and even local bases and personages, highlighting personal aspirations of the protagonists and/or poetic compositional earmarks accomplished by the composers of their eulogies. A few examples may be cited from different phases of the provincial history.

An early instance is available from the already discussed Gadag inscription of 1037 CE,[66] which contains the eulogy of the locally eminent scion of the *seṭṭi* family, Damodara in classical terms, likening him to Karṇa, Hariścandra, Nala, Dadhīchi, Śibi, Vikramāditya, Cārudatta and Gutta. Apart from the epic-purāṇic figures like Karṇa, Hariśchandra, and the like, drawing the example of legendary mythological characters like Vikramāditya was not unusual if we look at the pan-Indian tradition, which is to say, that this tradition had percolated down to the local levels. Gutta possibly refers to the name of an eminent local governing family claiming descent from the classical North Indian Gupta dynasty which is perhaps the intended reference here.[67] The reference to Cārudatta is significant. We note a similar instance in another record, found on the right side of the sanctum in the Mallikārjuna temple at Sudi, dated 1058 CE.[68] This inscription includes a list of administrative officials or *Karaṇa*, headed by a *Nāyaka* or minister whose name however is effaced from the record for some reason we can only guess at. But what is left is an elaborate description and eulogy of this person. The *Nāyaka* is said to be devoted to the major and minor disciplines, scripture reading and so on. But, more importantly, he is described as a supporter of the cultured, the agreeable, the eulogists, heralds, witty poets, readers, disputants and orators. He has been described as equal in character not only to the epic characters Bali, Karṇa, Śivi, Dadhīci, but also to such figures from fictional compositions as Cārudatta and Jimūtavāhana. In both the records presented here, classical figures from legends and fictions were invoked for claiming excellence. But Cārudatta and Jimūtavāhana were characters from early historic plays, Bhāsa's Cārudatta or the later *Mṛcchakaṭikā* and Harṣa's *Nāgānanda*. Familiarity with these early literary creations is suggestive of wide cultural currents whose waves reached the provincial town in the early medieval context. Barnett, while looking for clues to the dissemination of such cultural ideas into the western Chalukyan provincial circuit, cites Pandit Gaṇapati Śāstri to suggest this to be a reflection of the tradition of dramatic performances of the *chākyars* or actors who enacted Bhāsa's plays in the temple festivals.[69] This is the *Kuṭiyaṭṭam* tradition of male dancers, performing Sanskrit plays which was prevalent since the 10th century and continues to this day in Kerala. But closer to home in Karnataka one notes Kālidāsa, Bhavabhuti and Harṣa's plays being quoted in the works on poetics composed by the 10th century author Jayakīrti and the reputed 12th century Kannaḍa authors like Nāgavarma II. Ranna and other litterateurs had referred to dramas in various manners, which indicate thorough familiarity with styles, categories and rules of Sanskrit poetics including plays. Play enactments, especially in the royal court, could naturally have been prevalent in Karnataka as indicated in the writings of Durgasiṁha, the 11th century author of Kannaḍa *Pañcatantra*.[70] The records cited here showcase an overall cultural environment trickling into the local spheres, beyond the royal circuit and even the political world, to vitalise socio-religious conceptualisations, so far as internalisation of literary Sanskrit and intellectual traditions is concerned.

A different kind of example of innovative uses of classical parameters to glorify provincial identity comes late in the 12th century. This last example is from an inscription found at Sudi, dated to the 38th year of Vikramāditya VI's reign, that is, about 1113–1114 CE,[71] which provides quite a wonderful genealogy of a local ruling family. The family of the Mahāmaṇḍaleśvara Daḍigarasa IV of the Bappurasa family ruling over Kisukāḍ especially recalling the origin of the dynasty. We are introduced to the family of a feudatory in laudatory terms. This family was stated to be the Bappura family of Bāli race, harking back to the epics and Paraśurāma and the heroes of Kiṣkindhā who were claimed as ancestors, indicating a resurrected Kṣatriya lineage after Paraśurāma's extermination of the race. The conception of a sacred space with reference to Kiṣkindhā continued to prevail in the region around Hampi in the Vijaynagara times. It is still associated with the Añjaneyādri Hill, the Hanuman temple and the Pampa Sarovar area termed Hanumanahalli, with its ancient Lakṣmī temple, a little more than 100 km southeast of Sudi in the Koppal District.

Apart from the strategies of cultural legitimation by drawing similes, the composers of eulogies also invoked moral rectitude as a new device for claiming excellence on behalf of local potentates and sub-regional communities. For example, in a record dated 1179 from Ron,[72] the status of the Sinda Mahāmaṇḍaleśvara was sought to be glorified with the invocation of epic traditions. But, more importantly, his court was said to resonate with pleasant discussions—*sukha-saṁkatha-vinoda*, where the lines from Manu evidently impacted upon the benevolent actions of the protagonist of the record. These epigraphic markers relate a cultural paradigm with additions and modifications where the local came to feature amidst the classical on the scene in the late 11th–12th centuries, irrespective of the direct patronage of the central political authority. Regional polities with their integral ties with the principal and local bases of power saw these cultural transactions branching in and out between the ever-shifting centres and peripheries, especially through the varied rituals, cultural and philanthropic programmes associated with religious establishments at the community level.

Religious preceptors as icons and intellectual–spiritual motifs

From the late 11th century onward, a new category of protagonists was emerging on the scene with the concentration of temple building in the subregion and community actions in and around the precincts of these temples. These were the distinctive scholar-preceptors prominently featuring within the religious orbit. These preceptors, as we have noted, were often associated with single and even multiple religious establishments. The situation was similar for Jainism as well as Śaivism, as already noted. This trend would gain in degrees of importance and intensity. With time the preceptor-based sectarian developments spread across multiple sites of power and religious bases. The beginnings could be traced to the figures like those of Mūrti Śivācārya in Sudi in the early 10th century. The rising eminence and material status of the designation is remarkable when we look at the late 11th century CE manifestations. Closely associated with this was the transition in the perception of spiritual and scholastic qualities desired in such august personages, which was clearly articulated in the epigraphic compositions. Since these compositions were evidently meant for public consumption, the words carried wider intents of public authority in dispersing a certain religio-cultural paradigm. The general cultural spirit of the community, closely reflected in the built religious space dotted by temples, tanks and *maṭhas*, went to characterise this whole paradigm. The concentration of such spaces in our select zone highlights this aspect of the provincial history (Figure 10.5).

To come back to the articulation of icons of spiritual excellence in epigraphs a single instance would be the rise of the priest-preceptor-scholar, *śaivācarya* Someśvara-paṇḍita-deva as a figure of sacerdotal authority in inscriptions from Sudi, dated from 1060 CE to 1084–1085 CE. Eulogies of this preceptor supply a glimpse of the imaginings related to the sacred.

The tone of praise in the earliest record (1060 CE)[73] in which we encounter the priest might initially appear almost similar to that of the tone in which Someśvara Bhaṭṭa, the Minister of Vikramāditya VI Tribhuvanamalla, would be lauded in the 1098 CE inscription from Gadag.[74] But there are distinct differences in spelling out the augustness of the priest from Sudi. Not only was the Śaiva preceptor lauded as a great scholar, one who could set all masters of philosophical schools to shame, an Akṣapāda in logic and a Kaṇāda in metaphysics, but there was more of a religious, especially Śaiva overtone in the way the qualities were described and projected. We note the entry of new qualities of ascetic merit, deep attachment and devotion to the god: *Śiva-pūjā-vyāptigaṁ tac-Chiva-mahima-mahā-bhoga-saṁpat-padakkaṁ Śiva-yogīndra-brajakkaṁ Śiva-pada-yugaḷ ānamna-vidyārtthigaḷgaṁ.*[75] Later in a 1075 CE inscription[76] Someśvara-paṇḍita-deva, now enjoying the high status of the Ācārya over the Pañca-liṅga, is described with divine characteristics. He is like the primal Buddha to the Buddhists and a Jina to an Akalaṅka (the Jain theologists). But that was not all. He had to be physically likened to Śiva. It was said that, although he lacked the token appearances and devices sported by the god, the braided locks, the fiery eye and tiger skin, yet he was Īśvara, without peer. The panegyrist rests his case, as he could not praise enough the mastery of the preceptor over the doctrines of the Lākuliśa *āgama*.[77] Thus notions of sacerdotal superiority were clearly pronounced. The attributes also reveal a specific attempt to take in the best references from all sects and religious orders. The ritual qualities were reiterated to the extent of a typified set of attributes: *svasti yama-niyama-svādhyāya-dhyāna-hāraṇa-maunānuṣṭhāṇa-japa-samādhi-sampanna.*[78] There was thus a clear indication at Sudi for a shift in the perception of intellectual superiority, moving away from general scholarly attainments to ascetic and ritual-liturgical excellence.

The Pañca-liṅga mentioned in the 1075 CE record could actually denote a religious complex with the several Śaiva shrines at Sudi, like Baddegeśvara, Akkeśvar, Nāgeśvar, Achaleśvar and Chākeśvara, mentioned in earlier and current inscriptions. The tradition of Śaiva preceptors and temples as centres of religious learning continued to flourish with the entry of new personages like Kalyāṇaśakti in Sudi in the late 11th century and a number of *śaivācāryas* in Lakkundi through the 12th century. At Gadag too there was a steady rise in the activities of the religious establishments of Śaiva orientation and affiliations. But the trends were quite different at nearby Lakkundi, where epigraphic as well as architectural evidence indicate the growth of multiple sects, with continued prevalence of Jainism as well as the rise of various Śaiva, Vaiṣṇava and other local faiths and institutions (Figs. 10.3–4).

However, the dominance of the Śaiva Kālāmukha sect since the early 12th century brought in a different and intense religious experience in and around the Beḷvola country. The trends were initiated especially at Abbalūr/Ablūr in the present-day Haveri district adjacent to the Shirhaṭṭi tāluka of Gadag

District in ancient Beḷvola Three-Hundred. Two inscriptions of 1101 and 1104[79] of the time of the Chalukya monarch Vikramāditya VI indicate the growing dominance of the sect at the zonal level in Bānavāsi Twelve-Thousand and Nagarakhaṇḍa-Seventy with the preeminence of *Lākulasiddhānta* and a long line of hereditary Śaiva *ācāryas* of the Parvatāvali and Śaktiparişe sects.[80] The waves of this development tided over the nearby Gadag, Lakkundi and Ron *tāluka* in the subsequent times. Political dynasties came and went, but the religious establishments continued to prevail in these zones. Intellectual trends were also impacted by these developments, as the sect adhered to Śaiva *āgama* on the one hand and the principles of Vaiśeṣika and Nyāya philosophies on the other, as intellectual frames of monasticism.[81] Dominance of these philosophies was already manifest in late 11th century, with the rising status of the Śaiva preceptors and is reflected in the manner that Someśvarapaṇḍitadeva has been described positively as '*vaiśeṣika-cūḍāratna*', '*naiyāyika-sarasija-mārttaṇḍa*', '*śāṁkhya-prabhāvādhika*', but in a negative stance as a '*gotra trāsi*' or 'searer of mountains or families' so far as the Mīmāṁsakas were concerned. This is mentioned in the 1060 CE inscription from Sudi.[82] The statement runs counter to the earlier observed orientation toward Mīmāṁsakas as the prime philosophical base of the academic curriculum of the region.

One notes the rise of the Kālāmukha establishment at Roṇā (modern Ron) in Kisukāḍ-Seventy, locally named Kalla-Maṭha. The earlier mentioned record of 1179 CE from Ron refers to the powerful Pārvata school trustees and members of the sectarian establishment along with local sanctuaries of Chāmeśvara and Māḷeśvara as recipients of endowments from the Sinḍa brothers, Mahāmaṇḍaleśvara Vikramāditya Devarasa or Vikkāyyā and Bijjala or Vīra-Bijjaṇa-Devarasa.[83] Patronage and adherence to locally dominant religion were important means of tackling the local and provincial power equations. Awareness in this regard is spelt out in the reiteration of a verse from Manu in the inscription as '*subhāṣita vacanaṁ*': '*Dharmma eva hato haṁti dharmmo rakṣati rakṣitaḥ [1] tasmād- dharmmo na haṁtavya[s]sarvv-aiśvaryya-phaḷ-epsubhiḥ*'.[84] This *vacana* emanating from *Manusmṛti*[85] and possibly popularly making the local circuit, was said to be heard by the Mahāmaṇḍaleśvara Vikkayya in the course of discussions in the *sabhā* at Erambarage and evidently directed his attention towards the utmost importance of adhering to the cause of religion if one desired fruits of paramountcy. Continued devotion and material patronage to the locally dominant Kālāmukha sect were intimately linked with political manoeuvres of the rival dynasties in the 12th century. However, this tendency also establishes the fact that the religious establishments with all their services to the community and the sentiments derived thereof served as the anchor in sustaining ravages of time and changes in political dynamics just as the local potentates and power bases sustained changes in central political setups.

The story of the emergence of the Trikūṭeśvara temple at Gadag is a case in example. The temple rose to substantial prominence in the sub-regional sphere, amply registered through locating in its precincts least about nine stone inscriptions found in its precincts, belonging to various times with varied political affiliations, reported by Fleet in the late 19th century. All are connected to the interesting history of this establishment as well as the sub-region. One can still locate one of them at the back of the vestibule of the older part of the shrine. The temple of Svayambhūdeva at Kratuka/Kardugu/Gadag, as already noted, had been a recipient of royal patronage since the early days in 11th century CE (1002 CE) during Irivibeḍeṅgadeva's time.[86] This continued to the mid-11th century, as attested by the 1037 CE record, mentioning the temple of Traipuruṣadeva at Kratuka.[87] These two records hint at the genesis of the Śaiva institution at Gadag.[88] More than one and a half centuries later, the Śaiva establishment reached eminence in the local circuit as noted in a record of 1191 CE during the short period of independent Seuṇa Yādava rule under Bhillāmadeva and his steward Jaitasiṁha. We hear of elaborate gifts made by the victorious king to the famed temple of Svayaṁbhū-Trikūṭeśvara under the *sthānācārya*, the holy chief Siddhānticandrabhūṣaṇadeva, hailing from an illustrious lineage of preceptors.[89] The political dynamics changed within a year in these times of intense political contestations in the region. The Hoysalas under Biṭṭideva or Viṣṇuvardhana and later, especially under Vīra-Ballāla II, challenged the might of the Western Chalukyas and spread from Gaṅgavāḍi in Malnad region via Talakaḍu into the northern parts of the Beḷvola country, setting up the northern victory camp at Lakkundi.[90] The Sanskrit record of Vīra-Ballāla I/Ballāla II dated 1192 CE,[91] found in a slab against the back wall of the temple concerned, illuminates the victorious Hoysalas' negotiations with the dominant Śaiva establishment and the growing concentration of religious activities at Trikūṭeśvara temple under the aforementioned *ācārya*. It not only registers the victorious Hoysala King's show of devotion to Siddhānticandrabhuṣaṇadeva, the Kālāmukha *sthānācāraya* of the shrine of Svayambhū-Trikūṭeśvara at Kratuka, but goes on to praise the *ācārya* in terms that bestow divinity on his personage. Epigraphic records continue to throw light on the temples, their emergence as ritual and cultural centres and their association with political events and potentates. Looking beneath the surface, this trajectory of history indicates the necessity of turning attention toward the region beyond dynastic frames of history, to observe its people, their cultural practices and institutions to get the pulse of the historical rhythms in the context. A close look at the micro-level ideational specificities as reflected in the imaging of the cultural space would reveal a complex cultural scene rendering a prism of nuanced history. We note at least two distinct trends here.

The sacred space: making of a complex cultural region

The makings of a sacred space and imbuing it with locally grown traditions is a part of what we have noted so far. The idea of the sacred is deep and complex which is found to have been manifest in varied ways through diverse material and abstract creations comprising built landscapes and associated cultural traditions.[92] Following the scheme set by Himanshu Prabha Ray, we note the archaeological landscape around the Beḷvola and Kisukāḍ provinces emerging as a lived space with its natural and built environment integrated into the imagination of the community. The landsacape was nuanced with a sense of deeprooted identity, invested with glory, imbued with a sense of sacred and cultural excellence. This play of the real and the virtual, as we get from the monuments and the epigraphs, evokes the more complex picture of the sub-regional cultural history.

To begin with, the dominant trend in the sub-regional and even local religious sphere is reflected in the transition of the Śaiva Trikūṭeśvara temple of Gadag and its rise to the status of a *tīrtha* by the 12th century CE. The manifestation is noted in the temple building activity. According to M A Dhaky, the main temple in the complex may have been conceived of as a *tirtha* which came later as an addition to the older and starker northern shrine of early 11th century at the site. The two were connected by a large columner hall.[93] But it was not only the temple site that was invested with sacred glory. The 1192 CE record of Vīra-Ballāla II spells out the emerging concept of a wider sacred geography associated with the god Svayambhū-Trikūṭeśvara, lord of the three stationary *liṅgas*, symbolic of three peaks—Kāleśvara, Śrīsaila and Bhimeśvara. These marked the boundaries of the country, Triliṅga. The *sthānācārya* is described as the fourth and 'living' *liṅga*, with whose addition the phenomenon attains the glory of *catuḥkuṭeśvara*.[94] The concept thus linked the immediate spatial sphere of the god at Trikūṭeśvara with multiple famed religious centres in a wider sacred geography, lending the sub-regional cultural space a heightened sense of glory. The building of the edifices, the old and the later structures of the temple as well as the often-overlooked stepwell at the Trikūṭeśvara complex also suggest simultaneous evolution of the notions and related constructional activities at Kratuka.

Vīra-Ballāla II and his ministers would continue to bestow benevolence on the shrine with its long line of eminent Kālāmukha Śaivācāryas as revealed through the records of his times dated 1199 CE discovered at the concerned shrine in Gadag with the same illustrious sthānācāraya still gracing the scene at Svayambhūprasannatrikūṭeśvara.[95] The establishment continued to receive patronage from the Yādava rulers in the early 13th century when Siṅghana II stepped in as the independent ruler in the Beḷvola nāḍu, wresting power from the Hoysalas around 1202 CE, as evident from the records of Sudi in that year. A 13th century inscription dated in Śaka 1135 (1213 CE) indicates the continued evidence for the Śaiva establishment prevailing with its status in the local circuit under Yādava Siṅghanadeva.[96] The aspect of the sacred geography was enhanced with divinity ascribed to the river in the form of Tuṅgabhadrādevī, bathing in whose sacred waters was the special ritual which opened the sacred portals for Hoysala Mahāmaṇḍaleśvara Rāyadeva, who bestowed gifts to the *devī* and the god Svayambhūprasannatrikūṭeśvara.[97] The river, already hailed as the *Dakṣiṇagaṅgā* of the south, was described in the late 11th century inscription from Gawarwad to be conspicuous with 'series of holy sites of salvation, enjoying renown, praise and prosperity on its banks'.[98]

It was however, a complex cultural scene in Beḷvola Three-Hundred. In Lokkigundi, the community went for multiple expressions of religious faith and practices, not oriented to religious preceptors or even to Śaivism alone. This is the second trend noted especially at the *mahāgrahāra*, where multiple layers of socio-religious practices and participation of different categories of social agents could be observed. The epigraphic visibility of the site was manifest throughout the 12th to the early 13th century. Although we note the contiguity of Lakkundi and Gadag and the spillover of Śaiva affiliation, yet Lakkundi was vibrant with the presence of common folks, minor elites and their multiple faiths, emerging as a commercial-cum-administrative and minting centre (Figure 10.4). This phenomenon actually throws open the matter of a historiography focusing either on Saivism or Jainism in ancient Karnataka to critical review. Closer to the sentiments of the community were the cultural practices associated with religion, whatever the affiliation, which sustained and in fact flowered into a vibrant regional identity, the making of which was a community activity, a spontaneous growth out of felt experiences and sentiments.[99]

The fame of the *mahāgrahāra* had grown evidently from the end of the 11th century as reflected in the inscription from Gadag of 1098 CE,[100] where it was described as a beauty spot of sandal-wood upon the brow of the lady Beḷvola. Lokkigundi, a space spelt with distinctly different material, intellectual as well as sacred qualities, was a gift of the supreme lord, a support of the Chalukya realm, splendid as Devendra's brilliant Amarāvatī, or Alakāpura, or the serpent-king's seat—'*phaṇīndra neleyappa Bhogavati tān =ene raṁjisugaṁ*'.[101] A sacred site par excellence, it was a holy mine of Brahmins, its sky encompassed by banners of several temples, where Brahmins enjoyed the combination of essentials of good religion, wealth and pleasure, with all that is right and victorious gracing the town. Most importantly, the spot is clearly hailed the best as it housed the dwellings of diverse gods,[102] inhabited and supervised by the Thousand Mahājānas who are especially declared to be uniform to the four (churches): '*Samayaṁ nālkakkaṁ*'.[103] Barnett took the phrase to indicate uniform patronage shown to the four churches of 'Śaivas, Vaiṣṇavas, Jains, and Buddhists'.[104] Information in inscriptions would indicate that the Mahājanas were in charge of looking after all categories of religious affairs in the *agrahāra*.[105] Unlike the dominance of sectarian preceptors and their lineages at Suṇḍi and Kardugu, at Lakkundi we note the eminent Thousand Mahājanas, famously cited repeatedly in inscriptions as protecting the religious establishments of the neighbourhood in conjunction with all the residents of the place.

Position of the Mahājanas continue to emerge as essential in the socio-religious life of Lakkundi and possibly also stretched to Kardugu under the changing rules of the Western Chalukyas, Kalachuryas, Yādavas and finally the Hoysalas through the 12th century.[106] The continued prevalence of Jainism and Jain establishments, although much less conspicuous than the Śaiva establishments, is evident from epigraphic records of late 12th century and early 13th centuries CE.[107] It would seem that the *mahāgrahāra* had evolved into a complex socio-economic zone, and its activities included the presence of a population of various denominations from the days of the Chalukyas of Kalyāni to those of the Hoysalas, who paid homage to diverse gods and bestowed honours to the Mahājanas. The local faiths were expressed through devotion to multiple deities named in the 12th to early 13th century records from Lakkundi, not all of which were identifiable, many possibly local and some definitely affiliated to Śaiva, Vaiṣṇava and Jain sects. The coexisting faiths and associated rituals were integral to the historical rhythm of the provincial orbit. The region and its people undergoing shifting power dynamics and changing political rules, negotiated the times within the cultural environment they sought to build, where ritual and cultural engagements sustained them and imbued them with an identity transcending transient political fate.

The evidence from the ancient *tālukas* of the Gadag District thus evokes a complex sub-regional and local scene with socio-religious dynamics, which sought to lend overarching cultural identity to the zone. This complex cultural phenomenon had distinct ideational roots drawn from the locally reinvented Brahmanical and epic-puranic symbolism and the newly emerging sectarian liturgical-esoteric philosophy and practices imbued with vernacular sensitivities. In the creation of this culture it was the ritual and material role of the local players that appear to emerge as the most significant. Possibly the distinctive local architectural idiom at Lakkundi and Gadag and the classic derived style at Sudi exemplify the plural roots of the phenomenon, where continuities and innovations came together in a harmonious exuberance. Although the gradual receding of the generic Vedic culture was apparent in the face of corresponding rise of the regional cult derivatives of Śaivism, there were significant degrees of assimilation of the two trends. On the other hand, there were vivid and varied manifestations of popular faiths representing the spontaneous rise of the local. These trends converged in lending specificities to the complex prism of the sub-regional cultural ethos and idiom at the ground level at the three centres in Beḷvola and Kisukāḍ nāḍu.

Notes

1 J. F. Fleet, *The Dynasties of the Kanarese Districts of the Bombay Presidency from the Earliest Historical Times to the Muhammadan Conquest of A.D. 1318*, Bombay: Government Central Press, 1882, p. 42 fn1.

2 Adam Hardy, *Indian Temple Architecture: Form and Transformation. The Karṇāṭa Drāviḍa Tradition 7th to 13th Century*, New Delhi: Indira Gandhi National Centre for the Arts, Abhinav Publications, 1995, pp. 157–8.

3 Convergence of semiotics and meanings in the creation of spatial identity of communities in given geographical frames have been emerging within the disciplines of environmental studies and cultural geography especially with the rise of the new discourses on 'Place Identity' in modern contexts. The phenomenon is crucially relevant in the present context here. The theoretical parameters for the study of creation of cultural dimensions of place identity through ritual practices are only currently entering into the academic discourses of South Asia's pre-modern history. In this context the idea has been explored in some depth in the works cited here. Himanshu Prabha Ray, 'Introduction', in Himanshu Prabha Ray (ed), *Negotiating Cultural Identity*, London: Routledge, 2015, pp. xi–xiii; Susan Verma Mishra and Himanshu Prabha Ray (eds), *The Archaeology of Sacred Spaces: The Temple in Western India (2nd Century BCE to 8th Century CE)*, Oxon and New York: Routledge, 2017, pp. 1–13. For a further reading on the conceptual frame of such formations of cultural identities, see Kunal Chakravarti, 'Cult Region: The Purāṇas and the Making of the Cultural Territory of Bengal', *Studies in History*, 2000, 16(1): 1–16.

4 L. D. Barnett, 'Tuppad-Kurhatti Inscription of the Reign of Akalavarsha Krishna III: Saka 868', *Epigraphia Indica* (henceforth *EI*), 1917–18, XIV(28): 364–6; C. R. Krishnamacharlu, R. S. Panchamukhi, and N. Lakshmi Narayana Rao (eds), *South Indian Inscriptions*, vol. XI, Part I (henceforth *SII*, XI. I), Madras: Superintendent, Government Press, 1940, No. 45 (B. K. No. 231 of 1928–29), p. 30.

5 These two adjacent provinces were often jointly referred as *Erad arunuru* in ancient times. See N. Lakshmi Narayana Rao (ed), *South Indian Inscriptions*, vol. XVIII (henceforth *SII*, XVIII), New Delhi: Director General Archaeological Survey of India, reprint 1975, p. xxiv.

6 L. D. Barnett, 'Kalas Inscription of the Rastrakuta Govinda IV: Saka 851', *EI*, 1915–16, XIII(29): 326–38.

7 *SII*, XI. I, No. 35 (B. K. No. 13 of 1927–28), p. 20; also cited in R. N. Nandi, *Religious Institutions and Cults in the Deccan, C. A.D. 600—A.D. 1000*, New Delhi: Motilal Banarsidass, 1973, p. 5.

8 *SII*, XI. I, No. 37 (B. K. No. 126 of 1926–27), p. 20.

9 *Ibid*, No. 39 (B. K. No. 72 of 1926–27), p. 24.

10 *Ibid*, No. 38 (B. K. No. 182 of 1926–27), p. 23.

11 *Ibid*, 'Introduction', pp. vi–vii.

12 *Ibid*, No. 45 (B. K. No. 231 of 1928–29), p. 30.

13 L. D. Barnett, 'Inscriptions of Sudi', *EI*, 1919–20, XV(6, B): 74–5.

14 *Ibid*, No. 6, C, pp. 75–6.

15 *SII*, XI. I, No. 48 (B. K. No. 10 of 1926–27), pp. 32–4.

16 *Dharwar District Gazetteer (Including Gadag and Haveri Distircts)*, rev. edn, Bangalore: Chief Editor, Karnataka Gazetteer, 2002, p. 824.

17 *SII*, XI. I, No. 72 (B. K. No. 13 of 1926–27), p. 62.

18 S. Settar (ed), *Archaeological Survey of Mysore, Annual Reports: 1912, A Study*, rev. edn, Mysore: Department of History and Archaeology, Karnatak University, 1977, p. 23; Kelleson Collyer, *The Hoysala Artists: Their Identity and Styles*, Mysore: Directorate of Archaeology and Museums, 1990, pp. 26–7, 48–9; C. Hayavadana Rao (ed), *Mysore Gazetteer*, vol. II, Part 2, Bangalore: Government Press, 1930, pp. 1324–9, 1342–3.

19 L. D. Barnett, 'Gadag Inscription of the Reign of Jayasimha II: Saka 959', *EI*, 1927–28, XIX(37): 217–22.

20 *SII*, XVIII, No. 70 (B. K. No. 189 of 1932–33), pp. 62–5.
21 Barnett, 'Inscriptions of Sudi', No. 6, C & D, pp. 75–80.
22 *Ibid*, No. 6, E (1), pp. 80–3.
23 *Ibid*, No. 6, E (2), pp. 83–5.
24 *SII*, XVIII, No. 104 (B. K. No. 192 of 1932–33), pp. 110–11.
25 *Ibid*, No. 340, p. 435.
26 *SII*, XI. I, No. 39 (B. K. No. 72 of 1926–27), p. 24.
27 *Ibid*, No. 41 (B.K. No. 21 of 1926–27), p. 25.
28 *Ibid*, No. 47 (B. K. No. 111 of 1926–27), p. 32.
29 *Ibid*, No. 48 (B. K. No. 10 of 1926–27), pp. 32–4.
30 *Dharwar District Gazetteer*, p. 825.
31 R. S. Mugali, *The Heritage of Karnataka*, Bangalore: Satyasodhana Publishing House, 1946, p. 157.
32 Barnett, 'Inscriptions of Sudi', No. 6, B & C, pp. 75–7.
33 *SII*, XI. I, No. 56 (B. K. No. 129 of 1926–27), p. 27; R. S. Panchamukhi, 'Kotavumachgi Inscription of Vikramaditya V', *EI*, 1929–30, XX(6): 64–70.
34 R. F. Kittel, *Kannaḍa—English Dictionary*, Mangalore: Basel Misson Book & Tract Depository, 1894, p. 6.
35 *EI*, XX, 65fn1.
36 *Ibid*, fn2.
37 These ascetics were known to be committed to perpetual chastity. See David N. Lorenzen, *The Kāpālikas and Kālāmukhas: Two Lost Śaivite Sects*, New Delhi: Thomson Press (India) Limited, 1972, p. 157.
38 George Cardona, *Pāṇini: A Survey of Research*, New Delhi: Motilal Banarsidass, Reprint 1997, pp. 154–5.
39 Nandi, *Religious Institutions*, p. 84; Subodh Kapur, *The Philosophy of Śaivism*, New Delhi: Cosmo Publications, 2004, pp. 57–9; K. K. Handiqui, *Yaśastilaka and Indian Culture*, Sholapur: Jaina Samskriti Samrakshaka Sangha, 1949, pp. 184–5.
40 N. Lakshmi Narayana Rao (ed), *South Indian Inscriptions*, vol. XI, Part II (henceforth *SII*, XI. II), Madras: Superintendent Government Press, 1952, No. 146 (B. K. No. 132 of 1926–27), pp. 176–8.
41 P. B. Desai, *Jainism in South India and Some Jaina Epigraphs*, Sholapur: Gulābchand Hirāchānd Doshi, 1957, pp. 136–8.
42 *SII*, XI. I, No. 38 (B. K. No. 182 of 1926–27), p. 23.
43 *Ibid*, No. 52 (B. K. No. 28 of 1926–27), p. 46; No. 53 (B. K. No. 29 of 1926–27), p. 47.
44 Ajith Prasad, 'Jainism in Dharwad: A Cultural Study' (unpublished Ph.D. thesis, Karnatak University, Dharwad, 1996), Chap. 2, pp. 36–7.
45 Barnett, 'Inscriptions of Sudi', No. 6, E (1), pp. 80–3.
46 *SII*, XI. I, No. 52, p. 46.
47 Cited in Prasad, Chap. 3, p. 74fn35: Kamalā Hampanā, *Attimabbe and Chalukyas*, Bangalore: Paṇḍitaratna E. Śāntirājaśāstri Trāst, 1995, p. 12.
48 *SII*, XI. I, No. 52 (B. K. No. 28 of 1926–27), p. 46.
49 *Ibid*, No. 64 (B. K. No. 100 of 1926–27), p. 53.
50 Barnett, 'Inscriptions of Sudi', No. 6, F, p. 88.
51 *Ibid*, pp. 85–94.
52 See Kittel, *Kannaḍa-English Dictionary*, p. 568.
53 Barnett, 'Inscriptions of Sudi', No. 6, F, pp. 90, 93.
54 *Ibid*, No. 6, H, pp. 96–100.
55 *Ibid*, No. 6, I, pp. 100–3.
56 L. D. Barnett, 'Two Inscriptions from Gawarwad and Annigeri, of the Reign of Someśvara II: Saka 993 and 994 AD', *EI*, XV(23) *1919–20*, Calcutta: Government of India, 1923, pp. 337–47.

57 L. D. Barnett, 'Gadag Inscription of Vikramaditya VI: The 23rd Year', *EI*, XV(24) *1919–20*, Calcutta: Government of India, 1923, pp. 348–63.
58 *Ibid*, p. 355; Kittel, *Kannaḍa-English Dictionary*, p. 1454.
59 R. Narasimhacharya, *History of Kannada literature*, Mysore: Government Press, 1934, p. 18; K. A. Nilakanta Sastri, *A History of South India from Prehistoric Times to the Fall of Vijayanagar*, 2nd edn, New Delhi and London: Oxford University Press, 1958, p. 383.
60 Narasimhacharya, *History of Kannada Literature*, pp. 19, 65, 68; Nilakanta Sastri, *A History of South India*, p. 383; Suryanath U. Kamath, *A Concise History of Karnataka: From Pre-Historic Times to the Present*, Bangalore: Jupiter Books, 2001, p. 115.
61 Kamath, *A Concise History of Karnataka*, pp. 114–15.
62 Sheldon Pollock, *Language of Gods in the World of Men: Sanskrit, Culture, Power in Premodern India*, Berkeley: University of California Press, 2006, pp. 26–7.
63 Mugali, *The Heritage of Karnataka*, pp. 177–8.
64 Barnett, 'Gadag Inscription of Vikramaditya VI', pp. 352–4, 359–61.
65 Daud Ali, *Courtly Culture and Political Life in Early Medieval India*, Cambridge: Cambridge University Press, 2004.
66 Barnett, 'Gadag Inscription of the Reign', pp. 217–22.
67 *Ibid*, pp. 220–22.
68 Barnett, 'Inscriptions of Sudi', No. 6, E (2), pp. 83–5.
69 *Ibid*, pp. 83–4.
70 H. K. Ranganatha, *The Karnatak Theatre*, Dharwar: Karnatak University, 1960, pp. 13–18.
71 Barnett, 'Inscriptions of Sudi', No. 6, K, pp. 105–8.
72 L. D. Barnett, 'Two Inscriptions from Ron, of Saka 944 and 1102', *EI*, XIX, No. 38, B: 226–36.
73 Barnett, 'Inscriptions from Sudi', No. 6, F, pp. 85–94.
74 Barnett, 'Gadag Inscription of Vikramaditya VI', pp. 348–63.
75 Barnett, 'Inscriptions from Sudi', No. 6, F, p. 92.
76 *Ibid*, No. 6, H, pp. 96–100.
77 *Ibid*, pp. 98–9.
78 *Ibid*, No. 6, I, pp. 100–3.
79 J. F. Fleet, 'Inscriptions at Ablūr', *EI*, 1898–99, V(25, A & B): 213–31.
80 Lorenzen, *The Kāpālikas and Kālāmukhas*, pp. 97–9.
81 Nandi, *Religious Institutions*, pp. 84–5.
82 Barnett, 'Inscriptions of Sudi', No. 6, F, verse 11, pp. 89, 92.
83 Barnett, 'Two Inscriptions from Ron', pp. 226–36.
84 *Ibid*, verse 25, p. 231.
85 *Manusmṛti*, VIII. 15 cited in *ibid*, p. 235fn2.
86 *SII*, XI. I, No. 48 (B. K. No. 10 of 1926–27), pp. 32–4.
87 *Ibid*, No. 72 (B. K. No. 13 of 1926–27), p. 62.
88 *Dharwar District Gazetteer*, p. 824.
89 F. Kielhorn, 'Gadag Inscription of the Yadav Bhillama: Saka-Samvat 1113', *EI*, 1894–95, III(30): 217–20.
90 William Coelho, *The Hoysala Vamsa*, Bombay: Indian Historical Research Institute, St Xaviers College Bombay, 1950, pp. 150–7; J. D. M. Derrett, *The Hoysaḷas: A Medieval Indian Royal Family*, London: Oxford University Press, 1957, pp. 88–93.
91 H. Lüders, 'Gadag Inscription of Vira-Ballala II: Saka-Samvat 1114', *EI*, 1900–01, VI(10): 89–97.

92 Ray, 'Introduction', pp. xi–xiii; Verma Mishra and Ray, *The Archaeology of Sacred Spaces*, pp. 1–13.
93 M. A. Dhaky, *Encyclopaedia of Indian Temple Architecture, South India: Upper Drāviḍadeśa, Later Phase*, vol. I, Part 3, New Delhi: American Institute of Indian Studies, 1996, pp. 102–10.
94 Lüders, 'Gadag Inscription', verse 39, p. 96; J. F. Fleet, 'Notes on Inscriptions at Gaddak, in the Dambal Tālukā of the Dharwar District', *Indian Antiquary*, October 1873, 2: 300.
95 Fleet, 'Notes on Inscriptions at Gaddak', p. 298; Anon, 'Calculations of Hindu Dates', No. 36, Miscellanae, *Indian Antiquary*, 1890, XIX: 155–6.
96 Fleet, 'Notes on Inscriptions at Gaddak', p. 297; Shrinivas Ritti, *The Seunas: The Yadavas of Devagiri*, Dharwar: Department of Ancient Indian History and Epigraphy, 1973, pp. 133–4.
97 Anon, 'Calculations of Hindu Dates', pp. 155–6.
98 Barnett, 'Two Inscriptions', verse 16, pp. 341, 345.
99 Chakravarti, 'Cult Region'.
100 Barnett, 'Gadag Inscription of Vikramaditya VI', pp. 348–63.
101 *Ibid*, verse 68, p. 355.
102 *Ibid*, verses 57–60, p. 355.
103 *Ibid*, pp. 355, 362. Kittel's *Dictionary* defines '*nāluku*' as 'four' and '*nālku*' as 'the state of being four' or simply 'four'. More importantly Kittel also states that the term is used in the sense of 'all'. Kittel, *Kannaḍa-English Dictionary*, p. 860.
104 Barnett, 'Gadag Inscription of Vikramaditya VI', p. 362fn2.
105 P. B. Desai (ed), *South Indian Inscriptions*, vol. XV (henceforth *SII*, XV), New Delhi: Manager of Publications, Archaeological Survey of India, 1964, No. 103 (B. K. No. 209 of 1928 20), p. 167.
106 *SII*, XI. II, No. 202 (B. K. No. 49 of 1926–27), pp. 257–8; *SII*, XV, No. 48 (B. K. No. 54 of 1926–27), pp. 64–5, No. 119 (B. K. No. 30 of 1926–27), pp. 149–50, No. 125 (B. K. No. 41 of 1926–27), pp. 158–9.
107 *SII*, XV, No. 119 (B. K. No. 30 of 1926–27), pp. 149–50, No. 556 (B. K. No. 31 of 1926–27), p. 374, No. 557 (B. K. No. 34 of 1926–27), p. 374; *SII*, XVIII, No. 401 (B. K. No. 75 of 1934–35), p. 473.

INDEX

Abu'l Fazl 39–41, 43–4
Afghan 58–60, 76
Afghanistan 76, 108, 119, 123, 137n117
āgama 172, 175, 179, 181, 188n33, 269, 278–9
agrahāra 260, 263, 265, 267–8, 269, 273, 275, 282–3; *see also* Mahāgrahāra
agriculture 234, 236, 245–6, 248–52; *see also* land grant
Ahmed Shah Durrani 58–9
Ajātaśatru 107, 129n18
akala (distant time, or 'traditional') 95–7
Akbar 40–1, 43–6, 51, 56, 58, 61–2
akka bakka (ritual gate) 85, 88–90, 92–3, 97
Alagarkoyil 166–7, 179–80, 184–5, 188n37
Alluru 198
ancestors 30, 89–90, 92, 115, 222–3, 229, 276
Āndhradeśa 194–5, 200, 202, 204, 208–9, 211
animal sacrifice 21
annual birthday celebration 142, 156
annual festival 9, 84, 90–1, 93, 95, 146, 148, 151, 156, 161n24, 162n38, 165n79, 172
annual ritual 90, 142
Antal (Āṇṭāl) 149–52, 154, 157, 164n72, 164n77, 168, 178
Apracarāja 113, 115, 117–22, 136n97, 137n114, 137n115
Aravenu 84
Arbman, Ernst 23–5, 29, 35n34
artist 11, 47, 70–1, 187n26, 215, 217, 223, 226, 228–30
Aryanist ideology 5, 25, 29–30
Aryans 27–8, 31
Ashmolean Museum 50, 58–60, 62, 65, 68, 73–5
Aśoka 107–10, 112, 118, 129n22, 132n48, 132n52, 134n68, 134n69, 134nn72–3, 235
Aśokāvadāna 10, 107–10, 112–13, 129n22, 132n47
astronomy 41, 269
ātman 19
avadāna 109, 112, 134n69

Badaga 83–91, 93–7
Badayuni 43, 51–2
Bajaur 113–14, 117, 119–21
Barakā (blessing) 68, 77
Beragani 87–93
Bhādrayanīya school 206
bhakti 169
Bharhut 5
Bhāsa 276
Bhīmā 193–4
Bhutanatha temple 216, 219–20, 222, 226
Bilhana 274
birthday ritual 144
Bodleian Library 70–1
Brahmā 224–7, 270
Brahma-merit (*brāhmapuṇya*) 118, 140n159
Brahman 19, 146
Brāhmī 5, 104, 109, 235
Brahmin 19–20, 22, 25, 27, 29, 51, 107, 142, 151, 154, 158, 164n77, 194, 210, 243, 246, 264–5, 272, 282
British Museum 44, 48–50, 54, 76, 187n22, 188n38
Butkara I 109, 116, 133n62, 135n81

Haruva 86
hatti (satellite village) 86, 88–91, 93–4
Hauer, Jakob Wilhelm 26, 28, 29, 30
Held, George 26, 27, 28, 29, 36n56
Hethai *see* Hette
Hette 9, 86–95, 97
Hireodeya 9, 86–92, 94–7
Hockings, Paul 87
Hodivala, S. H. 40, 44, 46, 50–1, 58, 62–5
Höfler, Otto 26, 29
Homo Ludens 21, 26
Hoysaḷa 236, 238, 258–9, 265, 274, 280–1, 283
Huizinga, Johan 21, 26, 27, 29
Humayun 41, 51, 56–8

ikala (present time, or 'modern') 95–6
Ikṣvākus 115–16; of Vijayapurī 194–5, 200, 202, 204
Indo-Greek(s) 109–12, 115, 119
Indo-Parthian(s) 110–13, 122, 136n97
Indo-Scythian(s)110–13, 119–20
Indravarma I 117–18, 120–1; Indravarma II 121
inscription, dedicatory 115–16
invented tradition 39, 78
Iron Age 233, 235, 247–9, 251
irrigation 12, 184, 233–4, 237, 242–3, 245, 250–1, 253, 253n6
Islam, Islamic 40–3, 46, 54, 63, 68, 77

Jahangir 41, 43–55, 63–6, 70, 72–4, 77–9, 80n29, 81n45
Jain, Jaina, Jainism, Jains 5, 12, 186n3, 221, 228, 231n24, 263–5, 268–70, 272–4, 277–8, 282–3; Jain *basaḍis* 263
Jamison, Stephanie 20
Jihoṇika 112, 136n100

kāhāpana 130n30, 198–9, 201–2, 209–10, 212n12
Kakatiya(s) 236, 238–9, 241, 244, 251
Kālidāsa 276
kamma (measuring unit) 243, 246
Kanheri 203, 206–9, 213n25
Kaniṣka I 112, 134n70, 136n109, 136n110, 138n135
Kannada 229, 260, 268–70, 274, 276
Karnataka 11–12, 215, 234–5, 237, 241, 244, 247, 252, 254n9, 255n21, 256n59, 258–9, 262, 268–9, 271, 276, 282
Karṇaṭaka Bhāṣābhūṣaṇa (Kannada grammar) 274
kārṣapāṇa see kāhāpana
Kashmir smast 193
Kāśyapīya 111
Kavirājamārga 274
Kerala kings 149, 151–2, 157–9, 163n54, 163n58, 163n60, 164n72
Kharoṣṭhī 5, 10, 109–10, 112, 133n64, 136n100, 137n115
Khilat (robes) 55–6, 77
Khutbā 42
kingship 39–42, 46, 50, 54, 70, 77, 79; divine 8, 40–1, 43, 77; Mughal 40, 42, 63, 77, 79
Kota(s) 84, 93
Kṛṣṇa 154, 172, 183
Kṣatrapa(s) 112, 124, 126, 193–4, 200, 203, 207
kula devaru 'own god' 86–7, 90, 92, 95–6
Kurumba(s) 84–5, 91, 93, 97
Kuṣāṇa 110–13, 115, 123, 134n70, 137n117, 194, 208
kuutu (central council) 93–6

Lakkundi 260, 262, 265, 270–1, 273, 278–80, 282–3
land: agriculture 234, 236, 245–6, 248–52; donation 10, 12, 144, 148, 207, 211, 234, 242–3, 245–6, 251; grant 11–12, 143–5, 147–8, 151, 154, 156–7, 160n3, 164n77, 207, 213n26, 233–4, 242–4, 246, 252, 267, 269; measurement *(mattar)* 245, 246; ritualised 234, 252; types of 246, 252, 253
Lincoln, Bruce 29, 32, 33n2
liṅga 11, 169, 182, 218–21, 223, 225, 230n8, 272, 281
Lingayat(s) 85–7, 89
Louvre *see* Musée du Louvre

Madurai 143, 159n1, 160n3, 160n6, 160n12, 161n13, 164n71, 166, 174, 177, 181–2, 184, 231n24
Mahābhārata 6, 26–8, 193
Mahāgrahāra 260, 273, 275, 282–3; *see also agrahāra*
Mahājanas 243, 264–5, 267, 268, 273, 282–3
mahākṣatrapa see Kṣatrapa(s)

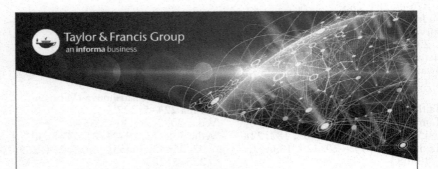